GRID COMPUTING FOR DEVELOPERS

GRID COMPUTING FOR DEVELOPERS

VLADIMIR SILVA

CHARLES RIVER MEDIA, INC.
Hingham, Massachusetts

Cover Design: Tyler Creative

CHARLES RIVER MEDIA, INC.
10 Downer Avenue
Hingham, Massachusetts 02043
781-740-0400
781-740-8816 (FAX)
info@charlesriver.com
www.charlesriver.com

This book is printed on acid-free paper.

Vladimir Silva. *Grid Computing for Developers.*
ISBN: 1-58450-424-2

Library of Congress Cataloging-in-Publication Data
Silva, Vladimir, 1969-
Grid computing for developers / Vladimir Silva.
p. cm.
Includes index.
ISBN 1-58450-424-2 (alk. paper)
1. Computational grids (Computer systems) 2. Computer software--Development. I. Title.
QA76.9.C58S56 2005
004'.36--dc22
2005026627

Printed in the United States of America
05 7 6 5 4 3 2 First Edition

CHARLES RIVER MEDIA titles are available for site license or bulk purchase by institutions, user groups, corporations, etc. For additional information, please contact the Special Sales Department at 781-740-0400.

Requests for replacement of a defective CD-ROM must be accompanied by the original disc, your mailing address, telephone number, date of purchase and purchase price. Please state the nature of the problem, and send the information to CHARLES RIVER MEDIA, INC., 10 Downer Avenue, Hingham, Massachusetts 02043. CRM's sole obligation to the purchaser is to replace the disc, based on defective materials or faulty workmanship, but not on the operation or functionality of the product.

To my dear parents Manuel and Annissia
who raised me with love and values;
and to my brothers Natasha, Alfredo, Ivan, and Sonia
from whom I drew inspiration for this project.

Contents

Preface

BOOK RATIONALE

The goal in writing this book is to share the knowledge I have acquired as a software engineer in the new and exciting field of grid computing. I have been lucky to participate in such projects as the IBM's internal grid initiative and The IBM Grid Toolbox product for on-demand and grid computing. I have also collaborated with engineers of the Globus Alliance in development efforts related to the Globus Toolkit, the de facto standard for grid computing.

This book focuses on three main areas:

- Provision of a "Swiss Army knife" of small programs and tools covering most of today's grid middleware protocols and sample grid services. These tools can be used to build bigger components in a grid environment.
- Middleware-scheduler integration: I have personally found this topic to be very obscure with little or no documentation available.
- In parallel systems development using the Message Passing Interface (MPI), and its integration with grid middleware specifically the Globus Toolkit.

TARGET AUDIENCE

Primary audience: Grid computing is quickly expanding to all the fields of technology and thus this book would be useful for all the following:

- *Computer Science students, developers, researchers, and professors:* This particular group would benefit from the vast array of tools provided to cover all major grid middleware protocols. IT professionals and application developers should be able to exploit the code to build grid services for their organizations.
- *System administrators:* This group will benefit from the installation transcripts and especially from the middleware-backend integration explored in Part II.

Secondary audience: This group is composed of system administrators and grid computing enthusiasts. Although this book is very technical, the first part has lots of theory and concepts.

- *Other IT related developers:* Although this book requires strong programming skills, it includes theory on distributed computing and grid market report information that could be of interest to strategists and distributed business market analysts.

BOOK OVERVIEW

Each chapter includes plenty of source code listings, installation transcripts, figures, and troubleshooting tips. The book is divided in four parts:

Part I: Theory and Foundations

This part provides a very simple and short introduction to the history of high-performance computing and grid computing concepts including the following:

- A time table of high-performance computing (HPC)
- Grid computing concepts such as computational economy, resource management, peer-to-peer (P2P), and enterprise computing.
- Current grid computing initiatives in science and technology

This part is intentionally short because it is not my goal to cover theory but, rather, practical grid middleware algorithms and tools.

Part II: Grid Middleware

This part covers two key middleware grid technologies: the Open Grid Services Architecture (OGSA) and Resource Management software (Schedulers)

OGSA explores all the protocols used to implement grid services with a real-world service implementation: A grid service for large integer factorization (a very popular subject among cryptographers and HPC developers).

Resource management explores today's most popular open source schedulers and their integration with OGSA.

Part III: The Globus Toolkit

The Globus Toolkit is the de facto standard for grid computing [Globus03]. It is being supported by major companies such as IBM, Sun, and Hewlett-Packard. This part explores the four major protocols used by the toolkit with source code samples in the areas of

- Public Key Infrastructure (PKI), including tools for X509 certificate and key generation, the Grid Security Infrastructure (GSI), and the Community Authorization service (CAS)
- Resource allocation and management programs and tools for Web Services (WS-GRAM) and pre–Web Services (GT2)
- Data management and transfer using GridFTP, Replica Location Services (RLS), and Reliable File Transfer (RFT)
- Information services, covering the Globus Monitoring and Discovery Services (WS-MDS and MDS2)
- Commodity Grid Kits, which provides code listings for commodity frameworks and toolkits in cooperation with grid technologies to enhance the functionality, maintenance, and deployment of grid services
- Web Services Resource Framework (WSRF), which covers the latest grid and web services standards.

Part IV: The Message Passing Interface (MPI) Standard

This part covers the MPI standard used to write parallel applications. MPI has been adopted by all major software vendors as the standard for multiprocessor parallel programs. Applications presented in this part are as follows:

- Simple examples of parallel programs such as numerical integration calculations, factorial computations, Fibonacci sequences, and so on.
- A parallel algorithm for large integer factorization (LIF) based on the number field sieve (NFS).

This part differs from other MPI books because integration with OGSA protocols will be explored, including the following:

- A provider for OGSA information services: Monitoring and Discovery Services (MDS3)
- Integration with the Resource Management Protocol (WS-GRAM)

Appendix A: Source Code

Appendix A, available on the companion CD-ROM, includes source code used for X.509 Certificate manipulation and signature with the following features:

- A simple Certificate Authority (CA) implementation for the Java language. (Used for security configuration of protocols such as GSI)
- X509 Certificate request (CSR) and key generation
- Certificate signatures
- Web tools for these programs

A GRID-ENABLED APPLICATION CHECKLIST

According to Foster and Kesselman [GridAnatomy01], when thinking about grid computing, one should think in terms of applications rather than of frameworks. I couldn't agree more; rushing to build a grid framework without considering potential users and applications may lead to a significant waste of resources in the long run. As a software engineer, I worked in many grid-related projects in this fashion that lead to powerful grids, but that were incapable of running any real applications. Three characteristics define a grid-enabled application (see Figure P.1): Distributed resources, Open source standards and protocols, and quality of service (for example, response time, throughput, availability, and security).

Distributed resources: This means resources that are not subject to centralized control. These resources might be scattered across your organization or among multiple virtual organizations. Well-known examples of such applications are media distribution networks such as Kazaa, Napster, and Gnutella. Kazaa and Napster fail to comply with the second characteristic, so they cannot be considered grids. Examples of programs that some people believe to be grids but fail in this regard are cluster management systems such as Portable Batch System (PBS), Sun Grid Engine (SGE), and LoadLeveler. Such systems are not grids themselves, although because of their centralized control of the hosts, they manage centralized control of system state, user requests, and individual components.

Open standards and general-purpose protocols: To address issues such as authentication, authorization, resource discovery, and resource access. Open standards are necessary for interoperability and industry acceptance. Kazaa and Napster fail in this regard too. On the other hand, the Gnutella network is built on open standards and delivers quality of service so it can be considered a media distribution grid.

Quality of service (QoS): To satisfy user demands. This QoS could be in the form of response time, throughput, availability, or security.

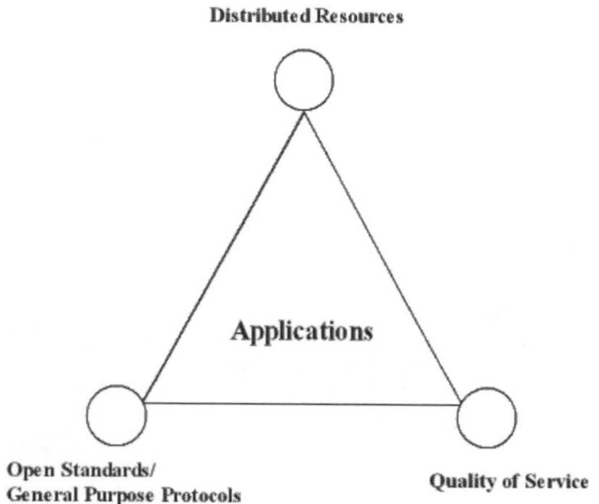

FIGURE P.1 The basic foundation of a grid-enabled application.

Ultimately, a grid should be considered in terms of applications and quality of service, rather than frameworks. Installing grid middleware in all the servers within your organization will only leave you with a networked cluster but nothing to run on it. As a software engineer, I faced this problem many times where significant time and resources were spent on installing grid software in all available machines without considering what type of applications could take advantage of such an environment. Focusing on applications and quality of service first will let you quickly identify potential solutions and put you on the right track to building a grid-enabled environment within your organization.

WILL GRID COMPUTING MAKE IT INTO THE ENTERPRISE?

Perhaps you find yourself wondering if you should go ahead and teach yourself grid computing—just to see what all the hype is about. After all, many IT vendors have invested significant resources to grid enable some of their products. Will grid computing make it into the enterprise? The answer is simple—we do not know; the future is uncertain. However, some numbers look encouraging, and there is indeed great momentum to push the technology into the mainstream.

The following sections will give you an overview of the grid computing market today. If you are a developer or software engineer eager to learn an exiting new technology, take a look at the market data in this section and draw your own conclusions. Consider the following market report from Insight Research (IR). In a study called "A Vertical Market Perspective 2003–2008," IR forecasts a growth in worldwide grid spending from $250 million in 2003 to $4.89 billion in 2008 (see Figure P.2). This is growth of 81.1% over the next five years [IRGridMarket03].

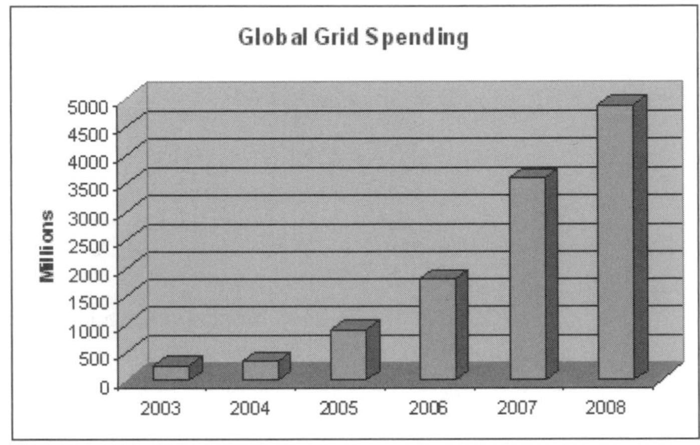

FIGURE P.2 Insight Research–grid computing: a vertical market perspective 2003–2008.

This study suggests grid computing as an emerging technology that will form the foundation of a fourth wave in IT comparable to the birth of the World Wide Web. Insight's market analysis examines the implications of grid computing on the telecommunications industry as the essential backbone for the success of grid computing.

MARKET SEGMENTATION

A report from Light Reading published in May 2003 indicates interest in grid computing from vertical markets such as life sciences, energy and oil, manufacturing, financial services, and government [LRReport03] (see Table P.1).

As with any emerging market, it is important to understand the market's segmentation. Although it is a bit early, several research firms have put numbers on the expected market size. For example, Grid Technology Partners, a firm specializing in grid computing, estimates the market (including hardware and software) growing as high as $4.1 billion by 2005 [IRGridMarket].

TABLE P.1 Grid Computing Market Segmentation

Market	*Applications*
Life Sciences	Drug discovery Development and testing for Bioinformatics
Energy	Gas and oil exploration Data-set visualization
Manufacturing	Chip design Simulation-based test and evaluation
Financial	Portfolio risk analysis
Government	Simulation and design Distributed database coordination Service utilities

The Light Reading report estimates most of the opportunity to be in education and short-term research. Regardless of market forecasts, the market is expected to spread into the enterprise through server aggregation and clusters, as well as enterprise data-center virtualization. This should translate into significant growth, although it will not be as quick as some may anticipate. Higher-growth opportunities will exist in the long term with the creation of grid services and service providers [LRReport03].

MARKET DATA

A study performed by IDC in 2003 estimates the worldwide software market in 2002 to be worth $169.8 billion based on software licensing revenue [IRGridMarket.] According to this study, the market where grid computing can make a significant impact can be partitioned as follows (see Figure P.3):

- System Infrastructure Software (29%—49.2 billion)
- System Management software (23%)
- Security software (14.3%)
- System Infrastructure (11.6%)

- Server-ware (5.4%—2.6 billion)
- Clustering software (13.6%)
- Web Server (10.9%)
- Filesystem software (3.6%)
- Virtual user interface software (71.9%)
- Mobile Infrastructure (1.3%)
- Operating environments (38.5%)
- Other (6%)
- Application Development and Deployment (22.1%)
- Applications (48.95)

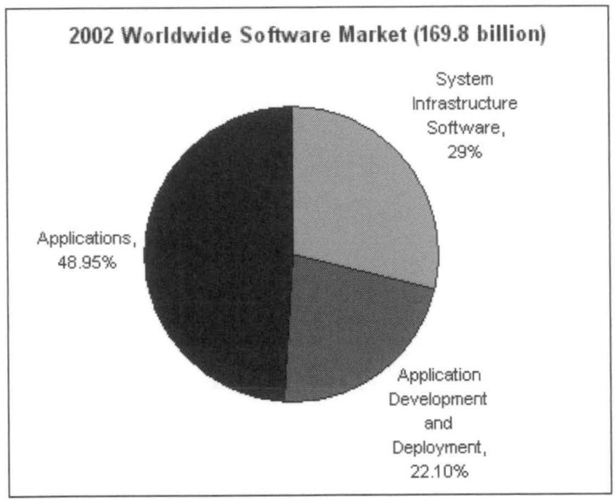

FIGURE P.3: IDC Software Market Report 2003 [LRReport03].

REFERENCES

[Globus03] Globus Project. University of Chicago, June 2003. *http://www.unix.globus.org.*

[GridAnatomy01] Ian Foster, Carl Kesselman, and Steven Tuecke. The Anatomy of the Grid. *International Journal of Supercomputer Applications*, 2001.

[IRGridMarket] Insight Research. "A Vertical Market Perspective 2003–2008." A market research study by Insight Research Corporation.

[LRReport03] Light Reading Research Corporation. "A Report on Grid Computing Market Outlook and Segmentation." May 07, 2003.

Part I Theory and Foundations

This part covers theory describing all the major initiatives in distributed and grid computing along with market reports and segmentation data, including the following:

Overview of High Performance Computing (HPC): Chapter 1 describes terminology used in distributed and grid computing and gives a quick summary of the evolution of grid technologies. It also describes current grid initiatives in science and technology.

Enterprise Computing: Chapter 2 explains distributed computing concepts focusing on the enterprise or virtual organization. Concepts such as infrastructures, shared services, business components, client state, pooled resources, and database concurrency. All these concepts play a role in today's competitive IT organization. Also in Chapter 2 is a discussion of computational economy, which is an emerging field in distributed computing. Its main goal is to drive grid technologies into the mainstream business world. This chapter describes exciting research conducted in the fields of resource management models, computational economy, and economy-driven grid applications on the enterprise.

Core Grid Middleware: Chapter 3 describes some of the middle tier technologies used on grid computing, including peer-to-peer (P2P) architectures, the Globus Toolkit, and research conducted on grid and business fields.

1 The Roadmap to High-Performance Computing

In This Chapter

- Evolution of Grid Technologies
- The Grid in a Nutshell
- Distributed Computing Models
- Computing on Demand (COD)
- Grids in Science and Technology
- Summary
- References

This chapter provides background information on the evolution of high-performance computing (HPC) from the early decades of networked computers to the latest technological advances in distributed systems. This chapter includes the following topics:

- A brief history of HPC
- An overview of the concept of the grid
- Explanations of the latest distributed computing models such as Internet computing, peer-to-peer, and grid architectures
- A brief discussion of some of the latest grid projects in science and technology

1.1 EVOLUTION OF GRID TECHNOLOGIES

High-performance computing has its roots in the early 1940s with the *Manhattan Project* and early efforts by the Department of Energy (DOE) to develop advanced computing capabilities to solve critical problems of interest. In those days parallel computing was done by mathematicians and the type of problems that could be solved was very limited. Many algorithms and computational methods developed by the DOE are still used today. For example, the *Monte Carlo method*, where statistical samples are used to predict behaviors of a large group, was developed by John von Neumann and others in 1946, and it is still used today in stock market forecasting, medicine, traffic flow, and others fields.

In the early 1950s, researchers pushed the state of the art computing to the limits by building their own computers and looking into commercial models. Thanks to the groundbreaking work of mathematicians like Alan Turing, ideas on machine intelligence were developed.

Major milestones of the 1950s are the following:

- Vacuum tubes became a thing of the past to open the way for the transistor allowing for the mass production of computers.
- The invention of the modem allowed scientists to access systems remotely.
- The Department of Defense created ARPANET, the first nationwide network connecting labs together and allowing researches access to a wide area network of computing systems.

Also in that decade, computers were mostly built to solve specific applications. Companies pushed the bounds of computational research to the limits in their effort to achieve greater memory density. Physics discoveries such as the ion-channeling effect allowed chip manufacturers to draw transistors inside blocks of silicon. More powerful computers provided broader support for energy research in applications such as fusion plasma modeling and atmosphere and emissions modeling.

In the 1970s, computers were first linked by networks, thus giving birth to the idea of harnessing idle computing power. Scientists at the Xerox Palo Alto Research Center (PARC) created the first Ethernet network beginning the first experiments on distributed computing. Scientists John F. Shoch and Jon Hupp developed the famous Internet worm, which was designed to move around using idle CPU cycles for beneficial purposes. Software to perform computations and cooperate with other machines on the network was developed. In the early 1980s, more powerful computers were developed, leaving researches with the task of writing their own operating systems. Advances such as *timesharing* (sharing computing power by multiple simultaneous users) were developed for Cray computers. NFSnet (that will later become the Internet) took center stage after researchers realized the critical role of networking on scientific computing. A common filesystem was developed, allowing remote computers to share storage resources. The first multiprocessor vector computers were built, allowing researchers to work on more complex problems using parallel systems.

The evolution of the Internet in the 1990s saw the creation of two groundbreaking distributed projects: The first was distributed.net, which used thousands of computers around the world to break encryption codes. The second, and one of the most successful, is the popular SETI@home project [SETI]. The goal of SETI is to look for radio signal fluctuations that could indicate a signal from intelligent life emanating from outer space. It originated at the University of California at Berkeley in 1999, becoming the most successful Internet distributed project with more than two million volunteers installing the SETI software agent.

As we jump into the 21st century, high-performance computing plays a phenomenal role in scientific advances: environmental simulations, unlocking the genetic code, exploring the basic structure of matter and the universe. All these accomplishments have been made possible through the advances in computing and simulation science. But we have only begun to grasp the future of what is to come in the next century!

1.2 THE GRID IN A NUTSHELL

As industry has become involved in distributed systems, the term *grid* has become a marketing slogan—so much so that any type of distributed filesystem can be called a storage grid, or a scheduler deployed in a cluster can be called a cluster grid, or if a user connects through a file-sharing application, he could be using a digital media distribution grid. Experts suggest that a grid must be evaluated for the applications, business value, and scientific results that it delivers, rather than for its architecture. Carl Kesselman [GridAnatomy01] defined the grid as a hardware and software infrastructure that provides dependable, consistent, pervasive, and inexpensive access to high-end computational capabilities. This definition suggests the idea of a form of on-demand access to computing, data, and services that evolved from early ideas of computer utilities. Indeed, in the 1960s, Len Kleinrock suggested the spread of computer utilities, similar to electric and telephone utilities that will service people [FosterChecklist02].

Foster and colleages suggested addressing social and policy issues with the idea of coordinated resource sharing and problem solving in dynamic, multi-institutional virtual organizations [GridAnatomy01]. This implies resource-sharing arrangements between providers and consumers resulting in a common purpose. This sharing of computers, software, data, and other resources is highly controlled by resource providers and consumers defining clearly what is shared, who is allowed, and the conditions under which sharing occurs. A logical group of resource providers and consumers is known as a virtual organization (VO) [FosterChecklist02].

Foster suggests the following checklist for characteristics of a grid-enabled application:

1. *Decentralized resource coordination:* A grid should integrate and coordinate resources and users in different domains and address issues of security, policy, payment, and membership.
2. *Standards and open source protocols:* These should be used for authentication, authorization, resource discovery, and resource access.
3. *Quality of service delivery:* Resources should be used in a coordinated fashion to deliver quality of service, response times, throughput, and availability to meet complex user demands.

1.2.1 What Can Be Called a Grid Application

According to this checklist, scheduler software such as Portable Batch System (PBS) or Sun Grid Engine (SGE), even though they deliver quality of service, don't constitute a grid because of their centralized host management policies. According to Foster and Kesselman, the Web is not yet a grid itself even though it is built on top of open, general-purpose protocols for access to distributed resources; it does not coordinate the use of those resources to deliver quality of service. Lately, schedulers such as Platform's MultiCluster can be called grids, as can distributed computing systems such as Condor®, SETI, and United Devices, which harness idle desktops; peer-to-peer (P2P) systems such as Gnutella, which support file sharing among participating peers, and the Storage Resource Broker, which supports distributed access to data resources [FosterChecklist02].

1.3 DISTRIBUTED COMPUTING MODELS

Modern distributed computing frameworks can be classified in three distinct branches: Internet computing, which seeks to harness idle CPU cycles; peer-to-peer for serverless communication; and grid to bridge the gap among client/server and Web Services. The following sections introduce concepts, similarities, and differences among these.

1.3.1 Internet Computing

Decentralized distributed models seek to harness the computing power of millions of devices worldwide, such as personal computers or pervasive devices such as personal digital assistants (PDAs), laptops, and others. Large-scale experiments such as Search for Extraterrestrial Intelligence (SETI) launched this model into the mainstream. By collecting radio telescope data delivered on tapes to SETI@home headquarters in Berkeley, California, researchers chop the raw data into small "work-units." These work-units are then distributed to users around the world, who analyze the data on their PCs.

This model is useful in environments where thousands and possibly millions of pervasive nodes, nodes with relatively low processing power, work in a transient manner. This basically means that users will be online-offline, connecting or disconnecting all the time. This method has the advantage of achieving a degree of sensitivity that could only be dreamed of by other methods such as mainframe processes. It also scales massively as millions of nodes connect and disconnect many times, generating low network latency.

On the other hand, the public nature of this model can raise serious security issues and can be prone to malicious attacks. This model also lacks advanced clustering features such as time sharing, resource management and brokering, information services, and search capabilities (see Figure 1.1).

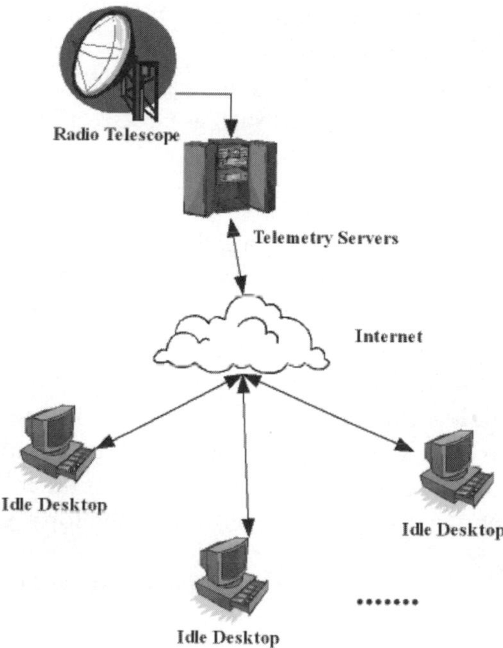

FIGURE 1.1 SETI@home architecture, a typical Internet computing application that harnesses idle desktop power.

1.3.2 Peer-to-Peer (P2P)

The infamous Napster software is the prime example of a P2P distributed model. In a P2P network, computers are called peers and take advantage of resources: storage, cycles, content, and human presence available in the Internet. Peers access decentralized resources in an environment of unstable connectivity and unpredictable IP addresses. Thus, P2P nodes operate outside the Domain Name System (DNS).

The main difference with this model is that peers have significant or total autonomy from central servers. This makes P2P unique. All distributed models seek to leverage unused resources, by aggregating cycles, sharing digital content, and working with the variable connectivity of possibly millions of devices.

1.3.2.1 Advantages and Disadvantages

An important goal in P2P networks is that the bandwidth of clients is aggregated, so the available download bandwidth for a given user grows with the number of nodes. Another advantage includes leveraging unused resources. Disadvantages include very high network latency, inefficient search mechanisms, and although peers claim to have autonomy from central servers, applications such as Napster and Kazaa rely on a centralized indexing server to store metadata about peers. P2P applications have caused serious legal controversies also by violating copyright laws on digital media distribution.

Besides file sharing, P2P is gaining ground in the online gaming industry and collaboration with applications such as Groove and others.

1.3.3 Grid Architectures

According to Foster and colleagues, three characteristics define a grid application: It should provide decentralized resource coordination, addressing issues of security, policy, payment, and membership. It should be based on standards and open source protocols for authentication, authorization, resource discovery, and access. Finally, it should deliver quality of service by using resources in a coordinated fashion, by providing low response times, and high throughput to meet user demands. A grid architecture should be extensible and an open structure designed to solve key VO requirements. Foster and colleagues suggest the following grid architecture, defined by a set of layers (from the bottom to the top) [GridAnatomy01]:

Fabric: This is the bottom layer and consists of resource and connectivity protocols, which facilitate the sharing of individual resources. This layer provides the resources (computational, storage systems, catalogs, and network resources) shared access mediated by grid protocols. Richer fabric functionality provides more sophisticated sharing operations. On the other hand, a simpler fabric simplifies the deployment of grid infrastructure. An example of this is advance reservation, which allows scheduling of resources in ways otherwise impossible to achieve. However, advance reservation increases the cost of incorporating new resources into a grid. At a minimum, the fabric layer should implement enquiry mechanisms for discovery of their structure, state, and capabilities, and resource management mechanisms to deliver quality of service. The types of resources manipulated by the fabric can be computational, storage, network, code repositories, and databases.

Connectivity: This layer defines communication and authentication protocols for network transactions. The goal is to provide easy and secure communications. Communication protocols include Internet (IP), transport (TCP, UDP), and application (DNS, and so on), with space for new protocols as the need arises. Authentication protocols should be able to provide the following: *single sign on* (log in once and access multiple resources defined by the fabric layer); *delegation*, to allow a program to run on the user's behalf so it is able to access the resources on which the user is authorized; *integration* with local security solutions; and *user-based trust relationships,* so resource providers are not required to interact before a user to access resources on either provider.

Resource: This layer defines protocols for secure negotiation, initiation, monitoring, control, accounting, and payment of sharing operations on individual resources. These protocols deal with individual resources and ignore global state and atomic actions across distributed collections that are handled by the collections layer. Resource layer protocols can be *information protocols* used to obtain information about configuration, load, or usage policies, and *management protocols* that negotiate access to shared resources by handling resource requirements and operation(s) to be performed. Management protocols ensure consistency of operations for a given shared resource.

Collective: This layer defines protocols and services global in nature and captures interactions across collections of resources. Examples of collective protocols are the following:

a. *Directory services:* for resource properties discovery.
b. *Coallocation, scheduling, and brokering services:* for allocation of one or more resources for a specific purpose and the scheduling of tasks.
c. *Monitoring and diagnostics:* for failure, intrusion detection, overload, and so on.
d. *Data replication services:* for storage management to maximize data access performance.
e. *Grid-enabled programming systems*: to provide a programming model for resource discovery, security, allocation, and others.
f. *Workload management systems:* for description and management of multicomponent workflows.
g. *Software discovery services:* for optimal software selection.
h. *Community authorization servers:* to enforce community policies governing resource access.
i. *Accounting/payment and collaboration services.*

Applications: This layer includes user applications that operate within a VO. Applications call on services defined at any layer—resource management, data access, resource discovery, and so forth—to perform desired actions. Applications rely on application programming interfaces (APIs) implemented by software development kits (SDKs), which in turn call grid protocols to interact with network services that provide capabilities to the end user. Protocols may implement local functionality or interact with other protocols.

A typical example of a grid-enabled framework should include some of the components specified in Figure 1.2.

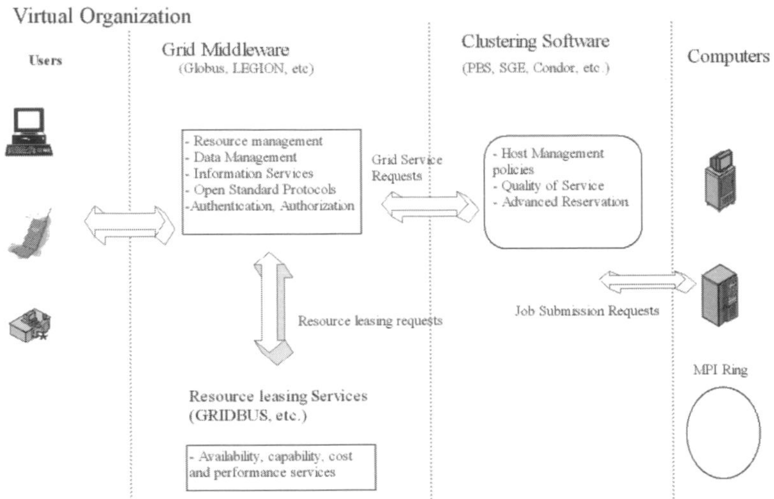

FIGURE 1.2 The typical framework of a grid-enabled application.

1.3.3.1 Virtual Organizations

Two or more organizations that share resources become a VO. The policies governing access to those resources vary according to the actual organizations involved, creating an environment of providers and consumers. Resources are made available by owners with constraints on when, where, and what can be done on them. Resource consumers may also place constraints on properties of the resources they are prepared to work with. For example, a consumer may accept a resource over a secure channel only.

This environment effectively creates a dynamic sharing relationship between providers and consumers. These dynamic relationships may be defined by policies that govern access to resources. Mechanisms for discovering and characterizing the nature of the relationships are required in this environment. For example, new users should be able to discover what resources are available in the VO and the quality of those resources. Because VOs enable disparate organizations or individuals to share resources in a controlled fashion to achieve a common goal, they are emerging as fundamental entities in modern computing [GridAnatomy01].

The management of a VO sharing relationships requires a new technology. This technology has been dubbed a grid architecture, which identifies components and how those components interact with one another.

1.3.3.2 The Need for Standards-Based Open Middleware

Interoperability is a central issue to be addressed in networked environments. Interoperability usually means common protocols which define the mechanisms by which users and resources connect, negotiate, and establish sharing relationships. A standards-based open architecture facilitates extensibility, interoperability, and portability making it easy to define standard services. This technology and architecture is also known as middleware. Interoperability is important because without it, users and applications are forced to use bilateral sharing arrangements, with no assurance that the mechanisms used will be extensible to other parties. This makes dynamic VO formation all but impossible. Standard protocols are fundamental for general resource sharing.

1.4 COMPUTING ON DEMAND (COD)

Computing on demand (COD) extends high throughput computing abilities to include a method for running short-term jobs on instantly available resources. Job management in COD-enabled systems includes interactive, compute intensive jobs, giving these jobs immediate access to the computing power they need over a relatively short period.

Many of the applications that are well suited for COD involve a cycle: blocking user input, computation burst to compute results, block again on user input, and so forth. When the resources are not being used for the bursts of computation to service the application, they should continue to execute long-running batch jobs. Examples of applications that require COD capabilities are the following [Condor04]:

- Graphics-rendering applications.
- Visualization tools for data mining.
- A large spreadsheet with lots of time-consuming complex formulas that take a lot of time to recalculate. When the user recalculates, the nodes work on the computation and send the results back to the master application.

1.4.1 How It Works

Resources on a pool of nodes run batch jobs. When a COD job appears at a node, the lower-priority (currently running) batch jobs are suspended allowing the COD job to run immediately. After completion, the batch jobs resume execution. Administratively, COD applications put claims on nodes. While the COD application does not need the nodes, the claims are suspended, allowing batch jobs to run [Condor04].

1.4.2 User Authorization

The system works by users putting claims on nodes for a COD job. A user with a claim on a resource can then suspend and resume a COD job at will. This gives the user a great deal of power on the claimed resource, even if it is owned by another user. Because of this, it is essential that users can be trusted not to abuse this power. Thus, privileges should be granted by cluster administrators and strong authentication methods used [Condor04].

1.4.3 Limitations

Support for COD in current schedulers faces a few limitations:

- Applications and data must be prestaged at a given node.
- Limits should be defined for how long a claim can be active, how often it is run, and so on.
- There is a lack of accounting for applications under COD claims.
- There is a lack of claim persistency on daemons.

COD provides high throughput computing abilities in an environment where short-term jobs should be run on instantly available resources. It provides computing power on demand for demanding environments such as visualization and graphics. COD capabilities are usually implemented by schedulers such as Condor [Condor04].

1.5 GRIDS IN SCIENCE AND TECHNOLOGY

The following is a compilation of popular grid computing related consortiums and projects aimed to provide the latest technologies as well as collaboration, news, documentation, and software standards in all things *grid*.

1.5.1 Grid Consortiums and Open Forums

The following forums contain the latest news and technologies related to grid initiatives all over the world.

1.5.1.1 Global Grid Forum (GGF)–*http://www.ggf.org/*

GGF is a community-initiated forum of individuals from industry and research aiming for a global standardization of grid technologies and applications.

GGF promotes the development, deployment, and implementation of grid technologies via documentation of "best practices"—technical specifications, user experiences, and implementation guidelines.

1.5.1.2 Peer-to-Peer Working Group (P2Pwg)–*http://p2p.internet2.edu/*

P2Pwg leads efforts to investigate and explore the many aspects of peer-to-peer, beyond the resource management issues that bring the most notoriety (e.g., Internet file downloads).

Its mission is as follows [P2PInternet]:

- Report on recent occurrences and future trends within P2P and distributed computing.
- Develop collaboration between the education community and corporate entities to investigate new P2P and distributed computing applications.
- Provide best practices for resource management and P2P technologies.

1.5.1.3 Asia Pacific Grid (ApGrid)–*http://www.apgrid.org/*

ApGrid aims at building an international grid test bed among organizations in the Asia Pacific region and provides venues for sharing and exchanging ideas and information, new projects, and collaboration and interfacing with global efforts such as the GGF [ApGrid04].

1.5.2 Grids in Science and Engineering

The general drive for most current grid projects is to enable the resource interactions that facilitate large-scale science and engineering projects such as bioinformatics, high-energy physics data analysis, climatology, large-scale remote instrument operation, and so forth.

In addition to government and military projects (NASA, DOE), grids are being developed by an increasing community of people who work together through coordinating organizations such as the GGF. From efforts such as this, grids will become a reality and an important component of the practice of science and engineering.

1.5.2.1 The DataGrid Project–*http://eu-datagrid.web.cern.ch/eu-datagrid/*

The DataGrid project is funded by the European Union (EU). The objective is to build the next generation computing infrastructure by providing intensive computation and analysis of shared large-scale databases, from hundreds of terabytes to petabytes, across widely distributed scientific communities. The DataGrid project will be included in the new EU grid project (Enabling Grids for E-sciencE [EGEE]).

EGEE aims to build a service grid infrastructure in Europe available to scientists 24 hours a day [EGEE04].

1.5.2.2 Grid Physics Network (GriPhyN)–*http://www.griphyn.org/*

The GriPhyN Project is developing grid technologies for scientific and engineering projects that must collect and analyze distributed, petabyte scale datasets. GriPhyN research will enable the development of Petascale Virtual Data Grids (PVDGs) through its virtual data toolkit (VDT). VDT is an ensemble of grid middleware that aims to make it as easy for users to deploy, maintain, and use grid middleware. VDT is composed by the following [GriPhyN05]:

- Basic grid services including Condor-G® and Globus®.
- Virtual data tools to work with virtual data, particularly the virtual data system.
- Utility software such as the Grid Security Infrastructure (GSI)–Enabled OpenSSH, software to update GSI certificate revocation lists, and monitoring software like MonaLisa.

1.5.2.3 Particle Physics DataGrid (PPDG)–*http://www.ppdg.net/*

The Particle Physics DataGrid Pilot (PPDG) is a collaboration of computer scientists with a strong record in grid technology and physicists with leading roles in the software and network infrastructures for major high-energy and nuclear experiments [PPDG04].

1.5.2.4 Petascale Data-Intensive Computing (Grid Datafarm)–*http://datafarm.apgrid.org/*

Grid Datafarm is a Petascale data-intensive computing project initiated in Japan. The project is the result of collaboration among the High Energy Accelerator Research Organization (KEK), the National Institute of Advanced Industrial Science and Technology (AIST), the University of Tokyo, and the Tokyo Institute of Technology.

The challenge involves the construction of a petascale to exascale parallel filesystems exploiting local storages of PCs spread over the worldwide grid [GridFarm04].

1.5.2.5 Resource Modeling and Simulation (GridSim)–*http://www.gridbus.org/gridsim/*

The focus of this project is to investigate effective resource allocation techniques based on computational economy through simulation. This project aims to simulate millions of resources and thousands of users with varied requirements and study the scalability of systems and algorithms, the efficiency of resource allocation policies and the satisfaction of users [GridSim04].

1.6 SUMMARY

The term *grid* suggests a computer paradigm analog to a power grid. In such an environment, a shared pool of resources is created for many consumers to access as needed. Resources include processors, memory, and storage. Grid computing is still in early development, but efforts are underway to develop open standards, thus promoting its mass adoption. Major software vendors are currently working actively on those efforts.

REFERENCES

[ApGrid04] Asia Pacific Grid. National Institute of Advanced Industrial Science and Technology (AIST). May 2004. Available online from *http://www.apgrid.org/*.

[Condor04] Condor Team. *Condor Version 6.6.6 Manual.* University of Wisconsin–Madison. Accessed online July 28, 2004, at *http://www.cs.wisc.edu/condor/manual/v6.6.6/*.

[EGEE04] The DataGrid Project. The European Union. Available online March 2004 from *http://eu-datagrid.web.cern.ch/eu-datagrid/*.

[FosterChecklist02] Ian Foster. *What is the Grid? A Three Point Checklist.* Argonne National Laboratory & University of Chicago, July 20, 2002.

[GridAnatomy01] Ian Foster, Carl Kesselman, and Steven Tuecke. "The Anatomy of the Grid." *International Journal of Supercomputer Applications, 15*(3), 200–222 (2001). Available online at *www.globus.org/research/papers/anatomy.pdf*.

[GridFarm04] Grid Datafarm for Petascale Data Intensive Computing. High Energy Accelerator Research Organization (KEK), National Institute of Advanced Industrial Science and Technology (AIST), the University of Tokyo, and the Tokyo Institute of Technology. Available online November 2004 from *http://datafarm.apgrid.org/*.

[GridSim04] Grid Computing and Distributed Systems. Department of Computer Science and Software Engineering. University of Melbourne, Australia. Available online 2004 from *http://www.gridbus.org/gridsim/*.

[GriPhyN05] GriPhyN (Grid Physics Network). University of Florida and Argonne National Laboratory. Available online February 2005 from *http://www.griphyn.org/*.

[P2PInternet] Peer-to-Peer Working Group. The Internet2 Consortium. Available online at *http://www.internet2.edu/*.

[PPDG04] Particle Physics Data Grid. Argonne National Laboratory, Brookhaven National Laboratory, California Institute of Technology, Fermi National Laboratory, Lawrence Berkeley National Laboratory, San Diego Supercomputer

Center, Stanford Linear Accelerator Center, Thomas Jefferson National Accelerator Facility, University of California at San Diego, University of Florida, University of Wisconsin–Madison, Harvard University, University of Manchester, University of Glasgow, State University of New York–Stony Brook, Boston University, University of Chicago, University of Texas–Arlington, University of Houston, University of Southern California Information Sciences Institute. Available online October 2004 from *http://www.ppdg.net/*.

[SETI] *The Search for Extraterrestrial Intelligence.* SETI@home. Accessed online 2001 at *http://setiathome.ssl.berkeley.edu/*.

2 Enterprise Computing

In This Chapter

- Existing Enterprise Infrastructures
- Integration with Grid Architectures
- Grid-Enabled Resource Management Models
- Enter Open Grid Services
- The Competitive IT Organization
- Computational Economy
- Summary
- References

Enterprise applications within IT units are responsible for information management, reporting, database and system administration, and supplying a consistent approach to management, coordination, and integration. Fortunately for today's enterprise, the past few years have seen this environment and landscape rapidly improve into one that can readily and effectively support modern enterprise demands and operational criteria [ShanRalph97]. This chapter includes information on the following topics:

- A discussion of existing enterprise infrastructures and their integration with grid architectures
- An overview of resource management models available to enterprise computing
- A discussion of the benefits provided by the latest Open Grid Services and Web Services Resource Framework technologies

Today's computing platforms are inexpensive and easy to use, and they are significantly more reliable and extensible than their predecessors. Public marketplace demands and the rapid pace of technological innovation dictate that today's management teams must embrace new mechanisms of providing their organizations with expandable tools to enhance existing tactical and strategic advantages.

The needs of enterprise computing in our world today are driven by the following:

- The need for flexible workload management systems to enhance existing computing environments
- Queuing and scheduling of computational workload across complex networks to optimize hardware and software utilization and minimize job turnaround times
- High-performance computing workload management
- Applications in a broad range of computing environments, such as engineering analysis, financial services, life sciences, visual effects, animation, meteorology, and others
- Reduction of operational expenses; improvement of operational efficiencies; increase in timeliness and accuracy of data collection and dissemination [Condor04]

Strategic factors play a role as well:

- The ability to stay closer to your customers, vendors, prospects, and partners
- The ability to efficiently and effectively capture operational metrics for quick, accurate, and informed strategic decision making
- Smooth and shortened turnaround for investment

As competition increases in the marketplace and companies seek to achieve a competitive advantage, one common issue is the reduction of costs without affecting the level of service or quality [Frankel03]. By allowing managers and teams to more quickly and accurately communicate information across a widespread workforce, productivity can be greatly increased while critical decision-making time can be dramatically reduced. The availability of accurate data over short periods and the capability to analyze it from any point or location can increase overall decision-making skills and provide a critical strategic advantage [Condor04].

2.1 EXISTING ENTERPRISE INFRASTRUCTURES

Today's enterprise infrastructure relies on back-end or legacy enterprise systems. Any successful business solution must be tightly coupled with the existing enterprise infrastructure to have an impact. This close coupling and integration is imperative for creating a solution that is powerful, effective, efficient, and widely accepted by the target audience. An overall strategy that can leverage such a tight integration is one that provides powerful solutions to complex business problems. The power of these types of applications lies almost entirely in the cohesiveness shared with the existing enterprise infrastructure, for it's the (often preexisting) infrastructure that provides the user access to mission-critical, line-of-business information needed to do a better job.

Subsequently, before you have a complete and integrated solution, many specific factors, such as network connectivity, database and knowledge base integration, intranet resources, and enterprise-level security must be carefully considered and properly addressed. Effective business links corporate-level resources such as enterprise resource planning systems, sales force automation tools, manufacturing and planning resources, and more [ShanRalph97].

A demanding marketplace has driven rapid enhancements in a number of areas such as usability, speed, size, and form. These areas will continue to improve, offering new alternatives as new development takes place.

2.2 INTEGRATION WITH GRID ARCHITECTURES

Enterprise computing systems provide standard resource interfaces, remote invocation mechanisms, and trading services for discovery to make it easy to share resources within an organization. Examples of enterprise computing systems are Common Object Request Broker Architecture (CORBA), Distributed Component Object Model (DCOM), Enterprise JavaBeans (EJBs), and Java 2 Platform Enterprise Edition (J2EE). These systems have the advantage of providing resource sharing and quality of service. On the other hand, these mechanisms address no specific virtual organization (VO) requirements such as the following [GridAnatomy01]:

- They lack dynamic reconfiguration of resources: for example, accessing data located on storage managed by two or more separate storage service providers (SSPs).
- They lack load sharing across resource providers.
- They cannot extend dynamically to encompass other resources and do not provide the remote resource provider with any control of when and whether to share its resources.

Other limitations include static resource sharing limited to a single organization, and interaction via client-servers, rather than the coordinated use of multiple resources. The addition of grid protocols can provide enhanced capability (for example, inter-domain security) and enable interoperability with other clients. Customers can negotiate access to particular resources and then use grid protocols to dynamically provision those resources to run customer-specific applications. Flexible delegation and access control mechanisms would allow customers to grant an application running on an application service provider (ASP) direct, efficient, and secure access to data on an SSP or to couple resources from multiple ASPs and SSPs with their own [GridAnatomy01]. Some of the issues related to enterprise computing and grid integration, discussed in the next section, include the following:

- Managing workload
- Managing shared services
- Using stateless business components
- Managing client state
- Handling pooled resources and lightweight server processes
- Maximizing database concurrency

2.2.1 Workload and Policy Management

Workload management means that the use of shared resources is controlled to best achieve an enterprise's goals such as productivity, timeliness, level-of-service, and so forth. Workload management is accomplished through managing resources and administering policies. Workload management should provide the following major capabilities [SGEUserGruide04]:

- Dynamic scheduling and resource management to enforce site-specific management polices.
- Dynamic collection of performance data to provide schedulers with up-to-the-minute job-level resource consumption and system load information.
- Enhanced security by encrypting messages sent between client and server.
- High-level policy administration for the definition and implementation of enterprise goals such as productivity, timeliness, and level of service.
- Support for *checkpoints* to migrate jobs from workstation to workstation without user intervention depending on system load.

Workload management provides users with the means to submit computationally demanding tasks to the grid for transparent distribution of the associated workload. Users can submit batch jobs, interactive jobs, and parallel jobs to the grid. Workload management software orchestrates the delivery of computational power that is based on enterprise resource policies set by the organization's staff. The system uses these policies to examine the available resources. It then gathers these resources and then allocates and delivers resources automatically, optimizing usage across the network. This functionality is achieved through cooperation of the different components of the workload management software. To enable this cooperation, resource owners must do the following:

- Negotiate policies
- Have flexibility in the policies for unique project requirements
- Have the policies automatically monitored and enforced

Effective workload management software should be capable of handling millions of jobs at a time without being concerned about where the jobs run.

2.2.2 Shared Services

Services are logical groupings of components that encapsulate behavior and data, accessible through a well-formed interface. Services are another way of providing general separation and compartmentalization by interacting with one another as peers. They provide scalability, ease of maintenance, transaction management, application partitioning and the capability to add service instances as the demand requires.

2.2.3 Stateless Business Components

Business services should be stateless to achieve scalability and make transactional components reusable by many requesters. For example, a system with multiple, active component instances for each user for a long period, won't scale very far.

Stateless business services mean two things:

- The state of the transaction must not be retained by service components across transaction boundaries.
- The state of the client must not be retained by the service components across transaction boundaries.

The way to solve this problem is to store the transaction state into a database or other storage medium. For example, if a customer order is missing data, the incomplete order can be stored for future retrieval into a database and the object instance(s) manipulating that order destroyed. The result is that fewer resources will be held for less time, which is the mission of a scalable system.

2.2.4 Client State Management

Managing the state on a server, without persisting it somewhere, is expensive. As you increase the number of clients in your system, the resources used will grow out of control [Frankel03]. Effective choices to manage the state that provide a reasonable programming model and scalability are the following:

Store the client state in the server: It may sound expensive, but it's one of the consequences of having a limited programming model on the client. Although there's extra overhead associated with reading and writing this object from and to the server, it will more than make up for it with increased scalability.

Use a client-side API such as ActiveX to manage the state locally: If this approach conforms to your strategy, it can be an effective alternative.

2.2.5 Pooled Resources and Lightweight Server Processes

Resource pools are created when the overhead associated with creating a sharable resource is expensive. Pooled resources can be used to gain efficiencies when using sharable objects such as sockets, CORBA objects, database connections and files. The idea behind pooling is to create the resource in advance and store it away so it can be reused [King02].

The behavior of a pooling framework is dictated by a set of policies such as the following:

Load balancing: It uses optimization algorithms such as round-robin, least-used, or other selection schemes.

Low-water/high-water: A minimum number of shared objects (low-water) are instantiated. On subsequent requests for the object, new resources will be created until the maximum (high-water) is reached.

Blocking versus no-wait: Using this method, if no objects are available on the pool, the client will wait for the first available resource (blocking) or an exception will be thrown to the client if a timeout is reached. A no-wait policy will throw an error back immediately if no resources are available on the pool.

Failed resource recovery: The framework attempts to recover pooled resources if a failure occurs such as network or I/O error system crashes, and so on.

Recycler idiom: The framework attempts to repair (recycle) failed objects into the pool. This alleviates the cost of removing and creating pooled objects from scratch.

Lightweight server processes, also called *server threads,* are single sequential flows of control within a program. Threads are used to isolate tasks that require significant processor time to run. They are useful for doing two or more tasks at once. However, they are difficult to handle and present many implementation challenges such as priority synchronization and life cycle management.

2.2.6 Database Concurrency Maximization

Concurrency control deals with the issues involved with allowing multiple people simultaneous access to shared entities such as objects, data records, or some other representation. The two big issues with concurrency are maximizing the number of clients through the database without compromising data integrity, and long-term locking across transactions for single-threaded objects [Frankel03]. To deal with these issues, concurrency control implementations focus on collisions and transactions.

2.2.6.1 Collisions and Transactions

A *collision* is said to occur when two activities, which may or may not be full-fledged transactions, attempt to change entities within a system of record. First, to deal with collisions a database management system (DBMS) can take a pessimistic locking approach that avoids collisions but reduces system performance. Second, you can use an optimistic locking strategy that enables you to detect collisions so you can resolve them. Third, you can take an overly optimistic locking strategy that ignores the issue completely [Ambler04].

Transactions are usually divided in business transactions and online transactions. A business transaction is an interaction in the real world, usually between an enterprise and a person, where something is exchanged. An online transaction is the execution of a program that performs an administrative or real-time function, often by accessing shared data sources, usually on behalf of an online user. An example of a transaction is a transfer of funds between two bank accounts. The transaction consists of debiting the source account, crediting the target account, and recording the facts. In modern software development projects, concurrency control and transactions are issues that affect all architectural tiers including databases, middle tiers, and client tiers [Ambler04].

Another concept that is becoming increasingly important for the enterprise system is the idea of coupling geographically distributed resources to solve large-scale problems. The management of these resources becomes complex when they are heterogeneous in nature, owned by different individuals within different organizations each having their own resource management policies. In this scenario, an efficient resource management model is required. Grid computing provides new ideas in this field that promise to change the way enterprises deal with this issue. The next section discusses such models.

2.3 GRID-ENABLED RESOURCE MANAGEMENT MODELS

Choosing the right model for resource management plays a major role in coupling resource producers and consumers and, thus, the success of your organization. There are a number of approaches for grid-enabled resource management. Among the most important are the following [ResMgrModels00]:

- Hierarchical Model
- Abstract Owner Model
- Market/Economy Model

2.3.1 Hierarchical

Hierarchical resource management introduces the idea of passive and active components. Passive components can be any of the following:

- *Resources* that can be shared by owners who may charge others for using them. Examples of resources are CPU, RAM, hard disk, network bandwidth, and so forth.
- *Resource Consumers*, also known as tasks. Tasks can be computational or noncomputational such as file staging and communication.
- *Jobs* that are logical groupings of one or more tasks.
- *Schedulers*, which are components that map jobs to resources over time.

Active components are the following:

- Information services used to describe resources, jobs, schedulers, and agents within the resource management system.
- Users that submit jobs for execution.
- Agents for the following: *domain control* (also known as local resource managers), which commits resources for use within a local domain; *deployment*, which implements schedules by negotiating with domain control agents to obtain resources and start tasks; *admission control* to accommodate or reject jobs depending on system load; and *job control* to coordinate between different components within the resource management system. For example, agents can be used to monitor job coordination within a local scheduler.

These components may interact with each other in many ways. For example, when a user submits a job, it is intercepted by the job control and admission agents who determine if it is safe to add the job to the work pool of the system. The job is sent then to the scheduler, which performs resource discovery and queries the domain control agents to determine resource availability. The scheduler then sends the job to the deployment agent who negotiates for the required resources, schedule, and obtains reservations for the resources. The reservations go back to the job control agent, which coordinates with the domain control agents to start the tasks. Monitors track the progress of the job and have capabilities to reschedule depending on load and performance [ResMgrModels00].

2.3.2 Abstract Owner Model (AO)

This model is based on the notion of abstract owners of resources, also known as brokers. In reality, users don't care who owns a specific resource. They are interested in access, cost, and means of payment for those resources. The entity the user deals with may not be the owner of the resource but a broker, who may in turn deal with the owners, or perhaps with other brokers. In any case, the broker is an abstraction for all the owners of the resource, an abstract owner [ResMgrModels00].

At the foundation of this model, all resources from individual processors and instruments to the grid itself are assigned abstract owners tightly related to schedulers. Clients negotiate with abstract owners or brokers by sending resource objects through remote procedure calls. Some of the information sent by the client includes resource object attributes, negotiation style, pickup approach, authorization, and so forth. The negotiation style specifies whether the job is to be run immediately, or the job status: pending, confirmed, canceled, and so on. The pickup approach specifies the protocol used between the AO and client for output delivery. Authorization is a capability or key that allows the AO to determine the authority of the client to access resources [ResMgrModels00].

The AO model requires more work in detail and functionality, for example, resource discovery between clients and brokers. Before an approach like AO has a likelihood of being accepted, it must address these challenges and should coexist with other contemporary approaches. Thus, it is important to understand how AOs and other systems can build upon or mimic each other.

2.3.3 Economy/Market Model

This model includes components of both hierarchical and AO models described earlier. It works well when resources are geographically distributed and owned by different organizations each with a different resource management model and price policies. It offers better incentives for resource owners to share resources by offering financial services for profit. This translates into return on investment for users/owners enhancing and expanding computational services thus effectively creating a market of supply and demand. In this market, resource owners want to maximize return on investment and resource users minimize their expenses [ResMgrModels00].

To achieve these goals, the economy model provides a resource management system with tools and services to allow both resource users and owners to express their requirements. Its basic components are user applications, grid resource broker, grid middleware, and local scheduler. The importance of market models for grid computing is that they tackle accounting and resource costs (for example, a price for idle processor cycles). This model is described in further detail in Computational Economy, later in this chapter.

2.4 ENTER OPEN GRID SERVICES

Open grid services aim for the integration of services across distributed and heterogeneous virtual organizations with disparate resources and relationships. Open Grid Services Architecture (OGSA) addresses these challenges by merging grid and Web

Services technologies. The goals of OGSA are to provide standard mechanisms for creating, naming, and discovering transient grid service instances; provide location transparency and multiple protocol bindings for service instances; and support integration with native platforms. This allows for the creation of sophisticated distributed systems to handle lifetime management, reliable invocation, authentication, authorization, and delegation of services [GridPhysiology04].

In the OGSA world, a grid is an extensible set of services that may be aggregated in different ways to meet the needs of VOs, which in turn operate and share those services. A grid service defines functionality to handle resource allocation and management for secure, reliable, service creation; information discovery through soft state registration; and a security infrastructure single sign on, delegation, and credential mapping. OGSA assigns a set of well-defined standard interfaces for managing transient service instances. These interfaces address the following [GridPhysiology04]:

- *Discovery:* to discover available services and their characteristics
- *Dynamic service creation:* to create and manage new service instances
- *Lifetime management:* to reclaim services and resources associated with failed operations
- *Notification:* for asynchronous notification of changes in the state among collections of dynamic, distributed services

A grid service also defines a set of service protocol bindings to address the following:

- *Authentication:* allow the identity of individuals and services to be established for policy enforcement. This is implemented as a transport protocol for mutual authentication of client and service instance, as well as the delegation of proxy credentials.
- *Reliable invocation:* This guarantees that a service has received a message. It gives the foundation for higher-level per-operation semantics, such as transactions.

The separation of standard interfaces functionality and protocol bindings increases the generality of the architecture without compromising its functionality. On the other hand, OGSA has received many critiques from the Web Services community. According to Foster and colleagues [WSRF04], OGSA is a too-bulky and complex architecture that is too object-oriented and lacks of support for the latest WSDL 2.0 extensions. These issues coupled with the emerging Web Services standards have given rise to the latest Web Services Resource Framework specification.

2.4.1 Grids on the Enterprise

Adoption of grid computing on the enterprise remains modest. A research study conducted by *Nucleus* in 2003 interviewed *Fortune 500* companies but found none that was using some form of grid technology. Furthermore, 80% of IT managers said they had no immediate plans to implement grids [GridEconomy].

However, awareness is growing; according to an *Insight Research* survey, 37% of the responders said they are planning to evaluate grid technologies. Investments on grid computing are expected to grow to US $4.9 billion in 2008, a 20-fold increase from US $250 million in 2003. The pace of grid computing adoption is expected to mimic rates of Internet penetration within corporations. *Enabling Grids for E-sciencE in Europe* (EGEE), a project started in April 2004 with more than 70 institutions from 27 countries, reports that 10 of its members are from private industry. Other

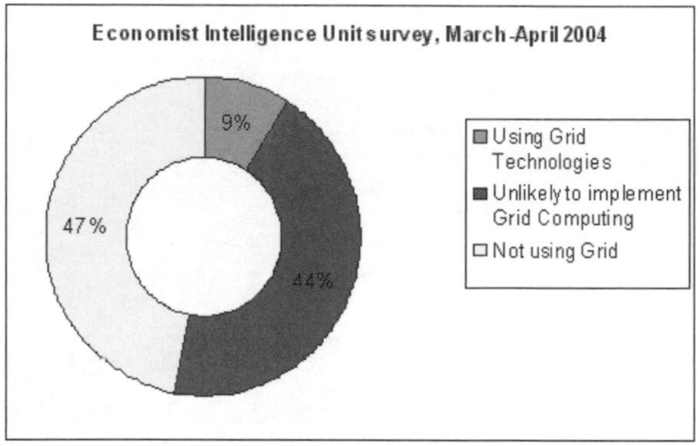

FIGURE 2.1 Economist Intelligence Unit (EIU) survey of grid computing penetration within *Fortune 500* companies.

projects such as the Singapore National Grid initiative will be used in science, research, and education, as well as for commercial purposes (see Figure 2.1).

Business sectors with large computing needs such as manufacturing and financial services are among the early adopters. According to a 2003 study on the use of grids in the financial services market conducted by the *Tabb Group*, grid computing expenditures are expected to rise to US $683 million in 2008 from US $54 million in 2003. This is a 60% increase within five years [GridEIU04].

Other early adopters include energy, pharmaceuticals, aerospace, life sciences, telecommunications, automotive, and chemical companies. Such projects include, among others: seismic interpretation applications and financial-risk calculations in life insurance research.

Growing corporate interest on grids is driven by the following:

- Business continuity improvements
- The ability to shift computing power easily
- Flexibility provided by breaking calculations among many machines

- Cost savings
- Ability to cope cost effectively with spikes

A survey by Economist Intelligence Unit (EIU) on IT managers conducted from 177 *Fortune 500* companies indicate that *cost savings* tops the list of advantages sought by corporations. Companies showed an overall satisfaction; in the EIU survey, 84% said they were satisfied with grids, and 11% said they were extremely satisfied [GridEIU04] (see Figure 2.2).

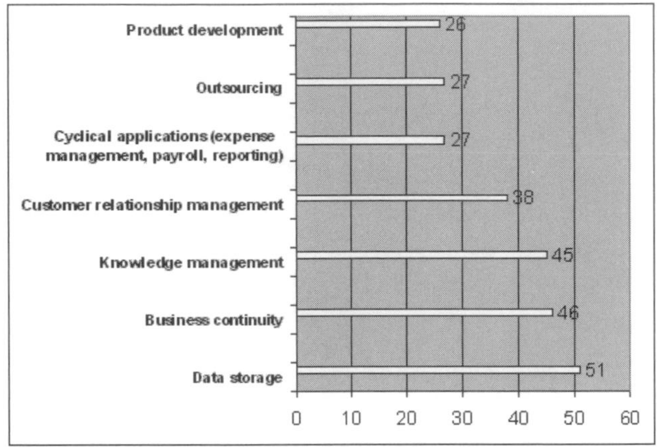

FIGURE 2.2 Business areas where grid computing is expected to have the greatest impact. Source: Economist Intelligence Unit survey, March–April 2004.

2.4.2 Challenges Facing Grid Computing on the Enterprise

Harnessing unused CPU cycles can give huge benefits to corporations and provide cost benefits too. Nevertheless, companies planning the move toward a grid-enabled infrastructure face many challenges:

- Changing IT environments without disrupting the business can be very challenging.
- Modifying applications to run on the grid may require significant hardware and software resources.
- Grid-enabled applications take more time to deploy than traditional applications.
- Complex monitoring as well as security and quality-assurance controls are required.
- Many mainstream enterprise applications aren't yet modified to run on a grid, and many grid vendors are small and unknown.

- Many companies are resistant to the changes grid computing will bring.
- There are concerns that the grid's promise and capabilities may be overhyped.
- Management may be reluctant to accept the advantages of a grid.

As with any new technology, there are many concerns to address including security, business continuity, implementation costs, financial benefits, standardization, and market understanding. Furthermore, the potential for competing standards could leave those who've adopted a losing standard in the dust. Nearly three-quarters of the EIU survey respondents named lack of agreement or momentum for open standards for grid computing as a significant roadblock to grid computing commercial use. According to this survey, grid computing corporate adoption is still years off, but ultimately will be driven by concrete business needs—for cost savings, faster processing time, and greater resilience [GridEIU04].

2.4.3 The Jump to Web Services Resource Framework (WSRF)

In 2004, the WSRF was proposed as an evolution of OGSI to exploit the new Web Services standards such as WS-Addressing. WSRF partitions OGSI functionality into five distinct specifications [WSRF04]:

- **WS-ResourceProperties:** Associates stateful resources and their properties with Web Services. It includes operations to retrieve, change, and delete resource properties.
- **WS-ResourceLifetime:** Creates or destroys a WS-Resources immediately or in the future.
- **WS-RenewableReferences:** Retrieves a new endpoint reference to a service.
- **WS-ServiceGroup:** Manipulates collections of Web Services.
- **WS-BaseFault:** Describes types for error reporting.
- **WS-Notification:** Uses publish and subscribe technologies for notification.

These specifications capture all of the functionality provided by OGSI, but do so in a way that integrates with evolving Web Services standards. In addition, the WSRF expresses the OGSI definition in a more consistent way more familiar to Web Services developers in general. Furthermore, changes required to port OGSI to WSRF services are simple and straightforward [WSRF04].

Grid services evolved from a need for collaboration, data sharing, and other new modes of interaction that involve distributed resources, focusing on the interconnection of systems across enterprises. In addition, companies have realized that they can save costs by outsourcing elements of their IT environment to various service providers. These new requirements for distributed applications have led to the development of grid technologies with a successful adoption in the scientific and technical fields.

2.5 THE COMPETITIVE IT ORGANIZATION

All the factors mentioned in prior sections influence the way enterprises handle their computing needs and represent the challenges enterprises face when modeling business processes. Enterprises face challenges of managing mission-critical applications in networked computing environments. Some of the key factors for building a competitive IT organization include the following:

- Focus on people issues and challenges, organization structure, and processes.
- Build a cost-effective and competitive infrastructure with an infrastructure development life cycle (IDLC).
- Use key methodologies for implementing and supporting a global IT organization.
- Partner with the business and become part of the business rather than being apart from the business.
- Recognize and communicate value to the enterprise.

The implementation of an ideal IT organization extends well beyond technology. Companies must ensure that their IT initiatives are closely aligned with their business objectives. And surprisingly, technology is the easy part. The key is taking a comprehensive approach that truly includes people, process, and organizational disciplines.

2.6 COMPUTATIONAL ECONOMY

Experts predict that global computational grids are expected to drive the economy of the 21st century similar to the way the electric power grid drove the economy of the 20th century. The need for an economy-driven resource management and scheduling system comes as the next logical step in the evolution of this new technology. Just as a decade or so ago when the idea of networking computers together gave rise to the World Wide Web, so will grid computing make the leap into a global economy market. Whether the grid-enabled computational economy will become the next killer application is yet to be seen. In the mean time, this section describes research work conducted in the following topics:

- A rationale for computational economy
- Resource management models for economy-driven grids
- A general discussion on the grid architecture for computational economy (GRACE) research project
- Information about market studies on the penetration of grids in the commercial world, including market data and projections

2.6.1 Why Computational Economy?

The transition of grid computing into the business world requires the development of a new information technology model—a new way of thinking if you will. Such a way of thinking has been called computational economy. Computational economy expands on the concepts of resource management and scheduling. It deals with the coupling of heterogeneous resources distributed across various organizations and administrative domains [GridEconomy].

The motivations or incentives for contributing resources toward building grids, to date, has been driven by public good, prizes, fun, or fame. Public Internet computing research projects that harness idle desktops, such as SETI@home [SETI] and Distributed.net [DistNet04] have been motivated by prizes or collaborative advantage. The chances of gaining access to such computational grids for solving commercial problems are low. Furthermore, access to all other resources is not guaranteed (contributing your PC CPU cycles to SETI@home will not give you access to the rest of CPUs on the project).

Some kind of collaboration is needed. A business model that encourages resource owners to let others use their resources is *computational economy.* In such a model, users are charged for access at a variable rate, buying computing power on-demand from computational grids or resource owners. A grid computing environment needs to support this *economy of computations* by allowing users and resource owners maximize their profits (i.e., the owners want to earn more money and the users want to solve their problems within a minimum possible cost). In a commercial computational grid, the resource owners' act as sellers and the users act as buyers. The pricing of resources will be driven by supply and demand [GridEconomy].

According to the work of computational economy researchers, economy-based resource management provides the following benefits:

- Helps in building large-scale computational grid because it motivates resource owners to contribute their idle resources for others to use and profit from it.
- Provides fair basis for access to grid resources for everyone.
- Helps in regulating the demand and supply.
- Offers an incentive for users to back off when solving low-priority problems and, thus, encourages the solution of time-critical problems first.
- Offers uniform treatment to all resources. That is, it allows trading of everything including computational power, memory, storage, network bandwidth and latency, and devices or instruments.
- Helps in developing scheduling policies that are user centric rather than system centric.
- Offers an efficient mechanism for allocation and management of resources.

- Helps in building a highly scalable system because the decision-making process is distributed across all users and resource owners.
- Places the power with both resource owners and users because they can make their own decisions to maximize utility and profit.

2.6.2 Economy-Driven Grid Resource Management

Economy-driven grid resource management architectures define the following entities that interact with each other [GridEconomy]:

Resources: These are geographically distributed and owned by different individuals or organizations. They have their own access policies and cost mechanisms.

Resource owners: Resource owners manage resources using their own local scheduler and specific policies. They charge a variable price for resource usage.

Grid users: Grid users consume resources based on the policies established by the *resource owners.*

All these entities interact to achieve their goals (see Figure 2.3). Resource owners by maximizing profits and grid users by minimizing the cost required to run their applications. This architecture includes the following components for a resource management system:

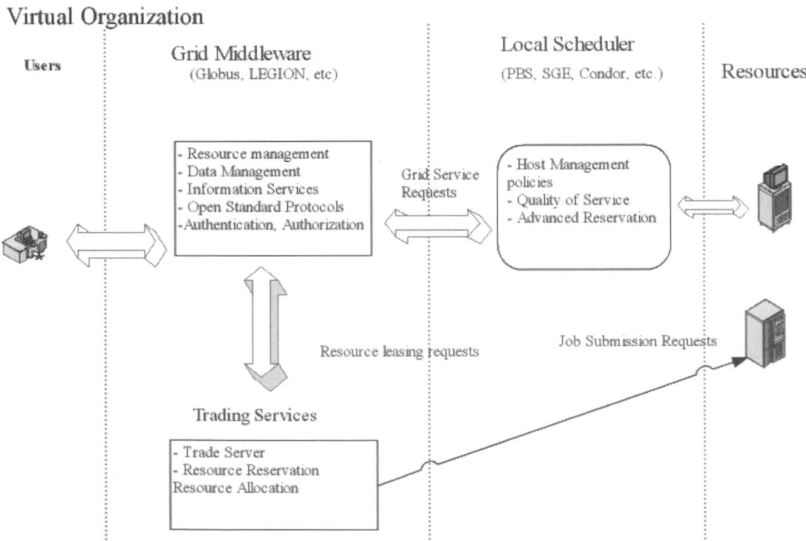

FIGURE 2.3 Components of an economy-driven grid resource management system.

2.6.2.1 Meta Scheduler

The Meta Scheduler, also known as *Grid Resource Broker,* provides a layer between users and resources via middleware services. Its main duties are resource selection and computation initiation. It provides the user a view of the grid as a single entity [GridEconomy01].

2.6.2.2 Grid Middleware

Grid middleware offers services that allow the Meta Scheduler to interact with the local resource schedulers. Among the services provided are resource allocation, data transfer, security, authorization and authentication services, storage allocation, information, and resource reservation services. Software such as Globus [Globus05] implements many of these services.

2.6.2.3 Local Scheduler

Local schedulers are responsible for executing user's requests/programs on local resources. They obey a predefined set of policies imposed by resource owners and may offer access to local devices, hardware and software. Examples of local schedulers are Portable Batch System (PBS), Platform's Local Scheduler Framework (LSF), Sun Grid Engine (SGE), and Condor.

2.6.2.4 User Applications

User applications are the set of programs to be executed by local schedulers on specific resources. Applications may be *sequential* if they execute a set of instructions one after the other, *parametric* if they take a set of input parameters, or *parallel* if they are capable of running instructions in parallel.

2.6.3 Resource Management Models

Resource management models are tightly integrated to a *resource scheduler* design. A resource scheduler or, simply, scheduler is a software component that accounts for the following:

- Number of resources to manage
- Location of those resources
- Types of jobs, and the computations to be performed

Common scheduling models include centralized, decentralized, and hierarchical.

2.6.3.1 Centralized

In this model, centralized resource management is capable of scheduling single or multiple resources on single or multiple domains. This is suitable for queuing systems and supports uniform policies. It is not, however, suitable for grid scheduling because it is expected to honor policies imposed by the resource owner.

2.6.3.2 Decentralized

In this model, multiple schedulers interact to decide which job should be applied to a specific resource. There is no central scheduler. This model has the advantages of being highly scalable and fault tolerant. It has the disadvantages of being difficult to implement and having potential scheduling optimization problems. However, it suits the grid computing model.

2.6.3.3 Hierarchical

This model is a combination of the centralized and decentralized models. A resource broker or super scheduler sits on top of local schedulers or resources. This broker allows remote resource owners to enforce their own policies on external users, thus it is suitable for grid computing.

Grid-enabled economies such as GRACE build on resource management models to bridge the gap between the scientific and business worlds.

2.6.4 Grid Architecture for Computational Economy (GRACE)

Low-cost high-performance machines have transformed the Internet into a ubiquitous commodity communication media. With the emergence of grid computing from the scientific into the business fields, the concept of *computational economy* is emerging to address the transition [GridEconomy01]. Scientists from the GRACE project have proposed the following requirements of a computational grid economy-driven framework:

- The need for resource discovery, brokering, and economy of computations.
- Cost-based scheduling mechanisms driven by user-supplied application deadlines and resource access budgets.
- Dynamic resource trading services required to facilitate flexible application scheduling
- A middleware infrastructure for trading resources to support dynamic scheduling capabilities.

GRACE addresses these issues with economy-driven resource management features [GridEconomy]. GRACE provides services for trading resources dynamically and complements the resource management features provided by middleware such as the *Globus Toolkit*.

2.6.4.1 GRACE Components

The GRACE framework has been designed to support the computational economy by means of resource brokering and dynamic trading capabilities. GRACE works with middleware services such as Globus and may have the following components:

2.6.4.2 Trade Manager and Trade Server

The Trade Manager (TM) interacts with the trade server to provide access to resources at low cost. It uses resource selection algorithms to identify access costs. The Trade Server (TS) is an agent that negotiates with users and sells access to resources. It uses pricing algorithms to maximize resource utility and interacts with the accounting system to track resource usage.

2.6.4.3 Grid Trading Protocols

The trading protocols define the rules for exchanging messages between the TM and TS under the GRACE architecture. Messages can contain formation such as quote/bid, resource requirements, or a deal template (DT). The contents of DT include CPU time units, expected usage duration, storage requirements, and so on.

2.6.4.4 Grid Open Trading APIs

Trade APIs are a set of application programming interfaces provided by GRACE to support software development for computational economy. Clients may use these functions to communicate with trade agents to perform connections, request resource quotes and negotiate trades.

2.7 SUMMARY

According to the EIU survey, a substantial number of IT managers expect grid computing to have a major impact on business around the world within the next decade. One-third of the respondents said they expect grid computing to have a significant impact on their industry in the next five years, 4% said they expect the impact to be massive [GridEIU04] (see Figure 2.4).

To calculate the potential impact of grids on the enterprise, one just needs to look back a decade or so ago. Those who remember how LANs developed in companies years before the Web was born can easily get a picture of how grid computing in corporations may change in the years to come. In the early days of the Internet, there was a strong opposition to linking computers together in a network. Ultimately, however, the Internet has become a ubiquitous tool, and many experts predict the same outcome for grid computing on the enterprise. There are still concerns to consider and obstacles to be overcome, but the momentum behind corporate grid computing is quickly gathering pace.

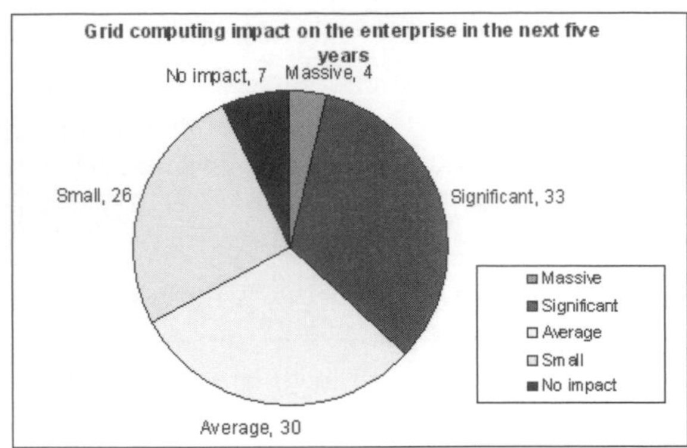

FIGURE 2.4 Survey of the impact belief of grids by IT managers on their core business.

The integration of grid technologies into enterprise computing systems can provide a much richer range of possibilities. For example, grid services and protocols can be used to achieve decoupling of hardware and software, portable adaptors could use the grid resource management protocol to access resources spread across a VO; or grid information services could be used by naming and trading services to query distributed information sources. This integration should provide enhanced capabilities and interoperability to meet current VO demands.

REFERENCES

[Ambler04] Scott W. Ambler, *Concurrency Control, Bringing Data Professionals and Application Developers Together.* John Wiley & Sons, 2004, summary of Chapter 17.

[Condor04] Condor Team. *Condor Version 6.6.6 Manual.* University of Wisconsin–Madison. Accessed online July 28, 2004, at *http://www.cs.wisc.edu/condor/manual/v6.6.6/.*

[DistNet04] Distributed.Net Distributed Computing Network. Accessed online May 2004 at *http://www.distributed.net/.*

[Frankel03] David S. Frankel. *Model Driven Architecture: Applying MDA to Enterprise Computing.* John Wiley & Sons, 2003.

[Globus05] The Globus Alliance. University of Chicago. Accessed online January 2005 at *http://www.globus.org/.*

[GridAnatomy01] Ian Foster, Carl Kesselman, and Steven Tuecke. "The Anatomy of the Grid." *International Journal of Supercomputer Applications, 15*(3), 200–222 (2001). Available online at *www.globus.org/research/papers/anatomy.pdf.*

[GridEconomy] Rajkumar Buyya, David Abramson, and Jonathan Giddy. *Economy Driven Resource Management Architecture for Global Computational Power Grids.* School of Computer Science and Software Engineering Monash University and CRC for Enterprise Distributed Systems Technology University of Queensland. Melbourne, Australia.

[GridEconomy01] Rajkumar Buyya, Jonathan Giddy, and David Abramson. *An Evaluation of Economy-based Resource Trading and Scheduling on Computational Power Grids for Parameter Sweep Applications.* School of Computer Science and Software Engineering Monash University and CRC for Enterprise Distributed Systems Technology, University of Queensland, Melbourne, Australia.

[GridEIU04] Grid Computing Corporate Prospects. *The Economist* Intelligence Unit survey, March–April 2004.

[GridPhysiology04] Ian Foster, Carl Kesselman, Steven Tuecke, and Jeffrey Nick. *The Physiology of the Grid, An Open Grid Services Architecture for Distributed Systems Integration.* Mathematics and Computer Science Division, Argonne National Laboratory, Argonne, IL 60439. Department of Computer Science, University of Chicago, Chicago, IL 60637. Information Sciences Institute, University of Southern California, Marina del Rey, CA 90292. IBM Corporation, Poughkeepsie, NY 12601. *http://www-unix.globus.org/ogsa/docs/alpha/physiology.pdf.*

[King02] Paul King. "Object Resource Pooling." Object Computing, Inc. (OCI) *Java News Brief* Available online at *http://www.ociweb.com/jnb/jnbMar2002.html*, March 2002.

[ResMgrModels00] Rajkumar Buyya, Steve Chapin, and David DiNucci. "Architectural Models for Resource Management in the Grid." Intl. Conf. on Parallel and Distributed Processing Techniques and Applications (PDPTA 2000), USA.

[SETI] The Search for Extraterrestrial Intelligence. SETI@home. Accessed online 2001 at *http://setiathome.ssl.berkeley.edu/*

[SGEUserGruide04] *N1 Grid Engine 6 User's Guide.* Sun Microsystems, 2004.

[ShanRalph97] Yen-Ping Shan and Ralph H. Earle. *Enterprise Computing with Objects: From Client/Server Environments to the Internet.* Addison-Wesley Professional, 1997, Ch 1, 3, 5.

[WSRF04] K. Czajkowski, D. Ferguson, I. Foster, J. Frey, S. Graham, T. Maguire. *From Open Grid Services Infrastructure to WSResource Framework: Refactoring & Evolution.* Copyright Fujitsu Limited, International Business Machines Corporation and The University of Chicago 2003, 2004. All Rights Reserved. Available online at *http://www.chinagrid.net/dvnews/upload/2005_04/05040200359561.pdf.*

3 Core Grid Middleware

In This Chapter

- P2P
- Globus
- Grid Computing and Business Technologies (GRIDBUS)
- Summary
- References

Grid middleware offers services that couple users with remote resources through resource brokers. The services offered include services for remote process management, co-allocation of resources, storage access, information, security, authentication, and quality of service (QoS) such as resource reservation and trading. Depending on the needs of your organization, different types of grid middleware are available. Among the most popular are peer-to-peer (P2P), Globus, and grid-economy architectures. This chapter discusses the most popular grid middleware available today, including:

- A discussion of the characteristics and structure of peer-to-peer networks, as well as benefits and drawbacks
- The Globus toolkit, which is emerging as the de facto standard for grid middleware
- Grid Computing and Business Technologies (GRIDBUS), a framework that merges grid technology with business requirements

P2P goes beyond client-server sharing modalities and computational structures, and it has much in common with grid technologies. Nevertheless, P2P and the grid have not yet overlapped. This is because P2P vendors have not defined common protocols that would allow for shared infrastructure and interoperability in their quest to achieve monopoly over their competitors. Another disadvantage of P2P is limited sharing capabilities targeted by applications. For example, file sharing with no access control and computational sharing with a centralized server.

Grid middleware such as Globus provides the following benefits:

- Resource allocation and process management
- Authentication and security services
- Resource information and discovery services
- Remote access to data via sequential and parallel interfaces
- Advanced resource reservation

On the other hand, Globus lacks certain important features such as a centralized management system for security credentials. Currently, grid security infrastructure (GSI) certificates are scattered all over the resource locations. Globus also lacks advanced resource reservation features to deliver quality of service. The Globus project has been working to address such drawbacks with projects such as Community Authorization Service (CAS) and Advanced Reservation (GARA).

Moreover, the OGSA framework has faced intense criticism from the Web Services community claiming that OGSA is too bulky (there is too much stuff in the specification); it does not work well with existing Web Services and XML tooling; it is too object oriented, and it lacks support for WSDL 2.0 capabilities. Current Globus efforts aim to move OGSA to the latest Web Services specification called Web Services Resource Framework (WSRF), which simplifies and clarifies some ideas expressed in OGSA such as transport-neutral mechanisms to address Web Services and mechanisms for obtaining information about a published service, its WSDL description, XML schema, and policy information.

An economy-based grid architecture expands these services by providing additional features, such as dynamic resource trading services. These services allow trade for the best resources based on price and performance available and schedule computations on these resources to meet user requirements. This requires a dynamic interaction between resource brokers and resource owners using standard and open protocols. The benefits of this economy are that it does the following:

- Regulates the demand and supply by providing a fair basis for resource access by everyone
- Helps in building a large computational grid and encourages owners to contribute their resources

- Helps in developing scheduling policies that are user centric rather than system centric
- Offers uniform treatment to all resources by using efficient mechanisms for resource allocation and management

3.1 P2P

P2P gained popularity in 2001 with the birth of Napster's music community on the Web. P2P later became infamous with the lawsuit of the music companies over digital rights management. Nevertheless, P2P is increasingly becoming an important technique in areas such as distributed and collaborative computing. It has received attention from many industrial partners such as Intel, Hewlett Packard, Sony, and a number of startup companies. Open source P2P initiatives such as Sun's JXTA are leading the way, and a number academic events are dedicated to P2P. Many P2P projects are in progress at universities and research institutes.

P2P computing goes beyond the client-server architecture by using enhanced sharing modalities and computational structures. For this reason, P2P has much in common with grid technologies, although the domains have not overlapped. One reason is the lack of common P2P protocols that would allow shared infrastructure and interoperability, typical of a market where participants want to acquire a monopoly. Another is the lack of access control, and computational sharing with centralized servers. As the need for interoperability and standards arises, we will see a strong convergence of P2P, Internet, and grid computing technologies. For example, single sign-on, delegation, and authorization may become important for resource sharing interoperability as the access policies to those resources become more complex.

3.1.1 Definition

P2P can be defined as a set of software applications that consume distributed resources (computing power, content, network bandwidth, and presence—computers, human, and other resources) to perform *functions* in a decentralized manner. These functions may include distributed computing, data and content sharing, communication and collaboration [P2PComputing02].

3.1.2 Advantages and Disadvantages

As with any software system, the goal of P2P is to support applications that satisfy the needs of users. According to Milojicic and colleagues [P2PComputing02], this technology offers the following advantages:

- *Low cost of interoperability* by aggregating resources through decentralization
- Low *cost of ownership* by using existing infrastructure and distributing maintenance costs
- *Privacy* by allowing peers an autonomous control over data and resources

However, P2P raises the following concerns or disadvantages:

- It is a relatively new technology still in development and lacks standards.
- Legal and accountability concerns for businesses (for example, lawsuits with music companies over digital rights management).
- Networking issues: P2P applications drain significant bandwidth resources in such a way that most companies currently forbid the use of P2P applications within their intranets.

3.1.3 P2P Versus the Client-Server Model

The client-server model is built on a centralized single or small cluster of servers and many clients, whereas P2P presents an alternative in which autonomous peers depend on other peers. Peers are not controlled by each other or by the same authority and depend on others to get information, resources, sending and receiving requests, and so on.

3.1.3.1 Scalability and Reliability

The client-server model relies on a strong central authority (server) where the server manages clients. In contrast, P2P presents a self-organized model that has no concept of server; rather, all participants are *peers*. A client-server application is organized in a hierarchical manner; it is usually static, configured, and depends on a server.

P2P, on the other hand, resembles a mesh structure where all nodes can connect to each other. It is dynamic and ad hoc and relies on independent lifetime of its peers.

3.1.3.2 Interoperability

P2P creates a highly dynamic network of peers with complex topology unrelated to the physical network. This topology defines an overlay network created ad hoc where resources are aggregated or removed as peers connect or disconnect from the network.

3.1.3.3 Autonomy and Privacy

P2P allows that all data and work be performed locally. The client-server model requires persistent connections for any kind of work. Because local nodes can do the work, P2P provides a higher degree of privacy, whereas in the client-server model, the server is able to identify the client by IP address and other information.

3.1.3.4 Network Structure and Fault Tolerance

In P2P, resources such as nodes will be entering and leaving the network continuously, effectively creating an ad hoc topology. This is a natural fit for P2P. The client-server model, on the other hand, implements a hierarchical model where clients connect to a central server and all traffic gets routed trough the central node. This model has the disadvantage that if the central server goes down, so does the network. A P2P network is fault tolerant in the sense that if a node goes down, it gets replaced dynamically by the network itself.

3.1.4 P2P Architectures

A Survey of Peer-to-Peer File Sharing Technologies by Stephanos Androutsellis-Theotokis classifies P2P architectures by their degree of centralization and network structure. *Degree of centralization* refers to the level at which they rely on central servers for peer interaction. *Network structure* refers to how content is located relative to the network topology (e.g., preconfigured versus ad hoc networks). According to the degree of centralization, P2P architectures can be classified as [SurveyP2P02] hybrid decentralized, pure decentralized, and partially centralized.

3.1.4.1 Hybrid Decentralized

This architecture is not really considered a P2P system because peers rely on a central server to store metadata about the users connected to the network and the files they share. The central server facilitates peer interaction by performing lookups and tracking the nodes on the network where files live. Once a specific file has been located on a node, the peers open a direct connection and proceed with a file transfer.

Hybrid systems have the advantage of being simple and having the ability to perform searches quickly and efficiently. Major disadvantages include being vulnerable to attacks and failures because of its centralized nature. Furthermore, hybrid systems are not scalable and are limited by the size of their database and query capacity. An example of a hybrid P2P system is *Napster*.

3.1.4.2 Pure Decentralized

In the *pure decentralized* model, applications act as both client and servers, with no centralization of the activities in the network. This model builds a virtual overlay network with its own routing mechanisms. An example of this model is the Gnutella network, which works as a distributed storage system, allowing users to specify the directories they want to share with their peers [SurveyP2P02].

Because of its unstructured nature, the pure decentralized model uses random searches when probing for resources over the network. Under this architecture, peers have no way of guessing where a specific file resides. For example, in a Gnutella network, messages are forwarded to all neighbors as soon as received and, to avoid flooding the network with messages, a Time to Live (TTL) value is attached to each message. On each node hop, this value is decreased, and once a file has been identified on a target system, a direct transfer between the peers is initiated. This system has the disadvantage that the TTL value segments the network creating a threshold beyond which messages cannot reach. This causes scalability problems although alternative communication methods are described. Another disadvantage is that significant network traffic is generated with each query. Proposed solutions to this problem include using parallel random walks and other node discovery methods [SurveyP2P02].

3.1.4.3 Partially Centralized

Partially centralized systems introduce the concept of *super nodes*. These are nodes in charge of servicing subsections of the peer network. Super nodes are selected based on bandwidth and CPU power, and some of their duties include indexing and caching files. When a client connects to the network, a list of super nodes to connect to is queried from a central server.

An advantage of this network is the reduction of node discovery times compared with pure decentralized systems. Another advantage is a high degree of *fault tolerance* as super nodes can be dynamically replaced in case of system failures. Examples of this model include the popular Morpheus and Kazaa programs (see Figure 3.1).

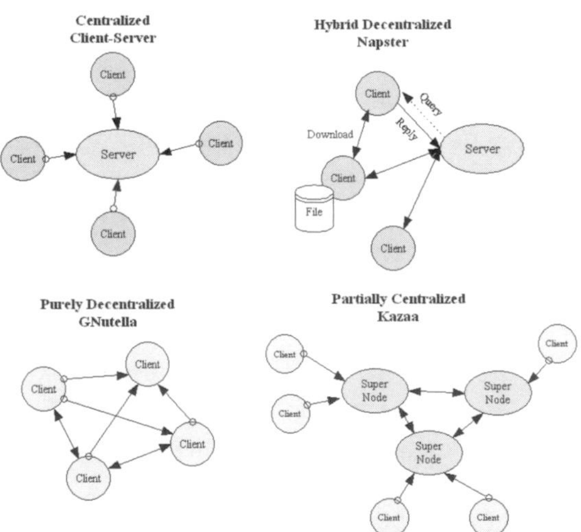

FIGURE 3.1 Client-server and P2P architectures.

According to the network structure or topology, P2P systems can be classified as unstructured, structured, and loosely structured.

3.1.4.4 Unstructured

In unstructured networks, the placement of files is independent of the overlay topology. Because there is no central repository for resource information, clients have no way of knowing where a file resides. Thus searches rely on random walks, generating a significant amount of traffic with each query. The advantage is that it can easily accommodate transient node populations. The disadvantage is poor scalability and high network query traffic.

3.1.4.5 Structured

Structured networks emerged to address the scalability issues from unstructured networks. In a structured network, resources such as files are closely tied to the network topology; they use distributed routing tables to map files to their respective locations. This model has the disadvantage of maintainability of the structure of the routing tables for temporary node populations where nodes join and leave at high rates [SurveyP2P02].

3.1.4.6 Loosely Structured

Loosely structured sits between the previous two models. It uses a mix of routing tables and random walks to locate files over the network. An example of this model is the open project *Freenet.com.*

3.2 GLOBUS

The Globus Toolkit (GT) (*www.globustoolkit.org*) is one of the exciting middleware software products that helped to launch grid computing onto center stage. Researchers from Argonne National Laboratory at the University of Illinois, Chicago, created GT in late 1994 when the director of the mathematics and computer science division and the director of the Electronic Visualization Laboratory proposed establishing temporary links between 11 high-speed research networks to create a national grid (the "I-WAY") during the Supercomputing '95 conference.

This successful experiment led to funding from the Defense Advanced Research Projects Agency (DARPA), and 1997 saw the first version of the Globus Toolkit, which was soon deployed across 80 sites worldwide. The U.S. Department of Energy (DOE) pioneered the application of grids to science research, the National Science Foundation (NSF) funded creation of the National Technology Grid to connect university scientists with high-end computers, and NASA started similar work on its Information Power Grid.

The Globus Toolkit has been called the de facto standard for grid computing by the *New York Times*. In 2002, the project earned a prestigious R&D 100 award, given by *R&D Magazine* in a ceremony where the Globus Toolkit was named "Most Promising New Technology" among the year's top 100 innovations.

In recent months, the Globus Toolkit has seen widespread adoption in commercial grounds as well in the scientific community. Since 2000, companies like Avaki, DataSynapse, Entropia, Fujitsu, Hewlett-Packard, IBM, NEC, Oracle, Platform, Sun, and United Devices have pursued grid strategies based on the Globus Toolkit. The project has spurred a revolution in the way science is conducted. Nevertheless, Globus is committed to preserving the open-source, nonprofit ideology on which this project was built on, while seeding commercial grids based on open standards.

3.3 GRID COMPUTING AND BUSINESS TECHNOLOGIES (GRIDBUS)

GRIDBUS (*www.gridbus.org*) merges grid technology with business requirements. The project was started by Grid Computing and Distributed Systems (GRIDS) Laboratory at the University of Melbourne in Australia. The GRIDBUS project team is developing middleware, tools, and applications that deliver end-to-end quality of services depending on user requirements. Its main components are the following:

- Economic Grid Scheduler: A local scheduler to lease services on distributed resources depending on their availability, performance, cost, and users' quality-of-service requirements
- Cluster Scheduler (Libra): An economy-based scheduler for clusters
- GridSim: A toolkit for modeling and simulation
- A Data Grid broker: A component for scheduling of distributed applications across multiplatform (Windows/Unix) grid resources
- GridBank: An accounting, authentication, and payment management infrastructure
- GUI tools for workflow management and composition

3.4 SUMMARY

Grid middleware helps in building a highly scalable system because the decision-making process is distributed across all users and resource owners. This places the power in the hand of both resource owners and users so they can make their own decisions to achieve the goals of their organizations. When thinking about grid middleware, you should think of applications and quality of service, rather than of frameworks. If you find yourself with the task of building a grid within your organization, ask yourself what application that is already available can take advantage of resource sharing and quality of service? Is it possible to build a component or service to coordinate those resources? Is user authorization/authentication a requirement? What about open standards of protocols? Once you identify such an application, the most difficult part is over. On the other hand, thinking only of frameworks could leave your organization with many interconnected resources and services, but nothing to run on them.

REFERENCES

[P2PComputing02] D. Milojicic, V. Kalogeraki, R. Lukose, K. Nagaraja, J. Pruyne, B. Richard, S. Rollins, and Z. Xu. *Peer-to-Peer Computing.* HP Laboratories Palo Alto. HPL-2002-57. Accessed online March 8th, 2002, at *http://www.cs.umbc.edu/~pmundur/courses/CMSC691M-04/p2p-survey.pdf.*

[SurveyP2P02] Stephanos Androutsellis-Theotokis. "A Survey of Peer-to-Peer File Sharing Technologies," Athens University of Economics and Business, Greece, Copyright 2002. Accessed online at *http://duch.mimuw.edu.pl/~alx/ask/androutsellis-theoto02survey.pdf.*

Part II Grid Middleware

This part covers a comprehensive description of the components of a grid-enabled framework. There is plenty of source code and figures, including the following:

Grid Portal Development: Chapter 4 describes software for grid portal environments. Source code and applications are included for two of the main grid protocols: resource management and data management. The software is written for two popular portal servers: Apache Jetspeed and IBM WebSphere Portal Server. This chapter includes plenty of source code, figures, and troubleshooting tips.

Schedulers: Schedulers are at the foundation of any grid system. Their job is to schedule programs or jobs in clusters of machines among others. Chapter 5 describes development for many open source schedulers, including OpenPBS, Sun Grid Engine (SGE), Condor, and others. This chapter also includes integration concepts with the Managed Job Factory Service (MJS) provided by the Globus Toolkit and troubleshooting tips.

Open Grid Services Architecture (OGSA): Open Grid Services Architecture is the middle-tier software that glues grid clients and scheduler services together. Chapter 6 provides a comprehensive overview of OGSA, including service models, interfaces, factories, lifetime management, service discovery, notifications, and higher level services.

The chapter also describes the relationship of grid services and Web Services within a virtual organization (VO) and the role the Globus Toolkit plays in that scenario. Software described in this chapter includes a grid service for large integer factorization using a quadratic sieve.

4 Grid Portal Development

In This Chapter

- Resource Management
- Data Management Portlets
- Troubleshooting
- Summary
- References

This chapter provides information on development of portals that use the APIs provided by the Globus toolkit. All source code provided here is available from the companion CD-ROM along with installation and deployment information: source code, binaries, read-me files, and so on. Topics in this chapter include the following:

- Resource management (Globus Resource Allocation Manager [GRAM]) portlets for Apache Jetspeed and IBM WebSphere Portal Server (WPS)
- Data Management portlets implementing all major data transfer protocols: GridFTP, Globus Access to Secondary Storage (GASS), and HTTPS
- An extensive troubleshooting section on installation, deployment, and testing of all the code implemented in this chapter

To run the programs in this chapter, the following software is required:

- *WebSphere Studio Application Developer 5.1.x with the Portal Toolkit or Apache Tomcat with Jetspeed portal engine*
- *Globus Toolkit version 2.x or 3.2.x*

Installation Instructions

- *IBM WPS: Import the folder CH04_WPSPortlets into your workspace directory or create a new portlet project and then copy the files to your favorite location, right-click the project name and select run on server.*

Make sure the Portal Toolkit is properly installed and the imported project is a portlet project. All the files should be visible within your project workspace.

- *Apache Jetspeed: Make sure Tomcat with Jetspeed is properly installed in your system and then follow the simple instructions provided in the Jetspeed sections on this chapter on copying the required files to the proper locations.*

Portals are important components in grid computing that provide an open, standards-based user interface to grid middleware. An enterprise portal consists of middleware, applications (called portlets), and development tools for building and managing business-to-business (B2B), business-to-consumer (B2C), and business-to-employee (B2E) portals. A portal is a Web site that provides users with a single point of access to Web-based resources by aggregating those resources in one place and by requiring that users log in only to the portal itself, and not to each portlet they use. An enterprise portal makes network resources such as applications and databases available to end users. The user can access the portal via a Web browser, Wireless Application Protocol (WAP)-phone, pager, or any other device. The portal acts as the central hub where information from multiple sources is made available in an easy-to-use manner [IBMWPS04].

One of the advantages of a portal is that the data presented is independent of content type. This means that content from XML, RSS, or SMTP can be integrated with the portal itself. The actual presentation of the data is handled via Extensible Stylesheet Language Transformations (XSLT) and delivered to the user via the combination of Java Server Pages (JSPs) and HTML. An enterprise portal provides a tool for both portal developers as well as for user interface designers that facilitate building an XML portlet and content syndication.

4.1 RESOURCE MANAGEMENT

The following section explores a series of JSP portlets for the GRAM protocol used for remote *job submission* against a remote node on a grid. Portlets for two popular platforms are implemented: Apache Jetspeed and IBM WebSphere Portal Server.

4.1.1 Apache Jetspeed

Jetspeed is an open source implementation of an Enterprise Information Portal using Java and XML. It supports the following features as described in Apache Portals—Jetspeed [JetSpeed04]:

- Template-based layouts, including JSP and Velocity
- Remote XML content feeds via Open Content Syndication
- Custom configuration
- Database user authentication
- Rich Site Summary (RSS) support for syndicated content
- Wireless Markup Language (WML) support
- XML-based configuration registry of portlets
- Full Web Application Archive (WAR) support
- Profiler Service to access portal pages based on user, groups, roles, access control lists (ACLs), media types, and language
- Skins that allow users to choose colors and display attributes
- Customizer, which allows users to select portlets and define layouts for individual pages
- User, group, role, and permission administration via Jetspeed security portlets.
- Role-based security access to portlets

4.1.2 A Resource Management JSP Portlet for Jetspeed

A JSP Portlet in Jetspeed is straightforward, and requires two files:

- A JSP implementation of the portlet itself *(gram.jsp)*. This file must be placed in the Jetspeed portlets directory [JETSPEED_HOME]\WEB-INF\templates\jsp\portlets\html
- A portlet registry descriptor *(gram.xreg)*, which contains portlet metadata information such as name, implementation class, and so on. This file must be placed in the Jetspeed configuration directory [JETSPEED_HOME]\WEB-INF\conf.
- GRAM client implementation Java classes in the portlet binaries directory [JETSPEED_HOME]\WEB-INF\classes.

4.1.2.1 GRAM Client UML Diagram

Our first JSP GRAM portlet requires a set of Java clients to access resources via the Globus GRAM protocol. The client programs presented here include the following functionality:

- Support for GRAM2 protocol from the Globus Toolkit 2.2.x using Resource Scripting Language (RSL) templates

- Support for GRAM3–Master Job Factory Service (MMJFS) using XML-based templates
- Support for batch and nonbatch job submission modes, dry run submissions, and staging of executables

The following Unified Modeling Language (UML) diagram depicts the relationships between these client programs implemented as four classes in the Java language (see Figure 4.1).

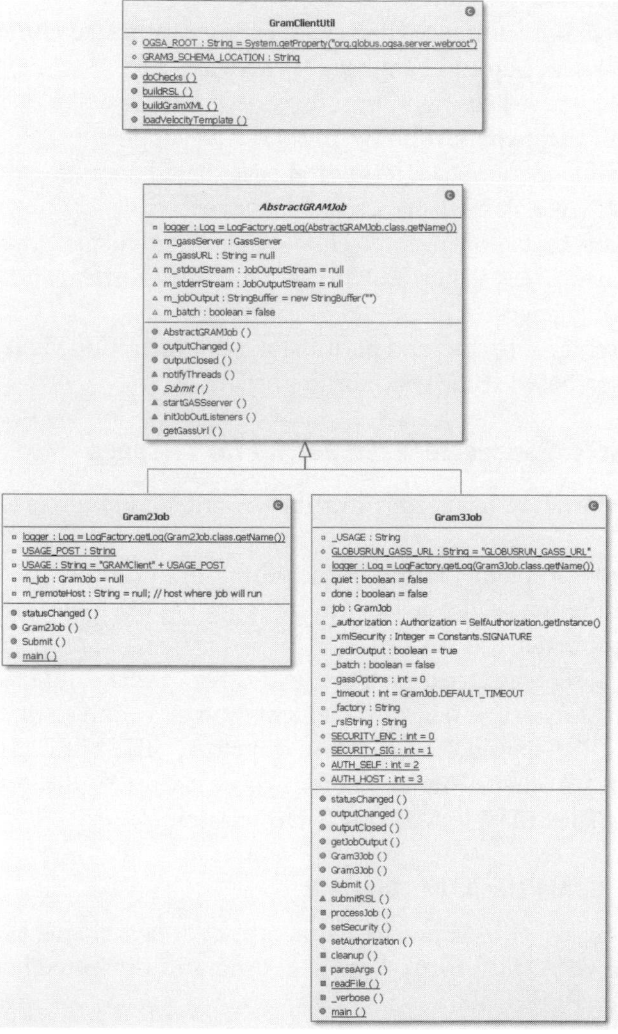

FIGURE 4.1 UML diagram of the JAVA clients used by the GRAM portlets.

4.1.2.2 GRAM Client Programs

The programs in the following sections assume familiarity with the Globus Toolkit resource management protocol as well as terminology such as RSL, and the Globus command-line interface (CLI), specifically the inner workings of the *globus-run* command. Further information is available at the Globus project Web site.

The client code is implemented in two straightforward Java classes, one per protocol version, with common functionality implemented in an abstract base class. The abstract program shown in Listing 4.1 implements the common functionality.

LISTING 4.1 AbstractGRAMJob.java—Abstract Java Class That Implements Common Functionality for the GRAM2 and GRAM3 Client Programs

```
package gram.client;

/**
 * <p>Title:AbstractGRAMJob </p>
 * <p>Description: Abstract Class for the GRAM 2.x 3.x protocol</p>
 * @author Vladimir Silva
 * @version 1.0
 */

import org.globus.io.gass.server.*;

import org.apache.commons.logging.Log;
import org.apache.commons.logging.LogFactory;

public abstract class AbstractGRAMJob
    // listen for job output from GASS server
    implements JobOutputListener
{
  private static Log logger =
      LogFactory.getLog(AbstractGRAMJob.class.getName());

  // GASS Server: required to get job output
  GassServer m_gassServer;

  // URL of the GASS server
  String m_gassURL = null;

  // Job output variables:
  // Used for non-batch mode jobs to receive output from
  // gatekeeper through the GASS server

  JobOutputStream m_stdoutStream = null;
  JobOutputStream m_stderrStream = null;
```

```
  // job output as string
  StringBuffer m_jobOutput = new StringBuffer("");

  // Submission modes:   batch=do not wait for output
  boolean m_batch = false;

// Globus job id on the form:
// https://server.com:39374/15621/1021382777/

  public AbstractGRAMJob() {
  }

  /**
   * It is called whenever the job's output
   * has been updated.
   *
   * @param output new output
   */
  public void outputChanged(String output) {
    m_jobOutput.append(output + "\n");
  }

  /**
   * It is called whenever job finished
   * and no more output will be generated.
   */
  public void outputClosed() {
  }

  void notifyThreads() {
    synchronized (this) {
      notify();
    }
  }

  public abstract String Submit(String rsl);

  /**
   * Start the GASS Server
   * Used to transfer data between MJFS and GRAM client
   */
  boolean startGASSserver(int gassOptions) {
    logger.debug("Starting the GASS server.");
    try {
```

```
      m_gassServer = new GassServer();
      if (gassOptions != 0) {
        m_gassServer.setOptions(gassOptions);

      }
      m_gassServer.registerDefaultDeactivator();
      m_gassURL = m_gassServer.getURL();

      // Listen for GASS stdout/stderr output
      initJobOutListeners();

    }
    catch (Exception e) {
      logger.error(
          "Exception while starting the GASS server: ", e);
      return false;
    }
    logger.info(m_gassServer.toString());
    return true;
  }

  /**
   * Init job out listeners for non-batch mode jobs.
   */
  void initJobOutListeners() throws Exception {
    if (m_stdoutStream != null) {
      return;
    }
    // job output vars
    m_stdoutStream = new JobOutputStream(this);
    m_stderrStream = new JobOutputStream(this);

    m_gassServer
        .registerJobOutputStream("err", m_stderrStream);
    m_gassServer
        .registerJobOutputStream("out", m_stdoutStream);

    return;
  }

  public String getGassUrl() {
    return m_gassServer.getURL();
  }

}
```

Listing 4.1 defines the Java class `AbstractGRAMJob` with common methods used by both GRAM2 and GRAM3 protocols. When the protocol negotiation starts, the GASS service is required. GASS allows transferring job information back and forth between client and server. The GASS server can be started as follows:

```
GassServer m_gassServer = new GassServer();

// A deactivator is used for GASS shutdown
m_gassServer.registerDefaultDeactivator();
```

The next step is to enable the client to listen for job output (`initJobOutListeners`). For example, the following code will listen for standard input and error from the server:

```
JobOutputStream m_stdoutStream = new JobOutputStream(this);
JobOutputStream m_stderrStream = new JobOutputStream(this);

// Register stdin/stderr with GASS
m_gassServer.registerJobOutputStream("err", m_stderrStream);
m_gassServer
.registerJobOutputStream("out", m_stdoutStream);
```

To allow `AbstractGRAMJob` to listen for server output, the interface Job OutputListener must be implemented. This interface defines the methods

```
public void outputChanged(String output)
public void outputClosed()
```

These methods will be called whenever the output changes or is closed by the server, thus allowing the client to receive it. The next code listing, defines the class Gram2Job, which extends `AbstractGramJob` and submits a job against GT2.

4.1.2.3 GRAM2 Protocol Client Program

The GRAM2 client program (see Listing 4.2) acts essentially as a *globus-run* command in GT2. It supports most of the functionality of the *globus-run* command including the following:

- Job Submission modes: batch versus nonbatch
- RSL
- Staging of the executable and standard input files

LISTING 4.2 Gram2.java –Client for the GT 2.x GRAM Protocol

```
package gram.client;

/**
 * <p>Title: </p>
 * <p>Description: Job Submission client program for GT 2.x</p>
 * @author Vladimir Silva
 * @version 1.0
 */
import org.globus.gram.*;
import org.globus.io.gass.server.*;
import org.globus.util.deactivator.Deactivator;

import org.apache.commons.logging.Log;
import org.apache.commons.logging.LogFactory;

/**
 * GT2 - GRAM2 Job Submission client program
 */
public class Gram2Job
    extends AbstractGRAMJob
    //listen for job status messages
    implements GramJobListener
{
  private static Log logger =
      LogFactory.getLog(Gram2Job.class.getName());

  private static String USAGE_POST =
      " [GRAM Contact] [RSL String]\n"
      + "Example:\n"
      + "\tGRAM Contact"
      + " => 192.168.74.131:32779:/O=Grid/OU=GlobusTest/"
      + "OU=simpleCA-vm-rhl8-2.ibm.com/OU=ibm.com/Cn=Globus"
      + "\n\tRSL String => &(executable=/bin/date)(directory=/bin)";

  private static String USAGE = "GRAMClient" + USAGE_POST;

  // GRAM JOB to be executed
  private GramJob m_job = null;

  // host where job will run
  private String m_remoteHost = null;
```

The java class `Gram2Job` implements the interface `GramJobListener`, which listen for job status changes; for example if the job fails or completes. This interface will then fire the method `statusChanged` (`GramJob` job) where logic needs to be inserted to handle the different job statuses. In this particular instance, if the job succeeds, then the waiting thread will be notified as to continue execution. If the job fails, an error message will be appended to the output:

```
/**
 * This method is used to notify the caller when the status of a
 * GramJob has changed.
 *
 * @param job The GramJob whose status has changed.
 */
public void statusChanged( GramJob job )
{
  try
  {
    if ( job.getStatus() == GramJob.STATUS_DONE )
    {
      // notify waiting thread when job ready
      if ( m_batch )
        m_jobOutput.append( "Job sent. url=" + job.getIDAsString() );

      // if notify enabled return URL as output
      this.notifyThreads();
    }

    if ( job.getStatus() == GramJob.STATUS_FAILED )
    {
      m_jobOutput.append( "GRAM Job Failed because "
           + GramException.getMessage( job.getError() )
           + ". (error code " + job.getError() + ")" );
      this.notifyThreads();
    }

  }
  catch ( Exception ex )
  {
    System.out.println( "statusChanged Error:" + ex.getMessage() );
  }
}
```

The class `constructor` is in charge of initialization. It requires a *Contact* string, which defines the remote GT2 gatekeeper. The contact can include a server name or IP as well as a port number and a credential subject. For example, the contact string

```
foo.com:32779:/O=Grid/OU=GlobusTest/Cn=Globus
```

will contact the GT2 gatekeeper running at server foo.com in port 32779 using the credential subject `/O=Grid/OU=GlobusTest/Cn=Globus`. The port and credential information are optional arguments.

```
/**
 * Constructor
 * @param Contact remote host
 *         example: "192.168.74.131:32779:
 *                 /O=Grid/OU=GlobusTest
 *                 /OU=simpleCA-vm-rhl8-2.ibm.com
 *                 /OU=ibm.com/Cn=Globus"
 * @param batch Job Submission mode
 * @throws GramException
 */
public Gram2Job(String Contact, boolean batch) throws GramException {
  USAGE = this.getClass().getName() + USAGE_POST;

  // remote host
  m_remoteHost = Contact;

  // submission mode
  m_batch = batch;

  // Start GASS server
  if (!super.startGASSserver(0)) {
    throw new
        GramException("Unable to stat GASS server.");
  }
}
```

The heavy lifting of `GRAM2Job` is implemented in the *Submit* method. This method should at least perform the following tasks:

- Initialize the output listeners.
- Format the RSL string for submission to the server according to the submission mode. Submission modes can be batch and nonbatch. In batch mode, the client will submit the job and return immediately with a Job ID. This mode is useful

for long-lived jobs. A nonbatch submission will wait for the server to complete the job execution thus returning the output.

- Create an instance of a GramJob request and submitted.
- Wait for the job to complete if nonbatch mode is used.

```
/**
 * Submit MMJFS job
 * @param RSL example: &(executable=/bin/date)(directory=/bin)
 */
public synchronized String Submit(String RSL) {
  try {
    // setup Job Output listeners
    initJobOutListeners();

    // Append GASS URL to job String
    // so we can get some output back
    String newRSL = null;

    // if non-batch, then get some output back
    if (!m_batch) {
      newRSL =
          "&"
          + RSL.substring(0, RSL.indexOf('&'))
          + "(rsl_substitution=(GLOBUSRUN_GASS_URL "
          + m_gassURL
          + "))"
          + RSL.substring(
              RSL.indexOf('&') + 1, RSL.length())
          + "(stdout=$(GLOBUSRUN_GASS_URL)/dev/stdout)"
          + "(stderr=$(GLOBUSRUN_GASS_URL)/dev/stderr)";
    }
    else {
      // format batching RSL to retrieve output
      // later on using any GTK commands
      newRSL = RSL
          +
          "(stdout=x-gass-cache://$(GLOBUS_GRAM_JOB_CONTACT)stdout
anExtraTag)"
          +
          "(stderr=x-gass-cache://$(GLOBUS_GRAM_JOB_CONTACT)stderr
anExtraTag)";
    }
```

```
  logger.info("RSL:" + newRSL);
  m_job = new GramJob(newRSL);

  // if non-batch then listen for output
  if (!m_batch) {
    m_job.addListener(this);

  }

  logger.debug(
      "Sending job request to: "
      + m_remoteHost
      + " batch="
      + m_batch);

  m_job.request(m_remoteHost, m_batch, false);

  // Wait for job to complete
  if (!m_batch) {
    synchronized (this) {
      try {
        logger.debug("Waiting for output...");
        wait();
      }
      catch (InterruptedException e) {
      }
    }
  }
  else {
    // do not wait for job. Return immediately
    m_jobOutput.append(
        m_job.getIDAsString() + "\n");
  }
}
catch (Exception ex) {
  if (m_gassServer != null) {
    m_gassServer.unregisterJobOutputStream("err");
    m_gassServer.unregisterJobOutputStream("out");
  }
  m_jobOutput.append(
      "Error submitting job: "
      + ex.getClass()
      + ":"
      + ex.getMessage());
```

```
    }
    // cleanup
    Deactivator.deactivateAll();
    return m_jobOutput.toString();
  }
```

Finally, the main subroutine will parse command-line arguments and submit the job appropriately. For example, the following call will submit a date command to a remote GT2 gatekeeper:

```
  /**
   * Main sample call:
   *  java gram.clientGram2Job gt2.acme.com & (executable = /bin/date)
   */
    public static void main(String[] args) {
    // Sample Job
    // String RSL = "&(executable=/bin/date)(directory=/bin)";
    // String GRAMContact = "192.168.74.131:32779:
    //        /O=Grid/OU=GlobusTest
    //        /OU=simpleCA-vm-rhl8-2.ibm.com
    //        /OU=ibm.com/Cn=Globus";

    if (args.length != 2) {
      System.err.println(USAGE);
    }
    else {
      try {
        // args[0] = GRAM Contact
        // args[1] = RSL string
        Gram2Job Job1 = new Gram2Job(args[0], false);
        System.out.println(Job1.Submit(args[1]));
      }
      catch (Exception ex) {
        System.err.println(
            "Error:"
            + ex.getClass()
            + ":" + ex.getMessage());
      }
    }
   }
   // end class Gram2Job
  }
```

4.1.2.4 GRAM3-MJS Protocol Client Program

The GRAM3 protocol has many similarities with its version 2 counterpart. Both use the GASS API to transfer job output between the client and server. Both also implement the same interfaces to listen for server events. However, job information in GT3 is represented as XML. The program in Listing 4.3 implements a GRAM client for the MMJFS for the Globus Toolkit 3.x.

LISTING 4.3 Gram3Job.java—A Client for MMJFS Protocol

```
package gram.client;

/**
 * <p>Title: Custom GRAM client for GT 3.x</p>
 * @author Vladimir Silva
 * @version 1.0
 */
import java.io.*;
import java.net.URL;

import org.globus.io.gass.server.*;
import org.globus.gram.GramException;

import org.globus.ogsa.impl.base.gram.client.*;
import org.globus.ogsa.base.gram.types.JobStateType;
import org.globus.ogsa.impl.security.authentication.Constants;
import org.globus.ogsa.impl.security.authorization.Authorization;
import org.globus.ogsa.impl.security.authorization.HostAuthorization;
import
org.globus.ogsa.impl.security.authorization.IdentityAuthorization;
import org.globus.ogsa.impl.security.authorization.SelfAuthorization;

import org.apache.commons.logging.Log;
import org.apache.commons.logging.LogFactory;

/**
 * GRAM MMJFS client Java program
 * Sample call:
 * java gram.client.Gram3Job
 *  -factory http://192.168.74.131:8080/ogsa/
 *     services/base/gram/MasterForkManagedJobFactoryService
 *  -file C:/GridBookSource/GRAMClients/etc/echo.xml -o
 */
```

```
public class Gram3Job
    // listen for job status messages
    extends AbstractGRAMJob implements GramJobListener
{
  private String _USAGE =
      "-factory <URL> -file <RSL file> [options] "
      + "\nOptions:"
      + "\n\t-help      Help"
      + "\n\t-auth      Authorization: "
      + "[host,self,(identity)e.g. /ou=ACME/o=globus/cn=John Doe"
      +
      "\n\t-o       Redirect output from the GASS server to the GRAM
client"
      + "\n\t-sec   sig' for XML signature 'enc' for XML encryption"
      + "\n\t-b     Submit in 'batch' mode. Mutually exclusive with -o"
      + "\n\t-quiet No verbose messages";

  /**
   * The variable name to use in input RSL when referring to the URL
   * of the local GASS server, if started.
   */
  public static final String GLOBUSRUN_GASS_URL =
      "GLOBUSRUN_GASS_URL";

  private static Log logger =
      LogFactory.getLog(Gram3Job.class.getName());

  boolean quiet = false;
  private boolean done = false;

  //    private GassServer m_gassServer;
  private GramJob job;

  // Cmd line arguments
  private Authorization _authorization =
      SelfAuthorization.getInstance();

  private Integer _xmlSecurity = Constants.SIGNATURE;

  // Redirect output from GASS must be true to receive GASS output
  // batch and out redir are mutually exclusive
  private boolean _redirOutput = true;
  private boolean _batch = false;
```

```
private int _gassOptions = 0;
private int _timeout = GramJob.DEFAULT_TIMEOUT;

private String _factory; // MJFS service factory URL
private String _rslString; // RSL file path

// Security
public static final int SECURITY_ENC = 0;
public static final int SECURITY_SIG = 1;

// Authorization
public static final int AUTH_SELF = 2;
public static final int AUTH_HOST = 3;

/**
 * Callback as a GramJobListener.
 * Will not be called in batch mode.
 */
public void statusChanged(GramJob job) {
  String stringStatus = job.getStatusAsString();
  if (!quiet) {
    System.out.println(
        "========== Status Notification ==========");
    System.out.println("Status: " + stringStatus);
    System.out.println(
        "=========================================");
  }

  if (stringStatus.equals(JobStateType._Failed)) {
    m_jobOutput.append(
        "GRAM Job Failed because "
        + job.getFault().getDescription(0));
  }

  synchronized (this) {
    if (stringStatus.equals(JobStateType._Done)
        //this class should be hidden from this layer?
        || stringStatus.equals(JobStateType._Failed)) {
      this.done = true;
      notifyAll();
    }
  }
}
```

```
/**
 * It is called whenever the job's output
 * has been updated.
 *
 * @param output new output
 */
public void outputChanged(String output) {
  m_jobOutput.append(output);
}

/**
 * It is called whenever job finished
 * and no more output will be generated.
 */
public void outputClosed() {
  //System.out.println("outputClosed");
}

/**
 * Return the output from the GRAM job submission
 */
public String getJobOutput() {
  return m_jobOutput.toString();
}
```

As with Gram2Job, Gram3Job extends `AbstractGramJob` and implements the `GramJobListener` interface to listen for job status messages. Job submission modes apply for both GT2 and GT3. The next method, *submitRSL* is very different. In GT3, RSL is represented as XML whereas in GT2, RSL is represented as plain text. This method must also deal with OGSA authentication and XML security that allow for XML encryption.

Dealing with Security

It's important for custom clients to handle OGSA features such as authorization and XML security. Authorization can be one of host, self, or identity. XML security defines the way XML is encrypted: signature or XML encryption.

Example for setting authorization:

```
Authorization authorization = SelfAuthorization.getInstance();
GramJob job = new GramJob();
job.setAuthorization(authorization);
```

```
Integer xmlSecurity = Constants.SIGNATURE;
job.setMessageProtectionType(xmlSecurity);
```

Apart from these differences, the submit method works in the same way as in the GT2 version. The submission mode should be checked, the GASS server started, a request sent, and the output handled appropriately.

```
/**
 * Constructor
 */
public Gram3Job(String[] args) throws Exception {
  if (parseArgs(args)) {
    submitRSL(
        _factory,
        _rslString,
        _authorization,
        _xmlSecurity,
        _batch,
        _gassOptions,
        _redirOutput,
        _timeout);
  }
}

/**
 * Constructor
 * @param factory Service factory
 * example: http://192.168.74.131:8080/ogsa/services/base
 *    /gram/MasterForkManagedJobFactoryService
 * @param batch Submission mode
 * @throws Exception
 */
public Gram3Job(String factory, boolean batch) throws Exception {
  _factory = factory;
  _batch = batch;
  _redirOutput = !batch;
}

/**
 * Submit MMJFS to the back end server
 * @param RSL job xml string
 */
```

```
public String Submit(String RSL) {
  submitRSL(
      _factory,
      RSL,
      _authorization,
      _xmlSecurity,
      _batch,
      _gassOptions,
      _redirOutput,
      _timeout);
  return m_jobOutput.toString();
}

/**
 * GRAM Submission sub
 * @param factoryUrl: URL of the MJS factory
 * @param rslString: RSL string as XML
 * @param authorization: Host, Self or Identity
 * @param xmlSecurity: sig for signature, enc for encryption
 * @param batchMode: Batch submission (don't don't wait for job)
 * @param gassOptions: GASS server options
 * @param redirOutput: Redirect GASS output to the client
 * @param timeout: Job timeout in milliseconds
 */
void submitRSL(
    String factoryUrl,
    String rslString,
    Authorization authorization,
    Integer xmlSecurity,
    boolean batchMode,
    int gassOptions,
    boolean redirOutput,
    int timeout) {

  _batch = batchMode;
//In multi-job, -batch is not allowed. Dryrun is.

  if (batchMode) {
    _verbose(
        "Warning: Will not wait for job completion, " +
        "and will not destroy job service.");
  }

  this.job = new GramJob(rslString);
  job.setTimeOut(timeout);
```

```
    job.setAuthorization(authorization);
    job.setMessageProtectionType(xmlSecurity);

    //now must ensure JVM will exit if uncaught exception:
    try {

      startGASSserver(gassOptions);

      //check isSubstitutionReferenced?
      //move XML string building to GramJobAttributes
      //or JobAttributesImpl
      String xmlValue =
          "<rsl:urlElement value=\"" + m_gassServer.getURL() + "\"/>";
      job.setSubstitutionDefinition(GLOBUSRUN_GASS_URL, xmlValue);
      //check isSubstitutionDefined

      if (redirOutput) {
        //add output path to GASS redirection
        _verbose(
            "Adding output path to GASS redirection");
        job.addStdoutPath(
            GLOBUSRUN_GASS_URL, "/dev/stdout");
        job.addStderrPath(
            GLOBUSRUN_GASS_URL, "/dev/stderr");
      }

      processJob(job, factoryUrl, _batch);
    }
    catch (Exception e) {
      cleanup();
      logger.error("Caught exception: ", e);
      m_jobOutput.append(
          "Job Failed:"
          + e.getClass() + ":" + e.getMessage());
    }
  }

  /**
   * processJob Send the actual GRAM request
   */
  private void processJob(GramJob job, String factoryUrl, boolean batch)
   throws GramException
  {
```

```
try {
  logger.debug("Factory URL " + factoryUrl);
  job.request(new URL(factoryUrl), batch);

}
catch (Exception e) {
  throw new GramException(
      "error submitting job request: "
      + e.getMessage());
}

if (batch) {
  _verbose(
      "CREATED MANAGED JOB SERVICE WITH HANDLE: "
      + job.getHandle());
  m_jobOutput.append(job.getHandle());
}
else {
  _verbose("Added job listener (this).");
  job.addListener(this);
}

try {
  logger.debug("Starting job");
  job.start(); //leave this free to interrupt?
}
catch (GramException ge) {
  logger.error("Error starting job", ge);
  throw new GramException(
      "Error starting job: " + ge.getMessage());
}

logger.debug("Job has started.");

if (!batch) {
  _verbose("WAITING FOR JOB TO FINISH");
  synchronized (this) {
    while (!this.done) {
      try {
        wait();
      }
      catch (InterruptedException ie) {
```

```
                logger.error(
                    "interrupted waiting for job to finish",
                    ie);
            }
        }
    }
    if (this.job.getStatusAsString()
        .equals(JobStateType._Failed)) {
      cleanup();
      throw new GramException(
          "Job Fault detected: "
          + this.job.getFault());
    }
  }

  // GRAM submission complete. Cleanup: Stop GASS server
  cleanup();
}

/**
 * Set job security
 * @param security
 */
public void setSecurity(int security) {
  switch (security) {
    case SECURITY_ENC:
      _xmlSecurity = Constants.ENCRYPTION;
      break;
    case SECURITY_SIG:
      _xmlSecurity = Constants.SIGNATURE;
      break;
    default:
      break;
  }
}

/**
 * Set job authorization
 * @param auth
 */
public void setAuthorization(int auth) {
  switch (auth) {
    case AUTH_HOST:
```

```
        _authorization =
            HostAuthorization.getInstance();
        break;
      case AUTH_SELF:
        _authorization =
            SelfAuthorization.getInstance();
        break;
      default:
        break;
    }
  }

  /**
   * Cleanup: Shut down GASS server
   */
  private void cleanup() {
    if (m_gassServer != null) {
      m_gassServer.shutdown();
    }
  }
```

Finally, this class can be called with the following arguments:

```
$ java gram.clientGram3Job
-factory http://192.168.74.131:8080/ogsa/services/base/gram/
MasterForkManagedJobFactoryService
-file echo.xml -o
```

The file `echo.xml` describes the job arguments. For example, the following file defines a simple echo command that redirects `stdout` and `stderr` to local files in the user's home directory:

```
<?xml version="1.0" encoding="UTF-8"?>
<rsl:rsl xmlns:rsl="http://www.globus.org/namespaces/2003/04/rsl"
  xmlns:gram="http://www.globus.org/namespaces/2003/04/rsl/gram"
  xmlns:xsi="http://www.w3.org/2001/XMLSchema-instance"
  xsi:schemaLocation="
              http://www.globus.org/namespaces/2003/04/rsl
              c:/ogsa-3.0/schema/base/gram/rsl.xsd
              http://www.globus.org/namespaces/2003/04/rsl/gram
              c:/ogsa-3.0/schema/base/gram/gram_rsl.xsd">
  <gram:job>
    <gram:executable>
      <rsl:path>
```

```
        <rsl:stringElement value="/bin/echo" />
      </rsl:path>
    </gram:executable>
    <gram:stdin>
      <rsl:path>
        <rsl:stringElement value="/dev/null" />
      </rsl:path>
    </gram:stdin>
    <gram:stdout>
      <rsl:pathArray>
        <rsl:path>
          <rsl:substitutionRef name="HOME" />
          <rsl:stringElement value="/stdout" />
        </rsl:path>
      </rsl:pathArray>
    </gram:stdout>
    <gram:stderr>
      <rsl:pathArray>
        <rsl:path>
          <rsl:substitutionRef name="HOME" />
          <rsl:stringElement value="/stderr" />
        </rsl:path>
      </rsl:pathArray>
    </gram:stderr>
  </gram:job>
```

The final section of the Gram3Job.java client program from Listing 4.3 defines three utility methods to parse the program arguments, reads a file from the filesystem, and displays debug output.

```
/**
 * Parse command line args
 */
private boolean parseArgs(String[] args) throws Exception
{
  if (args.length == 0) {
    System.err.println(_USAGE);
    return false;
  }
  for (int i = 0; i < args.length; i++) {
    if (args[i].equalsIgnoreCase("-help")) {
      System.err.println(_USAGE);
      return false;
    }
```

```
if (args[i].equalsIgnoreCase("-factory")) {
  _factory = args[++i];
}
else if (args[i].equalsIgnoreCase("-file")) {
  _rslString = readFile(args[++i]);
}
else if (args[i].equalsIgnoreCase("-o")) {
  _redirOutput = true;
  _batch = false;
}
else if (args[i].equalsIgnoreCase("-b")) {
  _redirOutput = false;
  _batch = true;
}
else if (args[i].equalsIgnoreCase("-sec")) {
  if (args[++i].equalsIgnoreCase("sig")) {
    _xmlSecurity = Constants.SIGNATURE;
  }
  else if (args[i].equalsIgnoreCase("enc")) {
    _xmlSecurity = Constants.ENCRYPTION;
  }
  else {
    throw new Exception(
        "Invalid xml security arg:" + args[i]);
  }
}
else if (args[i].equalsIgnoreCase("-auth")) {
  if (args[++i].equalsIgnoreCase("host")) {
    _authorization =
        HostAuthorization.getInstance();
  }
  else if (args[i].equalsIgnoreCase("self")) {
    _authorization =
        SelfAuthorization.getInstance();
  }
  else {
    _authorization = new
        IdentityAuthorization(args[i]);
  }
}
else if (args[i].equalsIgnoreCase("-quiet")) {
  quiet = true;
}
```

```
        else {
          throw new Exception("Invalid arg:" + args[i]);
        }
      }
      return true;
    }

    /**
     * Read a text file from disk
     * @param path
     * @return
     * @throws IOException
     * @throws FileNotFoundException
     */
    private static String readFile(String path) throws IOException,
        FileNotFoundException
    {
      RandomAccessFile f =
          new java.io.RandomAccessFile(path, "r");
      byte[] data = new byte[ (int) f.length()];
      f.readFully(data);
      return new String(data);
    }

    private void _verbose(String text) {
      if (!quiet) {
        System.out.println(
            this.getClass().getName() + ": " + text);
      }
    }

    // End Gram3Job.java
    }
```

4.1.2.5 Generating RSL and Job XML with the Velocity Template Engine

A tedious task when writing a user interface to a GRAM client is generating the RSL script or the XML required for job submission. A template engine such as Velocity (*http://jakarta.apache.org/velocity/*) can provide great assistance. Velocity allows for generation of files from templates on the fly by encoding parameters dynamically and manipulating those parameters within the template. The result, a simple RSL or XML template, can generate submission files for both versions of the GRAM protocol (see Listing 4.4).

LISTING 4.4 A Velocity Template to Generate an RSL Script

```
## ------------------------------------------------------
## Velocity Template for the Resource Scripting Language (RSL)
## http://jakarta.apache.org/velocity/
## Statements begin with a single (#)
## Comments with (##)
## ------------------------------------------------------

#if ( $t.get("stage:executable") &&
$t.get("stage:executable").booleanValue() )
&(executable=$(GLOBUSRUN_GASS_URL)
  # "$t.get("gram:executable")")
#else
&(executable="$t.get("gram:executable")")
#end

##
## Arguments
##
#if ( $t.get("gram:arguments")
   && !$t.get("gram:arguments").equals("") )
(arguments = "$t.get("gram:arguments")")
#end

##
## Directory
#if ( $t.get("gram:directory")
  && !$t.get("gram:directory").equals("") )
(directory = $t.get("gram:directory"))
#end

##
## Environment
#if ( $t.get("gram:environment") &&
!$t.get("gram:environment").equals("") )
(environment = $t.get("gram:environment"))
#end

##
## Standard Input (STDIN)
#if ( $t.get("gram:stdin")
  && !$t.get("gram:stdin").equals("") )
    #if ( $t.get("stage:stdin").booleanValue() )
```

```
(stdin = $(GLOBUSRUN_GASS_URL) # $t.get("gram:stdin"))
   #else
(stdin = $t.get("gram:stdin"))
   #end
#end

##
## STDOUT
##
#if ( $t.get("gram:stdout")
  && !$t.get("gram:stdout").equals("") )
(stdout = $t.get("gram:stdout"))
#end

##
## STDERR
##
#if ( $t.get("gram:stderr")
  && !$t.get("gram:stderr").equals("") )
(stderr = $t.get("gram:stderr"))
#end
```

The template in Listing 4.4 can generate an RSL script compatible with the Globus Toolkit 2.2.x by using simple Java code such as shown in Listing 4.5.

LISTING 4.5 Code for Loading the Template from Listing 4.4

```
/**
 * Build RSL string by loading a Velocity template
 * @param params Job parameters
 * For Example:
 * params.put("gram:executable", "/bin/echo");
 * params.put("stage:executable", new Boolean(true) );
 * params.put("gram:directory", "/bin");
 * params.put("gram:arguments", "Hello World");
 * params.put("gram:stdin","/dev/null");
 * params.put("stage:stdin", new Boolean(true) );
 * params.put("gram:stdout","/dev/null");
 * params.put("gram:stderr","/dev/null");
 * @return GT2 RSL string
 */
public static String buildRSL(Hashtable params) throws Exception
{
  return loadVelocityTemplate(params, "templates/rsl.vm")
```

```
        .replace('\r', ' ')
        .trim();
  }

  /**
   * Load a Velocity template.
   * The engine must be setup to load templates from the class path.
   * By default it loads from the file system, not the class path
   * @param params Hash table of parameters passed to the template
   * @param name Template file name
   * @return String representation of the parsed template
   * @throws Exception if an error occurs
   */
  public static String loadVelocityTemplate(Hashtable params, String
  name)
    throws Exception
  {
    VelocityContext context = new VelocityContext();
    context.put("t", params);

    Template template = null;
    StringWriter sw = new StringWriter();

    // Load Velocity template
    template = Velocity.getTemplate(name);

    template.merge(context, sw);
    sw.close();

    return sw.toString();
  }
```

For the previous code to work, `Velocity` must be configured to load templates from the class path. By default, `Velocity` will load files from the filesystem, thus some initialization code is required (see Listing 4.6).

LISTING 4.6 `Velocity` **Class Path Resource Loader Initialization**

```
static
{
  // initialize Velocity Class path resource loader
  Properties props = new Properties();
  props.put("resource.loader", "class");
  props.put("file.resource.loader.description",
            "Velocity Classpath Resource Loader");
```

```
    props.put("class.resource.loader.class",
              "org.apache.velocity.runtime.resource." + ""loader.
              ClasspathResourceLoader ");

    try {
      Velocity.init(props);
    }
    catch (Exception ex) {
      System.err.println(
          "Unable to load Velocity Class resource Loader:"
          + ex.getMessage());
    }
  }
```

Once all the pieces are in place, RSL scripting can be generated by simple means, as shown in Listing 4.7.

LISTING 4.7 RSL Sample Script Generation Using `Velocity` and Sample Output

```
/*
 Sample Program Output:
 &(executable="/bin/echo")
 (directory = /bin)
 */
public static void main(String[] args)
{
  Hashtable params = new Hashtable();
  params.put("gram:executable", "/bin/echo");
  params.put("gram:directory", "/bin");

  try {
    System.out.println(buildRSL(params));
  }
  catch (Exception e) {
    System.err.println(e);
  }
}
```

The same technique is used to generate XML for Jobs using the GRAM3–MMJFS protocol. Such techniques are used by both GRAM portlets implemented throughout this chapter. At the time of this writing, the version of the `Velocity` *engine used from the Apache Jakarta project is 1.4.*

4.1.2.6 Portlet View JSP

With the client programs in place, we can work on the user interface of the portlet. A JSP portlet in Jetspeed is very easy to implement. It requires two files to be placed in the proper locations:

- A portlet registry descriptor (xreg) (see Listing 4.8): This file contains portlet arguments and metadata such as display name, implementation class, and others. The xreg file must be placed in the following folder: [JETSPEED_HOME]\WEB-INF\conf.
- A portlet JSP: This file contains the actual user interface as a Java Server Page (JSP) file.

LISTING 4.8 Jetspeed GRAM Portlet Registry Descriptor (xreg)

```
<?xml version="1.0" encoding="UTF-8"?>
<registry>
  <portlet-entry name="GramClient" hidden="false" type="ref"
    parent="JSP" application="false">
    <meta-info>
      <title>Gram Client</title>
      <description>Gram Client Portlet Example</description>
    </meta-info>
    <classname>
      org.apache.jetspeed.portal.portlets.JspPortlet
    </classname>
    <parameter name="template" value="gram.jsp" hidden="true"
      cachedOnName="true" cachedOnValue="true" />
    <media-type ref="html" />
    <url cachedOnURL="true" />
    <category group="Jetspeed">gram</category>
    <category group="Jetspeed">gram.demo</category>
  </portlet-entry>
</registry>
```

The user interface JSP (see Listing 4.9) reads job information such as server contact/factory, executable, arguments, directory, protocol type (GRAM2 or MMJFS), and options like security, authentication, and others. This file must be placed in the following folder: [JETSPEED_HOME]\WEB-INF\templates\jsp\portlets\html.

LISTING 4.9 Jetspeed GRAM Portlet JSP

```
<%@ page import="java.util.*" %>
<%@ page import="gram.client.*" %>
<%@ page import="gram.client.utils.*" %>
```

```
<%@ taglib uri='/WEB-INF/templates/jsp/tld/template.tld'
  prefix='jetspeed' %>

<%String jspeid = (String) request.getAttribute("js_peid");
String action = (String) request.getParameter("gram_action");
String error = null;
String output = null;

if (action != null) {
  /*
   * Call GRAM client here...
   */
  String factory = request.getParameter("FACTORY");
  String proto = request.getParameter("PROTOCOL");
  String exe = request.getParameter("EXE");
  String args = request.getParameter("ARGS");
  String dir = request.getParameter("DIR");
  String stdin = request.getParameter("STDIN");
  String stdout = request.getParameter("STDOUT");
  String stderr = request.getParameter("STDERR");
  String batch = request.getParameter("BATCH");
  String dryRun = request.getParameter("DRY");
  String sec = request.getParameter("SECURITY");
  String auth = request.getParameter("AUTH");


  String rsl = null;
```

For the Web developer, the code is straightforward. It defines HTML user interface with the arguments for job submission. For example, to extract the executable argument from the servlet request, use the following:

```
String exe = request.getParameter("EXE");
```

A nice feature of Listing 4.9 is the ability to build the RSL (GT2) or XML (GT3) by using a `Velocity` template. This avoids having to manually build a string, which can be very complicated in GT3. By setting a simple hash table with the submission arguments, the XML can be easily built.

```
Hashtable params = new Hashtable();
params.put("gram:count", new Integer(2));
params.put("gram:hostCount", new Integer(1));
params.put("gram:project", "Foo Project");
params.put("gram:jobType", "single");
```

```
// Built GT3 GRAM XML Using an Apache Velocity template
String XML = GramClientUtil.buildGramXML(params);
```

The rest of the portlet code is straightforward HTML that builds the user interface with the required arguments. See Figures 4.2 and 4.3 to view this code in action.

```
// Job parameters
Hashtable params = new Hashtable();

params.put("gram:executable", exe);
params.put("gram:directory", dir);
params.put("gram:arguments", args);
params.put("gram:stdin", stdin);
params.put("gram:stdout", stdout);
params.put("gram:stderr", stderr);

try {
  if (proto.equals("GRAM2")) {
    // GRAM 2
    rsl = GramClientUtil.buildRSL(params);

    if (dryRun == null) {
      Gram2Job job =
          new Gram2Job(factory, batch != null);
      output = job.Submit(rsl);
    }
    else {
      output = rsl;
    }
  }
  else {
    // GRAM3 - MMJFS
    params.put("schema.loc",
               GramClientUtil.
               GRAM3_SCHEMA_LOCATION.replace('\\', '/'));

    //params.put("gram:count", new Integer(2));
    //params.put("gram:hostCount", new Integer(1));
    //params.put("gram:project", "Foo Project");
    //params.put("gram:jobType", "single");

    rsl = GramClientUtil.buildGramXML(params);
```

```
    if (dryRun == null) {
      Gram3Job job =
          new Gram3Job(factory, batch != null);

      job.setSecurity(Integer.parseInt(sec));

      job
          .setAuthorization(Integer.parseInt(auth));

      output = job.Submit(rsl);
    }
    else {
      output = rsl;
    }
  }
}
catch (Exception e) {
  System.err.println(e);
  output = error = e.getClass() + ":" + e.getMessage();
}
}

%>

<script>
    function gram2Sample() {
            var f = document.forms.F1;
            f.FACTORY.value =
            "192.168.74.131:32774:/O=Grid/OU=GlobusTest /CN=Globus";
            f.EXE.value = "/bin/date";
    }

    function gram3Sample() {
            var f = document.forms.F1;
            f.FACTORY.value =
                    "http://192.168.74.131:8080/ogsa/" +

"services/base/gram/MasterForkManagedJobFactoryService";
            f.EXE.value = "/bin/date";
            f.PROTOCOL.options.selectedIndex = 1;
    }
</script>
```

```
<style type="text/css">
<!–
A, P, TD, INPUT, SELECT, OPTION, TEXTAREA {
    font-family: "Verdana";
    font-size: 9px;
    color: 000000
}
–>
</style>

Globus GRAM Portlet client compatible with GT 2.4.x and GT 3.2.x
<br />

<%    if (error != null) {%>
<FONT color="red"><%=    error%></FONT>
<%    }%>


<a href="javascript:gram2Sample()" style="font-size: 10">Gram2
sample</a>
  
<a href="javascript:gram3Sample()" style="font-size: 10">Gram3
sample</a>

<br />
```

The user interface of the portlet defines the job submission arguments for both GT2 and GT3. Common arguments are a remote executable, standard input, output error, and the protocol type. Other options include submission mode (batch/nonbatch), authorization, and security.

```
<FORM method="POST" name="F1">
 <input type="hidden" name=vgram_action"
  value="submit" />

<TABLE width="100%">
  <TR style="">
    <TD>Factory/GRAM Contact</TD>
    <TD><INPUT name="FACTORY" type="text" size="50" /></TD>
  </TR>
  <TR>
    <TD>Protocol</TD>
    <TD><SELECT name="PROTOCOL">
      <OPTION value="GRAM2">Gram 2</OPTION>
      <OPTION value="MMJFS_FORK">MasterFork (MMJFS)</OPTION>
```

```
  </SELECT></TD>
</TR>

<TR>
  <TD>Executable</TD>
  <TD><INPUT name="EXE" type="textv size="50" /></TD>
</TR>
<TR>
  <TD>Arguments</TD>
  <TD><INPUT name="ARGS" type=vtext" size="50" /></TD>
</TR>
<TR>
  <TD>Directory</TD>
  <TD><INPUT name="DIR" type="text" size="50" /></TD>
</TR>

<TR>
  <TD>StdIn</TD>
  <TD><INPUT name="STDIN" type="text" size="50" /></TD>
</TR>
<TR>
  <TD>StdOut</TD>
  <TD><INPUT name="STDOUT" type="text" size="50" /></TD>
</TR>
<TR>
  <TD>StdErr</TD>
  <TD><INPUT name=vSTDERR" type="text" size="50" /></TD>
</TR>
<TR>
  <TD colspan="2"><B>Job options</B></TD>
</TR>
<TR>
  <TD>Batch mode</TD>
  <TD><INPUT class="wpsEditField" name="BATCH" type="checkbox"
    value="true" />      Dry run (return rsl
  only) <INPUT name="DRY" type="checkbox" value="true" /></TD>
</TR>
<TR>
  <TD>Security (GT3)</TD>
  <TD><SELECT name="SECURITY">
    <OPTION value="0">Signature</OPTION>
    <OPTION value="1">Secure Conversation</OPTION>
  </SELECT></TD>
</TR>
<TR>
```

```
        <TD>Authorization (GT3)</TD>
        <TD><SELECT name="AUTH">
          <OPTION value="2">Self</OPTION>
          <OPTION value="3">Host</OPTION>
        </SELECT></TD>
      </TR>
    </TABLE>
    <br />

    <INPUT class="wpsButtonText" name="SUBMIT" value="Submit" type="submit"
    />
    </FORM>

    <%  if (output != null) {%>
    <b>Job Output</b>
    <br />
    <TEXTAREA rows="5" cols="50"><%=output%></TEXTAREA>
    <% } %>
```

For a preview of the portlet in Jetspeed 1.5, see Figures 4.2 and 4.3.

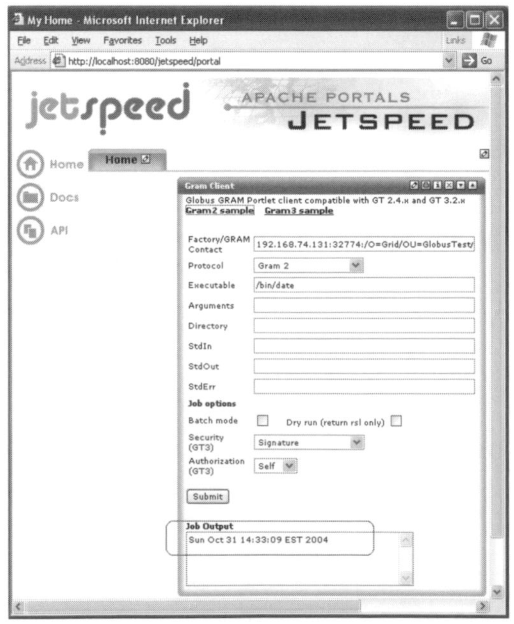

FIGURE 4.2 GRAM portlet in Jetspeed 1.5.

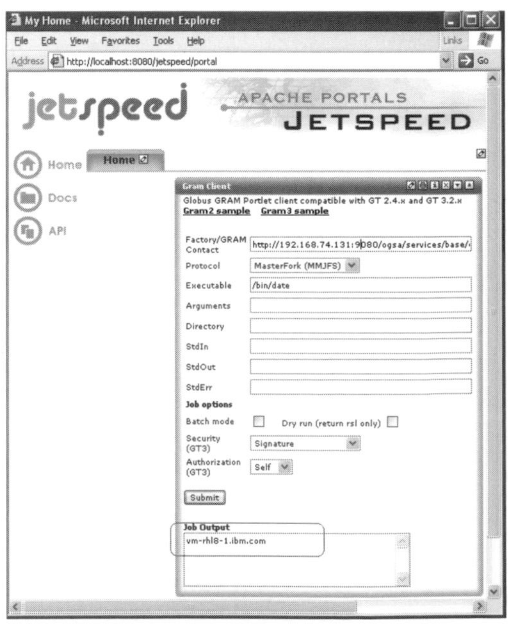

FIGURE 4.3 MMJFS Client Portlet for Jetspeed 1.5.

4.1.3 WebSphere® Portal Server v5.0 (WPS)

WebSphere Portal is IBM's infrastructure software for dynamic e-business. WebSphere Portal can deliver Web content to WAP-enabled devices and i-Mode phones, and to various Web browsers. WPS aims to deliver the following key features [IBMWPS04]:

Versatile framework: Allows users to define specific sets of applications presented in a single context. Applications are rendered depending on the requesting device.

Customization: Provides user and administrative portlets to customize look and feel, layout, and personalization.

Portlets: Allows portlets, which are small portal applications shown as small boxes in a Web page, to be developed, deployed, managed, and displayed independently allowing for Web page customization.

Content management: Allows for large-scale deployment, search, and delivery of personalized content. WPS supports syndicated content and integration with Web content management systems.

Application integration: Provides access to content, data, and services that are located throughout the enterprise.

Security: Provides administration of users and groups, third-party authentication, single sign-on (SSO), and credential vault.

Collaboration: Allows people in the organization to work together and share information to achieve their business goals.

4.1.4 IBM Portlet API

From the viewer's perspective, a portlet is a window on a portal site that provides a specific service or information, for example, a stock quotes feed or weather information. *Portlets* are a special type of *servlet.* The portlet class is an abstract entity that extends *HTTPServlet.* All portlets extend this abstract class and inherit from HTTPServlet.

IBM is working with other companies to standardize the Portlet API, making portlets interoperable between portal servers that implement the specification [IBMWPS04].

4.1.4.1 Deployment Descriptor

The deployment descriptor *(portlet.xml)* (see Listing 4.10) defines the portlet's capabilities to the portal server, including configuration parameters and general information all portlets provide.

LISTING 4.10 Sample WPS portlet Deployment Descriptor

```
<?xml version="1.0" encoding="UTF-8"?>
<!DOCTYPE portlet-app-def PUBLIC
  "-//IBM//DTD Portlet Application 1.1//EN"
  "portlet_1.1.dtd">
<portlet-app-def>
  <portlet-app uid="com.myCompany.myPortletApp.54321">
    <portlet-app-name>My portlet application</portlet-app-name>
    <portlet id="Portlet_1" href="WEB-INF/web.xml#Servlet_1">
      <portlet-name>My portlet</portlet-name>
      <supports>
        <markup name="html">
          <view output="fragment" />
        </markup>
      </supports>
    </portlet>
  </portlet-app>
  <concrete-portlet-app
    uid="com.myCompany.myConcretePortletApp.54321">
    <portlet-app-name>
      My concrete portlet application
    </portlet-app-name>
    <concrete-portlet href="#Portlet_1">
      <portlet-name>My concrete portlet</portlet-name>
      <default-locale>en</default-locale>
      <language locale="en_US">
        <title>My portlet</title>
      </language>
    </concrete-portlet>
  </concrete-portlet-app>
</portlet-app-def>
```

4.1.4.2 Portlet Life Cycle

The abstract portlet class defines the following life cycle methods:

`init()`: Called after construction and initialization. The portal instantiates only one instance of the portlet, and this instance is shared among all users, the same way a servlet is shared among all users.

`initConcrete()`: Called after construction and before the portlet is accessed for the first time.

`service()`: Called when the portlet renders its content. It is typically called many times.

`destroyConcrete()`: Used to take the portlet out of service, for example, if an administrator deletes a concrete portlet from the server.

`destroy()`: Called when the portal is terminating, it destroys the portlet and releases resources back to the system.

4.1.5 Job Submission Portlet for WPS

The WebSphere Studio Application Developer (WSAD) 5.1.2 environment makes the tasks of writing, compiling, and testing portlets easy. It includes a test environment that you can use to run and debug your portlets without having to manually deploy them to the server. Three components are required by a portlet in WPS:

- A portlet deployment descriptor (portlet.xml)
- A portlet implementation program that extends the abstract class Portlet Adapter
- A JSP file that contains the user interface of the portlet

WSAD automates these tasks with a series of easy-to-follow wizards, so we will discuss only the implementation here. For more information on WPS and WSAD, see the product documentation [IBMWPS04].

4.1.6 Portlet Program

The *GramPortlet.java* program implements the logic required to load the user interface to access the GRAM client programs described in the previous section. The *GramPortlet.java* program also handles the remote job submission against the remote server. When the server loads the portlet, the `doView()` method is called; it in turn loads the user interface (`GramPortletView.jsp`). When the submit button is pressed on the browser window, the `actionPerformed()` method fires and submits the GRAM job to the remote server, as shown in Listing 4.11.

LISTING 4.11 GramPortlet.java—WPS Portlet for the GRAM Protocol of GT2 and GT3-MMJFS

```
package portlet.gram;

import java.io.IOException;
import java.util.Hashtable;

import org.apache.axis.utils.ClassUtils;
import org.apache.jetspeed.portlet.*;
import org.apache.jetspeed.portlet.event.*;
import org.globus.gram.GramException;
```

```
import gram.client.*;
import gram.client.utils.GramClientUtil;

/**
 *
 * A sample portlet based on PortletAdapter
 *
 */
public class GramPortlet
    extends PortletAdapter implements ActionListener
{
  // JSP file name to be rendered on the view mode
  public static final String VIEW_JSP =
    "/portlet_gram/jsp/GramPortletView.jsp";
  // Action name for the orderId entry form
  public static final String FORM_ACTION =
    "portlet.gram.GramPortletFormAction";
  // Parameter name for general submit button
  public static final String SUBMIT = "portlet.gram.GramPortletSubmit";
  // Parameter name for general cancel button
  public static final String CANCEL = "portlet.gram.GramPortletCancel";

  /**
   * @see org.apache.jetspeed.portlet.Portlet#init(PortletConfig)
   */
  public void init(PortletConfig portletConfig) throws
UnavailableException
  {
    super.init(portletConfig);
  }

  /**
   * @see org.apache.jetspeed.portlet.PortletAdapter#doView
   */
  public void doView(PortletRequest request, PortletResponse response)
  throws PortletException, IOException
  {
    // Check if portlet session exists
    // Set actionURI in the view mode bean
    PortletURI formActionURI = response.createURI();
    formActionURI.addAction(FORM_ACTION);

    PortletSession session = request.getPortletSession();
    session.setAttribute("ACTION", formActionURI.toString());
```

```
    // Invoke the JSP to render
    try {
      getPortletConfig().getContext().
          include(VIEW_JSP, request, response);
    }
    catch (Exception e) {
      e.printStackTrace();
    }
  }

  /**
   * Portlet Action event handler method
   */
  public void actionPerformed(ActionEvent event) throws
PortletException {

    // ActionEvent handler
    String actionString = event.getActionString();

    // Add action string handler here
    PortletRequest request = event.getRequest();

    if (FORM_ACTION.equals(actionString)) {
      /*
       * Call GRAM client here...
       */
      String factory = request.getParameter("FACTORY");
      String proto = request.getParameter("PROTOCOL");
      String exe = request.getParameter("EXE");
      String args = request.getParameter("ARGS");
      String dir = request.getParameter("DIR");
      String stdin = request.getParameter("STDIN");
      String stdout = request.getParameter("STDOUT");
      String stderr = request.getParameter("STDERR");
      String batch = request.getParameter("BATCH");
      String dryRun = request.getParameter("DRY");
      String sec = request.getParameter("SECURITY");
      String auth = request.getParameter("AUTH");

      System.out.println("f=" + factory + ", proto=" + proto
                         + ", exe=" + exe + ", args=" + args
                         + ", dir=" + dir + ", stdin=" + stdin
                         + ", stdout=" + stdout + ", stderr=" + stderr
                         + ", batch=" + batch + " dry run=" + dryRun
                         + ", sec=" + sec + ", auth=" + auth);
```

```
// Job parameters
Hashtable params = new Hashtable();

params.put("gram:executable", exe);
params.put("gram:directory", dir);
params.put("gram:arguments", args);
params.put("gram:stdin", stdin);
params.put("gram:stdout", stdout);
params.put("gram:stderr", stderr);

String output = null;
String rsl = null;

try {
  if (proto.equals("GRAM2")) {
    // GRAM 2
    rsl = GramClientUtil.buildRSL(params);

    if (dryRun == null) {
      Gram2Job job =
          new Gram2Job(factory
                           , batch != null);
      output = job.Submit(rsl);
    }
    else {
      output = rsl;
    }
  }
  else {
    // GRAM3 - MMJFS
    params.put("schema.loc", GramClientUtil.
               GRAM3_SCHEMA_LOCATION.replace('\\', '/'));

    rsl = GramClientUtil.buildGramXML(params);

    if (dryRun == null) {
      Gram3Job job =
          new Gram3Job(factory, batch != null);

      job.setSecurity(Integer.parseInt(sec));
      job.
          setAuthorization(
              Integer.parseInt(auth));
```

```
              output = job.Submit(rsl);
            }
            else {
              output = rsl;
            }
          }
        }
        catch (Exception e) {
          e.printStackTrace();
          output = e.getClass() + ":" + e.getMessage();
        }

        // Set form text in the session bean
        request.
            getPortletSession().
            setAttribute("OUTPUT", output);
      }
    }
  }
```

4.1.7 Portlet View JSP

The Portlet View JSP (see Listing 4.12) renders the user interface elements to be used by the job submission clients when the request is submitted to the server.

LISTING 4.12 WPS GRAM Portlet View JSP

```
<%@ page session="false" contentType="text/html"
  import="java.util.*, portlet.gram.*"%>
<%@ taglib uri="/WEB-INF/tld/portlet.tld" prefix="portletAPI" %>

<portletAPI:init />

<%String actionURI =
  (String) portletRequest.getPortletSession().getAttribute("ACTION");
%>

<script>
function gram2Sample() {
  var f = document.forms.F1;
  f.FACTORY.value =

"192.168.74.131:32774:/O=Grid/OU=GlobusTest/OU=ibm.com/CN=Globus";
  f.EXE.value = "/bin/date";
}
```

```
function gram3Sample() {
  var f = document.forms.F1;
  f.FACTORY.value =
      "http://192.168.74.131:8080/ogsa/" +
      "services/base/gram/MasterForkManagedJobFactoryService";
  f.EXE.value = "/bin/date";
  f.PROTOCOL.options.selectedIndex = 1;
}
</script>

<DIV style="margin: 6px">Globus GRAM Portlet client compatible with GT
2.4.x and GT 3.2.x <br />
<a href="javascript:gram2Sample()" style="font-size: 10">Gram2
sample</a>
   <a href="javascript:gram3Sample()" style="font-size:
10">Gram3
sample</a>

<DIV style="margin: 12px; margin-bottom: 36px">


<!— viewBean.getFormActionURI() —>
<FORM method="POST" name="F1" action="<%=actionURI%>">
<TABLE width="100%">
  <TR>
    <TD>Factory/GRAM Contact</TD>
    <TD><INPUT class="wpsEditField" name="FACTORY" type="text"
      size="50" /></TD>
  </TR>
  <TR>
    <TD>Protocol</TD>
    <TD><SELECT name="PROTOCOL">
      <OPTION value="GRAM2">Gram 2</OPTION>
      <OPTION value="MMJFS_FORK">MasterFork (MMJFS)</OPTION>
    </SELECT></TD>
  </TR>

  <TR>
    <TD>Executable</TD>
    <TD><INPUT class="wpsEditField" name="EXE" type="text" size="50" />
    </TD>
  </TR>
  <TR>
    <TD>Arguments</TD>
```

```
    <TD><INPUT class="wpsEditField" name="ARGS" type="text" size="50" />
    </TD>
  </TR>
  <TR>
    <TD>Directory</TD>
    <TD><INPUT class="wpsEditField" name="DIR" type="text" size="50" />
    </TD>
  </TR>

  <TR>
    <TD>StdIn</TD>
    <TD><INPUT class="wpsEditField" name="STDIN" type="text" size="50" />
    </TD>
  </TR>
  <TR>
    <TD>StdOut</TD>
    <TD><INPUT class="wpsEditField" name="STDOUT" type="text" size="50"
/>
    </TD>
  </TR>
  <TR>
    <TD>StdErr</TD>
    <TD><INPUT class="wpsEditField" name="STDERR" type="text" size="50"
/>
    </TD>
  </TR>

  <TR>
    <TD colspan="2"><B>Job options</B></TD>
  </TR>
  <TR>
    <TD>Batch mode</TD>
    <TD><INPUT class="wpsEditField" name="BATCH" type="checkbox"
      value="true" />      Dry run (return rsl
    only) <INPUT name="DRY" type="checkbox" value="true" /></TD>
  </TR>
  <TR>
    <TD>Security (GT3)</TD>
    <TD><SELECT name="SECURITY">
      <OPTION value="0">Signature</OPTION>
      <OPTION value="1">Secure Conversation</OPTION>
    </SELECT></TD>
  </TR>
  <TR>
```

```
      <TD>Authorization (GT3)</TD>
      <TD><SELECT name="AUTH">
        <OPTION value="2">Self</OPTION>
        <OPTION value="3">Host</OPTION>
      </SELECT></TD>
    </TR>
  </TABLE>
  <br />

  <INPUT class="wpsButtonText"
    name="<portletAPI:encodeNamespace value='<%=GramPortlet.SUBMIT%>'/>"
    value="Submit" type="submit" /></FORM>

  <%String formText =
    (String) portletRequest.getPortletSession().getAttribute("OUTPUT");

  if (formText != null) {%> <b>Job Output</b> <br />
  <TEXTAREA rows="5" cols="80"><%=formText%></TEXTAREA> <%}%></DIV>
  </DIV>
```

4.1.8 Testing

This portlet was tested extensively in WPS 5.0 or later and OGSA 3.2.1. Before it can be run properly, certain system configuration is required.

The following system variables should be created in the server, for proper OGSA initialization:

```
-Djava.endorsed.dirs=[OGSA_LOCATION]\endorsed
-Dorg.globus.ogsa.server.webroot=[OGSA_LOCATION]
-Dorg.globus.ogsa.client.timeout=180000
-Djava.net.preferIPv4Stack=true
```

The following are the required OGSA libraries to run the GRAM clients:

Java Crypto Extensions (JCE): cryptix-asn1.jar, cryptix.jar, cryptix32.jar, jce-jdk13-120.jar, and puretls.jar

Apache Velocity Template Engine: Velocity1.4.jar

OGSA 3.2.1: jaxrpc.jar, jgss.jar, ogsa.jar, axis.jar, mjs.jar, grim.jar, filestreaming.jar, cog-axis, grim.jar, xalan.jar, xercesImpl.jar, xindice-1.1b3.jar, xml-apis-1.1.jar, xmlParserAPIs.jar, xmlrpc-1.1.jar, xmlsec.jar, and wsdl4j.jar

For a preview of the final application, see Figure 4.4.

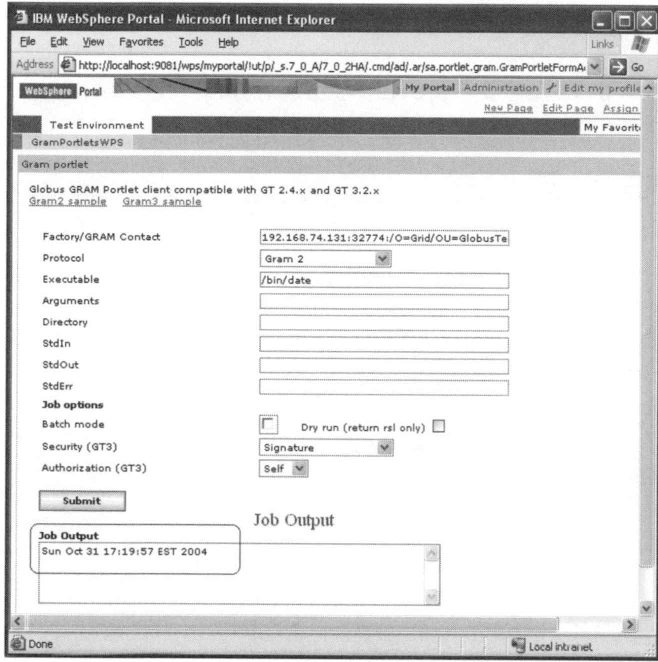

FIGURE 4.4 GRAM portlet for WPS.

4.2 DATA MANAGEMENT PORTLETS

The Globus Toolkit provides the following interfaces for remote access of data: GASS, GridFTP, Remote I/O, and GEM.

4.2.1 Global Access to Secondary Storage (GASS)

GASS provides read, write, and append operations to remote files. GASS is the protocol used by the resource management APIs to transfer job submission data back and forth between client and server. The GASS API has the following features:

- Eliminates the need to manually log in to sites and transfer files and to install a distributed filesystem
- Allows the reuse of programs that use Unix or standard C I/O with little or no modification
- Has simplistic design that is not meant to be another distributed filesystem
- Provides support for URL syntax including: HTTP, HTTPS, and FTP
- Provides support for a security model based on process-to-process authentication performed by grid security infrastructure (GSI)

- Provides access to SSL-authenticated FTP or HTTP servers.

The GASS API also provides support for a remote file caching mechanism with the following characteristics:

- Allows the use of local resource management facilities by associating caches with users
- Allows cache management by reference counting using tags on open and close operations
- Allows programs to access files through a cache API (no persistent cache daemon)
- Allows multiple caches per user, thus allowing the staging of data in different locations
- Allows remote cache management via GRAM requests: list contents, add items, delete items

4.2.2 GridFTP

GridFTP is a high-performance, secure, reliable data transfer protocol optimized for high-bandwidth wide area networks. The GridFTP protocol is based on the highly popular Internet file transfer protocol [GridFTP00]. The white paper "GridFTP: Universal Data Transfer for the Grid" describes the protocol in detail. The features can be summarized as follows:

- Based on GSI
- Multiple data channels for parallel transfers
- Partial file transfers
- Third-party (direct server-to-server) transfers
- Authenticated data channels
- Command pipelining

4.2.3 Remote I/O

Remote I/O is a distributed implementation of the Message Passing Interface (MPI)–IO, parallel I/O API.

4.2.4 Globus Executable Management (GEM)

GEM enables loading and executing a remote file through the GRAM resource manager.

4.2.5 Remote Data Access Portlet for Jetspeed

This remote data access JSP portlet is a client that allows users to transfer files (including third party—server to server) remotely (see Listing 4.13). It supports all the major data management protocols including GASS—HTTPS, GridFTP, HTTP, and FTP.

LISTING 4.13 Remote Data Access Portlet for Jetspeed

```
<%@ page import="org.globus.io.urlcopy.*" %>
<%@ page import="org.globus.util.*" %>
<%@ page import="org.globus.gsi.gssapi.auth.IdentityAuthorization" %>

<%@ taglib uri='/WEB-INF/templates/jsp/tld/template.tld'
prefix='jetspeed' %>

<%
/**
 * Listen for URL Transfer events
 */
class TransferListener implements UrlCopyListener
{
  Exception _exception;
  long transferedBytes;
  String transResult = "Transfer complete.";

  // fires multiple times
  public void transfer(long transferedBytes, long totalBytes) {
    this.transferedBytes += transferedBytes;
  }

  // fires if a transfer error occurs
  public void transferError(Exception e) {
    System.out.println("transferError:" + transResult);
    _exception = e;
  }

  // fires when transfer
  public void transferCompleted() {
    if (_exception == null) {
      transResult = "Transfer complete. Bytes: " + transferedBytes;
    } else {
      transResult = "Transfer failed: " + _exception.getMessage();
    }
  }
```

```
  public String getTransResult() {
    return transResult;
  }

}
%>

<%
TransferListener listener = new TransferListerner();
UrlCopy uc = new UrlCopy();
%>

<%
String jspeid = (String) request.getAttribute("js_peid");
String action = (String) request.getParameter("ra_action");
String error = null;
String output = null;

if (action != null && action.equals("submit")) {
  /*
   * Call GlobusUrlCopy here...
   */
  // From URL
  String fproto = request.getParameter("FPROTO");
  String fserver = request.getParameter("FSERVER");
  String fport = request.getParameter("FPORT");
  String ffile = request.getParameter("FFILE");

  // To URL
  String tproto = request.getParameter("TPROTO");
  String tserver = request.getParameter("TSERVER");
  String tport = request.getParameter("TPORT");
  String tfile = request.getParameter("TFILE");

  // opts
  String subject = request.getParameter("SUBJECT");

  // opts (ftp only)
  boolean thirdp = request.getParameter("TP") != null;
  boolean dcau = request.getParameter("DCAU") != null;

  try {
    String fromURL =
      (fproto.indexOf("file") >= 0)
        ? fproto + ffile
```

```
        : fproto + fserver + ":" + fport + "/" + ffile;

    String toURL =
      (tproto.indexOf("file") >= 0)
        ? tproto + tfile
        : tproto + tserver + ":" + tport + "/" + tfile;

    GlobusURL from = new GlobusURL(fromURL);
    GlobusURL to = new GlobusURL(toURL);

    uc.setSourceUrl(from);
    uc.setDestinationUrl(to);
    uc.setUseThirdPartyCopy(thirdp);
    uc.setDCAU(dcau);

    // set Authorization - subject (if any)
    if (subject != null && !subject.equals("")) {
      uc.setSourceAuthorization(new IdentityAuthorization(subject));
      uc.setDestinationAuthorization(
        new IdentityAuthorization(subject));
    }

    // fire transfer thread
    uc.addUrlCopyListener(listener);
    uc.run();

    // wait 4 output? - No need...
    // listener.waitForTransfer(10000);
    output = listener.getTransResult();
  } catch (Exception e) {
    //e.printStackTrace();
    System.err.println(e);
    output = error = e.getClass() + ":" + e.getMessage();
  }
}
%>
<script>
function Sample() {
  var f = document.forms.FRA;
  f.FPROTO.options.selectedIndex = f.TPROTO.options.selectedIndex = 1;
  f.FSERVER.value = f.TSERVER.value = "localhost";
  f.FPORT.value = f.TPORT.value = 4106;
  f.FFILE.value = f.TFILE.value = "c:/temp/myfile.txt";
}
```

```
function OnSubmit() {
  var f = document.forms.FRA;
  if (!f.FSERVER.value || !f.FPORT.value || !f.FFILE.value
      || !f.TSERVER.value || !f.TPORT.value || !f.TFILE.value) {
    alert("URL info is required.");
    return false;
  }
  return true;
}
</script>

<style type="text/css">
<!—
A, P, TD, INPUT, SELECT, OPTION, TEXTAREA {
    font-family: "Verdana";
    font-size: 9px;
    color: 000000
}
—>
</style>

Globus Remote Data Access Portlet client compatible with GT 2.4.x and
GT 3.2.x
<br />

<%if (error != null) {%>
<!— <FONT color="red"><%=error%></FONT> —>
<%}%>


<a href="javascript:Sample()" style="font-size: 10">Example</a>
  

<br />

<FORM method="POST" name="FRA" onsubmit="return OnSubmit()"><input
  type="hidden" name="ra_action" value="submit" />

<TABLE width="100%">
  <TR>
    <TD colspan="4"><B>From (URL)</B></TD>
  </TR>
  <TR>
    <TD>Protocol</TD>
```

```
      <TD>Server</TD>
      <TD>Port</TD>
      <TD>File</TD>
    </TR>
    <TR>
      <TD><SELECT name="FPROTO">
        <OPTION value="http://">Gass - http</OPTION>
        <OPTION value="https://">Gass - https</OPTION>
        <OPTION value="ftp://">ftp</OPTION>
        <OPTION value="gsiftp://">gsiftp</OPTION>
        <OPTION value="file:///">file</OPTION>
      </SELECT></TD>
      <TD><INPUT name="FSERVER" type="text" size="20" maxlength="50"
/></TD>
      <TD><INPUT name="FPORT" type="text" size="5" maxlength="50" /></TD>
      <TD><INPUT name="FFILE" type="text" size="20" maxlength="50"
/></TD>
    </TR>
    <TR>
      <TD colspan="4"><B>To (URL)</B></TD>
    </TR>
    <TR>
      <TD>Protocol</TD>
      <TD>Server</TD>
      <TD>Port</TD>
      <TD>File</TD>
    </TR>
    <TR>
      <TD><SELECT name="TPROTO">
        <OPTION value="http://">Gass - http</OPTION>
        <OPTION value="https://">Gass - https</OPTION>
        <OPTION value="ftp://">ftp</OPTION>
        <OPTION value="gsiftp://">gsiftp</OPTION>
        <OPTION value="file:///">file</OPTION>
      </SELECT></TD>
      <TD><INPUT name="TSERVER" type="text" size="20" maxlength="50"
/></TD>
      <TD><INPUT name="TPORT" type="text" size="5" maxlength="50" /></TD>
      <TD><INPUT name="TFILE" type="text" size="20" maxlength="50"
/></TD>
    </TR>
    <TR>
      <TD colspan="2"><B>Job options</B></TD>
    </TR>
    <TR>
```

```
        <TD> </TD>
        <TD colspan="2">Subject</TD>
        <TD><INPUT name="SUBJECT" type="text" size="20" maxlength="50"
/></TD>
      </TR>
      <TR>
        <TD> </TD>
        <TD colspan="2">Third party transfer (FTP Only)</TD>
        <TD><INPUT name="TP"v type="checkbox" checked="true" /></TD>
      </TR>
      <TR>
        <TD> </TD>
        <TD colspan="2">Data Channel Auth (DCAU - FTP Only)</TD>
        <TD><INPUT name="DCAU" type="checkbox" /></TD>
      </TR>
</TABLE>
<br />

<INPUT name="SUBMIT" value="Submit" type="submit" /></FORM>

<%if (output != null) {%>
<b>Job Output</b>
<br />
<TEXTAREA rows="5" cols="50"><%=output%></TEXTAREA>
```

The file above should be placed in the folder [JETSPEED_HOME]\WEB-INF\templates\jsp\portlets\html (for Jetspeed 1.5), and a registry descriptor should be created in [JETSPEED_HOME]\WEB-INF\conf, as shown in Listing 4.14.

LISTING 4.14 Remote Data Access Portlet Descriptor

```
<?xml version="1.0" encoding="UTF-8"?>
<registry>
    <portlet-entry name="RemoteAccessClient"
hidden="false" type="ref" parent="JSP" application="false">
        <meta-info>
            <title>Remote Access Client</title>
            <description>Remote Access Client Portlet</description>
        </meta-info>
        <classname>
org.apache.jetspeed.portal.portlets.JspPortlet
  </classname>
        <parameter name="template"
value="remote-access.jsp"
hidden="true" cachedOnName="true" cachedOnValue="true"/>
```

```
        <media-type ref="html"/>
        <url cachedOnURL="true"/>
        <category group="Jetspeed">Grid</category>
        <category group="Jetspeed">Grid.demo</category>
    </portlet-entry>
</registry>
```

Once the two files just described are setup correctly, you should be able to transfer files among your GASS or GridFTP servers (see Figure 4.5).

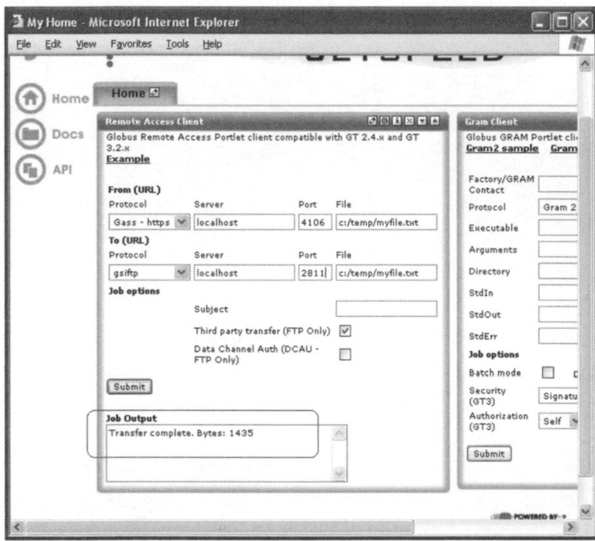

FIGURE 4.5 Remote data access portlet for Jetspeed 1.5.

4.2.6 Remote Data Access Portlet for IBM WPS

Portlets in WPS are built using the Model-View-Controller (MVC) model; thus, our remote data access portlet consists of a View JSP file and a controller JAVA class as shown in Listing 4.15.

LISTING 4.15 Remote Data Access View JSP for WPS

```
<%@ page import="portlet.remote.access.*"%>
<%@ taglib uri="/WEB-INF/tld/portlet.tld" prefix="portletAPI" %>
<portletAPI:init />

<%String actionURI =
  (String) portletRequest.getPortletSession().getAttribute("ACTION");
%>
```

```
<script>
function Sample() {
  var f = document.forms.FRA;
  f.FPROTO.options.selectedIndex = f.TPROTO.options.selectedIndex = 1;
  f.FSERVER.value = f.TSERVER.value = "localhost";
  f.FPORT.value = f.TPORT.value = 4106;
  f.FFILE.value = f.TFILE.value = "c:/temp/myfile.txt";
}

function OnSubmit() {
  var f = document.forms.FRA;
  if (!f.FSERVER.value || !f.FPORT.value || !f.FFILE.value
      || !f.TSERVER.value || !f.TPORT.value || !f.TFILE.value) {
    alert("URL info is required.");
    return false;
  }
  return true;
}
</script>

<a href="javascript:Sample()" style="font-size: 10">Example</a>
  
<br />

<FORM method="POST" action="<%=actionURI%>" name="FRA"
  onsubmit="return OnSubmit()"><input type="hidden" name="ra_action"
  value="submit" />

<TABLE>
  <TR>
    <TD colspan="4"><B>From (URL)</B></TD>
  </TR>
  <TR>
    <TD>Protocol</TD>
    <TD>Server</TD>
    <TD>Port</TD>
    <TD>File</TD>
  </TR>
  <TR>
    <TD><SELECT name="FPROTO">
      <OPTION value="http://">Gass - http</OPTION>
      <OPTION value="https://">Gass - https</OPTION>
      <OPTION value="ftp://">ftp</OPTION>
      <OPTION value="gsiftp://">gsiftp</OPTION>
```

```
    <OPTION value="file:///">file</OPTION>
  </SELECT></TD>
  <TD><INPUT class="wpsEditField" name="FSERVER" type="text"
    size="30" maxlength="50" /></TD>
  <TD><INPUT class="wpsEditField" name="FPORT" type="text" size="5"
    maxlength="50" /></TD>
  <TD><INPUT class="wpsEditField" name="FFILE" type="text" size="30"
    maxlength="50" /></TD>
</TR>
<TR>
  <TD colspan="4"><B>To (URL)</B></TD>
</TR>
<TR>
  <TD>Protocol</TD>
  <TD>Server</TD>
  <TD>Port</TD>
  <TD>File</TD>
</TR>
<TR>
  <TD><SELECT name="TPROTO">
    <OPTION value="http://">Gass - http</OPTION>
    <OPTION value="https://">Gass - https</OPTION>
    <OPTION value="ftp://">ftp</OPTION>
    <OPTION value="gsiftp://">gsiftp</OPTION>
    <OPTION value="file:///">file</OPTION>
  </SELECT></TD>
  <TD><INPUT class="wpsEditField" name="TSERVER" type="text"
    size="30" maxlength="50" /></TD>
  <TD><INPUT class="wpsEditField" name="TPORT" type="text" size="5"
    maxlength="50" /></TD>
  <TD><INPUT class="wpsEditField" name="TFILE" type="text" size="30"
    maxlength="50" /></TD>
</TR>
<TR>
  <TD colspan="2"><B>Job options</B></TD>
</TR>
<TR>
  <TD> </TD>
  <TD colspan="2">Subject</TD>
  <TD><INPUT class="wpsEditField" name="SUBJECT" type="text"
    size="30" maxlength="50" /></TD>
</TR>
<TR>
  <TD> </TD>
```

```
    <TD colspan="2">Third party transfer (FTP Only)</TD>
    <TD><INPUT class="wpsEditField" name="TP" type="checkbox"
      checked="true" /></TD>
  </TR>
  <TR>
    <TD> </TD>
    <TD colspan="2">Data Channel Auth (DCAU - FTP Only)</TD>
    <TD><INPUT name="DCAU" type="checkbox" /></TD>
  </TR>
</TABLE>
<br />

<INPUT class="wpsButtonText"
  name="<portletAPI:encodeNamespace
value='<%=RemAccessPortlet.SUBMIT%>'/>"
  value="Submit" type="submit" /></FORM>

<%String output =
  (String) portletRequest.getPortletSession().getAttribute("OUTPUT");

if (output != null) {
%>
<b>Job Output</b>
<br />
<TEXTAREA rows="5" cols="80"><%=output%></TEXTAREA>
<%}
%>
```

The controller Java class for the portlet is as shown in Listing 4.16.

LISTING 4.16 Remote Data Access Portlet Controller for WPS

```
package portlet.remote.access;

import java.io.IOException;

import org.apache.jetspeed.portlet.*;
import org.apache.jetspeed.portlet.event.*;

import org.globus.io.urlcopy.*;
import org.globus.util.*;
import org.globus.gsi.gssapi.auth.IdentityAuthorization;

/**
```

```
 * Remote Data Access Portlet for GT
 * Supports: GASS - HTTPS, GSIFTP, HTTP and FTP
 * Built with WebSphere Studio 5.1.2 (Portal Toolkit)
 * @author Vladimir Silva
 */
public class RemAccessPortlet
    extends PortletAdapter implements ActionListener {

  //       JSP file name to be rendered on the view mode
  public static final String VIEW_JSP =
      "/portlet_remote_access/jsp/RemAccessPortletView.jsp";
  //       Action name for the orderId entry form
  public static final String FORM_ACTION =
      "portlet.remote.access.RemAccessPortletFormAction";
  //       Parameter name for general submit button
  public static final String SUBMIT =
      "portlet.remote.access.RemAccessPortletSubmit";
  //       Parameter name for general cancel button
  public static final String CANCEL =
      "portlet.remote.access.RemAccessPortletCancel";

  /**
   * Listen for URL Transfer events
   */
  class TransferListerner
      implements UrlCopyListener {
    Exception _exception;
    long transferedBytes;
    String transResult = "Transfer complete.";

    // fires multiple times
    public void transfer(long transferedBytes, long totalBytes) {
      this.transferedBytes += transferedBytes;
      //System.out.println("transfer:" + transferedBytes);
    }

    // fires if a transfer error occurs
    public void transferError(Exception e) {
      System.out.println("transferError:" + e);
      _exception = e;
    }

    // fires when transfer is complete
    public void transferCompleted() {
```

```
    if (_exception == null) {
      transResult =
          "Transfer complete. Bytes: " + transferedBytes;
    }
    else {
      transResult =
          "Transfer failed: " + _exception.getMessage();
    }
  }

  public String getTransResult() {
    return transResult;
  }

}

/**
 * @see org.apache.jetspeed.portlet.Portlet#init(PortletConfig)
 */
public void init(PortletConfig portletConfig)
throws UnavailableException
{
  super.init(portletConfig);
}

/**
 * Fires when the portlet gets rendered
 * @see org.apache.jetspeed.portlet.PortletAdapter#doView
 */
public void doView(PortletRequest request,
                   PortletResponse response) throws PortletException,
    IOException {

  // Set actionURI in the view mode bean
  PortletURI formActionURI = response.createURI();
  formActionURI.addAction(FORM_ACTION);

  PortletSession session = request.getPortletSession();
  session.setAttribute("ACTION", formActionURI.toString());

  // Invoke the JSP to render
  getPortletConfig().getContext()
      .include(VIEW_JSP, request, response);
}
```

```
  /**
   * Fires when on form submission
   */
  public void actionPerformed(ActionEvent event) throws
PortletException {

    // ActionEvent handler
    String actionString = event.getActionString();
    PortletRequest request = event.getRequest();
    String output = null;

    if (FORM_ACTION.equals(actionString)) {
      /*
       * Call GlobusUrlCopy here...
       */
      // From URL
      String fproto = request.getParameter("FPROTO");
      String fserver = request.getParameter("FSERVER");
      String fport = request.getParameter("FPORT");
      String ffile = request.getParameter("FFILE");

      // To URL
      String tproto = request.getParameter("TPROTO");
      String tserver = request.getParameter("TSERVER");
      String tport = request.getParameter("TPORT");
      String tfile = request.getParameter("TFILE");

      // opts
      String subject = request.getParameter("SUBJECT");

      // opts (ftp only)
      boolean thirdp = request.getParameter("TP")
          != null;
      boolean dcau = request.getParameter("DCAU")
          != null;

      try {
        String fromURL =
            (fproto.indexOf("file") >= 0)
            ? fproto + ffile
            : fproto + fserver + ":"
            + fport + "/" + ffile;

        String toURL =
            (tproto.indexOf("file") >= 0)
```

```
            ? tproto + tfile
            : tproto + tserver + ":"
            + tport + "/" + tfile;

        System.out.println("from: "
                           + fromURL + ", to: "
                           + toURL +
                           ", Third party:"
                           + thirdp + ", dcau="
                           + dcau + ", sub:"
                           + subject);

        GlobusURL from = new GlobusURL(fromURL);
        GlobusURL to = new GlobusURL(toURL);
        TransferListerner listener =
            new TransferListerner();
        UrlCopy uc = new UrlCopy();

        uc.setSourceUrl(from);
        uc.setDestinationUrl(to);
        uc.setUseThirdPartyCopy(thirdp);
        uc.setDCAU(dcau);

        // set Authorization - subject
        if (subject != null && !subject.equals("")) {
          uc.setSourceAuthorization(
              new IdentityAuthorization(subject));
          uc.setDestinationAuthorization(
              new IdentityAuthorization(subject));
        }

        // fire transfer thread
        uc.addUrlCopyListener(listener);
        uc.run();

        // wait 4 output? - No need...
        // listener.waitForTransfer(10000);
        output = listener.getTransResult();
      }
      catch (Exception e) {
        //e.printStackTrace();
        System.err.println(e);
        output = e.getClass() + ":" + e.getMessage();
      }
```

```
            // Set form text in the session bean
            request.getPortletSession()
                .setAttribute("OUTPUT", output);
        }
    }
}
```

The portlet preview of the previous file can be seen in Figure 4.6.

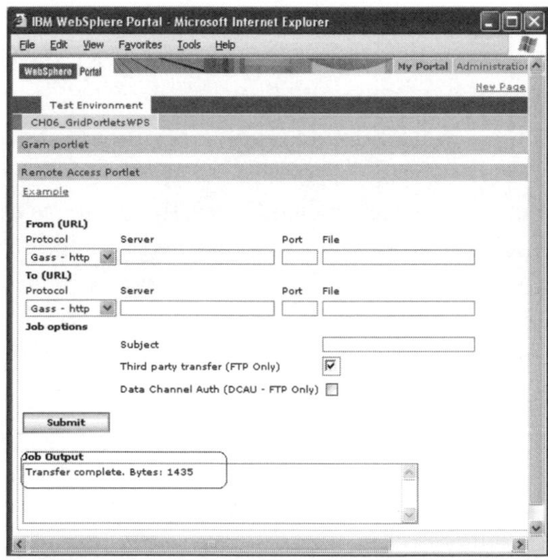

FIGURE 4.6 Remote data access portlet for WPS.

4.3 TROUBLESHOOTING

The following section explains the most common errors when running the programs in this chapter.

4.3.1 Certificate Not Yet Valid Errors

This error occurs when the time on the client and server are not synchronized. Some Linux/Unix servers do not use Network Time Protocol (NTP) to synchronize their clocks. Thus, if the time of a Win32 client happens to be out of sync with the server for 15 or more minutes, this error may be thrown.

4.3.2 Defective Credential Errors

Defective credential errors are thrown when either the user or host certificates are invalid. This error can occur when the client user certificates and host certificates are signed by two different Certificate Authorities (CAs). To check the integrity of your certificates, issue the following commands:

```
$ openssl verify [-CApath directory] [certificate1] [certificate2]
```

Where

[-CApath directory]: A directory of trusted certificates. The certificates should have names of the form: *hash.0*

[certificate1]: A user defined digital certificate

Trusted certificates, also called CA certificates, are the certificates used to sign both server and user certificates as explained in Chapter 8 in the section on GSI. More details on the OpenSSL documentation can be found at the Web site *http://www.openssl.org/*.

4.4 SUMMARY

Portals can provide an open standards-based user interface to grid middleware such as the Globus Toolkit. Portals have many features that make them the platform of choice for accessing grid services. They provide single point of access to Web-based resources and aggregate those resources in one place. A user can access the portal via a Web browser, WAP-phone, pager, or any other device. The portal acts as the central hub where information from multiple sources is made available in an easy-to-use manner.

An enterprise Portal consists of middleware, applications (called portlets), and development tools for building and managing business-to-business (B2B), business-to-consumer (B2C), and business-to-employee (B2E) portals. This chapter has introduced the development of portals that use the APIs provided by the Globus Toolkit.

REFERENCES

[GridFTP00] "GridFTP: Universal Data Transfer for the Grid." White paper. Copyright 2000, The University of Chicago and The University of Southern California. Accessed online September 5, 2000, at *http://www.globustoolkit.org/toolkit/docs/2.4/datagrid/deliverables/C2WPdraft3.pdf.*

[IBMWPS04] The Information Center for IBM WebSphere Portal for Multiplatforms Version 5.0.2. Copyright IBM Corporation 1994, 2004. All rights reserved.

[JetSpeed04] Apache Portals—Jetspeed. Apache Software Foundation 2004. Available online at *http://portals.apache.org/jetspeed-1/index.html.*

5 Schedulers

In This Chapter

- An Overview of Popular Schedulers and Grid Middleware Integration
- Portable Baatch System—OpenPBS
- Silver/Maui Metascheduler
- Sun Grid Engine (SGE)—B1 Grid Engine 6
- Condor-G
- MMJFS Integration with Other Job Schedulers
- Factors for Choosing the Right Scheduler
- Summary
- References

Schedulers are advanced resource management tools for heterogeneous distributed computing environments. The goal of schedulers is to allow organizations to best achieve the enterprise's goals such as productivity, timeliness, level of service, and so forth. Schedulers should support jobs in single system or in many systems grouped together; they should also provide the following functionality:

- Accept batch jobs
- Preserve and protect the job until run
- Run the jobs
- Deliver output back to the submitter

Schedulers use complex management polices and sophisticated scheduling algorithms to achieve such functionality as the following:

- Dynamic collection of performance data
- Enhanced security
- High-level policy administration
- Quality of service (QoS)
- Computationally demanding tasks
- Transparent distribution of the associated workload
- Advanced resource reservations
- Support for check-pointing programs

The topics covered in this chapter include the following:

- A description of the differences between job schedulers and job managers.
- An extensive guide of the integration of OpenPBS and Open Grid Services Architecture (OGSA), including installation, customization, and troubleshooting.
- Discussion about metascheduler software such as Silver/Maui.
- Integration of the Master Managed Job Factory Service (MMJFS) provided by OGSA with the most popular open source schedulers available today: OpenPBS, Sun Grid Engine (SGE), Condor, as well as others.

The chapter ends with a description of the factors you may face while choosing the right scheduler for your organization, always focusing on grid middleware integration.

5.1 AN OVERVIEW OF POPULAR SCHEDULERS AND GRID MIDDLEWARE INTEGRATION

This chapter starts with a feature description of the most popular schedulers available today. The discussion focuses in four major schedulers supported by the Globus Toolkit: OpenPBS/PBS Pro, Silver/Maui metascheduler, SGE, and Condor-G. Among the features covered are the following:

- Software Installation and service configuration
- Common features such as scheduling algorithms, job management policies, quality of service, and node allocation
- Usability: graphical and command-line user interfaces
- Grid middleware support: GT scheduler interface support and configuration

The chapter ends by looking at the factors that influence the selection of the right scheduler for your organization. You must weight the pros and cons of these software packages and select the one that bets fits the needs of your organization.

5.1.1 Job Schedulers versus Job Managers

The Globus Toolkit and OGSA provide a powerful standards-based framework for grid services. Among the services GT3 provides, the MMJFS is called a *job manager.* The function of MMJFS is to provide a single interface for requesting and using remote system resources for the execution of *jobs.* These sets of interfaces are called Globus Resource Allocation Manager (GRAM) and are designed to provide a flexible interface to scheduling systems—more like a remote shell with features if you will.

Job schedulers are networked systems for submitting, controlling, and monitoring the workload of batch jobs in one or more computers. The jobs or tasks are scheduled for execution at a time chosen by the subsystem according to an available policy and availability of resources. Popular job schedulers include Portable Batch System (PBS), Local Scheduler Framework (LSF), and LoadLeveler. This chapter discusses the most popular schedulers available today, focusing on job manager integration, specifically with grid middleware such as the Globus Toolkit.

5.2 PORTABLE BATCH SYSTEM—OPENPBS

OpenPBS is a popular open scheduler originally developed for the U.S. government and later commercialized by Altair Engineering.

5.2.1 Overview

PBS is *resource management* software, and was developed by NASA to conform to the Portable Operating System Interface for Unix (POSIX) Batch environment standards [PBSAdmin02]. PBS allows you to do the following:

- Accept batch jobs
- Control their attributes
- Preserve and protect the jobs until run
- Deliver jobs' output back to the caller

The four major components in PBS are the following:

Client side commands: These are used to submit, control, monitor, or delete jobs and can be installed in any supported platform. They include commands such as `qsub` and `qdel` and several graphical tools such as `xpbs`.

Server (`pbs_server`): This provides the main entry point for batch services such as creating, modifying, and protecting jobs against system crashes. All the clients and other daemons communicate with this server over TCP/IP.

Scheduler (`pbs_sched`): This controls the policies or set of rules used to submit jobs over the network. PBS was designed to allow each cluster to create its own scheduler or policies. When started, the scheduler queries with the server for jobs to be run and the executor for system resource availability.

Job Executor (`pbs_mom`): This is in charge of executing the job by emulating user sessions identical to the user's login session. It delivers the output back to the caller when directed.

In a typical cluster configuration, a `pbs_mom` would run on each system where jobs are to be run. The server and scheduler may run in the same machine, and the client commands can be placed on the machines that will submit the jobs. PBS provides an application programming interface (API) for sites that want to implement their own scheduling policies.

5.2.2 OpenPBS in Red Hat Linux (RHL) 9

In this chapter, we will set up an OpenPBS cluster in a Red Hat Linux (RHL) 9 Linux server. The best way is to install the Red Hat Package Manger (RPM) provided by the PBS Web site at *www.openpbs.org*. The PBSRPM version used is 2.3.2. Because this RPM requires Tool Command Language/Tool Kit (Tcl/Tk) and Wish 8.0 and was compiled for an older kernel, some tweaking is required to get PBS running (see Figure 5.1).

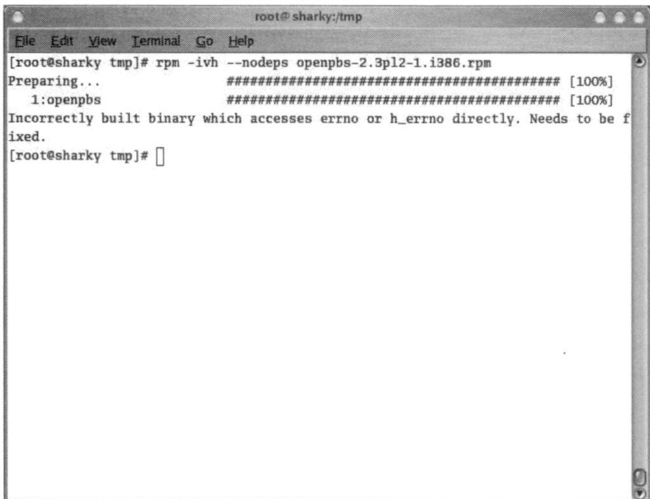

FIGURE 5.1 Installing OpenPBS 2.3.2 in Red Hat Linux 9.

As you can see in previous the figure, the rpm must be installed using the –nodeps flags because of the Tcl/Tk 8.0 requirements. OpenPBS should be up and running now, and a service automatically installed to start up at boot time. The next step is configuring the cluster.

5.2.3 Configuring PBS on a Single Machine Cluster

If the installation is successful, the next step is to configure the PBS cluster and start the daemons as shown in the following command sequence:

```
# export PATH=$PATH:/usr/pbs/bin:/usr/pbs/sbin
# pbs_mom
# pbs_server -t create (first time only)
# pbs_sched
```

The first line set the path to PBS binaries, `pbs_mom` starts the execution server. *The first time only,* start the server with the *-t create* option to initialize various files. While starting the servers, you may see the following message: "Incorrectly built binary which accesses `errno` or `h_errno` directly. Needs to be fixed." This is because the binaries built in an old kernel version. This message should not affect PBS execution in any way.

A faster way is to simply issue the command:

```
[root@sharky pbs]# service pbs start
Starting PBS daemons:
Starting pbs_mom:                                          [  OK  ]
Starting pbs_sched:                                        [  OK  ]
Starting pbs_server:                                       [  OK  ]
[root@sharky pbs]#
```

For simplicity, we have set up a *single execution system,* which means that the daemon and scheduling server run in the same machine and *no nodes* file is needed. For *multiple execution* systems where a nodes file is required see the OpenPBS Administration guide [PBSAdmin02]. Now log on to the system as root to configure the execution queue and activate the server:

```
# qmgr
Max open servers: 4
Qmgr: create queue dque queue_type=e
Qmgr: s q dque enabled=true, started=true
Qmgr: s s scheduling=true
Qmgr:
```

For more information on the `qmgr` options, see the OpenPBS administration manuals or man pages.

5.2.4 Tweaking PBS GUIs for RHL 9

Because the PBS GUI (`xpbs`) requires Tcl/Tk 8.0, some tweaking is required to make it work on RHL 9, which uses TCL 8.3 by default:

```
[root@sharky tmp]# /usr/pbs/bin/xpbs-bash: /usr/pbs/bin/xpbs:
/usr/bin/wish8.0:
bad interpreter: No such file or directory
[root@sharky tmp]# vi /usr/pbs/bin/xpbs
#!/usr/bin/wish8.0 -f
################################################################ xpbs-
gui: The GUI front end to the PBS user and operator commands.
#
# Written by Albeaus Bayucan
# History
#        Initial Date: 1/17/96
```

Change the line `#!/usr/bin/wish8.0 -f` to match your TCL version: **`#!/usr/bin/wish8.3 -f`** in our test system, then type *xpbs* to display the main window (see Figure 5.2).

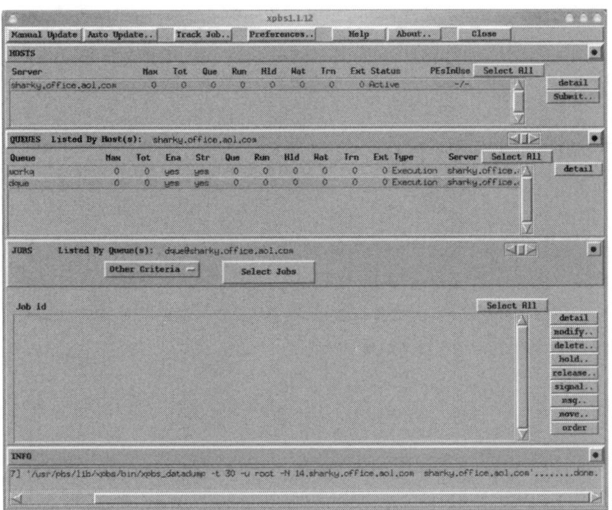

FIGURE 5.2 XPBS main GUI.

For the job submission dialog of *xpbs*, see Figure 5.3.

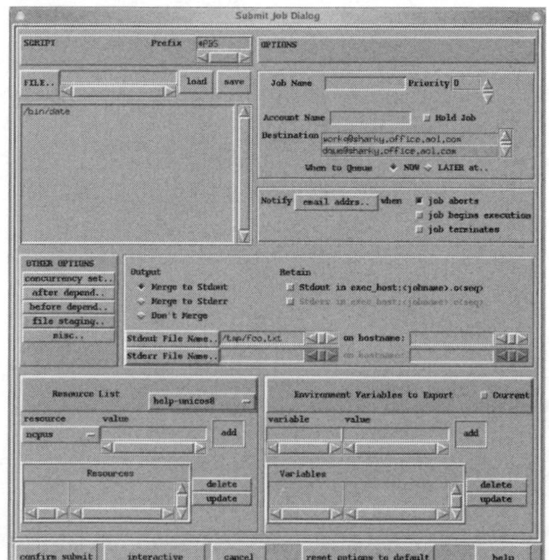

FIGURE 5.3 XPBS job scheduling dialog.

Type the command you want to run in the top right panel, and enter an output file name in the *Stdout File Name* text box, then click *confirm submit*. You should not run any jobs as root or you may see the error message: "Bad UID for job execution."

Try running a job in xpbs as any other user but root and you should get see the message *4.[my_host_domain]*, which indicates a successful submission. For this particular job, the output of the date command will be saved in /tmp/foo.txt.

5.2.5 Configuring the Globus Toolkit 3.2 PBS Job Scheduler

Now that PBS is up and running, the next step is to setup the Globus Toolkit 3.2 PBS job scheduler. For this step, we assume that GT3 has been successfully installed and GSI set up correctly, including the MMJFS, which is required to interface OGSA to the backend scheduler. The following command shows a quick way to test whether MMJFS is running properly:

```
$ grid-proxy-init
Your identity: /O=Grid/OU=GlobusTest/OU=simpleCA-
sharky.office.aol.com/OU=office.aol.com/CN=globus
Enter GRID pass phrase for this identity:
Creating proxy ................................. Done
Your proxy is valid until: Thu Jul 22 23:50:32 2004

$ bin/managed-job-globusrun -factory http://`hostname`:8080/ogsa/ser-
```

```
vices/base/gram/MasterForkManagedJobFactoryService -file
schema/base/gram/examples/test.xml -o
12 abc 34 pdscaex_instr_GrADS_grads23_28919.cfg pgwynnel was here
```

The following command sequence can be used to install the job scheduler bundles distributed with GT3:

```
[globus] cd schedulers
[globus] gpt-build scheduler-pbs-3.2-src_bundle.tar.gz gcc32dbg
[globus] gpt-postinstall
```

More information on installing or configuring GRAM services can be found in the Globus installation section at *www.globus.org*.

5.2.6 Customizing the PBS Job Manager

The file `$GLOBUS_LOCATION/lib/perl/Globus/GRAM/JobManager/pbs.pm` contains the configuration options used by Globus when submitting jobs to the backend scheduler. The following figure shows the PBS configuration options for GT3. These options may have to be changed to match your cluster configuration. For example, some clusters may use `ssh` instead or `rsh` (see Figure 5.4).

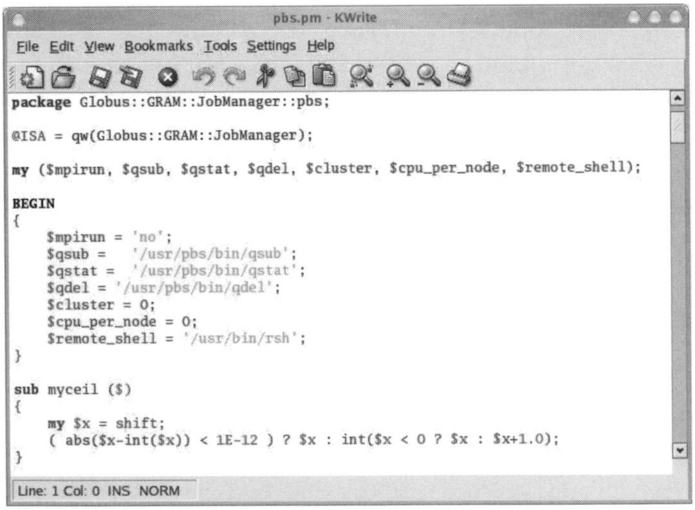

```
pbs.pm - KWrite
File Edit View Bookmarks Tools Settings Help
package Globus::GRAM::JobManager::pbs;

@ISA = qw(Globus::GRAM::JobManager);

my ($mpirun, $qsub, $qstat, $qdel, $cluster, $cpu_per_node, $remote_shell);

BEGIN
{
    $mpirun = 'no';
    $qsub =   '/usr/pbs/bin/qsub';
    $qstat =  '/usr/pbs/bin/qstat';
    $qdel = '/usr/pbs/bin/qdel';
    $cluster = 0;
    $cpu_per_node = 0;
    $remote_shell = '/usr/bin/rsh';
}

sub myceil ($)
{
    my $x = shift;
    ( abs($x-int($x)) < 1E-12 ) ? $x : int($x < 0 ? $x : $x+1.0);
}
Line: 1 Col: 0 INS NORM
```

FIGURE 5.4 OpenPBS Job Manager script—pbs.pm.

For an RHL 9 *single-execution* system, *mpirun* must be set to 'no,' *cluster* must be 0 (single execution). Failing to set the cluster variable to 0 on a single execution system will give the following error:

```
[globus@sharky gt32]$ cd $GLOBUS_LOCATION/
[globus@sharky gt32]$ bin/managed-job-globusrun
-factory
http://`hostname`:8080/ogsa/services/base/gram
  /MasterPbsManagedJobFactoryService
-file
 $GLOBUS_LOCATION/schema/base/gram/examples/pbs_gram_rsl_example_1.xml
 -o
[07/22/2004 12:54:13:389 ]
 org.globus.ogsa.impl.base.gram.client.GramJob
[setStatusFromServiceData:1216] ERROR:
 The executable could not be started.
 Error: Job failed: The executable could not be started.
```

5.2.7 Troubleshooting PBS MMJFS Runtime Errors

The following section contains a compilation of the errors we have found when working and installing MMJFS on Linux systems running on VMWare 4 workstations:

5.2.7.1 PBS Resource Scripting Language (RSL) Parsing Errors

The following error may be thrown by the MMJFS client:

```
org.globus.ogsa.impl.base.gram.client.GlobusRun
[submitRSL:1068] ERROR: Caught exception:
 org.globus.gram.GramException:
 The provided RSL could not be properly parsed
[Root error message: exception during RSL parsing
 Embedded exception class org.xml.sax.SAXParseException:
 cvc-elt.1: Cannot find the declaration of element 'rsl:rsl'.].
```

Possible cause: This error seems to occur when the `managed-job-globusrun` is run using absolute paths. For example, the following command should produce this error:

```
$GLOBUS_LOCATION/bin/managed-job-globusrun
-factory
http://`hostname`:8080/ogsa/services/base/
 gram/MasterPbsManagedJobFactoryService
-file
 /opt/gt32/schema/base/gram/examples/pbs_gram_rsl_example_1.xml
-o
```

Possible solution: Run the command from the `$GLOBUS_LOCATION` folder.

5.2.7.2 "The executable could not be started" Messages Returned by the MMJFS Client

Message:

```
ERROR: The executable could not be started.
Error: Job failed: The executable could not be started.
```

Source: This message sometimes appears when running the MMJFS test script

```
bin/managed-job-globusrun
-factory
 http://`hostname`:8080/ogsa/services/
 base/gram/MasterPbsManagedJobFactoryService
-file
 schema/base/gram/examples/pbs_gram_rsl_example_1.xml -o
```

Possible cause: Common mistakes in the PBS RSL xml script or the *Job Manager* configuration Practical Extraction and Report Language (PERL) script may throw this error. In this case, the error occurs when the *Job Manager* configuration file is set up to run in a cluster but the backend scheduler has been set up as a single execution system.

To figure out what is going on through the MMJFS execution process, the GT3 container can be set up in *debug* mode, displaying messages that can help you track down the problem.

1. Edit the file `$GLOBUS_LOCATION`/log4j.properties.
2. Add the lines shown in Listing 5.1 to debug the GRAM Job Manager.

LISTING 5.1 Enabling DEBUG for the MMJFS Job Manager

```
# DEBUG Job Manager Classes (PBS Fork)
#log4j.category.org.globus
 .jobmanager.JobManager=DEBUG
#log4j.category.org.globus
 .jobmanager.JobManagerService=DEBUG
#log4j.category.org.globus.ogsa.impl.base
 .gram.mmjfs.MasterManagedJobFactory=DEBUG
#log4j.category.org.globus.ogsa.impl.base
 .gram.jobmanager.ManagedJobFactoryImpl=DEBUG
#log4j.category.org.globus.ogsa.impl.base
 .gram.jobmanager.JobManager=DEBUG
log4j.category.org.globus.ogsa.impl.base
 .gram.jobmanager.JobManagerScript=DEBUG
#log4j.category.org.globus.ogsa.impl.base
```

```
 .gram.jobmanager.ManagedJobImpl=DEBUG
#log4j.category.org.globus.ogsa.impl.base
 .gram.jobmanager.ManagedJobFactoryImpl =DEBUG
```

3. Select the classes you want to debug by removing comments from their respective lines. For our purposes, the class `gram.jobmanager.JobManagerScript` is enough to see what is going on.

Before testing the changes, the *User Hosting Environment (UHE)* must be refreshed. There is no need to restart the GT container.

1. To refresh the UHE: `rm -Rf $HOME/.globus/uhe-*`
2. Rerun the PBS job and monitor the UHE logs: `$HOME/.globus/uhe-*` is created dynamically, then type `tail -f $HOME/.globus/uhe-*/log`

The UHE log file will show messages such as shown in Listing 5.2:

LISTING 5.2 UHE Job Manager Log

```
23010 [Thread-21] DEBUG org.globus.ogsa.impl
 .base.gram.jobmanager.JobManagerScript
- script is done, setting done flag
23010 [Thread-21] DEBUG org.globus.ogsa.impl
 .base.gram.jobmanager.JobManagerScript
- script is done, signaling callback
23019 [Thread-13] DEBUG org.globus.ogsa.impl
 .base.gram.jobmanager.JobManagerScript
- Initializing script thread
23022 [Thread-21] DEBUG org.globus.ogsa.impl
 .base.gram.jobmanager.JobManagerScript
- returned from callback
23023 [Thread-22] DEBUG org.globus.ogsa.impl
 .base.gram.jobmanager.JobManagerScript
- Executing /opt1/gt32/libexec/globus-job-manager-script.pl
 -m pbs -f /tmp/gram_job_mgr37073.tmp -c submit
23306 [Thread-22] DEBUG org.globus.ogsa.impl
 .base.gram.jobmanager.JobManagerScript
- Read line GRAM_SCRIPT_GT3_FAILURE_MESSAGE:
 qsub: Job exceeds queue resource limits
23306 [Thread-22] DEBUG org.globus.ogsa.impl.base
 .gram.jobmanager.JobManagerScript
- Read line GRAM_SCRIPT_ERROR:17
```

Greedy: Greedy behaves like *Bestfit,* but rather than attempting to start the best jobs one at a time, it attempts to determine the best possible combination of jobs that meet certain criteria.

Preempt: Backfill jobs are optimistically started even if they may potentially conflict with higher priority blocked idle jobs. Priority jobs may stop them and use their resources as soon as aggregate idle and preemptible resources become available. This policy overcomes many of the drawbacks of other backfill methods where job wall clock inaccuracies cause scheduling inefficiencies.

5.3.4 Job Prioritization

Job prioritization is defined by factors such as wall-clock time, queue duration, user's system usage, and others. Prioritization can be classified into categories such as the following:

Service factors: job service metrics, backfill time and queue time

Resource factors: processors, memory, swap, wall-time, and so on

Fairshare factors: system utilization or quality of service

Other factors: credential and scheduling targets, and so on

5.3.5 Throttling Policies

These are policies to control resource consumption. The goal is to prevent the system from being dominated by an individual user, group, account, or QoS, for example, restricting user *john-doe* to a total of 1 job and 4 processors at any time. If a user submits a job and exceeds its policy limits, then the job will be placed in a deferred state until the job is able to join the normal job queue.

5.3.6 Quality of Service (QoS)

This method allows the special consideration of classes of jobs, users, groups, and so on. QoS can be thought of as a container that holds privileges, such as job prioritization, policy exemptions, and resource access.

5.3.7 Node Allocation

Nodes are allocated according to rules such as minimum of resources, CPU load, last available, site priority, and speed.

```
23310 [Thread-22] DEBUG org.globus.ogsa.impl.base
 .gram.jobmanager.JobManagerScript
- script is done, setting done flag
```

Solution:

The message "Job exceeds queue resource limits" tells us that Globus is trying to submit a PBS script for a multiple execution system to a single cluster. Once the *cluster* flag is set to 0 in pbs.pm, the output will look something like the following:

```
[vsilva@sharky gt32]$ bin/managed-job-globusrun
 -factory
 http://`hostname`:8080/ogsa/services/base/gram/
   MasterPbsManagedJobFactoryService
 -file schema/base/gram/examples/pbs_gram_rsl_example_1.xml -o
12 abc 34 pdscaex_instr_GrADS_grads23_28919.cfg
```

Another possible cause for this error could be invalid paths to the PBS client executables in your job-manager script (pbs.pm). Edit this file and make sure the paths to the clients point to the proper locations. The script can be found in `$GLOBUS_LOCATION`/lib/perl/Globus/GRAM/JobManager /pbs.pm.

```
$qsub =   '/usr/pbs/bin/qsub';
$qstat =  '/usr/pbs/bin/qstat';
```

5.2.7.3 "Job failed" Errors Returned by the MMJFS Client

The following is a common error message reported by the MMJFS PBS client:

```
[01/19/2005 14:29:41:523 ]
org.globus.ogsa.impl.base.gram.client.GramJob [setStatusFromService-
Data:1226]
ERROR: Invalid ns1:value path
"/home".
Error: Job failed: Invalid ns1:value path "/home".
```

Possible cause: Mistakes in the job submission XML. For example:

- *An inexistent executable:* The following XML will produce this error if the executable does not exist:

```
<gram:executable>
    <rsl:path>
        <rsl:stringElement value="/home/bin/a.out"/>
    </rsl:path>
```

```
        </gram:executable>
```

- *An invalid directory:* Your job should print to a valid remote directory with the appropriate permissions:

```
<gram:directory>
    <rsl:path>
        <rsl:stringElement value="/home"/>
    </rsl:path>
</gram:directory>
```

- *Invalid standard input:* This is a major source of headaches. If your program does not read from STDIN make sure you set this values to /dev/null.

```
<gram:stdin>
    <rsl:path>
        <rsl:stringElement value="/dev/null"/>
    </rsl:path>
</gram:stdin>
```

5.2.8 Customizing PBS Scheduler Execution Parameters with RSL

The final step is to customize the RSL xml file that MMJFS uses to submit a job to the scheduling system. Arguments such as the executable, environment, and number of CPUs can be controlled as shown in the following xml snippets:

5.2.8.1 Executable and Arguments

For example, to run the program echo from the /bin directory with the arguments "Hello World" the submission XML should look like:

```
...
<gram:executable>
  <rsl:path>
    <rsl:stringElement value="echo" />
  </rsl:path>
</gram:executable>
<gram:directory>
  <rsl:path>
    <rsl:stringElement value="/bin" />
  </rsl:path>
</gram:directory>
<gram:arguments>
  <rsl:stringArray>
```

```
      <rsl:string>
        <rsl:stringElement value="Hello World" />
      </rsl:string>
    </rsl:stringArray>
  </gram:arguments>
  ...
```

5.2.8.2 Standard Input and Error

Setting the right parameters for your job input and output is important for preventing and debugging execution errors. If the program is not to use standard input, then the NULL device (/dev/null) can be used.

```
<gram:stdin>
    <rsl:path>
        <rsl:stringElement value="/dev/null"/>
    </rsl:path>
</gram:stdin>
<gram:stdout>
    <rsl:pathArray>
        <rsl:path>
            <rsl:stringElement value="./out"/>
        </rsl:path>
    </rsl:pathArray>
</gram:stdout>
<gram:stderr>
    <rsl:pathArray>
        <rsl:path>
            <rsl:stringElement value="./err"/>
        </rsl:path>
    </rsl:pathArray>
</gram:stderr>
```

5.2.8.3 Cluster Parameters

Cluster parameters specify the PBS standard scheduling options such as the following: host count, number of processor, execution queue, project name, CPU times, and so forth.

```
<!-- Number of PBS nodes -->
<gram:hostCount>
  <rsl:integer value="3" />
</gram:hostCount>

<!-- PBS Project Name -->
```

```
<gram:project>
  <rsl:string>
    <rsl:stringElement value="cgt::ws:demo_sc02" />
  </rsl:string>
</gram:project>

<!-- PBS Queue -->
<gram:queue>
  <rsl:string>
    <rsl:stringElement value="dque" />
  </rsl:string>
</gram:queue>

<!-- Wall clock time parameters -->
<gram:maxTime>
  <rsl:long value="60" />
</gram:maxTime>
<gram:maxWallTime>
  <rsl:long value="60" />
</gram:maxWallTime>
<gram:maxCpuTime>
  <rsl:long value="60" />
</gram:maxCpuTime>

<!-- Memory requirements -->
<gram:maxMemory>
  <rsl:integer value="2048" />
</gram:maxMemory>
<gram:minMemory>
  <rsl:integer value="1024" />
</gram:minMemory>
```

5.2.8.4 Job Type

The job type specifies how the PBS Job Manager should execute the requested job. Types supported by Globus are `single`, `multiple`, and `mpi`. Single means that the job will be dispatched into a single execution system. Multiple will be dispatched as a multinode PBS cluster and mpi will use the Message Passing Interface (MPI) manager (mpirun) to dispatch it into a parallel system.

```
<!-- jobType: single, multiple, mpi -->
<gram:jobType>
  <enum:enumeration>
    <enum:enumerationValue>
      <enum:mpi />
```

```
      </enum:enumerationValue>
    </enum:enumeration>
  </gram:jobType>

  <!-- GRAM arguments, better not touch -->
  <gram:gramMyJobType>
    <enum:enumeration>
      <enum:enumerationValue>
        <enum:collective />
      </enum:enumerationValue>
    </enum:enumeration>
  </gram:gramMyJobType>

  <!-- dryRun will not submit the job to the back end scheduler -->
  <gram:dryRun>
    <rsl:boolean value="false" />
  </gram:dryRun>
```

5.3 SILVER/MAUI METASCHEDULER

Maui was designed and written by the High Performance Computing Center to address limitations of resource managers of the time such as low system and job prioritization. It is now maintained by the Supercluster Research Group (*http://www.supercluster.org*). Maui is an external scheduler designed to work with resource managers such as PBS or LoadLeveler. Even though the resource manager is still responsible for managing resources, the Maui scheduler decides which nodes to use and the start time of the jobs. As with all external schedulers, Maui takes advantage of the scheduling API provided by the resource manager to retrieve job and node information. A set of policies or decisions is then applied to decide where and when jobs should run. The following policies are available [LoadLeveler00]:

- Reservations
- Fairshare
- Backfill
- Job prioritization
- Throttling policies
- Quality of service
- Node allocation

5.3.1 Reservations

Advanced reservation is a method of allocation resources for a specific period according to a resource list, start time, and a life time. The reservation is run against an access list. The scheduler enforces the access list for the lifetime of the reservation. There are two types of reservations: administrative and standing.

Administrative reservations are useful for situations of unpredictable nature such as system maintenance, reboots, or exclusive access to a set of nodes. *Standing reservations* are methods for repetitively reserving resources for a constant period. For example: serving login sessions, Monday through Friday between 9:00 A.M. and 5:00 P.M. This approach provides flexibility, allowing a resource to be dedicated to potentially fast job turnaround but at the expense of utilization [LoadLeveler00].

5.3.2 Fairshare

Fairshare is a method of allocating equal priority to all the jobs in a specific queue. Maui attempts to achieve fairshare by adjusting, not enforcing, a job's priority based on the historical system usage of the job's user, group, account, or quality of service. An example of fairshare would be an environment that allocates a specific number of processor seconds for each user. In such an environment, Maui will attempt to adjust the job priority of every job in an attempt to match each user's requirements for processor time.

5.3.3 Backfill

Backfill is used to improve job throughput and system utilization by allowing the scheduler to run lower priority jobs with available resources as long as the highest priority queued job is not delayed in running. In backfill, each job should have a wall-clock time allowing the scheduler to perform a look ahead to find out when the job will complete at the latest.

Maui orders the queue by priority creating a reservation when the job starts until a job that cannot be started is found. Maui prevents backfilled jobs from delaying the highest priority jobs from running. It then attempts to run jobs that will fit in available resource gaps without delaying reserved priority jobs. Backfill algorithms include the following:

Firstfit: Each entry in the list of candidate jobs is considered for backfill starting with the highest priority idle job.

Bestfit: From the list of eligible jobs, those that would fit in the current backfill window are considered for dispatch. The job that has the best degree of fit is started and the backfill window size is adjusted accordingly. This process continues while there are backfill jobs and free resources are available.

5.4 SUN GRID ENGINE (SGE)—N1 GRID ENGINE 6

For the delight of the open source community, powerful scheduling software dubbed N1 Grid Engine 6 has been released by Sun Microsystems. N1 Grid Engine is resource management software that accepts jobs submitted by users. It uses resource management policies to schedule jobs to be run on appropriate systems in the cluster. Users can submit millions of jobs at a time without being concerned about where the jobs run. The grid engine software delivers computational power that is based on enterprise resource policies set by the organization's staff. The grid engine system uses these policies to examine the available computational resources. The system gathers these resources and then allocates and delivers resources automatically, optimizing usage across the grid [SGEUSer04].

5.4.1 Workload Management

Heterogeneous distributed computing environments require advanced resource management tools. Workload management requires resource management and policy administration. SGE achieves workload management by controlling shared resources to best achieve an enterprise's goals such as productivity, timeliness, level of service, and so forth. Organizations can maximize usage and throughput by controlling system timeliness (job deadlines) and importance (user share and job priority).

The grid engine system provides the following major capabilities [SGEUSer04]:

- Advanced policy administration for enhanced productivity, timeliness, and level of service.
- Dynamic scheduling and resource management to enforce site-specific management polices.
- Dynamic collection of performance data to provide the scheduler with up-to-the-minute job-level resource consumption and system load information.
- Enhanced security by way of Certificate Security Protocol (CSP)–based encryption. Messages are encrypted with a secret key.

5.4.2 Architecture

SGE is built on client-server architecture that matches *resources to requests*. Different requests with different needs require different types of service. Needs are immediately recognized and then matched to available resources. The basic entities handled by SGE are *jobs and queues.* Each job has a different set of requirements such as memory, processors, and storage. By using requirement profiles, SGE determines what jobs are suitable for any given queue. The system immediately dispatches the job that has either the highest priority or the longest waiting time. Queues allow concurrent execution of many jobs. The grid engine system tries to start new jobs in the least-loaded and most-suitable queue [SGEUSer04].

5.4.2.1 Usage Policies

Policy management controls the use of shared resources in the cluster to achieve the best administration goals. The grid engine software monitors all job progress and adjusts their priorities accordingly with respect to the policy goals. Four types of policies are available [SGEUSer04]:

Urgency: Job priority is based on *urgency values* derived from resource requirements, deadlines, and waiting times.

Functional: Jobs are priced with special treatment by affiliation to groups or projects.

Share-based: Level of service depends on share entitlement, resource usage and user presence.

Override: Policies are controlled by manual intervention of a cluster administrator.

5.4.2.2 Ticket-Based Policies

Tickets are used to control functional, share-based, and override policies. A ticket is analog to company stocks. The more stocks employee "A" has, the more important he becomes. The more tickets assigned to a particular job, the higher priority it has. Administrators control the number of tickets assigned to each policy type, allowing the system to run on different policy modes.

5.4.2.3 Daemons

As with most scheduling systems, the grid engine system is composed of three daemons. *The Master Daemon* maintains information about hosts, jobs, queues, system load, and user permissions. *The Scheduler Daemon* connects to the server for a view of the status of the cluster. Its main duty is to query jobs from queues and dispatch them based on priorities, deadlines, and resources. The *Execution Daemon* is responsible for running the jobs on the remote resources. It periodically sends information to the server such as job status and system load.

5.4.3 Step-by-Step SGE Installation Transcript

The following installation transcript was used to perform an automatic install of SGE in a single machine cluster running Red Hat Linux. For a complete set of installation instructions, consult the installation guide available from the grid engine Web site at *http://gridengine.sunsource.net/*.

The following transcripts use the following hardware and software:

Hardware: IBM ThinkPad T30

Software: Red-Hat Linux 8 workstation running on VMWare 4.5

Install Type: automated

Shell: Bash

For the SGE software download and documentation, see *http://gridengine.sunsource.net/*

As user root:

- Create a user to administer the cluster:
```
useradd sge
passwd sge
```
- Create the root install folder `SGE_ROOT`:
```
mkdir /opt/sge6
```
- Download and unzip binaries. We assume the binaries are located in `/tmp`:
```
cd /opt/sge6
tar zxvf /tmp/sge-6.0-common.tar.gz
tar zxvf /tmp/sge-6.0-bin-lx24-x86.tar.gz
```
- Adjust file ownership:
```
chown -R sge /opt/sge6
```

As user sge:

- Create an automated install configuration script:
```
su - sge
cp ./util/install_modules/inst_template.conf
./util/install_modules/myconfig.conf
```
- Edit the configuration script `myconfig.conf` and adjust parameters:
```
vi ./util/install_modules/myconfig.conf
# Adjust parameters
SGE_ROOT="/opt/sge6"
SGE_QMASTER_PORT="536"
SGE_EXECD_PORT="537"
QMASTER_SPOOL_DIR="/opt/sge6/default/spool/qmaster"
EXECD_SPOOL_DIR="/opt/sge6/default/spool"
GID_RANGE="20000-20100"
ADMIN_HOST_LIST="[YOUR_HOSTNAME]"
SUBMIT_HOST_LIST="[YOUR_HOSTNAME]"
EXEC_HOST_LIST="[YOUR_HOSTNAME]"
EXECD_SPOOL_DIR_LOCAL=""
```
- Perform the automated install:
```
export SGE_ROOT=/opt/sge6
```

```
cd $SGE_ROOT
./inst_sge -m -x -auto ./util/install_modules/myconfig.conf
```

5.4.4 Installation Troubleshooting Tips

If your automated installation fails, log files are created in two places: under the /tmp folder as install.n and under $SGE_ROOT/default/spool/qmaster/messages. Listing 5.3 shows a sample installation failure log.

LISTING 5.3 SAMPLE SGE INSTALL FAILURE LOG

```
Starting qmaster installation!
Reading configuration from file ./myconfig.conf
Your $SGE_ROOT directory: /opt/sge6
Using SGE_QMASTER_PORT >536<.
Using SGE_EXECD_PORT >537<.
Using >default< as CELL_NAME.
Using >/opt/sge6/default/spool/qmaster< as QMASTER_SPOOL_DIR.
Using >true< as IGNORE_FQDN_DEFAULT.
If it's >true<, the domain name will be ignored.

Making directories
Setting spooling method to dynamic
Dumping bootstrapping information
Initializing spooling database

Using >20000-20100< as gid range.
Using >/opt/sge6/default/spool< as EXECD_SPOOL_DIR.
Using >none< as ADMIN_MAIL.
Reading in complex attributes.
Adding default parallel environments (PE)
Reading in parallel environments:
    PE "make".
Reading in usersets:
    Userset "defaultdepartment".
    Userset "deadlineusers".

   starting sge_qmaster
sge_qmaster didn't start!
Please check the messages file
   starting sge_schedd
error: getting configuration: unable to contact qmaster
 using port 536 on host "vm-rhl8"
```

```
error: can't get configuration from qmaster -- backgrounding

Adding ADMIN_HOST localhost
ERROR: unable to contact qmaster using port 536 on host "vm-rhl8"
Adding SUBMIT_HOST localhost
ERROR: unable to contact qmaster using port 536 on host "vm-rhl8"

Creating the default <all.q> queue and <allhosts> hostgroup
unable to contact qmaster using port 536 on host "vm-rhl8"

Command failed: ./bin/lx24-x86/qconf -Ahgrp /tmp/hostqueue1562

Probably a permission problem. Please check file access permissions.
Check root read/write permission. Check if SGE daemons are running.

Failure log file: $SGE_ROOT/default/spool/qmaster/messages
08/23/2004 12:05:40|qmaster|vm-rhl8|E|database directory spooldb
 doesn't exist
08/23/2004 12:05:40|qmaster|vm-rhl8|E|startup of rule
 "default rule" in context "berkeleydb spooling" failed
08/23/2004 12:05:40|qmaster|vm-rhl8|C|setup failed
```

Messages in these two files give us a clue of the reason for this failure. The *spooling* method seems to be wrong! It seems that we have set up the spooling method incorrectly in the configuration file `myconfig.conf`. The option `SPOOLING_METHOD="classic"` should fix the problem.

If your automated installation fails, try an interactive install and follow the prompts.

Master host interactive install:

```
export SGE_ROOT=/opt/sge6
cd $SGE_ROOT
./inst_sge –m
```

Execution Host interactive install:

```
./inst_sge –x
```

The Administration Guide for the SGE [SGEUSer04] software has a complete set of instructions and messages for interactive install.

5.4.5 Installation Verification

1. Make sure the three SGE daemons are running:
```
# ps -ef | grep sge
sge  16818  1  0 13:36 ? 00:00:00 /opt/sge6//bin/lx24-x86/sge_qmaster
sge  16836  1  0 13:36 ? 00:00:00 /opt/sge6//bin/lx24-x86/sge_sched
sge  17085  1  0 13:37 ? 00:00:00 /opt/sge6//bin/lx24-x86/sge_execd
2)2.    Start or stop the service daemons:
service sgemaster [start/stop]
service sgeexecd [start/stop]
```

2. Run simple verification commands:
```
$> . $SGE_ROOT/default/common/settings.sh
$> qconf -sconf
Output:
global:
execd_spool_dir              /opt/sge6//default/spool
mailer                       /bin/mail
xterm                        /usr/bin/X11/xterm
load_sensor                  none
prolog                       none
epilog                       none
shell_start_mode             posix_compliant
login_shells                 sh,ksh,csh,tcsh
min_uid                      0
min_gid                      0
user_lists                   none
xuser_lists                  none
projects                     none
xprojects                    none
```

3. Run simple jobs as user *sge:*
```
. $SGE_ROOT/default/common/settings.sh
sge> qsub $SGE_HOME/examples/jobs/simple.sh
```

Standard Error/Output files for this script can be found at `$HOME/simple.sh.e1` and `$HOME/simple.sh.o1` respectively.

4. Monitor the queue using the `qstat` command client:
```
>qstat -f
queuename     qtype used/tot. load_avg arch          states
-----------------------------------------------------------
all.q@vm-rhl8   BIP   0/1       3.31     lx24-x86      a
```

```
#######################################################################
- PENDING JOBS - PENDING JOBS - PENDING JOBS - PENDING JOBS
#######################################################################
 3 0.56000 data       root   qw    08/30/2004 12:45:34 1 1-3:1
 4 0.56000 data       globus qw    08/30/2004 12:52:01     1 1-3:1
 5 0.56000 data       sge    qw    08/30/2004 12:56:03     1 1-3:1
 6 0.56000 simple.sh  sge    qw    08/30/2004 13:00:03     1
```

5.5 CONDOR-G

Condor® is a software package developed by the University of Wisconsin–Madison. The primary focus of Condor is high throughput computing (HTC). HTC is a computing environment that delivers large amounts of computational power over a long time. In contrast, high-performance computing (HPC) environments deliver a tremendous amount of compute power over a short period [Condor04]. HTC is ideal for large-scale research and engineering projects where the goal is to complete as many jobs as possible over a long time instead of how fast they can complete them.

In early days, the scientific community relied on centralized mainframes or supercomputers to efficiently harness the use of all available resources. Such computers were insanely expensive, and users had limited mainframe time allocated. Even though such environments were inconvenient, system utilization was very high!

The world has moved away from centralized mainframes because the same goals can be achieved with many smaller more affordable PCs. In this world of *distributed ownership,* computational power is raised for the companies as a whole, but system utilization is very low because machines are idle most of the time.

Condor is a software system that creates an HTC environment. Condor tries to harness all available resources under distributed ownership to achieve this goal. Condor is capable of detecting machine availability on the network. It can checkpoint jobs and migrate them to idle resources to maximize the number of machines that can run a job. This allows machines across the enterprise, even in different domains, to run jobs. It uses remote system call technology to send read/write operations over the network and requires no account login on remote machines. Condor provides powerful resource management by matching resource owners with resource consumers. Condor acts as a broker by matching resource offer ads with resource request ads, making certain requirements in both ads are satisfied [Condor04].

5.5.1 Condor Features

Condor has the following features not commonly found in open schedulers:

Checkpoint and Migration: Allows condor to migrate jobs from busy resources to idle ones, ensuring that your job will eventually always run.

Remote System Calls: Allows Condor to transfer data files and executables across machines. The program behaves as if it were running as the user that submitted the job on the workstation where it was originally submitted, no matter on which machine it really ends up executing on.

Pool Flocking: Allows jobs executed in one pool to execute in other. Each pool can set policies over the conditions under which jobs are executed.

Owner sensitivity: Gives the owner of a machine complete priority over the use of the machine. Control is returned to the machine owner automatically.

Job ordering: Uses acyclic graphs where each job is a node in the graph.

ClassAds: Provide a flexible, expressive framework for matching resource requests with resource offers. Users can easily request both job requirements and job desires. Job requirements and preferences and resource availability constraints can be described by powerful expressions, resulting in Condor's adaptation to nearly any desired policy [Condor04].

5.5.2 Condor-MMJFS Installation Transcript

The following section contains a complete transcript of a Condor 6.6 installation and GT 3.2 MMJFS integration. Install was performed on a Red Hat Linux 8.0 system running on a VMWare workstation 4.x.

5.5.2.1 Condor Software Installation

To be performed as user *root*:

```
[tmp]# tar zxvf condor-6.6.6-linux-x86-redhat80.tar.gz
[tmp/condor-6.6] ./condor_configure
 --install
 --install-dir=/opt/condor-6.6.6/
 --type=submit,execute,manager
 --central-manager=`hostname`
 --owner=condor
```

Condor has been installed into

```
    /opt/condor-6.6.6
In order for Condor to work properly you must set your
CONDOR_CONFIG environment variable to point to your
Condor configuration file:
    /opt/condor-6.6.6/etc/condor_config
```

```
before running Condor commands/daemons.
```

5.5.2.2 Setup a Startup Condor Service

```
cp  /opt/condor-6.6.6/etc/examples/condor.boot /etc/init.d/condor
ln -s /etc/init.d/init.d/condor /etc/rc5.d/S86condor

[root@vm-rhl8 condor-6.6.6]# chkconfig --list | grep condor
condor          0:off   1:off   2:off   3:off   4:off   5:on    6:off

[root@vm-rhl8 root]# service condor start
```

Starting Condor:

```
[root@vm-rhl8 root]# ps -ef | grep condor_
condor    3222     1  0 13:14 ?        00:00:00 /opt/condor-
6.6.6/sbin/condor_ma
condor    3223  3222  9 13:14 ?        00:00:07 condor_startd -f
condor    3224  3222  0 13:14 ?        00:00:00 condor_schedd –f
```

5.5.2.3 Condor Install Verification

Listing jobs in a queue:

```
[condor@vm-rhl8 examples]$ condor_q

-- Submitter: vm-rhl8.ibm.com : <192.168.74.128:32788> : vm-
rhl8.ibm.com
 ID      OWNER            SUBMITTED     RUN_TIME ST PRI SIZE CMD
   1.0   condor          9/1  13:33   0+00:00:00 I  0   0.0  date

1 jobs; 1 idle, 0 running, 0 held
```

Checking the pool status:

```
[condor@vm-rhl8 condor-6.6.6]$ condor_status

Name          OpSys  Arch   State  Activity  LoadAv Mem   ActvtyTime

vm-rhl8.ibm.c LINUX  INTEL  Owner  Idle      1.040   249  0+00:00:20

         Machines Owner Claimed Unclaimed Matched Preempting

INTEL/LINUX  1      1       0         0       0          0

Total        1      1       0         0       0          0
```

5.5.2.4 Install the Condor MMJFS Scheduler

```
[globus@vm-rhl8 root]# cd /tmp/gt3.2.1-all-linux-glibc2.2-installer/
schedulers/
```

```
[globus@vm-rhl8 schedulers]$ /opt/gt32/sbin/gpt-build ./scheduler-condor-3.2-src_bundle.tar.gz gcc32dbg
```

The output should look like the following:

```
gpt-build ====> CHECKING BUILD DEPENDENCIES FOR globus_core
...

[globus@vm-rhl8 schedulers]$ /opt/gt32/sbin/gpt-postinstall
running /opt/gt32/setup/globus/setup-globus-gaa-authz-callout-message

**********************************************************************

Note: If you wish to complete the setup of the Globus
 GAA Authorization
Callout, you will need to run the following script as root:

/opt/gt32/setup/globus/setup-globus-gaa-authz-callout

This script will create the
 /etc/grid-security/gsi-authz.conf file if it does
not already exist and register the callout.
For further information on using the
 setup-globus-gaa_authz-callout script,
use the -help option.
The -nonroot can be used on systems where root access
 is not available.
...
running /opt/gt32/setup/globus/setup-condor-provider...
loading cache ./config.cache
checking for condor_q... /opt/condor-6.6.6/bin/condor_q
checking for condor_status... /opt/condor-6.6.6/bin/condor_status
updating cache ./config.cache
creating ./config.status
creating /opt/gt32/etc/globus-gram-condor-provider
running /opt/gt32/setup/globus/setup-mjs-condor...
Determining system information...

...

BUILD SUCCESSFUL
Total time: 32 seconds
```

5.5.2.5 Submit a Condor MMJFS Test Job

Make sure your GT 3.2 container is running and your system is properly configured. The output should look like the following:

```
[globus@vm-rhl8 gt32]$ bin/managed-job-globusrun -factory
http://192.168.74.128:8080/ogsa/services/base/gram/
CondorIntelLinuxManagedJobFactoryService -file schema/base/gram/exam-
ples/scheduler_gram_rsl_example_1.xml
WAITING FOR JOB TO FINISH
========== Status Notification ==========
Job Status: Pending
=========================================
========== Status Notification ==========
Job Status: Done
=========================================
DESTROYING SERVICE
SERVICE DESTROYED
```

At the same time the condor queue can be monitored with the following command:

```
[condor@vm-rhl8 condor]$ condor_q

-- Submitter: vm-rhl8.ibm.com : <192.168.74.128:33744> : vm-rhl8
 ID      OWNER     SUBMITTED      RUN_TIME ST PRI SIZE CMD
1.0   condor      9/1  13:33   0+00:00:00 I  0   0.0  date
2.0   condor      9/1  14:47   0+00:00:00 I  0   0.0  date
3.0   globus      9/1  19:00   0+00:00:00 I  0   0.0  echo 12 abc
3.1   globus      9/1  19:00   0+00:00:00 I  0   0.0  echo 12 abc
3.2   globus      9/1  19:00   0+00:00:00 I  0   0.0  echo 12 abc 34

8 jobs; 8 idle, 0 running, 0 held
```

5.6 MMJFS INTEGRATION WITH OTHER JOB SCHEDULERS

The Globus Project provides Grid Packaging Tool (GPT) bundles for several open source schedulers including PBS, LSF, and Condor. If you use a custom scheduler, for example SGE or LoadLeveler, you must write you own packaging bundle. That can be a very time-consuming process. This section explores some simple changes that will allow you to integrate your custom scheduler with MMJFS. For this exercise, a scheduler interface for SGE is implemented in the following sections. The code in this section is based on the SGE integration with Globus by the London e-Science Centre [SGEGlobus03].

5.6.1 Step 1: Create a Job Manager Script

The first step in the integration of MMJFS with SGE is to create a job manager PERL script that will be used by MMJFS to interface with the master daemon. The file should be called `lib/perl/Globus/GRAM/JobManager/`[SCHEDULER_NAME].pm. In this case, the file name will be `lib/perl/Globus/GRAM/JobManager/sge.pm`

This script must implement a set of standard methods used to interface with the SGE daemon. Among the most important are the following [WSGRAMScheduler04]:

Submit: This method takes care of dispatching the job to the server daemon. It should call the corresponding command line client, for example, qsub in PBS or SGE.

Poll: This method is used to poll for the status of the running job from the server. We may call a command such as `qstat`.

Cancel: This method allows MMJFS to cancel a submitted job.

The following listings present a basic scheduler interface for SGE that can be used as a template for integration with other popular schedulers. A complete SGE scheduler interface package for GT3 has been developed by the London e-Science Centre (*http://www.lesc.ic.ac.uk/projects/epic-gt3-sge.html*).

5.6.1.1 Initialization

Every scheduler script should have an initialization section where the paths to the client programs and global variables are defined. For example, the initialization subroutine for SGE may look like that shown in Listing 5.4.

LISTING 5.4 Sample SGE Scheduler Interface Initialization Segment

```
# SGE Initialization  parameters.
# This code is based on the SGE scheduler Interface
# by the London e-Science Centre
#
BEGIN
{
 # paths to the programs which interact with the scheduler
 $qsub        = '/opt/sge6/bin/lx24-x86/sge-qsub';
 $qstat       = '/opt/sge6/bin/lx24-x86/sge-qstat';
 $qdel        = '/opt/sge6/bin/lx24-x86/sge-qdel';
 $qselect     = '/opt/sge6/bin/lx24-x86/qselect';
```

```
    $qhost       = '/opt/sge6/bin/lx24-x86/qhost';
    $qconf       = '/opt/sge6/bin/lx24-x86/qconf';
    $qacct       = '/opt/sge6/bin/lx24-x86/qacct';

    # MPI arguments
    $mpirun      = 'no';
    $sun_mprun   = 'no';
    $mpi_pe      = 'no';

    $cat         = '/bin/cat';

    # SGE Environment
    $SGE_ROOT    = '/opt/sge6';
    $SGE_CELL    = 'default';
    $SGE_MODE    = 'SGE';
    $SGE_RELEASE = 'N1GE 6.0';
}
```

If you are planning to package your scheduler interface for distribution, you must write a set of GPT configuration scripts, and the previous section should be written as follows:

```
$qsub        = '@QSUB@';
$qstat       = '@QSTAT@';
$qdel        = '@QDEL@';
$qselect     = '@QSELECT@';
$qhost       = '@QHOST@';
$qconf       = '@QCONF@';
$qacct       = '@QACCT@';
```

For details on packaging the scheduler interface, see the section on *packaging advice*.

5.6.1.2 Overloading the Submit Method

The submit method (see Listing 5.5) is the longest and toughest to write. All scheduler modules must implement this method. This method gets called on job submission. The information in the original job request RSL string is available to the scheduler interface through the job description data member of its hash [WS-GRAMScheduler04].

LISTING 5.5 Sample Job Description Input Hash to the Submit Method

```
$description =
{
 'directory' => [ '/home/globus'] ,
 'stdin' => [ '/dev/null'] ,
 'count' => [ '1'] ,
 'jobtype' => [ 'multiple'] ,
 'grammyjob' => [ 'collective'] ,
 'environment' => [ [ 'X509_USER_PROXY'
 , '/home/globus/.globus/job/vm-rhl8-1/1775.1099013881/x509_up']
 , [ 'GLOBUS_LOCATION', '/opt/gt32']
 , [ 'GLOBUS_GRAM_JOB_CONTACT'
   , 'https://vm-rhl8-1.ibm.com:32911/1775/1099013881/']
   , [ 'GLOBUS_GRAM_MYJOB_CONTACT'
       , 'URLx-nexus://vm-rhl8-1.ibm.com:32912/']
   , [ 'HOME', '/home/globus'] , [ 'LOGNAME', 'globus']
    ] ,
 'dryrun' => [ 'no'] ,
 'executable' => [ '/bin/date'] ,
 'stdout' => [ '/dev/null' ],
 'stderr' => [ '/dev/null' ],
 'logfile' => [ '/dev/null' ],
 'uniqid' => [ '1775.1099013881' ],
 'cachetag' => [ 'https://vm-rhl8-1.:32911/1775/1099013881/' ],
 'jobdir' => [ '/home/globus/.globus/job/vm-rhl8-1/1775.1099013881' ],
filestagein => [ ],
filestageinshared => [ ],
filestageout => [ ]
};
```

The script in Listing 5.5 submits a `/bin/date` command to the backend scheduler in host `vm-rhl8-1.ibm.com` for user *globus* whose home directory resides in `/home/globus`. This script will be passed to the method shown in Listing 5.6, which will parse it and call the appropriate scheduler command (qsub for SGE).

LISTING 5.6 A Submit Method for the SGE Scheduler

```
#
# Submit method
# All scheduler modules must implement the submit method.
# This method is called when the job manager wishes to submit
# the job to the scheduler.
# The information in the original job request RSL string
# is available to the scheduler interface through the
# JobDescription data member of it's hash.
```

```
#
sub submit
{
    my $self = shift;
    my $description = $self->{JobDescription};
    my $tag = $description->cache_tag()
      or $ENV{GLOBUS_GRAM_JOB_CONTACT};
    my $status;
    my $sge_job_script;
    my $sge_job_script_name;
    my $errfile = "";
    my $queue;
    my $job_id;
    my $rsh_env;
    my $script_url;
    my @arguments;
    my $email_when = "";
    my $cache_pgm = "$Globus::Core::Paths::bindir/globus-gass-cache";
    my %library_vars;

    $self->log("Entering SGE submit");

    #
    # The first step is to check for a valid job type
    #
    if(defined($description->jobtype()))
    {
        if($description->jobtype !~ /^(mpi|single|multiple)$/)
        {
            return Globus::GRAM::Error::JOBTYPE_NOT_SUPPORTED;
        }
      elsif($description->jobtype() eq 'mpi' && $mpirun eq "no" )
    {
          return Globus::GRAM::Error::JOBTYPE_NOT_SUPPORTED;
    }
    }

    #
    # check directory
    #
    if( $description->directory eq "")
    {
    return Globus::GRAM::Error::RSL_DIRECTORY();
    }
```

```
chdir $description->directory() or
return Globus::GRAM::Error::BAD_DIRECTORY();

#
# check that executable exists and can be run
#
if( $description->executable eq "")
{
return Globus::GRAM::Error::RSL_EXECUTABLE();
}
elsif(! -f $description->executable())
{
return Globus::GRAM::Error::EXECUTABLE_NOT_FOUND();
}
elsif(! -x $description->executable())
{
return Globus::GRAM::Error::EXECUTABLE_PERMISSIONS();
}
elsif( $description->stdin() eq "")
{
return Globus::GRAM::Error::RSL_STDIN;
}
elsif(! -r $description->stdin())
{
return Globus::GRAM::Error::STDIN_NOT_FOUND();
}

#
# Times are given in minutes.
# They must be converted to (h:m:s)
#
$self->log("Job WALL time");
if(defined($description->max_wall_time()))
{
$wall_time = $description->max_wall_time();
    $self->log("  of $wall_time minutes");
}
elsif(defined($description->max_time()))
{
    $wall_time = $description->max_time();
    $self->log("  max_wall_time of $wall_time minutes");
}
else
{
```

```
$wall_time = 0;
    $self->log("  using default");
}

#
# max_cpu_time
#
$self->log("Job CPU time");

if(defined($description->max_cpu_time()))
{
    $cpu_time = $description->max_cpu_time();
    $self->log("  max_cpu_time of $cpu_time minutes");
}
elsif(defined($description->max_time()))
{
    $cpu_time = $description->max_time();
    $self->log("  max_cpu_time of $cpu_time minutes");
}
else
{
    $cpu_time = 0;
    $self->log("  using default");
}

#
# start building job script
# open the script file
#
$script_url = "$tag/sge_job_script.$$";
system("$cache_pgm -add -t $tag -n $script_url file:/dev/null");

$sge_job_script_name = `$cache_pgm -query -t $tag $script_url`;
chomp($sge_job_script_name);

if($sge_job_script_name eq "")
{
return Globus::GRAM::Error::TEMP_SCRIPT_FILE_FAILED();
}

$sge_job_script = new IO::File($sge_job_script_name, '>');

$self->log("JOB SCRIPT: $sge_job_script_name");

#
```

```
    # Script header
    #
    $sge_job_script->print("#!/bin/sh\n");
    $sge_job_script->print("# SGE job script built by ");
    $sge_job_script->print("Globus job manager\n");
    $sge_job_script->print("\n");
    $sge_job_script->print("#\$ -S /bin/sh\n");

    #
    # To Whom to send email
    #
    if($description->email_address() ne '')
    {
        $sge_job_script->print("#\$ -M "
          . $description->email_address() ."\n");
    }

    #
    # Queue used to execute this job
    #
    if(defined($description->queue()))
    {
        $sge_job_script->print("#\$ -q " . $description->queue() .
"\n");
        $self->log("QUEUE: " . $description->queue);
    }

    #
    # wall_time in minutes. Must be converted ti time format (h:m:s)
    #
    if($wall_time != 0)
    {
        $wall_m = $wall_time % 60;
        $wall_h = ( $wall_time - $wall_m ) / 60;

        $self->log("Using max WALL time (h:m:s)
          of $wall_h:$wall_m:00");
        $sge_job_script->print("#\$ -l h_rt=$wall_h:$wall_m:00\n");
    }

    #
    # Convert cpu_time to (h:m:s)
    #
    if($cpu_time != 0)
```

```
{
    $cpu_m = $cpu_time % 60;
    $cpu_h = ( $cpu_time - $cpu_m ) / 60;

    $self->log("Using max CPU time (h:m:s) of $cpu_h:$cpu_m:00");
    $sge_job_script->print("#\$ -l h_cpu=$cpu_h:$cpu_m:00\n");
}

#####
# RSL attribute for max_memory is given in Mb
#
$max_memory = $description->max_memory();
if($max_memory != 0)
{
    $self->log("Total max memory flag is set to $max_memory Mb");
    $sge_job_script->print("#\$ -l h_data=$max_memory" . "M\n");
}

#
# Standard output error
#
if(($description->jobtype() eq "single")
  && ($description->count() > 1))
{
  #
  # use job arrays for a single job
  #
  $sge_job_script->print("#\$ -o "
          . $description->stdout() . ".\$TASK_ID\n");
  $sge_job_script->print("#\$ -e "
          . $description->stderr() . ".\$TASK_ID\n");
}
else
{
  $sge_job_script->print("#\$ -o "
      . $description->stdout() . ".real\n");
  $sge_job_script->print("#\$ -e "
      . $description->stderr() . ".real\n");
}

#
# Load SGE settings
#
$sge_job_script->
```

```
     print(". $SGE_ROOT/$SGE_CELL/common/settings.sh\n");

    #
    # Change to directory requested by user
    #
    $sge_job_script->print("# Change to directory requested by
user\n");
    $sge_job_script->print('cd ' . $description->directory() . "\n");

    #
    # Job arguments
    # Quote and escape the strings in the argument list so that the
    # values of the arguments will be identical to those in the
    # initial job request
    # double-quote each argument, and escaping the backslash (\),
    # dollar-sign ($), double-quote ("), and single-quote (')
    # characters.
    #
    @arguments = $description->arguments();

    foreach(@arguments)
    {
        if(ref($_))
    {
            return Globus::GRAM::Error::RSL_ARGUMENTS;
    }
    }
    if($arguments[0])
    {
        foreach(@arguments)
        {
            $self->log("Transforming argument \"$_\"");
            $_ =~ s/\\/\\\\/g;
            $_ =~ s/\$/\\\$/g;
            $_ =~ s/"/\\\"/g;
            $_ =~ s/`/\\\`/g;
            $self->log("Transformed to \"$_\"");

            $args .= '"' . $_ . '" ';
        }
    }
    else
    {
        $args = '';
```

```
}

#
# JOB TYPE
# Depending on the job type of this submission, start either
# one or
# more instances of the executable, or the mpirun program which
# will start the job with the executable count
#
$self->log("JOB TYPE " . $description->jobtype());
if($description->jobtype() eq "mpi")
{
    #
    # Use mpirun
    #
$sge_job_script->print("$mpirun -np ". $description->count() . " "
                      . $description->executable() . " $args < "
                      . $description->stdin() . "\n");
}
elsif($description->jobtype() eq "multiple")
{
    #
    # Multiple job: Fork multiple requests
    #
    for(my $i = 0; $i < $description->count(); $i++)
    {
        $sge_job_script->
          print($description->executable() . " $args < "
                . $description->stdin() . "&\n");
    }
    $sge_job_script->print("wait\n");
}
else
{
    #
    # Single execution job
    #
    $sge_job_script->print($description->executable()
        . " $args < " . $description->stdin() . "\n");
}

#
# submit the job to the scheduler.
# Be sure to close the script file before trying to redirect
```

```
#
$sge_job_script->close();

if($description->logfile() ne "")
{
    $errfile = "2>>" . $description->logfile();
}

#
# Submit...
#
$self->log("Submitting...");

$ENV{"SGE_ROOT"} = $SGE_ROOT;

chomp($job_id = `$qsub $sge_job_script_name`);

if($? == 0)
{
    # Success, get job ID
    $job_id = (split(/\s+/, $job_id))[2];

return {JOB_ID => $job_id ,
        JOB_STATE => Globus::GRAM::JobState::PENDING };
}

# Comment this to prevent job script cleanup
system("$cache_pgm -cleanup-url $tag/sge_job_script.$$");

return Globus::GRAM::Error::INVALID_SCRIPT_REPLY;
}
```

5.6.1.3 Polling for Job Status

The purpose of this method (see Listing 5.7) is to check for updates of a job's status. This method receives as input a job ID returned from the submit method. It then uses the scheduler client (`qstat` for SGE) to query for the job status and reports back to the caller [WSGRAMScheduler04].

LISTING 5.7 Poll Method for the SGE Scheduler

```
# A poll method for the SGE scheduler
# It queries the job status by using the qstat command
#
```

```
sub poll
{
    my $self = shift;
    my $description = $self->{JobDescription};
    my $job_id = $description->job_id();
    my $state;
    my $status_line;
    my $job_out = $description->stdout();
    my $job_err = $description->stderr();

    # Separate  the job_out path from the job_id() string.
    # A workaround for the fact that job_out() and _err()
    # is missing
    $job_id =~ /(.*)\|(.*)\|(.*)/;
    $job_id = $1;
    $job_out = $2;
    $job_err = $3;

    $self->log("polling job $job_id");

    #
    # The env var SGE_ROOT is required by qstat
    $ENV{"SGE_ROOT"} = $SGE_ROOT;

    # Query job_id by number.
    my (@output) = `$qstat -j $job_id 2>&1`;

    # Obtain first line of output (STDOUT or STDERR)
    my ($notexist) = $output[0];

    #
    # Parse the Job status from the qstat command
    #
    if ($notexist =~ /do not exist/)
    {
      # Job no longer exists in SGE job manager.
      # It must have finished.
      $self->log("Job $job_id has completed.");
      $state = Globus::GRAM::JobState::DONE;

      $self->log("Writing job STDOUT and STDERR to cache files.");

      if(($description->jobtype() eq "single")
        && ($description->count() > 1))
```

```
        #
        # Jobtype is single and count>1. Therefore, we used job arrays
        # Merge individual output/error files into one.
        #
        {
          system ("$cat $job_out.* >> $job_out");
          system ("$cat $job_err.* >> $job_err");
        }
        else
        {
      #
      # Append the job output to the GASS cache file manually
      system("$cat $job_out.real >> $job_out");
        }

      }
      else
      {
      # Job has not completed yet.
      # Determine it's current state from the qstat output

      $_ = pop @output;
      # Obtain scheduler details from output, if any.

      # Look at the qstat output and return a job state
      if (/"error"/) {
        $state = Globus::GRAM::JobState::FAILED;
      }
      elsif(/queue|pending/) {
        $state = Globus::GRAM::JobState::PENDING;
      }
      elsif(/hold|suspend/) {
        $state = Globus::GRAM::JobState::SUSPENDED;
      }
      else {
        $state = Globus::GRAM::JobState::ACTIVE;
      }
      }

      return {JOB_STATE => $state};
}
```

5.6.1.4 Canceling a Job

As with the poll method, this method will be given a job ID. If the job was cancelled successfully, then its state can be changed to FAILED. Otherwise, return an empty hash reference, and let the poll method return the state change the next time it is called (see Listing 5.8).

LISTING 5.8 Cancel Method for SGE

```
sub cancel
{
    my $self = shift;
    my $description = $self->{JobDescription};
    my $job_id = $description->jobid();

    $self->log("cancel job $job_id");

    system("$qdel $job_id >/dev/null 2>/dev/null");

    if($? == 0)
    {
      return { JOB_STATE => Globus::GRAM::JobState::FAILED }
    }

    return Globus::GRAM::Error::JOB_CANCEL_FAILED();
}
```

5.6.2 Step 2: Update the GT 3.2 Deployment Descriptors

Two deployment descriptors must be updated with the SGE/MMJFS service factory description XML:

$GLOBUS_LOCATION/server-config.wsdd: This is the container (MHE) deployment descriptor.

$GLOBUS_LOCATION/local-server-config.wsdd: UHE deployment descriptor.

The service XML shown in Listing 5.9 must be included.

LISTING 5.9 OGSA Deployment Descriptor for SGE

```
<service
  name="base/gram/MasterSGEManagedJobFactoryService"
  provider="Handler"
  style="wrapped"
```

```
use="literal">
<parameter
  name="relabelOriginators"
  value="true" />
<parameter
  name="installPath"
  value="/opt/gt32" />
<parameter
  name="operationProviders"
  value="org.globus.ogsa.impl.ogsi.FactoryProvider
   org.globus.ogsa.impl.security.authentication
   .SecureNotificationSourceProvider" />
<parameter
  name="persistent"
  value="true" />
<parameter
  name="instance-schemaPath"
  value="schema/base/gram/managed_job_service.wsdl" />
<parameter
  name="activateOnStartup"
  value="true" />
<parameter
  name="baseClassName"
  value="org.globus.ogsa.impl.base
   .gram.mmjfs.MasterManagedJobFactoryService" />
<parameter
  name="sweeperFrequency"
  value="1000" />
<parameter
  name="schemaPath"
  value="schema/base/gram/mmjfs_service.wsdl" />
<parameter
  name="handlerClass"
  value="org.globus.ogsa.router.RedirectProvider" />
<parameter
  name="targetFactoryService"
  value="/ogsa/services/base/gram/SGEManagedJobFactoryService" />
<parameter
  name="className"
  value="org.globus.ogsa.base.gram.mmjfs
   .MasterManagedJobFactoryService" />
<parameter
  name="starterClass"
  value="org.globus.ogsa.impl.base
```

```
        .gram.mmjfs.proxyStarter.HostingEnvironmentStarter" />
    <parameter
      name="allowedMethods"
      value="*" />
    <parameter
      name="gridmap"
      value="/etc/grid-security/grid-mapfile" />
    <parameter
      name="factoryCallback"
      value="org.globus.ogsa.impl.base
       .gram.mmjfs.MasterManagedJobFactory" />
  </service>

  <service
    name="base/gram/SGEManagedJobFactoryService"
    provider="Handler"
    style="wrapped"
    use="literal">
    <parameter
      name="condorOs"
      value="" />
    <parameter
      name="instance-schemaPath"
      value="schema/base/gram/managed_job_service.wsdl" />
    <parameter
      name="condorArch"
      value="" />
    <parameter
      name="className"
      value="org.gridforum.ogsi.NotificationFactory" />
    <parameter
      name="operationProviders"
      value="org.globus.ogsa.impl.ogsi.FactoryProvider
       org.globus.ogsa.impl.security
        .authentication.SecureNotificationSourceProvider" />
    <parameter
      name="baseClassName"
      value="org.globus.ogsa.impl.ogsi.GridServiceImpl" />
    <parameter
      name="hostOsVersion"
      value="2.4.18-14" />
    <parameter
      name="hostCpuType"
      value="i686" />
```

```
<parameter
  name="instance-baseClassName"
  value="org.globus.ogsa.impl.base.gram
    .jobmanager.ManagedJobImpl" />
<parameter
  name="hostManufacturer"
  value="pc" />
<parameter
  name="sweeperFrequency"
  value="120" />
<parameter
  name="x509CertDir"
  value="/etc/grid-security/certificates" />
<parameter
  name="allowedMethods"
  value="*" />
<parameter
  name="instance-operationProviders"
  value="org.globus.ogsa.impl
    .security.authentication.SecureNotificationSourceProvider" />
<parameter
  name="instance-lifecycle"
  value="persistent" />
<parameter
  name="globusLocation"
  value="/opt/gt32" />
<parameter
  name="hostOsName"
  value="Linux" />
<parameter
  name="schemaPath"
  value="schema/ogsi/ogsi_notification_factory_service.wsdl" />
<parameter
  name="securityConfig"
  value="org/globus/ogsa/impl/base
  /gram/jobmanager/factory-security-config.xml" />
<parameter
  name="lifecycleMonitorClass"
  value="org.globus.ogsa.repository.DefaultServiceDeactivator" />
<parameter
  name="instance-deactivation"
  value="120000" />
<parameter
  name="instance-name"
```

```
    value="SGE ManagedJob" />
  <parameter
    name="persistent"
    value="true" />
  <parameter
    name="instance-className"
    value="org.globus.ogsa.base.gram.ManagedJobPortType" />
  <parameter
    name="managerType"
    value="sge" />
  <parameter
    name="handlerClass"
    value="org.globus.ogsa.handlers.RPCURIProvider" />
  <parameter
    name="factoryCallback"
    value="org.globus.ogsa.impl.base
      .gram.jobmanager.ManagedJobFactoryImpl" />
  <parameter
    name="jobMonitorType"
    value="scheduler" />
  <parameter
    name="instance-activateOnStartup"
    value="true" />
  <parameter
    name="instance-securityConfig"
    value="org/globus/ogsa/impl/base
      /gram/jobmanager/security-config.xml" />
  <parameter
    name="name"
    value="SGE ManagedJob Factory Service" />
</service>
```

5.6.3 Step 3: Verification

The final step is to start the GT 3.2 container, make sure the configuration is correct, and submit a sample job.

5.6.3.1 Start the GT 3.2 Container and Monitor the Standard Output:

```
bin/globus-start-container
...
http://192.168.74.128:8080/ogsa
 /services/base/gram/PbsManagedJobFactoryService
http://192.168.74.128:8080/ogsa
 /services/base/gram/ForkManagedJobFactoryService
```

```
http://192.168.74.128:8080/ogsa
 /services/base/gram/SGEManagedJobFactoryService
http://192.168.74.128:8080/ogsa
 /services/base/gram/MasterPbsManagedJobFactoryService
http://192.168.74.128:8080/ogsa
 /services/base/gram/MasterForkManagedJobFactoryService
http://192.168.74.128:8080/ogsa
 /services/base/gram/MasterSGEManagedJobFactoryService
```

Two services must show up in the standard output: `MasterSGEManagedJobFactoryService` and `SGEManagedJobFactoryService`. These are the managed job services for SGE. If they don't, stop and backtrack. You have done something wrong!

5.6.3.2 Check the User Hosting Environment (UHE) Propagation

Check the UHE deployment descriptor: `$HOME/.globus/uhe-[hostname]/server-config.wsdd`. Make sure an entry for `SGEManagedJobFactoryService` exists.

If the entry doesn't exist, refresh the UHE by removing its directory: `$HOME/.globus/uhe-`hostname``

5.6.3.3 Adjust Parameters in the Sample RSL Submission Script

The Globus Toolkit 3.2 provides a generic scheduler script that can be used to submit a sample job. *Note:* This script is not available on GT 3.0. Adjust the script parameters to match your system. Among the most common parameters are the following:

```
<gram:executable>
    <rsl:path>
        <rsl:stringElement value="/bin/echo"/>
    </rsl:path>
</gram:executable>
<gram:project>
    <rsl:string>
        <rsl:stringElement value="cgt::ws:demo_sc02"/>
    </rsl:string>
</gram:project>
<gram:queue>
    <rsl:string>
        <rsl:stringElement value="all.q"/>
    </rsl:string>
</gram:queue>
```

If you have GT 3.0, use the following generic MMJFS-scheduler script to run a sample job. The script in Listing 5.10 should work for any type of scheduler: PBS, SGE, Condor, LoadLeveler, and so on.

LISTING 5.10 MMJFS/SGE Sample RSL Script for Job Execution

```
<?xml version="1.0" encoding="UTF-8"?>
<rsl:rsl
  xmlns:rsl="http://www.globus.org/namespaces/2004/02/rsl"
  xmlns:enum="http://www.globus.org/namespaces/2004/02/rsl/enum"
  xmlns:gram="http://www.globus.org/namespaces/2004/02/rsl/gram"
  xmlns:xsi="http://www.w3.org/2001/XMLSchema-instance"
  xsi:schemaLocation="
  http://www.globus.org/namespaces/2004/02/rsl
  ./schema/base/gram/rsl.xsd
  http://www.globus.org/namespaces/2004/02/rsl/gram/scheduler
  ./schema/base/gram/scheduler_gram_rsl.xsd">
  <scheduler:job>

    <!-- Executable/Directory -->
    <gram:executable>
      <rsl:path>
        <rsl:stringElement value="/bin/echo" />
      </rsl:path>
    </gram:executable>
    <gram:directory>
      <rsl:path>
        <rsl:stringElement value="/tmp" />
      </rsl:path>
    </gram:directory>

    <!-- Job Arguments and Environment -->
    <gram:arguments>
      <rsl:stringArray>
        <rsl:string>
          <rsl:stringElement value="Hello World" />
        </rsl:string>
      </rsl:stringArray>
    </gram:arguments>
    <gram:environment>
      <rsl:hashtable>
        <rsl:entry name="GLOBUS_DUROC_SUBJOB_INDEX">
          <rsl:stringElement value="0" />
```

```
      </rsl:entry>
    </rsl:hashtable>
  </gram:environment>

  <!-- Standard Input/Error -->
  <gram:stdin>
    <rsl:path>
      <rsl:stringElement value="/dev/null" />
    </rsl:path>
  </gram:stdin>
  <gram:stdout>
    <rsl:pathArray>
      <rsl:path>
        <rsl:stringElement value="./out" />
      </rsl:path>
    </rsl:pathArray>
  </gram:stdout>
  <gram:stderr>
    <rsl:pathArray>
      <rsl:path>
        <rsl:stringElement value="./err" />
      </rsl:path>
    </rsl:pathArray>
  </gram:stderr>

  <!-- Cluster parameters -->
  <gram:count>
    <rsl:integer value="3" />
  </gram:count>
  <gram:hostCount>
    <rsl:integer value="3" />
  </gram:hostCount>

  <!-- Backend Execution Queue -->
  <gram:queue>
    <rsl:string>
      <rsl:stringElement value="all.q" />
    </rsl:string>
  </gram:queue>

  <!-- Job Wall clock and CPU time limits -->
  <gram:maxTime>
    <rsl:long value="60" />
  </gram:maxTime>
```

```
<gram:maxWallTime>
  <rsl:long value="60" />
</gram:maxWallTime>
<gram:maxCpuTime>
  <rsl:long value="60" />
</gram:maxCpuTime>

<!-- Memory limits -->
<gram:maxMemory>
  <rsl:integer value="2048" />
</gram:maxMemory>
<gram:minMemory>
  <rsl:integer value="1024" />
</gram:minMemory>

<!-- Miscellaneous arguments: Job type (single) -->
<!-- email address notifications, etc. -->
<gram:jobType>
  <enum:enumeration>
    <enum:enumerationValue>
      <enum:single />
    </enum:enumerationValue>
  </enum:enumeration>
</gram:jobType>
<gram:gramMyJobType>
  <enum:enumeration>
    <enum:enumerationValue>
      <enum:collective />
    </enum:enumerationValue>
  </enum:enumeration>
</gram:gramMyJobType>
<gram:dryRun>
  <rsl:boolean value="false" />
</gram:dryRun>
<scheduler:emailAddress>
  <rsl:string>
    <rsl:stringElement value="myaccount@somesystem.domain.com" />
  </rsl:string>
</scheduler:emailAddress>
<scheduler:emailOnAbort>
  <rsl:boolean value="true" />
</scheduler:emailOnAbort>
<scheduler:emailOnExecution>
  <rsl:boolean value="false" />
```

```
      </scheduler:emailOnExecution>
      <scheduler:emailOnTermination>
        <rsl:boolean value="true" />
      </scheduler:emailOnTermination>
    </scheduler:job>
  </rsl:rsl>
```

5.6.3.4 Run a Quick MMJFS/Scheduler Job

Finally, the moment of truth has come. Run the following command to test your configuration. In GT 3.2:

```
bin/managed-job-globusrun -factory
http://`hostname`:8080/ogsa/services/base/gram/
MasterSGEManagedJobFactoryService
-file schema/base/gram/examples/
scheduler_gram_rsl_example_1.xml -o
```

The output should look like:

```
12 abc 34 pdscaex_instr_GrADS_grads23_28919.cfg
```

5.6.4 Integration Troubleshooting

5.6.4.1 Service Not Found Errors

The most likely cause of these errors is that the service configuration has not been replicated from the MHE to the UHE. Check the UHE deployment descriptor and make sure the entry `SGEManagedJobFactoryService` is present.

5.6.4.2 `managed-job-globusrun` Job Failure Errors

Consider the following error message:

```
WAITING FOR JOB TO FINISH
[08/30/2004 12:10:46:805 ] org.globus.ogsa.impl.base.
gram.client.GramJob [setStatusFromServiceData:1226]
ERROR: The ns1:value mpi feature is not available
on this resource.
========== Status Notification ==========
Job Status: Failed
=========================================
Error: Job failed: The ns1:value mpi feature is not
available on this resource.
```

This error is most likely because of mistakes in the job XML. Common mistakes can be made in the executable, standard input and especially in the job type. For example, consider the XML:

```
<gram:jobType>
    <enum:enumeration>
        <enum:enumerationValue>
            <enum:mpi/>
        </enum:enumerationValue>
    </enum:enumeration>
</gram:jobType>
```

This XML is a common mistake made when installing both PBS and SGE MMJFS services. It requires your scheduler to use the MPI for job dispatching, which is most likely not to be installed in your cluster by default:

- Single machine clusters use`<enum:single/>`
- Multimachine clusters use `<enum:multiple/>`
- MPI-enabled clusters use `<enum:mpi/>`

Other common XML mistakes include the following:

1. Wrong job output folder:

```
<gram:directory>
    <rsl:path>
        <rsl:stringElement value="/tmp"/>
    </rsl:path>
</gram:directory>
```

2. Invalid input files:

```
<gram:stdin>
    <rsl:path>
        <rsl:stringElement value="/dev/null"/>
    </rsl:path>
</gram:stdin>
```

3. Invalid executable:

```
<gram:executable>
    <rsl:path>
        <rsl:stringElement value="/bin/echo"/>
```

```
            </rsl:path>
        </gram:executable>
```

5.6.4.3 The Jobs Are Put in Pending State

For example, some jobs take an unusual execution time and return the output:

```
WAITING FOR JOB TO FINISH
========== Status Notification ==========
Job Status: Pending
=========================================
```

A possible cause for this error is that the system load is too high. GT 3.2 requires significant computing power from your system. If you run the GT container and the scheduler daemons in the same host, this error is likely to occur.

To diagnose, you can monitor the queue using the client commands. For SGE, use the following command:

```
>qstat -f
queuename          qtype used/tot. load_avg arch    states
---------------------------------------------------------
all.q@vm-rhl8      BIP   0/1       3.31     lx24-x86      a

####################################################################
 - PENDING JOBS - PENDING JOBS - PENDING JOBS - PENDING JOBS
####################################################################
3 0.56000 data       root    qw    08/30/2004 12:45:34     1 1-3:1
4 0.56000 data       globus  qw    08/30/2004 12:52:01     1 1-3:1
5 0.56000 data       sge     qw    08/30/2004 12:56:03     1 1-3:1
6 0.56000 simple.sh  sge     qw    08/30/2004 13:00:03     1
```

As we can see, four jobs are in "Pending" state, thus unable to be dispatched. For example, to diagnose why job number 4 cannot be dispatched, run the following command for SGE:

```
>qstat -j 4
job_number:                 4
exec_file:                  job_scripts/4
submission_time:            Mon Aug 30 12:52:01 2004
owner:                      globus
uid:                        501
group:                      globus
gid:                        501
sge_o_home:                 /home/globus
```

```
sge_o_log_name:              globus
sge_o_workdir:               /tmp
sge_o_host:                  vm-rhl8
account:                     sge
stderr_path_list:            /home/globus/.globus
   /job/192.168.74.128/hash-32459003-1093884590771/stderr.$TASK_ID
hard resource_list:          h_rt=3600,h_cpu=3600,h_data=2048M
mail_list:                   myaccount@somesystem.domain.com
notify:                      FALSE
job_name:                    data
stdout_path_list:            /home/globus/.globus
   /job/192.168.74.128/hash-32459003-1093884590771/stdout.$TASK_ID
jobshare:                    0
hard_queue_list:             all.q
shell_list:                  /bin/sh
env_list:
script_file:                 /home/globus/.globus/.gass_cache
  /local/md5/97/6c7bd37461e926114d8a3d743f5c57/md5/aa
  /121153a3fc6e4e3ffe5218e813de28/data
job-array tasks:             1-3:1
scheduling info:             queue instance "all.q@vm-rhl8" dropped
  because it is overloaded:
  np_load_avg=2.730000 (no load adjustment) >= 1.75

All queues dropped because of overload or full

Reason: System load too high 2.73 >= 1.75
```

The reason this job cannot be dispatched is that the system load is over the threshold required for job submission by SGE. This can be easily fixed by stopping applications that are consuming high levels of system resources.

5.6.4.4 Troubleshooting the Scheduler Interface Script

If none of these suggestions fixes any errors, it is likely that there is a problem with the scheduler script. Fortunately, this can be easily tested from the command with a few easy scripts.

Scheduler Interface Test

When MMJFS attempts to submit a job to a backend scheduler, it runs the PERL script `globus-job-manager-script.pl` using the following format:

```
$GLOBUS_LOCATION/libexec/globus-job-manager-script.pl
-m <SCHEDULER> -f <SCRIPT_FILE> -c <METHOD>
```

Where SCHEDULER is the scheduler type: pbs, fork, lsf, or sge. SCRIPT_FILE is the Job description script file. METHOD is the scheduler method to be run: submit, poll, or cancel

By creating a simple wrapper to this command and a few input job scripts, you can write a generic script that can be used to test all the methods of any scheduler interface. (see Listing 5.11)

LISTING 5.11 Generic Scheduler Interface Test Script (test_scheduler.sh)

```
#
# Test a Scheduler interface
#
USAGE="$0 <job_description> <scheduler:pbs|lsf|...>
  <method:submit|poll|cancel>"

if [ -z $GLOBUS_LOCATION ] ; then
    echo "Must set GLOBUS_LOCATION"
    exit 1
fi

if [ "$1" == "" ] ; then
    echo "Scheduler script is required. $USAGE"
    exit 1
fi

script=$1;

if [ "$2" == "" ] ; then
    echo "Scheduler type is required. $USAGE"
    exit 1
fi

scheduler=$2

if [ "$3" == "" ] ; then
    echo "A method is required. $USAGE"
    exit 1
fi

method=$3

# run
$GLOBUS_LOCATION/libexec/globus-job-manager-script.pl
```

```
-m $scheduler -f $script -c $method
```

Testing the Submit Method

To test the submit method, a job description file is needed. For example, see Listing 5.12.

LISTING 5.12 Submit Method Job Description File (`submit_job_description.10465`)

```
$description = {
   'jobdir' => [ '/home/globus/.globus/job/192.168.74.131
     /hash-18618854-1106935620669' ],
   'count' => [ '1' ],
   'stdin' => [ '/dev/null' ],
   'cachetag' => [ 'http://192.168.74.131:33786/ogsa/services
     /base/gram/PbsManagedJobFactoryService
     /hash-18618854-1106935620669' ],
   'stderr' => [ '/home/globus/.globus/job/192.168.74.131
     /hash-18618854-1106935620669/stderr' ],
   'directory' => [ '/tmp' ],
   'environment' => [ [ 'GLOBUS_DUROC_SUBJOB_INDEX', '0' ]
    , [ 'PI', '3.141' ]
    , [ 'X509_USER_PROXY'
            , '/home/globus/.globus/job
               /192.168.74.131/hash-18618854-1106935620669/x509_up' ]
            , [ 'HOME', '/home/globus' ]
            , [ 'GLOBUS_LOCATION', '/opt/gt32' ]
            , [ 'X509_CERT_DIR', '/etc/grid-security/certificates' ]
            , [ 'LOGNAME', 'globus' ]
    ],
   'uniqid' => [ 'hash-18618854-1106935620669' ],
   'executable' => [ '/bin/echo' ],
   'arguments' => [ 'Hello World' ],
   'jobtype' => [ 'single' ],
   'grammyjob' => [ 'collective' ],
   'dryrun' => [ 'no' ],
   'stdout' => [ '/home/globus/.globus/job/192.168.74.131
     /hash-18618854-1106935620669/stdout' ],
   '_description_file' => '/tmp/gram_job_mgr2582.tmp',
};
```

To start the test for the submit method of the PBS scheduler, run

```
test_scheduler.sh submit_job_description.10465 pbs submit
```

Sample output:

```
GRAM_SCRIPT_GT3_FAILURE_MESSAGE:qsub: Job exceeds queue resource limits
```

```
    GRAM_SCRIPT_ERROR:17
```

This output is telling us that there is an error with the submit method or the initialization parameters in *pbs.pm*. It turns out that the section

```
BEGIN
{
 ...
    $cluster = 1;
    $cpu_per_node = 1;
    $remote_shell = '/usr/bin/ssh';
 ...
}
```

is invalid for PBS single-node systems. In this case, we ran this test in a single-node IBM ThinkPad, thus the value of `$cluster` should be 0 for single node systems and 1 for multimode. After an update to `pbs.pm`, the test displays the following:

```
./test_scheduler.sh submit_job_description.10465 pbs submit

GRAM_SCRIPT_JOB_ID:9.vm-rhl8-1.ibm.com
GRAM_SCRIPT_JOB_STATE:1
```

This indicates a successful submission with job ID 9.[`HOST_NAME`]

Testing the Poll Method

For the *poll* method, a different job description file is needed. For example, see Listing 5.13.

LISTING 5.13 Poll Method Job Description File (`poll_job_description.16898`) and Test Run

```
$description = {
   'jobid' => [ '9.vm-rhl8-1.ibm.com' ]
};
test_scheduler.sh poll_job_description.16898 pbs poll
GRAM_SCRIPT_JOB_STATE:8
```

In this particular case, a job state of 8 means that the job is finished (DONE).

5.6.5 Packaging Advice

If you want to distribute your scheduler interface, you must follow a significant set of steps to bundle the files using the GPT. For example, your script should not hard-code any paths; thus, the initialization section should be as shown in Listing 5.14.

LISTING 5.14 Scheduler Initialization for GPT

```
BEGIN
{
    $qsub         = '@QSUB@';
    $qstat        = '@QSTAT@';
    $qdel         = '@QDEL@';
    $qselect      = '@QSELECT@';
    $qhost        = '@QHOST@';
    $qconf        = '@QCONF@';
    $qacct        = '@QACCT@';

    $mpirun       = '@MPIRUN@';
    $sun_mprun    = '@SUN_MPRUN@';
    $mpi_pe       = '@MPI_PE@';

    $cat          = '@CAT@';

    $SGE_ROOT     = '@SGE_ROOT@';
    $SGE_CELL     = '@SGE_CELL@';
    $SGE_MODE     = '@SGE_MODE@';
    $SGE_RELEASE  = '@SGE_RELEASE@';
}
```

A set of configuration scripts must be created, including the following:

scheduler setup script: This script must perform the following steps:

- Install the GRAM scheduler PERL module and register a gatekeeper service.
- Install an RSL validation file defining extra scheduler-specific RSL attributes.
- Update the GPT metadata to indicate that the job manager service has been set up.

Packaging scripts: These are required by GPT to build and install your package and include a *configure* script, a package metadata file, auto-make, and bootstrap files. Globus provides an extensive set of documentation on packaging scheduler interfaces in the "Scheduler Tutorial" for the GRAM developer's guide available at *http://www-unix.globus.org/toolkit/docs/3.2/gram/ws/developer/scheduler.html.*

5.7 FACTORS FOR CHOOSING THE RIGHT SCHEDULER

There are many factors to consider when choosing the right scheduler for your organization. Among the most important are features; installation, configuration, and usability; user interfaces; support for open standards; interoperability; the organization's requirements; and support for grid middleware.

5.7.1 Features

All schedulers covered in this chapter are enough for the basic workload management functionality. That is, the job submission, collection of performance data, security, and management polices. For more advanced management policies such as metascheduling, reservations, and quality of service; SILVER/Maui Meta scheduler may be a good choice, although that requires advanced configuration that is not properly documented. The lack of good documentation seems to be a common problem for most open software. SGE provides other advanced features such as ticket-based policies, fairshare, and node allocation.

5.7.2 Installation, Configuration, and Usability

Easy installation can provide significant time-savings that will translate into productivity increases. Of the schedulers covered in this chapter, PBS offers the simplest and easiest installation. It is also the most widely used scheduler today. NASA pioneered PBS, and it has gained a large user base over the years. It is currently owned by Altair Engineering. SGE and Condor-G provide more complex installation processes. There are no binaries available, so they must be built from source.

5.7.3 User Interfaces

Good user interfaces improve usability, which translates into increased productivity. All schedulers support the basic command-line interface. Many of these commands have the same names (SGE and PBS), which is confusing when both packages are run on the same machine. Both OpenPBS and SGE provide an X Window–based graphical interface for job submission and miscellaneous monitoring and administration tasks. However, SGE, which is a commercial product by Sun Microsystems, offers the best features. PBS Pro includes support for windows systems and an extra Web-based interface for submission and monitoring.

5.7.4 Support for Open Standards

Workload management software was developed in the mainframe era for the mainframe. In those days, software companies were not interested in open standards but, rather, profit and competition. Almost every scheduler available uses a closed architecture. Client-server interaction is usually performed by sending messages in a proprietary binary format, thus providing no interoperability. Condor-G makes a nice attempt to support standards by allowing the output to be presented in XML format. It would be nice to find a scheduler that sends messages through Simple Object Access Protocol (SOAP) and includes support for the latest Web Services and Web standards.

5.7.5 Interoperability

If what your company is looking for is interoperability among different platforms, you will be very disappointed. By interoperability, we mean support for SOAP/Web Services, which will allow a scheduler to interact with virtually any Web Services–enabled application. None of the schedulers covered in this chapter includes support for any open standard, although OGSA can provide the glue between workload management and Web Services.

5.7.6 Organization's Requirements

Each organization has a different set of requirements when selecting the right approach to workload management. For example, some organizations may require a multiplatform environment (both Unix and Windows) system to be used. Others may be Unix only. The hardware available could be Intel-compatible only or it may be a cluster of multiprocessor machines:

- If your organization requires a multiplatform cluster (Windows/Unix), only PBS and its commercial sibling PBS Pro provide such functionality.
- For a Unix-only or a multiprocessor cluster, any package will suffice.

Budget is another important factor to consider when choosing the right scheduler. For companies with low budgets, open source is the way to go. All schedulers described here are freely available; although OpenPBS offers an enhanced commercial version (PBS Pro) that supports windows environments. PBS Pro is the only scheduler that can run on both Windows and Unix systems.

5.7.7 Support for Grid Middleware

Globus has included support for major schedulers through a *scheduler interface*. This interface is basically an OGSA or WSRF service that calls a set of PERL scripts, which in turn build a job definition file for submission by the scheduler CLI interface. Currently, Globus bundles out of the box support for PBS, LSF, Condor-G, and SGE, although other schedulers can be manually integrated. These factors should help you determine which package best fits your company's needs. Ultimately is up to the reader to weight the pros and cons of these packages and make the right selection.

5.8 SUMMARY

Schedulers are advanced resource management tools for heterogeneous distributed computing environments. The goal of schedulers is to allow organizations to best achieve enterprise's goals such as productivity, timeliness, and level of service. Schedulers use complex management polices and sophisticated scheduling algorithms to achieve a dynamic collection of performance data, enhanced security, high-level policy administration, and quality of service. Schedulers can handle computationally demanding tasks through the transparent distribution of the associated workload. This chapter has presented a comprehensive overview of popular schedulers and focused on the integration with grid middleware. Schedulers constitute one of the foundations under which Grid Services are built.

REFERENCES

[Condor04] Condor Team. *Condor Version 6.6.6 Manual,* University of Wisconsin–Madison, 2004.

[LoadLeveler00] Subramanian Kannan, Mark Roberts, Peter Mayes, Dave Brelsford, and Joseph F Skovira. *Workload Management with LoadLeveler.* pp 120–132.

[PBSAdmin02] Albeaus Bayucan, Robert L. Henderson, James Patton Jones, and Casimir Lesiak. *Portable Batch System Administrator Guide.* Release: OpenPBS 2.3, August, 2000.

[SGEGlobus03] *EPIC—Sun Grid Engine Integration with Globus Toolkit 3.* London e-Science Centre. Available online at *http://www.lesc.ic.ac.uk/projects/epic-gt3-sge.html,* 2003.

[SGEUSer04] Sun Microsystems. *N1 Grid Engine 6 User's Guide,* pp. 17–70. 2004.

[WSGRAMScheduler04] Scheduler Tutorial from the *WS GRAM: Developer's Guide.* Globus Project and Globus Toolkit are trademarks held by the University of Chicago. Available online at *http://www-unix.globus.org/toolkit/docs/3.2/gram/ws/developer/scheduler.html.*

6 Open Grid Services Architecture (OGSA)

In This Chapter

- Web Services versus Grid Services
- OGSA Service Model
- Standard Interfaces
- Other Service Models
- Service Factories
- Lifetime Management
- Handles and References
- Service Information and Discovery
- Notifications
- Network Protocol Bindings
- Higher-Level Services
- Otrher Interfaces
- Hosting Environments
- Virtual zorganizations (VOS)
- The Globus Toolkit
- Simple Grid Services: Large Interger Factorization
- Summary
- References

OGSA is a refinement and an extension of the Web Services architecture and the Web Service Description Language (WSDL). WSDL was designed to provide for extensions to the core language through a series of hooks to make that possible. OGSA defines extensions, including the concept of *service types*, that allow us to describe families of services defined by collections of ports of specific types. These extensions provide a mechanism to describe service semantic evolution and versioning [OGSAAnalysis]. The topics covered in this chapter include the following:

- OGSA service models
- Standard interfaces
- Service factories
- Lifetime management
- Handles and references
- Service information and discovery
- Notifications
- Network protocol bindings
- Higher-level services and Interfaces
- Hosting environments
- Virtual organizations
- Sample grid services

6.1 WEB SERVICES VERSUS GRID SERVICES

Web Services emerged from the need for a simple framework for business-to-business (B2B) computing. Web Services have created an exiting service provider industry that has been the goal of the business marketplace for distributed information management [OGSAAnalysis]. Web Services provide a standard means of interoperating between different software applications, running on a variety of platforms and frameworks. A Web Services architecture identifies global elements in a network that are required to ensure interoperability between Web Services [WebServices01].

A Web Service is designed to support interoperable machine-to-machine interaction over a network. It has an interface described by the WSDL. Other systems interact with the Web Service using Simple Object Access Protocol (SOAP) messages, typically using HTTP with an XML serialization in conjunction with other Web standards [SOAP1.2.1.03].

Message exchange is defined by a Web Service description (WSD). The WSD is a specification of the Web Service's interface, written in WSDL. It defines the message formats, data-types, transport protocols, and transport serialization formats that should be used between the requester agent and the provider agent. It also specifies one or more network locations at which a provider agent can be invoked and may provide some information about the message exchange pattern that is expected [URIRFC98].

The Web Services model is based on the following standards:

- SOAP defines the mechanism for message exchange though XML [SOAP1.2.1.03] . SOAP uses XML envelopes and a remote procedure call convention. SOAP is a protocol independent so it can exchange messages through HTTP, FTP, or any other network protocol.

- The WSDL defines the XML schema and language used to describe a Web Service. Each Web Service is an entity, which is defined by ports that are service *endpoints* capable of exchanging a set of messages defined by the port type [OGSAAnalysis].
- The Universal Description, Discovery and Integration (UDDI) and the Web Services Inspection Language (WSIL) provide the mechanism needed to discover WSDL documents [WebServices01]. UDDI is a specification for a registry that can be used by a service provider as a place to publish WSDL documents. Clients can then search the registry looking for services and fetch the WSDL documents needed to access them. WSIL provides a simple way to find WSDL documents on a Web site. These discovery mechanisms are equivalent to the Grid Information Services provided by Globus.

The Web Services model provides two advantages to grid services:

- Support for dynamic discovery and composition of services in heterogeneous distributed environments through WSDL. WSDL provides the mechanism for discovering and defining interface definitions and endpoint implementation descriptions [GridPhysiology02].
- The widespread adoption of Web Services mechanisms allows the framework to exploit new tools and technologies such as WSDL processors, workflow systems, language bindings, and hosting environments.

A *grid service* is a Web Service that provides a set of well-defined interfaces and that follows specific conventions. The interfaces address discovery, dynamic service creation, lifetime management, notification, and manageability [GridPhysiology02].

The basic characteristics that separate a grid service from a Web Service are the following [OGSAAnalysis]:

- A grid service must be an instance of a service implementation of some service type.
- It must have a grid services handle (GSH), which is a type of uniform resource identifier (URI) for the service instance. The GSH is not a direct link to the service instance but, rather, is bound to a grid service reference (GSR). The GSH provides a way to locate the current GSR for the service instance because the GSR may change if the service instance changes or is upgraded.
- A grid service instance must implement the *GridService* interface with three operations:
    a. *FindServiceData*: for service metadata discovery and information.

b. *Destroy:* for clients to destroy instances
c. *SetTerminationTime*: for service lifetime management

6.2 OGSA SERVICE MODEL

The OGSA service model represents computational resources such as filesystems, databases, programs, networks, and so forth as *services,* thus creating a virtual representation of the environment. Grid services are an enhancement of Web Services that follow a specific convention and a set of standard interfaces from which all services are implemented. In this way, services can be treated in a uniform manner proving a layer of abstraction [GridPhysiology02].

A grid service may implement many interfaces, which define a set of operations that exchange a defined sequence of messages. These interfaces correspond to PortTypes and are defined as extensions to the WSDL (Web Service Description Language). Grid services maintain internal state for the lifetime of the service through a *grid service instance.* Grid services interact by exchanging messages, and their interfaces are bound by a protocol to define delivery semantics. Another protocol binding behavior defines mutual authentication during communication.

6.3 STANDARD INTERFACES

A set of basic OGSA interfaces (WSDL PortTypes) can be used to manipulate service abstractions and provide a rich range of services. OGSA has defined the following table of standard interfaces [GridPhysiology02] (see Table 6.1).

TABLE 6.1 Standard OGSA Interfaces

PortType	Operation	Description
GridService	`FindServiceData`	Provides information about the service instance such as handle, reference, primary key, and service-specific information (e.g., service instances known to a registry). Provides extensible support for various query languages. →

	`SetTerminationTime`	Set termination time
	`Destroy`	Terminate service.
Notification-Source	`SubscribeTo-NotificationTopic`	Subscribe to notifications of service-related events, based on message type and interest statement. Allows for delivery via third-party messaging services.
Notification-Sink	`DeliverNotification`	Carry out asynchronous delivery of notification messages.
Registry	`RegisterService`	Soft state registration of GSH.
	`UnregisterService`	Unregister a GSH.
Factory	`CreateService`	Create new grid service instance.
HandleMap	`FindByHandle`	Return GSR associated with supplied GSH.

Besides these interfaces, OGSA includes other characteristics such as service discovery, factories, dynamic service creation and destruction, notification, and lifetime management.

6.4 OTHER SERVICE MODELS

The Web Service model provides OGSA with more interoperability than other more mature technologies such as Common Object Request Broker Architecture (CORBA) have. Many people have debated the use of CORBA as the OGSA model; however, CORBA has always focused on source code compatibility rather than on interoperability between different implementations, which leaves little flexibility. Because the Web Service model is primarily concerned with the specification of service properties such as interface and the specification of the port-to-protocol bindings, it allows great flexibility in the way the service's hosting environment is implemented.

New architectural styles for Open Grid Services and network-based software have received attention and are worth mentioning. One of these new ideas is called the representational state transfer (REST), which is based on the principles that have helped the Web achieve success. These principles include statelessness, low-entry barriers, and an emphasis on a small number of operations (`get`, `put`) applied to a large number of network URLs that constitute the Web [NetArch00].

Grid services are not stateless and rely on a small number of methods to retrieve data resulting in a more extensible and interoperable framework. Nevertheless, some problems with the Web Service model make OGSA less suitable for grid computing:

- The use of WSDL extensions to specify additional semantics may be risky to preserve interoperability with other WSDL clients. Some toolkits do not properly ignore extensibility elements that are not understood. It should be clearly stated, in the OGSA specifications, which WSDL extensions are required and which are not.
- Current extensibility mechanisms provided by Web Services may be inadequate. No community process exists to define new extensions in an orderly manner and no mechanisms exist for the discovery of new extensions.
- Ports are not separately addressable, but merely a different interface to the service. Thus, multiple ports with different names but the same port types are defined as *semantically equivalent*. This serves well for business transactions where the notion of port identity is meaningless. However, in the scientific world, we may need to access multiple instruments using multiple protocols, in which case port identity becomes relevant. For example, consider controlling an electron microscope possessing two electron guns, with identical characteristics, through a Web Service via two different protocols. The OGSA document for this service will now have four ports with the same PortType. No distinction can be made, however, between two ports that control the same electron gun via different protocols, or two ports that control different electron guns.

6.5 SERVICE FACTORIES

Service factories in OGSA are interfaces that create other services. They return the GSH and GSR for the new service instance. Factories do not define how instances are created. This gives the *hosting environment* the flexibility to define how interfaces are implemented, so service implementation is transparent to service factories. Factories can create other factories by delegation.

6.6 LIFETIME MANAGEMENT

Lifetime management defines when a service should be terminated so resources can be reclaimed by the system. Traditionally, services are created to perform a task and terminate on completion or by request of some other service or entity. In distributed systems, where services communicate through messages, services may fail, thus rendering other services unable to terminate. OGSA overcomes this issue by giving a service an initial lifetime. Lifetimes can be adjusted by the client or other service acting in the client's behalf. On lifetime expiration, either the hosting environment or the instance itself is at liberty to terminate the instance and release resources. Lifetime is defined by the *SetTerminationTime* in the *GridService* interface [GridPhysiology02].

Lifetime management in OGSA has been implemented with the following characteristics:

- Clients know when a service should terminate and control lifetime and status update requests.
- Hosting environments can terminate services if the lifetime has been exceeded.

6.7 HANDLES AND REFERENCES

Grid services are dynamic and stateful; thus, they can be created and destroyed dynamically. GSHs are unique identifiers used to distinguish instances from one another. GSH carries no instance or protocol-specific information such as network addresses or protocol bindings. Instead, this information is encapsulated into a GSR. Unlike a GSH, which is invariant, the GSRs for a grid service instance can change over that service's lifetime. A GSR carries expiration time and allows services to be upgraded during their lifetimes [GridPhysiology02].

GSR presents a challenge when dealing with obtaining references after the service creation operation expires. OGSA handles this issue by transforming handles to references using a *handle-to-reference mapper* interface. This interface can have access control so requests can be denied, but it does not guarantee the service can be contacted—for example, if the service failed or was explicitly terminated.

6.8 SERVICE INFORMATION AND DISCOVERY

Service information allows for the discovery of service characteristics through the concept of *service data*. Service data, or metadata, are a set of XML elements that describe characteristics of a service. Among the basic service data elements defined by

OGSA are the GSH, GSR, primary key, and handleMap. The *findServiceData* operation from the *GridService* interface can be used to query for service data, and it is extensible to allow any query language to be used [GridPhysiology02].

Service discovery is provided by a *registry* service. A GSH is capable of registering with the registry service, and the *findServiceData* operation from the *GridService* interface can be used to query for specific metadata.

6.9 NOTIFICATIONS

OGSA clients are capable of receiving notifications about particular messages delivered asynchronously. Clients wanting to receive notifications must implement the *NotificationSink* interface. Services wanting to accept subscriptions must implement *NotificationSource* to handle subscriptions. The notification process starts with a client requesting a subscription to the notification source sending the GSH of the sink. The source then will push messages that meet a certain criteria to the sink, which will respond with periodic keep-alive messages. The notification framework allows both for direct service-to-service notification delivery and for integration with various third-party services, such as messaging services commonly used in the commercial world, or custom notification services [GridPhysiology02].

6.10 NETWORK PROTOCOL BINDINGS

Web Services can use a variety of protocol bindings such as SOAP, HTTP, or SSL for security. OGSA addresses four requirements when selecting network protocol bindings:

- *Reliability* for transport service invocation.
- *Authentication and delegation.* As discussed earlier, the grid services abstraction can require support for communication of proxy credentials to remote sites. One way to address this requirement is to incorporate appropriate support within the network protocol binding, as for example in TLS extended with proxy credential support.
- *Ubiquity.* The grid goal of enabling the dynamic formation of VOs from distributed resources means that, in principle, it must be possible for any arbitrary pair of services to interact.
- *GSR Format.* Recall that the GSR can take a binding-specific format. One possible GSR format is a WSDL document; CORBA is another.

6.11 HIGHER-LEVEL SERVICES

The OGSA community is committed to providing many high-level services required by today's business and scientific applications including [GridPhysiology02]:

- Distributed data management services, supporting access to and manipulation of data such as databases or files. Services of interest include database access, data translation, replica management, replica location, and transactions.
- Workflow services, supporting the execution of multiple application tasks on multiple distributed grid resources.
- Auditing services, supporting the recording of usage data, secure storage of that data, analysis of that data for purposes of fraud and intrusion detection, and so forth.
- Instrumentation and monitoring services, supporting the discovery of "sensors" in a distributed environment, the collection and analysis of information from these sensors, the generation of alerts when unusual conditions are detected, and so forth.
- Problem determination services for distributed computing, including dump, trace, and log mechanisms with event tagging and correlation capabilities.
- Security protocol mapping services, enabling distributed security protocols to be transparently mapped onto native platform security services to support distributed authentication and access control mechanisms.

6.12 OTHER INTERFACES

Many optional interfaces have been proposed for OGSA. Among the relevant are a *manageability* interface to allows large amount of service instances be managed by consoles and other tools and a *concurrency* interface to provide concurrency control operations.

6.13 HOSTING ENVIRONMENTS

A hosting environment is required to instantiate grid services. The role of the hosting environment is to provide an implementation, programming model and language to the semantics of a grid service. OGSA delegates issues of implementation, programming model, language, tools, and execution to the hosting environment [GridPhysiology02]. The hosting environment of choice by Globus is an enhanced version of the *Apace Axis* Web Services container. Nevertheless, OGSA can be deployed in other servlet containers such as Tomcat, WebSphere, and others. A hosting environment should be able to do the following:

- Map grid service handles to platform-specific entities such as pointers or objects
- Dispatch grid invocations and notifications into implementation specific events or procedure calls
- Provide protocol processing and the formatting of data for network transmission
- Provide lifetime management of service instances and authentication

6.14 VIRTUAL ORGANIZATIONS (VOS)

In today's world where information is power, VOs are becoming ubiquitous. A VO can be defined as a geographically distributed organization whose members seek a long-term common interest, and who communicate and coordinate their work through information technology [NetVOs98].

VOs provide the following features:

- Team-based, and distributed structures
- Use informal communication methods such as email, instant messaging, and so on
- Decentralized and nonhierarchical
- Flexible and fast responses to changing business needs

Historically, virtual organizations have used electronic mail to share information and coordinate their work. Recently, new communication technologies have facilitated lateral communication with little regard for traditional hierarchy. VOs differ from traditional organizations by the degree of centralization and hierarchy they are built on. In many traditional organizations, the centralization or hierarchy is in the authority structure and is related to status and tenure differences.

Because VOs are highly decentralized structures, they are becoming an increasingly popular type of work environment. Enter the concept of grid computing. Grid computing enables and simplifies collaboration among the members of a VO. Evolved from many concepts on *distributed computing*, grids take these distributed capabilities even further through open standards to enable distributed heterogeneous systems to work together as a single virtual system. Users in a VO can access these resources by means of policies, information sharing, resource management, and security.

The users of a grid can be members of several real or virtual organizations. Grids enforce security rules and implement policies to resolve priorities among competing users. A grid virtualizes disparate and geographically disperse resources to present a simpler view to a virtual organization [IBMGrid02].

Virtual organizations can benefit from computational grids in the many ways:

- By providing access to increased quantities of computing resources and special devices thus increasing resource usage efficiency.
- By maximizing underutilized resources. It has been estimated that desktop machines are busy less than 5% of the time.
- By better balancing resource utilization. Organizations have activity peaks that demand more resources. Grids are capable of moving applications to underutilized machines during such peaks thus providing *dynamic load balancing*.
- By providing software-based *fault tolerance* against power failures. Current fault tolerance systems use expensive hardware to increase reliability. Grid management software can dynamically resubmit tasks to other machines when failures are detected.
- By providing advanced *resource management* to better manage a large and disperse IT infrastructure; for example, visualizing resource capacity and utilization, thus making it easier for an IT department to control expenditures of computing resources in a large organization.

One of the most attractive features provided by grid computing is the potential of massive parallel CPU capacity. Tapping into such powers is driving the evolution of many of today's industries such as biomedical, financial, oil, motion picture, and others.

6.15 THE GLOBUS TOOLKIT

The Globus Toolkit was conceived as an open community of architectures, services, and software libraries that support grids and grid applications [GridPhysiology02]. The *Globus Toolkit (GT)* software was created by the Globus Alliance, an R&D research group based at Argonne National Laboratory, the University of Southern California's Information Sciences Institute, the University of Chicago, the University of Edinburgh, and the Swedish Center for Parallel Computers. Its previous software, the Globus Toolkit 2.0 won the 2002 R&D 100 award from R&D magazine—a very impressive achievement for such a relatively new technology.

Because of this success, GT has been called the de facto standard for grid computing. It has been embraced by major vendors such as Compaq, Cray, SGI, Sun, Fujitsu, Hitachi, NEC, and IBM, which have implemented optimized versions of the toolkit for their systems.

The Globus Toolkit provides services in the following major areas of distributed systems: core services, security, and data management.

6.15.1 Core Services

Core services provide the basic infrastructure needed to create grid services, including authorization, message level security and system level services such as ping, log management and management services to monitor the current status, load, and shut down grid containers.

6.15.2 Security

Security is implemented in two components: the *grid security infrastructure* (GSI) and the *Community Authorization Service* (CAS). GSI lays the foundation for security in GT. It is built on top of open standards such as public key cryptography, digital signatures, certificates, mutual authentication, delegation, and single sign-on. CAS builds on GSI to provide communities with access control policies, delegating access control policy management to the community itself [CASGrid02]. The CAS server takes care of day-to-day policy administration tasks such as adding, deleting, and changing users.

6.15.3 Data Management

Data management is composed of four protocols: GridFTP, Reliable File Transfer (RFT), Replica Location Service (RLS) and Extensible Input/Output (XIO).

GridFTP: This is a high-performance, secure, and reliable data transfer protocol based on the standard FTP. GridFTP enhances the FTP standard with GSI security, multiple data channels for parallel transfers, third-party transfers, authenticated reusable data channels, and command pipelining.

Reliable File Transfer: RFT is an OGSA- compliant service that provides reliability and fault tolerance for file transfers. RFT can checkpoint and restart transfers in case of service failures. Users can query the service for transfer status or to receive completion notifications. For example, a system administrator in a VO may need to transfer hundreds of database files across multiple systems for many weeks. RFT is capable of keeping socket connections open for weeks and tracking the transfers by storing transaction data into a database. Finally, RFT can notify the user by email or other method when the transfer has completed.

Replica Location Service: RLS is designed as a component of the data grid architecture. RLS provides access to mapping information from logical names for data items to target names. Its goal is to reduce access latency, improve data locality, and increase robustness, scalability, and performance for distributed applications. RLS produces *local replica catalogs* (LRCs), which are mappings between *logical* and *physical* files scattered across storage system(s). An LRC can be indexed for faster performance.

XIO: The goal of Globus XIO is to provide a single API for input and output operations in all grid protocols. XIO has the following characteristics:

- It is extensible, simple, and intuitive. Implements open/close, read/write operations.
- It is designed to support new protocols in the form of *drivers*. Drivers are transparent to the application developer. No source code changes will be required if the underlying protocol driver changes.
- It relieves developers from the headaches of error checking, asynchronous message delivery, and timeouts in protocol implementation. For example, a GRAM driver can be written to run on TCP or UDP protocols.

The Globus Toolkit has been an evolutionary process dedicated to the open-source philosophy. Since its inception in 1996, Globus Toolkit has evolved from a monolithic remote shell-like interface to an open services infrastructure and beyond. With the soon-to-be released GT4, the Globus Toolkit is certainly at the vanguard of the open high-performance computing world.

6.16 SAMPLE GRID SERVICES: LARGE INTEGER FACTORIZATION

The following sections describe a sample grid service to factorize integers greater than 100 digits in size that may interest any reader involved in the field of cryptography.

6.16.1 Overview: Large Integer Factorization and Public Key Cryptosystems

Public-key algorithms use a pair of two related keys. One key is private and must be kept secret, whereas the other is public and can be distributed; it should also be infeasible to generate one key from the other. Diffie and Helman invented this concept in the 1970s. Since then, many public-key algorithms have been developed, among the simplest and most practical are RSA, elGamal, and Rabin. Of these three, RSA is the most popular and easiest to understand [Schneier96].

Public-key algorithms are slower than symmetric or single key algorithms and in reality are impractical for bulk data encryption. They are commonly used to encrypt random session keys, which in turn are used to encrypt the bulk of the data.

6.16.1.1 A Little Mathematical Background

One of the reasons large integer factorization samples are used throughout this book is due to their application in public-key cryptosystems (such as PKI). They are also ideal applications for a distributed or parallel computer system and easy enough to illustrate. Of all the PKI algorithms, RSA is the easiest to understand and implement. It is named after the inventors Ron Rivest, Adi Shamir, and Leonard Adleman. According to *Applied Cryptography* by Bruce Schneier, RSA gets its security from the difficulty of factoring large integers (in the range of 150 digits or more). Recovering the plaintext from the public key and the ciphertext is equivalent to factoring the product of the two primes [Schneier96].

The algorithm is as follows: to generate the keys, first choose two large primes p, q of equal length for maximum security. Then compute the product:

$$n = pq \tag{6.1}$$

Then choose a random encryption key *e* less than *pq*, and *e* and (P – 1)(Q – 1) are relatively prime, which means they have no prime factors in common. *e* does not have to be prime, but it must be odd. (P – 1)(Q – 1) can't be prime because it's an even number [RSAGuts01].

Finally, use the extended Euclidean algorithm to compute a decryption key, *d*, such that

$$ed = 1 \ (\text{mod } (p-1)(q-1)) \tag{6.2}$$

Thus, *e* equals,

$$d = e^{-1} \text{mod}((p-1)(q-1)) \tag{6.3}$$

To encrypt a message *m*, it should be divided into numerical blocks smaller than the modulus, *n*.

$$c = (m^e) \text{mod}\, n \tag{6.4}$$

where *c* is the ciphertext, and *m* is the plaintext, both expressed as positive integers. The message being encrypted, *m*, must be less than the modulus *n*. To decrypt the message *m*,

$$m = c^d \text{ mod}\, n \tag{6.5}$$

where *c* is the ciphertext, and m is the plaintext both expressed as positive integers. The following example based on [RSAGuts01] can illustrate this point.

Given the following:

```
p  = 61    p and q are primes and must remain secret
```

```
q  = 53
n = pq = 3233  modulus (available to others, discard p and q after)
e  = 17    public exponent
d  = 2753  private exponent (must be  secret)
The public key is (e, n).
The private key is d.
To encrypt the message 123:
   E(123) = (123^17) mod 3233
   = 337587917446653715596592958817679803 mod 3233
   = 855
To decrypt the ciphertext 855:
   D(855) = (855^2753) mod 3233
   = 123
```

Table 6.2 summarizes RSA.

TABLE 6.2 RSA

Public Key (n,e)
n = modulus, the product of 2 large primes, 150 or more digits. p and q must remain secret.
e = public exponent, relatively prime to (p – 1)(q – 1)
Private Key
$d = e^{-1} \bmod ((p-1)(q-1))$, d is the secret exponent
Encrypting
$c = (m^e) \bmod n,$
Decrypting
$m = c^d \bmod n$

6.16.1.2 Further Information on Large Integer Factorization Algorithms

Large integer factorization is a complex subject that requires some advanced mathematics, especially in the fields of linear algebra and modular arithmetic. We have attempted to give as much context as possible on the algorithms without confusing the reader. If you are looking for an in-depth study on the inner workings of the quadratic or number field sieves, we suggest [BriggsThesis98]as a beginner's guide to the number field sieve. For the more technical reader, [Cohen96, LenstraNFS,

ON THE CD

Lenstra93, Montgomery95] should keep you busy for a while. The CD-ROM provided with this book contains a Java implementation of the quadratic sieve, which is roughly 10,000 lines in size. Another open source algorithm studied in this book, public domain GNFS by Chris Monico, explained in Chapter 16, is 50,000 lines in size. This should give the reader an idea of the complexity of these algorithms.

6.16.2 Service Implementation

Good candidates for grid services are scientific applications in the fields of mathematics, biology, and business. For this implementation, we have chosen an application in the field of cryptography and *large integer factorization*. Cryptographic research requires intensive computational power, making it an ideal topic for a grid service. Grid services are designed for distributed systems; thus, our problem should be designed for such environments.

There are currently many algorithms for factorization tasks. Among the fastest is the quadratic sieve (QS) invented by Carl Pomerance in 1981, extending earlier ideas of Kraitchik and Dixon. The QS is the fastest algorithm for numbers up to 110 digits long [QuadSieve01].

6.16.3 Factorization with the Quadratic Sieve

The QS is a fairly complex factorization algorithm that requires understanding of several concepts of numerical analysis and modular algebra. The algorithm can be described by the following set of formulas:

$$x \equiv \pm y (\bmod n) \tag{6.6}$$

$$x \wedge 2 \not\equiv y \wedge 2 (\bmod n) \tag{6.7}$$

Where n is the number to factor, and x, y are two numbers that satisfy equations 6.1 and 6.2. From the previous equations, we obtain

$$(x-y)(x+y) \equiv 0 (\bmod n) \tag{6.8}$$

then we compute (x – y, n) sing the Euclidean algorithm to see if n is a nontrivial divisor. There is a 50% chance of this to be true. Then we define the following:

$$Q(x) = (x + \lfloor \sqrt{n} \rfloor)^2 - n = \tilde{x}^2 - n^2 \tag{6.9}$$

and compute $Q(x_1), Q(x_2), \ldots, Q(x_k)$. From the equations Q($x$), we pick a subset such that $Q(x_{i_1}), Q(x_{i_2}), \ldots, Q(x_{i_r}) \equiv (x_{i_1} x_{i_2} \ldots x_{i_r})$ is a square.

So finally, we have the equation:

$$Q(x_{i_1})Q(x_{i_2})...Q(x_{i_r}) \equiv (x_{i_1}x_{i_2}...x_{i_r})^2 (\bmod n) \tag{6.10}$$

If the conditions above hold, then we have found the factors of n [Quad-Sieve01].

6.16.4 Service Architecture

Our OGSA implementation of the large integer factorization service has the following components (see Figure 6.1):

- A standalone factorization engine implementing a quadratic sieve.
- An OGSA compliant layer composed of a service factory interface and a service implementation.
- A client program that can be used to call instances created by the GT3 container on a given host.

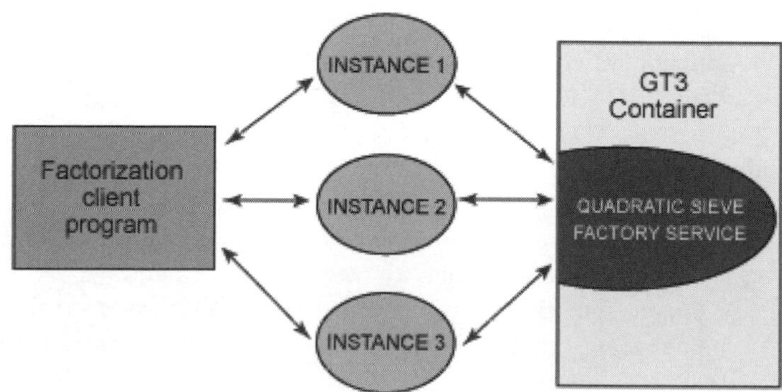

FIGURE 6.1 The quadratic sieve factorization service architecture.

6.16.5 Step 1: Obtaining Factorization Code

The factorization engine can be run in standalone mode and implements a QS algorithm in the Java language with code based from an elliptic curve algorithm available from Alpern's *Elliptic Curve Method Algorithm* [ECMAlg]. The algorithm is included in the companion CD-ROM of this book. To run the engine in standalone mode, the following commands can be used:

```
# Note: Your Java CLASSPATH must be set first!
# Linux :
export CLASSPATH=$CLASSPATH:./classes
```

```
# Win32:
set CLASSPATH=%CLASSPATH%;classes

java javax.math.factorization.Factorizer
 -n 2131231231231231213213123123 45
5 * 379 * 338999 * 3317591734291557 03289
```

6.16.6 Step 2: Building a Factorization Service Interface

We start our OGSA service by creating a "service interface" that defines a method to be called remotely by clients (see Listing 6.1).

LISTING 6.1 Factorization.java OGSA Service Interface for Large Integer Factorization

```
package factorization.service.impl;

/**
 * <p>Title: Factorization Library</p>
 * <p>Description: A factorization lib based on the quadratic
 * sieve</p>
 * @author Vladimir Silva
 * @version 1.0
 */
public interface Factorization {
  /**
   * Remote factorization method
   * @param bigNum Number to factorize
   * @param outFile Output file path (contains factors)
   * @param options: -verbose to display process output
   */
  public String factorize
    (String bigNum, String outFile, String options);
}
```

This method takes a number as the argument and dumps the output on the filesystem on the server. Because the factorization process can take months for large numbers, an XML status string is returned by the server. The server logs can be monitored for the actual process output.

6.16.7 Step 3: Creating the Service Implementation

The service implementation contains the actual code to be executed whenever a factory instance is executed. This code calls the QS factorization engine with the required arguments (see Listing 6.2).

LISTING 6.2 FactorizationImpl.java Service Implementation

```
package factorization.service.impl;

/**
 * <p>Title: Factorization Library</p>
 * <p>Description: Factorization Service Implementation</p>
 * @author Vladimir Silva
 * @version 1.0
 */

import org.globus.ogsa.impl.ogsi.GridServiceImpl;
import factorization.service.Factorization.FactorizationPortType;
import java.rmi.RemoteException;

import javax.math.factorization.Factorizer;

/**
 * Factorization service Implementation
 */
public class FactorizationImpl
    extends GridServiceImpl implements FactorizationPortType {
  public FactorizationImpl() {
    super("Factorization Service");
  }

  /**
   * Factorization Method
   * @param bigNum Number to factor
   * @param outFile Full path to the server side Output file.
    (Which Contains factors of the form pd(1)^ exp(1) * .....
   * @param options Use "-verbose" to display debug messages
   */
  public String factorize(String bigNum, String outFile
                          , String options)
  throws RemoteException
  {
    if (options == null) {
      options = "";
    }
    String[] args = {
      "-n", bigNum, "-out", outFile, options};

    try {
```

```
        Factorizer f = new Factorizer(args);
        // dump output: to the console or a file
        f.dumpOutput();
        return buildXML(false, "Out in: " + outFile);
      }
      catch (Exception ex) {
        return buildXML(true
          , ex.getClass().getName() + ": " + ex.getMessage());
      }

    }

    /*
     * An XML string is returned w/ service status
     */
    private String buildXML(boolean error, String text) {
      return "<xml><error>" + error
          + "</error><text>" + text + "</text></xml>";
    }
  }
```

6.16.8 Step 4: Creating a Service Deployment Descriptor

The service deployment descriptor tells the GT3 container where to find the service components such as schema (WSDL) files, service interface, and implementation (see Listing 6.3).

LISTING 6.3 Large Integer Factorization OGSA Service Deployment Descriptor

```
<?xml version="1.0"?>
<deployment
  name="defaultServerConfig"
  xmlns="http://xml.apache.org/axis/wsdd/"
  xmlns:java="http://xml.apache.org/axis/wsdd/providers/java">

  <service
    name="factorization/factory/FactorizationService"
    provider="Handler"
    style="wrapped">
    <parameter
      name="name"
      value="Factorization Service Factory" />
    <parameter
      name="instance-name"
```

```
      value="Factorization Service Instance" />
    <parameter
      name="instance-schemaPath"
      value="schema/factorization.service
      /Factorization/FactorizationService.wsdl" />
    <parameter
      name="instance-baseClassName"
      value="factorization.service.impl.FactorizationImpl" />

    <!-- Start common parameters -->
    <parameter
      name="allowedMethods"
      value="*" />
    <parameter
      name="persistent"
      value="true" />
    <parameter
      name="className"
      value="org.gridforum.ogsi.Factory" />
    <parameter
      name="baseClassName"
      value="org.globus.ogsa.impl.ogsi.PersistentGridServiceImpl" />
    <parameter
      name="schemaPath"
      value="schema/ogsi/ogsi_factory_service.wsdl" />
    <parameter
      name="handlerClass"
      value="org.globus.ogsa.handlers.RPCURIProvider" />
    <parameter
      name="factoryCallback"
      value="org.globus.ogsa.impl.ogsi.DynamicFactoryCallbackImpl" />
    <parameter
      name="operationProviders"
      value="org.globus.ogsa.impl.ogsi.FactoryProvider" />
  </service>
</deployment>
```

6.16.9 Step 5: Creating the Schema Files and Grid Archives (GARs)

Many steps are required before you can use this service within GT3. Fortunately, all steps can be automated using Ant and shell scripting.

Globus provides shell scripts written to build this service automatically. These scripts require the file `build.properties`, which contains system-dependent information such as the path to the GT installation and other parameters. This file must be changed to match your platform.

6.16.9.1 Tools for Building Grid Services

Globus provides scripts to automate the service build process. These tools perform calls to a series of Ant scripts. The shell script in Listing 6.4 can be used to build a service in Linux.

LISTING 6.4 Shell Script to Build an OGSA Service

```
#!/bin/bash

INTERFACE_PATH=$1

if [ ! -e $INTERFACE_PATH -o ! -f $INTERFACE_PATH ]
then
    echo "$INTERFACE_PATH does not exist or is not a file."
    exit 1;
fi

PATH_AUX=$(echo $INTERFACE_PATH | cut -f 1 -d .)
DESCRIPTION_TYPE=$(echo $INTERFACE_PATH | cut -f 2 -d .)

IFS=/
set -- $*
NUM_FIELDS=$#


i=1
for n in $PATH_AUX
do
    if [ $i -eq 1 ]
    then
    PACKAGE=$n
    NAMESPACE="$n"
    else
    if [ $i -eq $NUM_FIELDS ]
    then
        INTERFACE=$n
    else
        if [ $i -lt $[NUM_FIELDS-1] ]
        then
                NAMESPACE="$n.$NAMESPACE"
        PACKAGE="$PACKAGE.$n"
```

```
        fi
    fi
    fi
    i=$[i+1]
done
IFS=""

PACKAGE_DIR=$(echo $PACKAGE | sed "s/\./\//g")


case $DESCRIPTION_TYPE in
"java")
    ant -Djava.interface=true -Dpackage=$PACKAGE
     -Dinterface.name=$INTERFACE
     -Dpackage.dir=$PACKAGE_DIR -Dservices.namespace=$NAMESPACE
    ;;
"gwsdl")
    ant -Dgwsdl.interface=true -Dpackage=$PACKAGE
     -Dinterface.name=$INTERFACE -Dpackage.dir=$PACKAGE_DIR
    ;;
*)
    "$INTERFACE_PATH must be a Java interface or a GWSDL description."
esac
```

6.16.9.2 Ant Build Script

The Ant script in Listing 6.5 is very useful for building your grid service. It requires a configuration file (`build.properties`) with path and library information.

LISTING 6.5 `build.xml` Ant Script for Building OGSA Services

```
<?xml version="1.0"?>

<project
  default="all"
  basedir=".">

  <!-- Give user a chance to override without editing this file
    (and without typing -D each time it compiles it) -->

  <property file="build.properties" />
  <property file="${user.home}/build.properties" />

  <path id="classpath">
    <pathelement location="${java.home}/../lib/tools.jar" />
    <pathelement location="./" />
```

```
    <pathelement location="${build.dest}" />
    <fileset dir="lib">
      <include name="*.jar" />
    </fileset>
    <fileset dir="${ogsa.root}/lib">
      <include name="*.jar" />
    </fileset>
    <pathelement path="${java.class.path}" />
    <pathelement path="${factorizer.cp}" />
  </path>

  <property
    name="src.dir"
    value="./" />
  <property
    name="build.dir"
    value="./build" />
  <property
    name="build.lib"
    value="${build.dir}/lib" />
  <property
    name="build.stubs"
    value="${build.dir}/stubs" />
  <property
    name="build.dest"
    value="${build.dir}/classes" />
  <property
    name="build.schema"
    value="${build.dir}/schema" />
  <property
    name="build.services"
    value="${ogsa.root}/build-services.xml" />
  <property
    name="build.packages"
    value="${ogsa.root}/build-packages.xml" />
  <property
    name="schema.origin"
    value="${ogsa.root}/schema" />
  <property
    name="stubs.dest"
    value="../stubs" />
  <property file="${ogsa.root}/ogsa.properties" />
  <property
    name="mapping.file"
```

```
  value="namespace2package.mappings" />

<target name="copyFiles">
  <mkdir dir="${build.dest}" />
  <mkdir dir="${build.lib}" />
  <mkdir dir="${build.schema}" />
  <mkdir dir="${build.stubs}" />
  <mkdir dir="${lib.dir}" />
  <copy toDir="${build.schema}">
    <fileset dir="${schema.origin}" />
  </copy>
  <available
    file="${mapping.file}"
    property="mapping.file.present" />
</target>

<target
  name="mergeMapping"
  if="mapping.file.present">
  <ant
    antfile="${build.services}"
    target="mergePackageMapping" />
</target>

<target
  name="setenv"
  depends="copyFiles,mergeMapping" />

<target
  name="generateWSDLfromJava"
  if="java.interface"
  depends="setenv">
  <property
    name="schema.file"
    value="${interface.name}Service.wsdl" />
  <ant
    antfile="${build.services}"
    target="generateWSDL">
    <property
      name="interface"
      value="${package.dir}/impl/${interface.name}.java" />
    <property
      name="interface.package"
      value="${package}.impl" />
```

```
      <property
        name="interface.dir"
        value="${package.dir}/impl" />
      <property
        name="generated.dir"
        value="${package}" />
    </ant>
  </target>

  <target
    name="generateWSDLfromGWSDL"
    if="gwsdl.interface"
    depends="setenv">
    <property
      name="schema.file"
      value="${interface.name}_service.wsdl" />
    <copy
      todir="${build.schema}/${package}/${interface.name}"
      overwrite="true">
      <fileset dir="${package.dir}/schema" />
    </copy>

    <ant
      antfile="${build.services}"
      target="GWSDL2WSDL">
      <property
        name="build.schema.dir"
        value="${package}/${interface.name}" />
      <property
        name="wsdl.root"
        value="${interface.name}" />
    </ant>

    <ant
      antfile="${build.services}"
      target="generateBinding">
      <property
        name="binding.root"
        value="${interface.name}" />
      <property
        name="build.schema.dir"
        value="${package}/${interface.name}" />
      <property
        name="porttype.wsdl"
```

```
        value="${interface.name}.wsdl" />
    </ant>
  </target>

  <target
    name="stubs"
    unless="stubs.present"
    depends="setenv, generateWSDLfromJava, generateWSDLfromGWSDL">
    <ant
      antfile="${build.services}"
      target="generateStubs">
      <property
        name="schema.file.dir"
        value="${package}/${interface.name}" />
      <property
        name="schema.file"
        value="${schema.file}" />
    </ant>
  </target>

  <target
    name="compileStubs"
    depends="stubs">
    <javac
      srcdir="${build.stubs}"
      destdir="${build.dest}"
      debug="${debug}"
      deprecation="${deprecation}"
      classpathref="classpath">
    </javac>
  </target>

  <target
    name="compile"
    depends="compileStubs">
    <javac
      srcdir="${package.dir}/impl"
      destdir="${build.dest}"
      debug="${debug}"
      deprecation="${deprecation}"
      classpathref="classpath">
    </javac>
    <javac
      srcdir="${factorization.engine}"
```

```
      destdir="${build.dest}"
      debug="${debug}"
      deprecation="${deprecation}"
      classpathref="classpath">
    </javac>

  </target>

  <target
    name="stubjar"
    depends="compile">
    <jar
      jarfile="${build.lib}/${package}.${interface.name}-stub.jar"
      basedir="${build.dest}">
      <include name="**/${package.dir}/**" />
      <exclude name="**/${package.dir}/impl/**" />
      <exclude name="**/${package.dir}/client/**" />
      <exclude name="**/${package.dir}/schema/**" />
    </jar>
  </target>

  <target
    name="jar"
    depends="stubjar">
    <jar
      jarfile="${build.lib}/${package}.${interface.name}.jar"
      basedir="${build.dest}">
      <include name="**/${package.dir}/impl/**" />
      <exclude name="**/${package.dir}/impl/${interface.name}.class" />
      <include name="${factorization.engine}/**" />
    </jar>
  </target>

  <target
    name="gar"
    depends="jar">
    <copy todir="${build.lib}">
      <fileset dir="${lib.dir}">
        <include name="**/*.jar" />
      </fileset>
    </copy>
    <ant
      antfile="${build.packages}"
      target="makeGar">
```

```
      <property
        name="gar.name"
        value="${build.lib}/${package}.${interface.name}.gar" />
      <property
        name="garlib.dir"
        value="${build.lib}" />
      <property
        name="garserverdeployment.file"
        value="${package.dir}/${interface.name}.wsdd" />
      <property
        name="garschema.origin"
        value="${build.schema}/${package}" />
      <property
        name="garschema.path"
        value="${package}" />
    </ant>
  </target>

  <target
    name="compileClient"
    depends="setenv">
    <javac
      srcdir="${src.dir}"
      destdir="${build.dest}"
      debug="${debug}"
      deprecation="${deprecation}"
      classpathref="classpath">
    </javac>
  </target>

  <target name="clean">
    <delete dir="${build.dir}" />
  </target>

  <target
    name="all"
    depends="gar" />
</project>

<!-- **********************************************
  A sample Ant configuration file (build.properties)
  for the above script may look like:
  ogsa.root=c:/ogsa-3.2.1
  factorizer.cp=../classes
```

```
  factorization.engine=javax/math/factorization
**************************************************-->
```

6.16.9.3 Building the Service Using the Ant Tools

The shell script and Ant build files described earlier allow the grid service build process to be automated by running the simple command:

```
build_service.sh [SERVICE_INTERFACE_NAME]
```

In this case:

```
build_service.sh factorization/service/impl/Factorization.java
```

6.16.10 Step 6: Deploying the Service to the GT3 Container

The final step before using this service is to deploy it into a GT3 grid services container. A command such as the following can be used:

- To deploy:

```
ant deploy
–Dgar.name=[PATH_TO_GAR]factorization.service.Factorization.gar
```

- To undeploy:

```
ant undeploy –Dgar.id=factorization
```

Make sure the GLOBUS_LOCATION *environment variable has been set up on your system and the binaries are included in your* PATH *variable.*

Make sure the all the JAR libraries are included in your CLASSPATH. *Globus provides a class path setup script (globus-devel-env) under* GLOBUS_LOCATION/etc/. *For example in Linux:*

```
export GLOBUS_LOCATION=/opt/gt32
export PATH=$PATH:$GLOBUS_LOCATION/bin
. $GLOBUS_LOCATION/etc/globus-devel-env
```

Once the service has been successfully deployed, the service browser GUI can be used to look at the service and create an instance (see Figure 6.2)

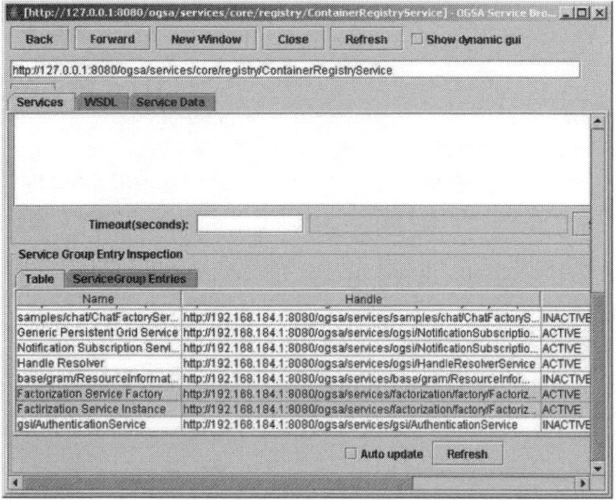

FIGURE 6.2 OGSA service browser showing the deployed factorization service.

6.16.11 Step 7: Writing a Service Client

The service client is the program used to call remote instances of the factorization service on a given host (see Listing 6.6).

LISTING 6.6 FactorizationClient.java, the Client Program to Access the Factorization Service

```
package factorization.client;

/**
 * <p>Title: Factorization Library</p>
 * <p>Description: A factorization lib based on the quadratic sieve</p>
* @author Vladimir Silva
 * @version 1.0
 */

import factorization.service.Factorization.FactorizationServiceGridLo-
cator;
import factorization.service.Factorization.FactorizationPortType;
import java.net.URL;

/**
 * Factorization Service client
 * Usage: FactorizationClient
-factory [URL] -n [BIG_NUM] -out [OUTFILE_PATH] {-verboseServer}
 *  {-verboseServer} : optional
```

```
 */
public class FactorizationClient
{
  private static final String PROGRAM_NAME = "FactorizationClient";
  private static final String USAGE =
     PROGRAM_NAME + " -factory URL -n [NUMBER2FACTOR] “" +“
     - "-out [OUT_FILE_PATH] [-verboseServer]";

  // Factorization factory service URL.
  // Example:
  // http://localhost:8080
  //  /ogsa/services/factorization/FactorizationService/{INSTANCE-NAME}
  private URL _GSH = null;

  // Big Number to factor
  private String _number = null;

  // Server side output file
  private String _outFile = null;
  private String _options = "";
  private String _message = null;

  /* * Constructor */
  public FactorizationClient( String[] args ) throws Exception
  {
    if ( !parseArgs( args ) )
      throw new Exception( _message );
    if ( !validateArgs() )
      throw new Exception( _message );

    // Get a reference to the MathService instance
    FactorizationServiceGridLocator loc =
       new FactorizationServiceGridLocator();
    FactorizationPortType fac = loc.getFactorizationService( _GSH );

    // call remote Method: factorize (num, out file, options)
    String ret = fac.factorize( _number, _outFile, _options );

    // display remote serv  out
    System.out.println( "Factorization Service returned:" + ret );
  }

  /* * Parse input args */
  boolean parseArgs( String args[] ) throws Exception
```

```
{
  String arg;
  for ( int i = 0; i < args.length; i++ )
  {
    arg = args[i].trim();
    if ( arg.length() == 0 ) continue;

    if ( arg.equals( "-factory" ) )
      _GSH = new URL( args[++i] );
    else if ( arg.equals( "-n" ) )
      _number = args[++i];
    else if ( arg.equals( "-out" ) )
      _outFile = args[++i];
    else if ( arg.equals( "-verboseServer" ) )
      _options = "-verbose";
    else
    {
      _message = "Invalid argument(s): " + args[i];
      return false;
    }
  }
  return true;
}

/* * Validate program arguments */
boolean validateArgs()
{
  if ( _GSH == null || _number == null )
  {
    _message = "Service factory and number are required.\n"
       + USAGE;
    return false;
  }
  if ( _number.length() == 0 )
  {
    _message = "A valid number is required.\n" + USAGE;
    return false;
  }
  return true;
}

static void usage()
{
  System.out.println( USAGE );
```

```
    }

    /* * Main Sub */
    public static void main( String[] args )
    {
      try
      {
        FactorizationClient c = new FactorizationClient( args );
      }
      catch ( Exception ex )
      {
        System.err.println( ex );
      }
    }
}
```

6.16.12 Step 8: Running the Factorization Client

The client program can be used to factorize numbers by submitting remote calls to instances created on specific containers. As shown here:

```
%GLOBUS_LOCATION%\etc\globus-devel-env
java factorization.client.FactorizationClient-factory
http://localhost:8080/ogsa/services/
factorization/factory/
FactorizationService/hash-19521418-1093629122756
    -n 123
    -out c:\temp\out.txt
    -verboseServer
```

For this client to run, your OGSA environment should be set up properly including the required environment variable `GLOBUS_LOCATION` and the OGSA Java libraries in your class path.

6.17 SUMMARY

Today's enterprise IT infrastructures have become increasingly concerned with the need for management and creation of distributed resources and services. These *virtual organizations* (VOs) seek common goals such as quality of service, common security, distributed workflow, resource management, coordinated fail-over, problem determination, and other metrics. Thus, the need arises for a mechanism to provide those goals in practical settings. Enter the *Open Grid Services Architecture,* which supports the creation, maintenance, and application of ensembles of services maintained by VOs [GridAnatomy01]. This became the foundation for building enterprise-level grids.

REFERENCES

[BriggsThesis98] Matthew E. Briggs. "An Introduction to the General Number Field Sieve." Thesis submitted to the Faculty of the Virginia Polytechnic Institute and State University, Blacksburg, Virginia, April 17, 1998.

[CASGrid02] L. Pearlman, V. Welch, I. Foster, C. Kesselman, and S. Tuecke. A Community Authorization Service for Group Collaboration. *Proceedings of the IEEE 3rd International Workshop on Policies for Distributed Systems and Networks,* 2002.

[ECMAlg] Dario Alejandro Alpern. *Elliptic Curve Method Algorithm.* Available online at *http://www.alpertron.com.ar/ECM.htm.*

[GridAnatomy01] Ian Foster, Carl Kesselman, and Steven Tuecke, "The Anatomy of the Grid: Enabling Scalable Virtual Organizations." *International Journal of High Performance Computing Applications, 15*(3), 200–222. 2001. Available online at *http://www.cs.utk.edu/~angskun/cns04/02-anatomy.pdf.*

[GridPhysiology02] Ian Foster, Carl Kesselman, Jeffrey Nick, and Steven Tuecke, *The Physiology of the Grid: An Open Grid Services Architecture for Distributed Systems Integration.* Globus Project, 2002, Available online at *http://www-unix.globus.org/ogsa/docs/alpha/physiology.pdf.*

[IBMGrid02] Viktors Berstis, Fundamentals of Grid Computing. *IBM Redbooks Paper.* Available online at *http://www.redbooks.ibm.com/redpapers/pdfs/redp3613.pdf,* November 11, 2002.

[MonicoGNFS] GGNFS. A public domain implementation of GNFS by Chris Monico. *http://www.math.ttu.edu/~cmonico/software/ggnfs/index.html.*

[Lenstra93] A. Lenstra and H. Lenstra, H. (Eds.), "The Development of the Number Field Sieve." *Lecture Notes in Mathematics 1554,* Springer-Verlag, Berlin, 1993.

[NetArch00] Roy Thomas Fielding, *Architectural Styles and the Design of Network-based Software Architectures,* Ph.D. Dissertation, University of California, Irvine, 2000.

[NetVOs98] Manju K. Ahuja and Kathleen M. Carley "Network Structure in Virtual Organizations." JCMC-3-(4) June 1998.

[OGSAAnalysis] Dennis Gannon, Kenneth Chiu, Madhusudhan Govindaraju, and Aleksander Slominski. *An Analysis of the Open Grid Services Architecture.* Department of Computer Science, Indiana University, Bloomington, IN.

[QuadSieve01] Eric Landquist. The Quadratic Sieve Factoring Algorithm. *MATH 488: Cryptographic Algorithms.* December 14, 2001. Available online at *http://www.math.uiuc.edu/~landquis/quadsieve.pdf*

[RSAGuts01] Francis Litterio. *The Mathematical Guts of RSA Encryption.* 1999–2001. Available online at *http://world.std.com/~franl/crypto/rsa-guts.html,* 2001.

[Schneier96] Bruce Schneier. *Applied Cryptography,* 2nd edition. John Wiley & Sons, 1996.

[SOAP1.2.1.03] M. Gudgin, M. Hadley, N. Mendelsohn, J-J. Moreau, and H. Nielsen, *SOAP Version 1.2 Part 1: Messaging Framework, W3C Recommendation.* Available online at *http://www.w3.org/TR/2003/REC-soap12-part1-20030624/,* 24 June 2003.

[SOAP1.2.2.03] SOAP M. Gudgin, M. Hadley, N. Mendelsohn, J-J. Moreau, and H. Nielsen, *Version 1.2 Part 2: Adjuncts, W3C Recommendation.* Available online at *http://www.w3.org/TR/2003/REC-soap12-part2-20030624/,* 24 June 2003.

[URIRFC98] T. Berners-Lee, R. Fielding, L. Masinter, *Uniform Resource Identifiers (URI): Generic Syntax,* IETF RFC 2396, August 1998.

[WebServices01] M. Paolucci, N. Srinivasan, and K. Sycara, OWL Ontology of Web Service Architecture Concepts. Available online October 2004 at *http://www.daml.org/services/swsa/note/swsa-note_v2.html.*

Part III The Globus Toolkit

This part includes a comprehensive study of the main grid protocols from a developer's perspective. This part has plenty of source code and figures including the following:

Core: Core grid services provide basic interfaces and functionality for hosting environments. Chapter 7 describes integration for two popular hosting environments including Apache Tomcat and IBM WebSphere. This chapter also includes configuration and troubleshooting tips for both environments as well as others.

Security: Security is one of the foundations of grid computing. This chapter includes an overview of the grid security infrastructure (GSI) as well as software to take advantage of all the GSI features. This chapter goes beyond traditional development guides providing a set of Web components to exploit all GSI features including certificates, private keys, grid proxies, certificate requests, and signature. It also includes troubleshooting advice when for integrating GSI with Web application software such as WebSphere.

Resource Management: Resource management allows running jobs remotely as well as monitoring, and terminating a job. It also provides fault tolerance and interfaces for integration with resource schedulers. Chapter 9 describes the Globus Resource Allocation Manager (GRAM) with plenty of source code, installation scripts, and troubleshooting tips.

Data Management: The goal of data management is the implementation of high-performance, secure, robust data transfer mechanisms for computational grids. Chapter 10 includes a comprehensive guide to developing applications that used the GridFTP protocol for data transfer. Source code is described for connecting and transferring data between hosts as well as third-party transfers and other techniques.

Information Services: Information Services provide for resource discovery, selection, and optimization. The protocol described in Chapter 11 is the Monitoring and Discovery Service (MDS) and its use within virtual organizations (VOs) to obtain a view of the capabilities and services provided by a computational grid. Source code for this chapter includes custom data providers for the MD3 and MD2 families as well as default providers.

Commodity Grid Kits (CoGs): Commodity frameworks are designed to provide service reusability and integration with grid services to enhance their functionality, maintenance, and deployment. In Chapter 12, the most popular language bindings are explained, including Java, Python, and Practical Extraction and Report Language (PERL). Source code for the APIs of the Java CoG kit is included for resource and data management as well as security.

Web Services Resource Framework (WSRF): WSRF attempts to make the transition from stateless services into stateful services. A stateful service is able to keep track of the changes made to its state through the propagation of Simple Object Access Protocol (SOAP) messages between client and server. WSRF represent the evolution of Web services and their convergence with grid services to form the next generation of distributed systems. Source code for Chapter 13 includes a WSRF-enabled large integer factorization service as well as deployment, testing, and troubleshooting instructions.

7 Core

In This Chapter

- Concepts
- Architecture
- Hosting Environments
- Summary
- References

This chapter provides background information on the core component of the Globus Toolkit. The topics discussed here include the following:

- Basic concepts on the structure of the core and its architecture
- A set of installation transcripts for the GT core and Tomcat and WebSphere application server hosting environments
- Common installation errors as well as troubleshooting tips for the core installation

7.1 CONCEPTS

Grids are environments that enable software applications to integrate devices, displays, and computational and information resources that are managed by diverse organizations in geographically dispersed locations. Grid computing enables sharing resources that are located in different places based on heterogeneous architectures and belonging to different management domains. Computer grids create a powerful pool of computing resources capable of running the most demanding scientific and engineering applications required by researchers and businesses today.

The Globus Toolkit is considered by many to be today's de facto standard for grid applications. The Globus Toolkit is an open architecture, open source software package that focuses on the following areas: resource management, data management and access, application development environments, information services, and security.

Resource management focuses on providing uniform and scalable mechanisms for naming and locating computational and communication resources on remote systems, and for incorporating these resources into parallel and distributed computations.

Data management focuses on handling large amounts of data (terabytes or petabytes). Next generation applications may also require access to distributed data applications, such as collaborative environments, Grid-enabled RDBMS systems, and so on [GridRDT04].

Information services require high-performance execution in distributed computing environments with careful selection and configuration of computers, networks, and other resources as well as of the protocols and algorithms used by applications.

Security establishes secure relationships between a large number of dynamically created objects and across a range of administrative domains, each with its own local security policy.

7.2 ARCHITECTURE

The hosting environment is the component that implements the Web server functionality (see Figure 7.1). Tomcat or WebSphere are examples of hosting environments. Within the hosting environment, the Grid Services Container is an Open Grid Services Infrastructure (OGSI)–compliant runtime that provides a layer of abstraction from specific implementation settings such as persistence mechanisms. It also controls the lifecycle of services, and the dispatching of remote requests to service instances. The main design goal of the Grid Services Container is to make it as implementation independent as possible. Within the service container, the OGSI component implements standard grid service interfaces such as GridService, Fac-

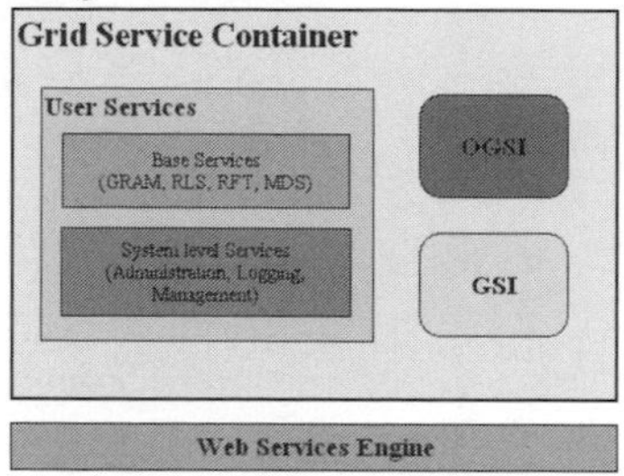

FIGURE 7.1 GT3 Core architecture.

tory, Notification, HandleResolver, and ServiceGroup. Service providers do not interact with the interfaces directly but, rather, configure them for the provided services [SandholmGawor03].

Grid security infrastructure (GSI) implements transport-level and message-level security. Transport-level security is provided for compatibility with previous C clients. Globus discourages its use and does not guarantee its support in future versions. Instead, Globus recommends message-level security based on WS-Security, XML-Signature, and XML-Encryption standards. Other standards used by GSI include Public Key Infrastructure (PKI), X509 certificates, Java Cryptography Extensions (JCE) and Java Authentication and Authorization Service (JAAS) [SandholmGawor03].

GT3 ships with a set of user services built on top of OGSI and GSI. These services are divided into system-level services and base services. System-level services are general-purpose services designed to facilitate the use of other services. They encapsulate tasks such as administration, logging, and management. Base services provide functionality in the areas of remote execution (GRAM), data management (RFT, RLS, GridFTP), and information services (MDS3). Base services are built on top of the system services, OGSI and GSI.

7.3 HOSTING ENVIRONMENTS

The purpose of this chapter is to explore the deployment of the GT3 OGSA service container in popular hosting environments also known as application servers. Integration of the OGSA container with custom application servers such as WebSphere or JBoss can be a time-consuming process. OGSA provides a built-in hosting environment and supports Apache Tomcat out of the box (see Figure 7.1). Integration with WebSphere and other Java-based containers can cause many headaches especially if the container uses its own implementation of the JCE for security.

7.3.1 Apache Tomcat

Deploying the OGSA services container in Apache Tomcat is as simple as running the following command:

```
C:\ogsa-3.2.1>ant deployTomcat
-Dtomcat.dir=
"C:\Program Files\Apache Software Foundation\Tomcat 5.0"
```

This command will deploy the required libraries and deployment descriptors to the proper locations and set things up (see Figures 7.2 and 7.3).

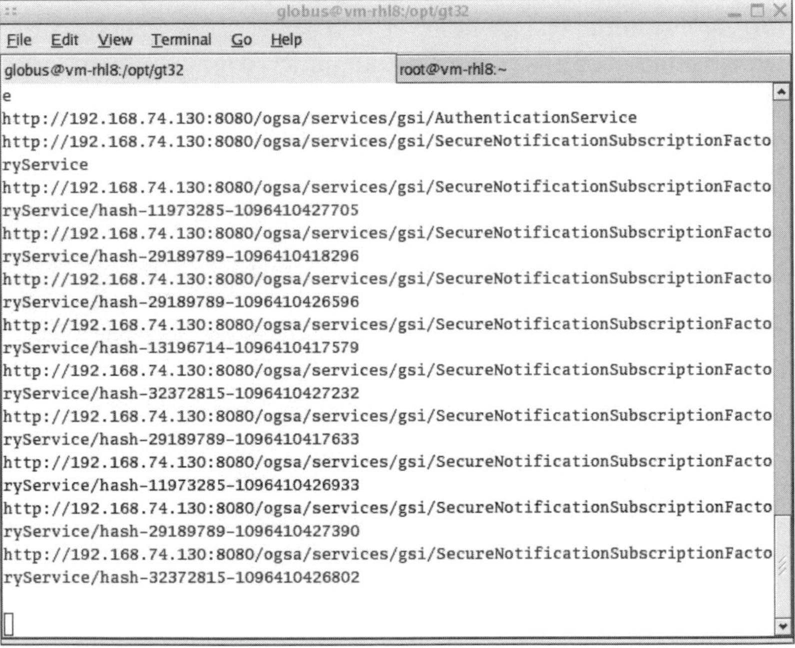

FIGURE 7.2 OGSA default hosting environment.

7.3.2 WebSphere Application Server v5.1

Deploying your OGSA container in IBM WebSphere represents a bit more of a challenge. Many developers might be temped to just create a *web project* for OGSA and copy the required libraries from the Globus distribution. This approach will certainly create a hosting environment for your services container, but it will create problems when dealing with GSI, specifically when you try to decrypt private keys. Follow these steps to set up your OGSA container within WebSphere:

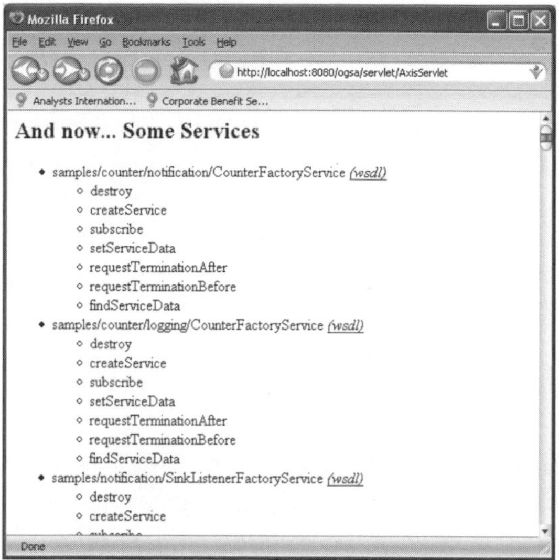

FIGURE 7.3 OGSA services container under Apache Tomcat.

Step 1: Create a Web Project and Enterprise Application for the OGSA Services Container

Copy the required libraries, schema files, and deployment descriptors from your OGSA distribution to the enterprise application. This step can be easily done within the WebSphere Studio Application Developer (see Figure 7.4).

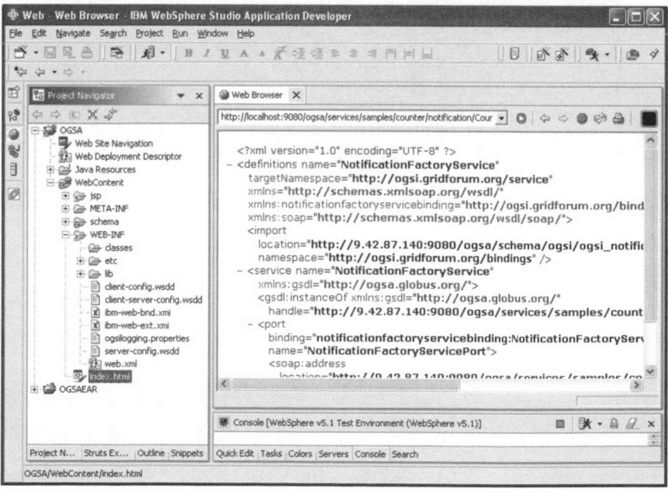

FIGURE 7.4 An OGSA enterprise application under WebSphere Studio v5.1.1.

Start the WebSphere server and verify this step by opening a Web browser to the local container at *http://localhost:9080/ogsa/services/*. The Axis welcome page should be displayed. Look at the Axis servlet and make sure the list of deployed services shows up and that the Web Service Description Language (WSDL) for the services can be displayed as shown.

When creating the enterprise application, make sure you set the context root of the project to OGSA.

Step 2: Create a Shared Library Location for GSI Security Libraries

At this point, you should be able to start your GT3 service browser and run services *without* security. Before running secure services, you should create a *shared library* for GSI to prevent many security problems explained in the troubleshooting section. Log in to your *WebSphere Administration Console,* under *Environment-Shared Libraries,* create a shared library location for GSI, then add the required JCE libraries (see Figure 7.5).

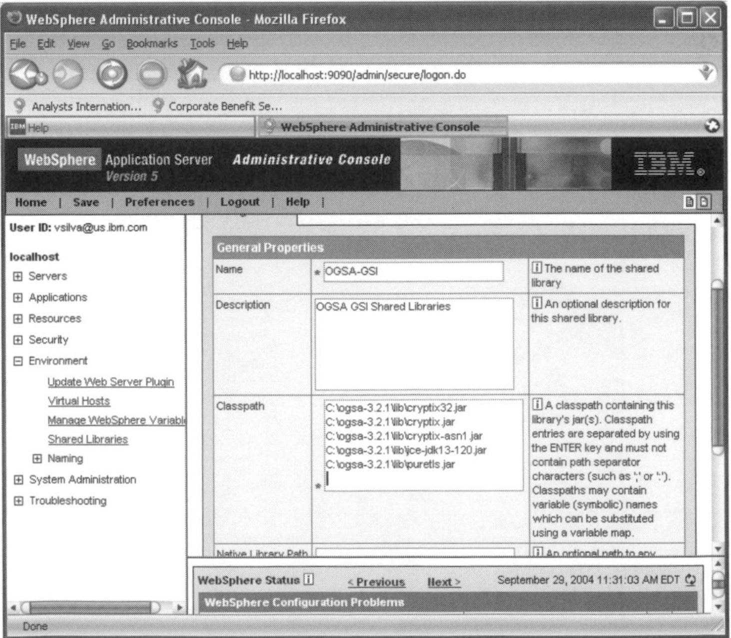

FIGURE 7.5 A shared library location for GSI under WebSphere Application Server 5.1.

Step 3: Associate the New Shared Library with the Enterprise Application

Now a reference must be created to link the new *shared library* to the *OGSA enterprise application*. In the administrator console, click *Applications/Enterprise Applications/OGSA*, then scroll down to *shared libraries* and add a reference to the newly created GSI library (see Figure 7.6).

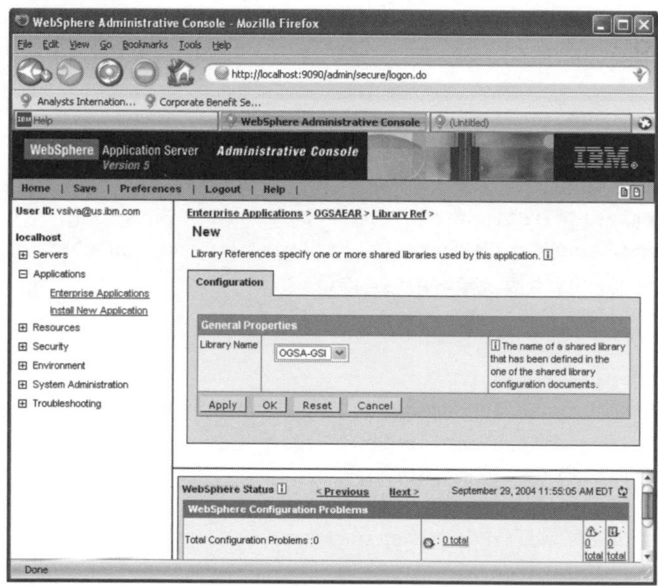

FIGURE 7.6 Shared library location reference to the OGSA enterprise application.

If you are an experienced WebSphere system administrator or you don't have the administrator console available to your distribution, these changes can be done manually. Simply look for the files libraries.xml and deployment.xml under the WebSphere installation directory. Libraries.xml contains the library class paths in the following form:

```
<?xml version="1.0" encoding="UTF-8"?>

<libraries:Library xmi:version="2.0"
xmlns:xmi="http://www.omg.org/XMI"
xmlns:libraries =
"http://www.ibm.com/websphere/appserver/schemas/5.0/libraries.xmi"
xmi:id="Library_1096472200839"
name="OGSA-GSI"
description="OGSA GSI Shared Libraries">
```

```
  <classPath>C:\ogsa-3.2.1\lib\cryptix-asn1.jar</classPath>
  <classPath>C:\ogsa-3.2.1\lib\puretls.jar</classPath>
  <classPath>C:\ogsa-3.2.1\lib\jce-jdk13-120.jar</classPath>
  <classPath>C:\ogsa-3.2.1\lib\cryptix32.jar</classPath>
  <classPath>C:\ogsa-3.2.1\lib\cryptix.jar</classPath>

</libraries:Library>
```

Deployment.xml contains a reference to the created library:

```
<?xml version="1.0" encoding="UTF-8"?>
<appdeployment:Deployment
  xmi:version="2.0"
  xmlns:xmi=http://www.omg.org/XMI
  xmlns:appdeployment="http://www.ibm.com/websphere/appserver
  /schemas/5.0/appdeployment.xmi"
  xmi:id="Deployment_1">

  <deployedObject
    xmi:type="appdeployment:ApplicationDeployment"
    xmi:id="ApplicationDeployment_1"
    startingWeight="10"
    binariesURL="${WS_EAR_OGSAEAR}"
    useMetadataFromBinaries="true"
    reloadInterval="0"
    reloadEnabled="false">

    <targetMappings
      xmi:id="DeploymentTargetMapping_1"
      enable="true"
      target="ServerTarget_1" />

    <modules
      xmi:type="appdeployment:WebModuleDeployment"
      xmi:id="WebModuleDeployment_1"
      startingWeight="10000"
      uri="OGSA.war">

      <targetMappings
        xmi:id="DeploymentTargetMapping_2"
        target="ServerTarget_1" />
    </modules>
```

```
    <classloader
      xmi:id="Classloader_1"
      mode="PARENT_FIRST">
      <libraries
        xmi:id="LibraryRef_1096473578961"
        libraryName="OGSA-GSI" />
    </classloader>
  </deployedObject>

  <deploymentTargets
    xmi:type="appdeployment:ServerTarget"
    xmi:id="ServerTarget_1"
    name="server1"
    nodeName="localhost" />

</appdeployment:Deployment>
```

7.3.3 Troubleshooting WebSphere

The following section contains an overview of some the errors found when deploying OGSA on WebSphere and especially when attempting to run secure services. This overview can help you set up your OGSA environment in WebSphere.

7.3.3.1 Class Loader Errors

Message:

```
E SRVE0026E: [Servlet Error]-
[Error while defining class:
 org.globus.axis.transport.GSIHTTPTransport
This error indicates that the class:
Error while defining class: org.globus.axis.gsi.GSIConstants

This error indicates that the class:
org.globus.gsi.GSIConstants
could not be located while defining the class:
  org.globus.axis.gsi.GSIConstants
This is often caused by having the class at a
higher point in the classloader hierarchy
```

Possible Cause: This message is thrown by the Axis servlet when attempting to display a service WSDL. It is probably caused by missing OGSA libraries in the classpath.

Solution: Make sure all required OGSA libraries are included in your enterprise application classpath.

7.3.3.2 Configuration Errors (`InvalidHandlerFaultType`)

Message:

```
Failed to obtain WSDL:
org.gridforum.ogsi.InvalidHandlerFaultType:
http://127.0.1:8080
/ogsa/services/core/registry/ContainerregistryService
```

Possible Cause: This error is thrown by the *service browser* client when attempting to connect to the OGSA container. It might be caused by an invalid hostname or port number.

Solution: Make sure all required OGSA libraries and schema and configuration files are placed in the right locations. Also check that the hostname and port number are correct in the connection URL.

7.3.3.3 Application Server Errors (`Class Cast Exceptions`)

Message:

```
TRAS0014I: The following exception was logged
java.lang.ClassCastException:
com.ibm.ws.webservices.engine.Message at
org.apache.axis.MessageContext.setMessage(MessageContext.java:607)
```

Possible cause: This error is thrown by the application server when running a secure service from the Globus service browser. Its probable cause is a collision between the Axis and the WebSphere Application Server (WAS) Web Services implementations.

Solution: One solution is to rename the WebSphere Web Services implementation library (webservices.jar) to avoid the collision. Rename the file: `$WAS_ROOT\webservices.jar` *to* `$WAS_ROOT\webservices.jar.old`.

7.3.3.4 Security Errors (`NoSuchAlgorithm`)

Message:

```
java.lang.InternalError:
java.security.NoSuchAlgorithmException:
class configured for Cipher:
com.ibm.crypto.provider.DESedeCipher
is not a subclass of xjava.security.Cipher
at
```

```
COM.claymoresystems.crypto.PEMData.writePEMObject
(PEMData.java:172)
    at
COM.claymoresystems.crypto.EAYEncryptedPrivateKey
  .writePrivateKey (EAYEncryptedPrivateKey.java:83)
    ...
```

Possible cause: This error has been a major source of headaches for many people involved in OGSA and WebSphere. It is thrown because the GSI security libraries have not been properly configured. If you take at look at the directory structure of the OGSA deployment under Tomcat, you will notice the GSI security libraries cryptix.jar, cryptix32.jar, cryptix-asn1.jar, jce-jdk13-120.jar and puretls.jar have been saved under the `$TOMCAT_ROOT/common/lib` folder. A similar configuration is required for all hosting environments.

Solution: The JCE should be loaded at server boot time to prevent these errors. To fix this error, a *shared library* directory must be created in WebSphere with the JCE libraries as explained in the previous section.

7.3.4 Other Hosting Environments

When attempting to install the OGSA Web Services container in other hosting environments, keep in mind that all the libraries, deployment descriptors, configuration files, and schema files must be placed in the correct locations. Most hosting environments will require a *context root,* which should be OGSA. The security libraries are a major source of problems and should be the first thing to look into if any problems are found. Looking at the OGSA installation under Apache Tomcat has been a valuable template of how and where the files should be placed.

7.4 SUMMARY

Grids are environments that enable software applications to integrate devices, displays, and computational and information resources that are managed by diverse organizations in geographically disperse locations. Grid computing enables sharing resources that are located in different places based on heterogeneous architectures and belonging to different management domains. This chapter has introduced the core component of the Globus Toolkit including basic concepts, installation transcripts, common installation errors, and troubleshooting tips.

REFERENCES

[GridRDT04] W. E. Allcock, I. Foster, and R. Madduri. "Reliable Data Transport: A Critical Service for the Grid." Building Service Based Grids Workshop, Global Grid Forum 11, June 2004.

[SandholmGawor03] Thomas Sandholm and Jarek Gawor. *Globus Toolkit 3 Core—A Grid Service Container Framework.* Accessed online July 2, 2003 from *http://www-unix.globus.org/toolkit/3.0/ogsa/docs/gt3_core.pdf.*

8 Security

In This Chapter

- Grid Security Infrastructure (GSI) Overview
- Certificate Basics
- Java Certificate Services—Web Tools for X.509 Certificates
- Globus Toolkit 3 Security Libraries
- Summary
- References

This chapter includes the following topics:

- An overview of the Grid Security Infrastructure (GSI).
- An explanation of the basic structure of a digital certificate (also known as an X.509 certificate) along with a set of programs for certificate, key, and grid proxy generation and signature.
- A sample Web-based application for certificate manipulation very similar in functionality to a certificate authority (CA) along with command-line tools and installation transcripts for two popular application servers: Apache Tomcat and IBM WebSphere.
- Tips on the integration of the Globus Toolkit security libraries and other Open Grid Services Architecture (OGSA) hosting environments along with common error messages and troubleshooting.

8.1 GRID SECURITY INFRASTRUCTURE (GSI) OVERVIEW

GSI enables secure authentication and communication over computer networks. It is a Globus Toolkit component that provides a number of useful services for grids, including mutual authentication and single sign-on.

GSI is based on proven standards such as public key encryption, X.509 certificates, and the Secure Sockets Layer (SSL). Extensions to these standards have been added for single sign-on and delegation [GridPhysiology02].

Manipulating grid certificates using the Globus Toolkit 3.0 in windows environments is an uncomfortable situation. It usually requires system administrators or users to install GT3 on Linux systems, then use the command-line scripts to generate certificates and move those certificates to their windows systems. An easier alternative, provided by the Java Cog Kit [CogKit01], is to write your own certificate generation software as demonstrated by the Java programs throughout this chapter. These programs are used to create certificate requests and sign them, or to create user or host certificates or self-signed (CA) certificates, and grid proxies.

8.2 CERTIFICATE BASICS

One of the main concepts in GSI authentication is certificates. Users and services are identified on grid environments via certificates, which contain information about that user or service such as an identity, time stamp, a signature, and others.

A GSI certificate includes information such as the following about a subject [GSIGlobus03]:

- Identifies the person or object that the certificate represents.
- The public key that belongs to the subject.
- The identity of a CA that has signed the certificate. CAs certify that the public key and the identity both belong to the subject.
- The digital signature of the named CA.

A third-party certificate authority is used to certify the link between the public key and the subject in the certificate.

8.2.1 Understanding X.509 Certificates

Certificates are data structures that bind public key values to subjects by having a trusted CA digitally sign each certificate. A certificate has a limited valid lifetime that is indicated in its signature; they are usually distributed via nontrusted communications and can be stored in unsecured media. Certificates can be concatenated in chains. Thus, a certificate for *user A* signed by one CA can have additional certificates of CAs signed by other CAs. Such chains or certification paths are required when the public key user does not already hold a guaranteed copy of the public key of the CA that signed the certificate. For example, if user A has a certificate signed by CA1 but requires a signature by CA2, then a certification path can be established by signing user A cert with CA1 and then signing CA1 with CA2 certificate [X509Pki99].

8.2.2 Typical Public Key Infrastructure (PKI) Model

A public key infrastructure is composed of several entities that interact with each other in different fashions (see Figure 8.1).

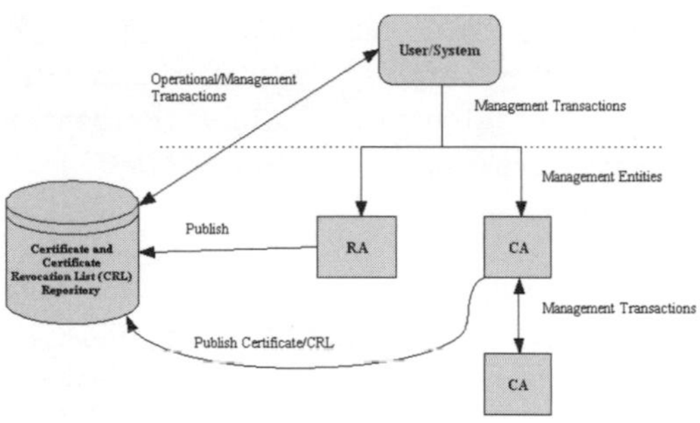

FIGURE 8.1 Typical PKI infrastructure.

Certification Authorities (CAs): Trusted third-party entities that sign certificates and establish a chain of trust between two entities.

Revocation Authority (RA): Optional entity to which a CA delegates management functions. RAs are in charge of invalidating certificates when the validity period expires or other circumstances occur such as change of name, employee termination resulting on the private key being compromised, and so on. Revocation is accomplished with a time-stamped list (certificate revocation list or CRL) identifying revoked certificates signed by a CA and freely available in a public repository [X509Pki99].

Operational Protocols: Used to deliver certificates via Lightweight Directory Access Protocol (LDAP), HTTP, FTP, or X.509.

Management Protocols: Management protocols provide interactions between PKI users and management entities (CAs), or between two CAs that cross-certify each other. This functionality includes the following:

1. *Registration:* Where the user makes itself aware to the CA.
2. *Initialization:* Where the user key pairs are initialized and public keys among the participating entities are exchanged.
3. *Certification:* Where a CA issues a certificate to a given user or system.
4. *Key pair recovery:* Where backup systems are provided for public and private keys.
5. *Revocation and cross-certification:* Where certificates are invalidated, and two CAs exchange certificate information.

8.2.3 Certificate Fields

An X.509 v3 certificate is composed of the following sequence of fields [X509Pki99]:

```
Certificate  ::=  SEQUENCE  {
        tbsCertificate       TBSCertificate,
        signatureAlgorithm   AlgorithmIdentifier,
        signatureValue       BIT STRING  }


TBSCertificate  ::=  SEQUENCE  {
        version         [0]  EXPLICIT Version DEFAULT v1,
        serialNumber         CertificateSerialNumber,
        signature            AlgorithmIdentifier,
        issuer               Name,
        validity             Validity,
        subject              Name,
        subjectPublicKeyInfo SubjectPublicKeyInfo,
        issuerUniqueID  [1]  IMPLICIT UniqueIdentifier OPTIONAL,
                             -- If present, version shall be v2 or v3
        subjectUniqueID [2]  IMPLICIT UniqueIdentifier OPTIONAL,
                             -- If present, version shall be v2 or v3
        extensions      [3]  EXPLICIT Extensions OPTIONAL
                             -- If present, version shall be v3
        }
```

Certificates are usually instantiated using certificate factories. The JCE provide this functionality and make the tasks of using such factories simple. For example, the following code demonstrates how to instantiate an X.509 certificate:

```
InputStream in= new FileInputStream("cert-filename");
CertificateFactory cf= CertificateFactory.getInstance("X.509");
X509Certificate cert= (X509Certificate)cf.generateCertificate(in);
in.close();
```

8.2.4 GSI Proxies

A proxy is a data structure used by GSI to provide: mutual authentication, confidential communication delegation, and single sign-on on grid environments. Internally, a proxy is composed of a new certificate (with a public key) containing the owner's identity slightly modified to identify it as a proxy, and an unencrypted private key. The certificate is signed by the owner, rather than a CA, and it has an associated lifetime. Because the private key is unencrypted, it must be kept secure. However, because the proxy has a lifetime or expiration time, the private key doesn't have to be kept as secure as the owner's private key. Thus, the proxy can be stored in local media as long as the access permissions on the file prevent unauthorized access. GSI uses the proxy certificate and private key for mutual authentication without entering a password [GSIGlobus03].

8.2.4.1 Mutual Authentication

For mutual authentication to occur between two users A and B, both entities must have copies of each other's CA certificates besides their own certificate and key pair [GSIGlobus03]. A connection must be established to proceed with the authentication steps (see Figure 8.2).

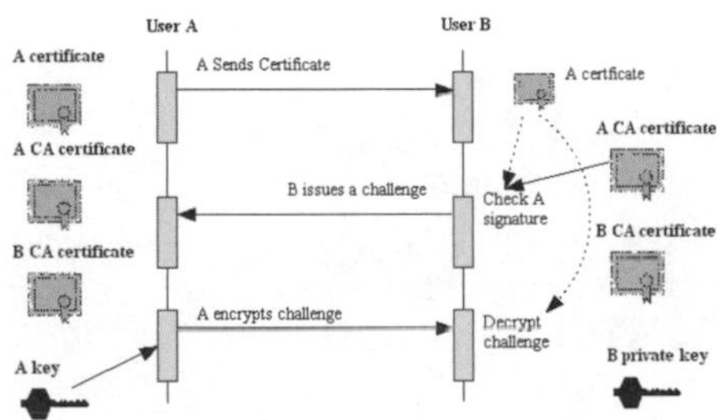

FIGURE 8.2 GSI mutual authentication.

1. A establishes a connection and sends its certificate and public key.
2. B checks A's certificate for tampering by validating the signature using A's CA certificate, a technique known as nonrepudiation.
3. B issues a random challenge to be encrypted by A.
4. A encrypts B's challenge using its private key (A) and sends it back.
5. B decrypts the challenge using A's public key.
6. If successful, then B has authenticated A.

The same process is repeated for user B to authenticate user A. The process finishes when both entities have authenticated each other.

8.2.4.2 Confidentiality

By default, GSI does not encrypt the data sent across mutual parties. Once mutual authentication has completed, no data will be encrypted. This is to improve performance and reduce communication overhead. However, GSI can be easily used to implement a key exchange algorithm for confidentiality (data encryption) [GSIGlobus03].

8.2.4.3 Integrity

Message integrity prevents unauthorized third parties from sniffing communications and then changing the message contents. GSI provided built-in message integrity.

8.2.5 Certificate Generation

The program in Listing 8.1 demonstrates the APIs available in the Java CoG kit 1.1, part of GT3, to generate a user certificate or certificate request, sign certificates and create proxies. CoG can serve as the basis for a Java CA implementation, if you don't want to use the Unix-based simple CA available at the Globus Web site. We will start by creating a certificate generator class.

LISTING 8.1 CertificateGenerator.java, a Program to Generate X.509 Certificates

```
package com.gsi;

import java.io.*;
import java.net.*;
import java.util.Properties;
import java.util.Vector;
import java.security.*;
import java.security.cert.*;

import org.globus.gsi.*;
import org.globus.gsi.gssapi.*;
import org.globus.gsi.bc.*;
import org.globus.util.Base64;

// for cert rq generation
import COM.claymoresystems.cert.*;
import cryptix.util.mime.Base64OutputStream;

/**
 * A class to automate the Globus Proxy creation process
 * analog to: setp-gsi script in Linux
 *
 */
```

```
public class CertificateGenerator {
      private final boolean DEBUG = false;

      // Common Name + Org Unit used to create X509 DNs
      private String m_CommonName = null;
      private String m_OrgUnit = null;

      // Certs in PEM format
      private String m_PEMUserCert = null;
      private String m_PEMUserKey = null;

      /**
       * Constructor for CertificateGenerator
       * @param cn X509 Common Name, such as an email address
       * @param orgUnit, Organization Unit
       * Arguments are used to create an X509 DN (Distinguished Name)
       */
      public CertificateGenerator(String cn, String orgUnit)
throws Exception
      {
              m_CommonName = cn;
              m_OrgUnit = orgUnit;
      }
```

8.2.6 Creating a Self-Signed User Certificate and Private Key

The first step in setting up GSI is to create a signed used certificate and a private key. These two arguments can later be used to generate a Globus credential also known as "proxy" that provides access to your grid resources. In Unix systems, the `$GLOBUS_LOCATION`/setup-gsi.sh script will start by creating a "certificate request" that must be submitted to the Globus CA for signature. A certificate authority testifies that indeed you are the person you claim to be. In this sample class, we will use the `COM.claymoresystems.cert.CertRequest` class to make a "self-signed" user certificate along with a private key encrypted with a user's password. This technique is demonstrated by the code in Listing 8.2.

LISTING 8.2 Creating a Self-Signed Certificate and Private Key

```
/**
 * CertKeyGenerator: Creates a Signed User certificate and a private
key
 * by generating a self signed user certificate.
 * The Private key is encrypted with Pwd
 * @param Pwd = Challenge pwd (used to encrypt the key)
 */
```

```
public void createUserCertAndKey(String Pwd)
    throws NoSuchAlgorithmException, Exception
{
  debug("CertKeyGenerator OrgUnit="
        + m_OrgUnit
        + " CommonName="
        + m_CommonName + " Pwd=" + Pwd);

  // sw/bw are buffers for the priv key PEM
  StringWriter sw   = new StringWriter();
  BufferedWriter bw = new BufferedWriter(sw);

  // generate a 512 bit RSA key pair
  KeyPair kp = CertRequest.generateKey(
      "RSA", 512, Pwd, bw, true);

  // certs are valid for 1 year: 31536000 secs
  byte[] reqBytes = CertRequest.makeSelfSignedCert(kp,
      makeGridCertDN(m_OrgUnit, m_CommonName), 31536000);

  // buffer for the key
  m_PEMUserKey = sw.toString();

  // encode cert in PEM format
  m_PEMUserCert = writePEM(reqBytes,
                           "-----BEGIN CERTIFICATE-----\n",
                           "-----END CERTIFICATE-----\n");
}
```

A call to `CertRequest.generateKey("RSA", 512, Pwd, bw, true);` should do trick. The arguments to this call represent: a cipher used for generation (RSA), the strength of the certificate keys in bits (512), a password used to encrypt the private key, and a buffered writer to store the private key. This class is contained in the *puretls.jar* archive distributed with GT3/Java CoG kit.

This call will return a key pair object (from the `java.security` package) that can be then used by the following instruction to generate a self-signed certificate: `CertRequest.makeSelfSignedCert(kp, makeGridCertDN(m_OrgUnit, m_CommonName), 31536000)`. Both user certificate and private key are encoded in base 64 —Privacy Enhanced Mail (PEM) format (take a look at the *writePEM* function).

8.2.7 Creating Credentials from User Certificates

With a user certificate and private key, we are ready to create a GSI proxy. Note that the package *org.globus.security.** has been deprecated and replaced with *org.globus.gsi.**

that uses the open Generic Security Service Application Program Interface (GSS-API) [GSS-API93]. The method shown in Listing 8.3 will create a credential compatible with GT3 or GT 2.2x.

LISTING 8.3 Creating a Globus Proxy

```
/**
 * Create a Globus proxy required to run jobs on the Grid.
 * This method is used to create a proxy if you have a cert file
 * and a key file encoded in PEM format. Certs come from input streams.
 * @param inUserCert User Cert input stream
 * @param inUserKey private key
 * @param pwd Password used to decrypt the private key
 * @param bits Strength of the proxy
 * @param hours Proxy lifetime
 */
public static GlobusCredential createGlobusProxy(
InputStream inUserCert, /* certificate */
InputStream inUserKey,  /* private key */
String pwd,             /* key passphrase */
int bits,               /* cert strength 512, 1024, etc… */
int hours               / lifetime in hrs */
)
throws Exception

{
  // Load cert and key
  X509Certificate userCert = CertUtil.loadCertificate(inUserCert);
  OpenSSLKey key = new BouncyCastleOpenSSLKey(inUserKey);

  if (key.isEncrypted()) {
    try {
      key.decrypt(pwd);
    }
    catch (GeneralSecurityException e) {
      throw new Exception("Wrong password or other security error");
    }
  }

  PrivateKey userKey = key.getPrivateKey();

  // Load certificate factory
  BouncyCastleCertProcessingFactory factory =
      BouncyCastleCertProcessingFactory.getDefault();
```

```
  return factory.createCredential(
new X509Certificate[] {userCert},
userKey,
bits,
hours * 3600,
GSIConstants.GSI_2_PROXY, null
);
}
```

If you have a PEM-encoded proxy file (downloaded from your Unix system), the utility method shown in Listing 8.4 can be used to build a `GlobusCredential` object.

LISTING 8.4 Creating a Credential from a PEM-Encoded File

```
/**
 * Create a Globus proxy from a PEM encoded proxy string
 * @param sProxyPEM: Globus proxy as a PEM encoded string
 */
public static GlobusCredential
    createGlobusCredFromPEM(String sProxyPEM)
    throws Exception
{
  // user certificate IS
  ByteArrayInputStream is = new
      ByteArrayInputStream(sProxyPEM.getBytes());

  TrustedCertificates trustedCerts = null;
  GlobusCredential p = null;

  try {
    // load default trusted (CA) certificates
    TrustedCertificates.loadDefaultTrustedCertificates();
  }
  catch (Exception e) {
    throw new
        Exception("Unable to load trusted certs: "
                  + e.getMessage());
  }

  // generate a grid proxy
  try {
    p = new GlobusCredential(is);
  }
```

```
  catch (Exception e) {
    throw new Exception("Unable to load Proxy:"
                        + e.getMessage());
  }
  return p;
}
```

8.2.8 Creating a Certificate Request

If you just want to submit your certificate request to be signed by another CA, you can create it by using the function shown in Listing 8.5.

LISTING 8.5 Creating a Certificate Request

```
/**
 * Cert request Generator.
 * @param CommonName Common name
 * @param OrgUnit Organization Unit
 * @param Pwd Password
 * @return a PEM encoded string (Certificate request)
 */
public static String createCertRequest(
    String CommonName
    /* Certificate owner example: John Doe */
    , String OrgUnit
    /* Organizational Unit. Example: Info Technology */
    , String Pwd
    /* Certificate passphrase, used to encrypt the key */
    )

throws IOException, NoSuchProviderException, NoSuchAlgorithmException

{
  StringWriter sw = new StringWriter();
  // Private key PEM buffer
  BufferedWriter bw = new BufferedWriter(sw);

  // generate a 512 bit  RSA key pair
  KeyPair kp = CertRequest.generateKey("RSA", 512, Pwd, bw, true);

  // certificate bytes buffer
  byte[] req = CertRequest.makePKCS10Request(kp,
      makeGridCertDN(OrgUnit, CommonName)
      );
```

```
    ByteArrayOutputStream bos = new ByteArrayOutputStream();
    org.globus.util.PEMUtils.writeBase64(bos,
      "-----BEGIN CERTIFICATE REQUEST-----\n",
      req,
      "-----END CERTIFICATE REQUEST-----\n");

    // return the cert as a PEM encoded string
    return writePEM(req
                    , "-----BEGIN CERTIFICATE REQUEST-----\n"
                    ,
                    "-----END CERTIFICATE REQUEST-----\n");
  }
```

Our certificate generator is complemented with the utility functions (see Listing 8.6) used for tasks such as the following:

- Encoding certificate bytes in PEM format
- Creating X.509 distinguished names (DN) for generation purposes

LISTING 8.6 Certificate Encoding Utility Methods

```
/** Write a sequence of bytes as a PEM encoded string */
public static String writePEM( byte[] bytes, String hdr, String ftr )
   throws IOException
   {
     ByteArrayOutputStream bos = new ByteArrayOutputStream();
     Base64OutputStream b64os = new Base64OutputStream( bos );
     b64os.write( bytes );
     b64os.flush();
     b64os.close();

     ByteArrayInputStream bis =
        new ByteArrayInputStream( bos.toByteArray() );
     InputStreamReader irr = new InputStreamReader( bis );
     BufferedReader r = new BufferedReader( irr );

     StringBuffer buff = new StringBuffer();
     String line;
     buff.append( hdr );

     while ( ( line = r.readLine() ) != null )
     {
       buff.append( line + "\n" );
```

```
        }
        buff.append( ftr );
        return buff.toString();
    }

    /**
     Create an X509 Certificate distinguished name
     @param OrgUnit Organizational Unit
     @param CommonName Certificate owner
    */
    private static X509Name
       makeSimpleDN( String OrgUnit, String CommonName )
       {
         Vector tdn = new Vector();
         String[] o1 = new String[2];
         String[] o2 = new String[2];
         String[] ou = new String[2];
         String[] cn = new String[2];
         String[] cn1 = new String[2];

         o1[0] = "O";
         o1[1] = "IBM";
         o2[0] = "O";
         o2[1] = "Grid";
         ou[0] = "OU";
         ou[1] = OrgUnit;
         cn[0] = "CN";
         cn[1] = CommonName;

         tdn.addElement( o1 );
         tdn.addElement( o2 );
         tdn.addElement( ou );
         tdn.addElement( cn );

         // COM.claymoresystems.cert (puretls.jar)
         return CertRequest.makeSimpleDN( tdn );
    }

    private void debug( String text )
    {
      if ( DEBUG )
        System.out.println( this.getClass() + ": " + text );
    }
```

```
public String getUserCert()
{
  return m_PEMUserCert;
}

public String getUserKey()
{
  return m_PEMUserKey;
}
```

Finally, a certificate generator main function for testing purposes can be seen in Listing 8.7.

LISTING 8.7 Certificate Generator Test Function

```
/**
 * For testing purposes only
 */
public static void main(String[] args) {
  try {
    // Test 1: cert request
    String rqPEM = CertificateGenerator.
createCertRequest("Vladimir Silva", "ACME", "test");

    System.out.println("Cert Request\n" + rqPEM);

    // Test 2: User Cert & encrypted Private key (PEM encoded)
    CertificateGenerator gen =
new CertificateGenerator("Vladimir Silva",
        "ACME");

    gen.createUserCertAndKey("secret");

    System.out.println("User Cert\n" + gen.getUserCert());
    System.out.println("User Key\n" + gen.getUserKey());

    // Test 3: Globus Proxy (Credential) from Cert and Key
    ByteArrayInputStream inCert =
new ByteArrayInputStream(gen.getUserCert().
                    getBytes());
    ByteArrayInputStream inKey =
new ByteArrayInputStream(gen.getUserKey().
                    getBytes());
```

```
    GlobusCredential cred =
        createGlobusProxy(inCert, inKey, "testpwd", 512, 12);

    // Test 4: save proxy in pem format
    ByteArrayOutputStream bos = new ByteArrayOutputStream();
    cred.save(bos);

    System.out.println("Globus Credential Info\n" + cred.toString());
    System.out.println("Globus Credential PEM\n" + bos.toString());

    // load a proxy from PEM encoded string
    GlobusCredential cred1
= CertificateGenerator.createGlobusCredFromPEM(
bos.toString()
);
    System.out.println(
"Globus Credential Verification\n" + cred1.toString());

  }
  catch (Exception ex) {
    System.err.println("Main Error: " + ex.getMessage());
  }
}
```

The previous code requires the following libraries to be in your Java classpath:

- Commodity Grid Kit: `cog-jglobus.jar`, `log4j-core.jar`
- OGSA Security (JCE): `cryptix32.jar`, `cryptix-ans1.jar`, `jce-jdk13-117.jar`, `and puretls.jar`.

Both these libraries are included in the GT distribution. A run of the main program will produce output such as the following:

```
Cert Request
-----BEGIN CERTIFICATE REQUEST-----
MIH7MIGmAgEAMEUxDDAKBgNVBAoTA0lCTTENMAsGA1UEChMER3JpZDENMAsGA1UE
CxMEQUNNRTEXMBUGA1UEAxYOVmxhZGltaXIgU2lsdmEwWjALBgkqhkiG9w0BAQED
SwAwSAJBAK2XHqN5dYgCgJ1ZVs/6JmijnLlUSl7RVMVV0ECf7dHg0mVGbwA1ZEJQ
RaL0yGCYUv7rOF3MyGxRobfzkO6NkrMCAwEAATANBgkqhkiG9w0BAQUFAANBAGyF
F1UBdVnO9qpT6pf2zeSDLM5JY5nSLeaR/eau1BkyBDJ2hgrcqnroHAxcJ8MfCMJO
A2THH/cPIyrxPtRqnWw=
-----END CERTIFICATE REQUEST-----
```

```
User Cert
-----BEGIN CERTIFICATE-----
MIIBcjCCARwCAQAwDQYJKoZIhvcNAQEFBQAwRTEMMAoGA1UEChMDSUJNMQ0wCwYD
VQQKEwRHcmlkMQ0wCwYDVQQLEwRBQ01FMRcwFQYDVQQDFg5WbGFkaW1pciBTaWx2
YTAeFw0wMzA4MDkxNTEzNDFaFw0wNDA4MDgxNTEzNDFaMEUxDDAKBgNVBAoTA0lC
TTENMAsGA1UEChMER3JpZDENMAsGA1UECxMEQUNNRTEXMBUGA1UEAxYOVmxhZGlt
aXIgU2lsdmEwWjALBgkqhkiG9w0BAQEDSwAwSAJBAK2/BQtVdEgdORfCFkIupxyC
La/duZuN5Xln3Hw4B/eScyJKd4JpCxLlbBOywXZ/By63UFEww+CwkJnIg1sTMbcC
AwEAATANBgkqhkiG9w0BAQUFAANBAIJELfGdC2NS54EWMTrySLgqjjN/5/PP6tKV
APReCBMjOhAPFK19EOP+DtM/2G52WwXzZDL7z+U6laziNoKSu/s=
-----END CERTIFICATE-----

User Key
-----BEGIN RSA PRIVATE KEY-----
Proc-Type: 4,ENCRYPTED
DEK-Info: DES-EDE3-CBC,A94D69693CBB8D86

1qKvARBYM+Dz72nzcc5ZzYrzXHkIox1pbBjwrK4L1VQqZVM8s9/Tbau/W84guQOy
fcTVNJ4CBVonYdgiT5kTyYsamzHQKCiVCpC/XWOw7PTuiHODWl2gDXoEHH7SPkAg
wRuZdFhO281HfmKjICOOBtIndBW4+98dFc9usRXBVPNLNW7GELxqFueGISueLPOY
yOzsYVTs1ReZX1XgAV7vLgx/I939UHrpaoHS4i4orqTENsbLUUfcCYraU4cwiBZ2
AwCPLKCMV6hTanK/JlTOJParsC7TXwgCgSo27Jfv7Ioq2OqPR8ZiMlJ+Rxuepnox
zH2AlxXPy9X6Cx+VNDDIw4WVUE22D/aEaBQQaumiVEMCiKU7zdXWYtirpod8Lg9w
MWX9BUTrSphW7xb7PYYjudPGU7xfSpaaimnnJtwxTBA=
-----END RSA PRIVATE KEY-----

Globus Credential Info
subject    : O=IBM,O=Grid,OU=ACME,CN=Vladimir Silva,CN=proxy
issuer     : O=IBM,O=Grid,OU=ACME,CN=Vladimir Silva
strength   : 512 bits
timeleft   : 43199 sec
proxy type : full legacy globus proxy
Globus Credential PEM
-----BEGIN CERTIFICATE-----
MIIBhzCCATGgAwIBAgIBADANBgkqhkiG9w0BAQUFADBFMQwwCgYDVQQKEwNJQk0x
DTALBgNVBAoTBEdyaWQxDTALBgNVBAsTBEFDTUUxFzAVBgNVBAMWDlZsYWRpbWly
IFNpbHZhMB4XDTAzMDgwOTE1MDg1MFoXDTAzMDgxMDAzMTM1MFowVTEMMAoGA1UE
ChMDSUJNMQ0wCwYDVQQKEwRHcmlkMQ0wCwYDVQQLEwRBQ01FMRcwFQYDVQQDFg5W
bGFkaW1pciBTaWx2YTEOMAwGA1UEAxMFcHJveHkwWjANBgkqhkiG9w0BAQEFAANJ
ADBGAkEAnrnvlZ4tOOa+8pfiHzyVRTn+PAyezGzAbSNH9DX45VTiSAQe/WW1EczR
VTuIeRcnz8fXPiu/q55l3rVWhipdUwIBETANBgkqhkiG9w0BAQUFAANBAKRvKN8c
DRbswd8fDJoPonyiwnQUpk3OarmVeyaDxEcreMHKZwbDEBPh/KGAzyrRjSKNXuEM
YapXoT8UqCziJtg=
-----END CERTIFICATE-----
```

```
-----BEGIN RSA PRIVATE KEY-----
MIIBOQIBAAJBAJ6575WeLTjmvvKX4h88lUU5/jwMnsxswGOjR/Q1+OVU4kgEHv1l
tRHMOVU7iHkXJ8/H1z4rv6ueZd61VoYqXVMCARECQEFbnuNBIa4EqPp6xoVVLmfM
ldx9qsylQCzwaOwWOU9eiU1Ls+d2dDSkxXL2viEjvhB5S5hCko8y1o6pdxzDllkC
IQC4A6cCD75zj2JntByMZUDkqEQ8WmZOm2MOHzZ/Uwu19wIhANzRydW7h5UCkRxl
WgnDWuNIpixx/zGOdrxlB9p/jMyFAiEAjLd/tkhGWF6Wi4m7emuL+iZSTEUhDu9L
v4FHyscI9I8CIE3vsKXJt2HEq6+rTPRjEQTsduKClk3HOPcyt3pLIqKJAiEAgLoE
bcj8OkwKXcCTlJE1WxK+Dk4IK/XQNi/jtpUZs4g=
-----END RSA PRIVATE KEY-----

Globus Credential Verification
subject     : O=IBM,O=Grid,OU=ACME,CN=Vladimir Silva,CN=proxy
issuer      : O=IBM,O=Grid,OU=ACME,CN=Vladimir Silva
strength    : 512 bits
timeleft    : 43198 sec
proxy type  : full legacy globus proxy
```

8.3 JAVA CERTIFICATE SERVICES—WEB TOOLS FOR X.509 CERTIFICATES

The following sections describe a Web and command-line application called Java Certificate Services (JCS) included in the companion CD-ROM of this book. JCS is a set of Web and command-line tools created to assist system administrators and developers with the tedious task of managing user and host certificates in development grids. JCS is written to work specifically with the Globus and the Java CoG Toolkits, and it demonstrates techniques for certificate, key, and proxy generation.

8.3.1 Overview

JCS provides the following functionality:

- Certificate signing request (CSR) creation
- CSR signature
- X.509 certificate creation (useful for GT3 user for host certificates)
- Self-signed (CA) certificate creation services

JCS is built on top of the JCE used by GT3 to implement the GSI. The providers used currently are Cryptix (*http://www.cryptix.org*) and the Legion of the Bouncy Castle *http://www.bouncycastle.org*.

8.3.2 Installing JCS on a Windows or Linux Host

ON THE CD

Source and binary bundles for JCS are provided in the companion CD-ROM.

To install JCS, download the source bundle and decompress it into a folder on your host:

- On Windows systems, unzip the binary into a working folder such as C:\
- On Linux systems, untar the binary bundle: `tar zxvf cert-services.tar.gz –directory=/opt`

Look for the jCertServices-1.1 folder created and look at the *Readme.txt* or readme.html files for an in-depth description of this software.

8.3.3 Deploying the Web-Based Tool on Tomcat

JCS provides a very convenient Web-based tool that can be easily deployed on Apache Tomcat (*http://www.apache.org/*) or any J2EE/servlet container for that matter. JCS has been tested with Tomcat 4.1.27 and IBM WebSphere 4.x/5.x. To deploy the Web-based tool and build the source you will need *Apache Ant* from *http://ant.apache.org/*.

On Windows or Linux hosts, at the command prompt, type the following:

- In Linux: `cd /opt/jCertServices-1.1`
- In Windows: `cd c:\jcertServices-1.1`
- In Windows/Linux: `ant-Dtomcat.dir=<tomcat root> deployTomcat`

Make sure to replace `<tomcat root>` with the full path to your Tomcat installation, for example: `/opt/tomcat-4.1-27` in Linux.

8.3.4 Accessing the Web-Based Tool

To access the JCS Web-based tool, start your Tomcat server (assuming the tomcat server is installed and configured on your system. See the server documentation for how to do this.) Once the server is running, open a browser to the following URL: *http://localhost:8080/certservices/*. You should see the CA certificate installation dialog. A CA certificate must be configured first. This certificate will be used later on to sign any subsequent CSR request or X.509 certificate (see Figure 8.3).

After the "root" CA certificate is installed, the main JCS menu will be displayed, as in Figure 8.4.

8.3.5 Creating a Certificate Request

To create a certificate request, click on the JCS "Certificate Request" main menu and fill all the fields on the form. Save the output of your certificate request and pri-

FIGURE 8.3 CA certificate installation page.

FIGURE 8.4 The JCS Web-tool main menu.

vate key in two different files such as `usercert_request.pem` and `userkey.pem` (see Figure 8.5).

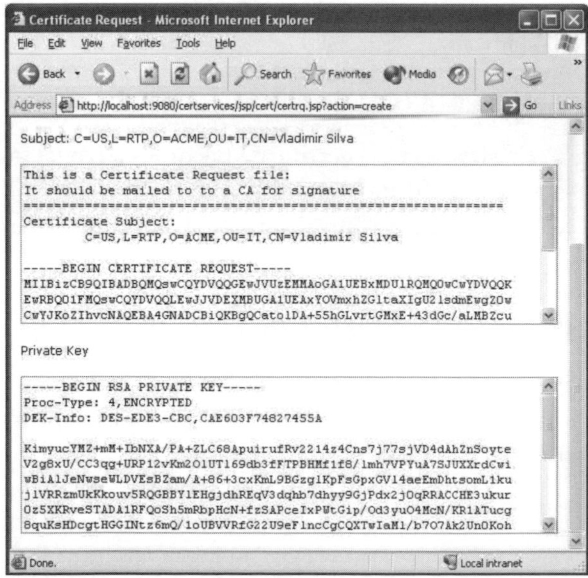

FIGURE 8.5 Certificate request sample output.

8.3.6 Signing a Certificate Request

To sign a certificate request, click "Sign cert request" from the main menu, upload your CSR PEM encoded file, and save the output to a file. For example, `usercert.pem` (see Figure 8.6).

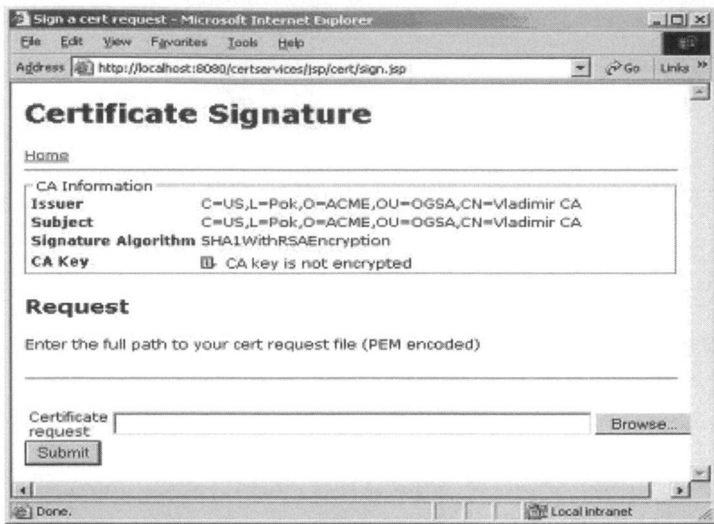

FIGURE 8.6 Certificate request signature.

8.3.7 Creating a Self-Signed (CA) Certificate and Private Key

Creating a self-signed (CA) certificate becomes a trivial task with JCS. Simply click the "Self-signed certificate" link from the main menu, fill in the form values, and save the certificate and private key contents into two separate files: `cacert.pem` and `cakey.pem`.

8.3.8 Using the Command-Line-Based Tools

JCS provides command-line tools similar to GT3's openssl executable. These tools provide similar functionality to the Web application, including CSR generation and signature plus certificate information.

To enable certificate signature, a trusted or CA certificate (`cacert.pem`) *and private key* (`cackey.pem`) *must exist on* `$HOME/.globus/CA`.

8.3.9 Creating a Certificate Request from the Command Line

To create a certificate request, the following command can be used in Windows/ Linux (make sure the `JCS_INSTALL_PATH` environment variable is set to the installation directory):

```
jcs req –out /tmp/rq.pem –keyput /tmp/key.pem –pwd "mypwd"
```

Optional arguments are *–dn "O=Grid, OU=OGSA, OU=IT, CN=John Doe" –bits 1024* (Note: O, OU, CN are case sensitive).

8.3.10 Signing a Certificate Request from the Command Line

To sign a certificate request run the following command from your OS prompt (Windows/Linux):

```
jcs ca –rq /tmp/req.pem –out /tmp/cert.pem
```

For this command to work, a trusted (CA) certificate must be installed in the user's "`.globus/CA`" directory, thus, `$HOME/.globus/CA` must exist and have two files: `cacert.pem` and `cakey.pem`.

Optional arguments are `-cacert` <path to CA cert>, `-cakey` <path to the CA key>, and `-capwd` <CA pwd>

8.3.11 Getting Information on an X.509 Certificate

To get information on an X.509 certificate, use the following command (Windows/Linux):

```
jcs x509 –in /tmp/cert.pem –info
```

A sample output of this command would be

```
Subject: C=US, O=Grid, OU=simpleCA, CN=John Doe
Hash: 945769
```

8.3.12 Creating a Binary Distribution from Source

To build JCS from source, you will need Apache Ant configured in your system:

- Unzip the source distribution in your filesystem.
- Change to the source directory: `cd jCertServices`

- Type: `ant all`
- The binary distribution can be found within the source directory as `build/jCertServices-1.1`

8.4 GLOBUS TOOLKIT 3 SECURITY LIBRARIES

GT3 uses a completely new security library provided by the Java CoG Kit 1.1. The new security library is based on GSS-API and is implemented entirely with open-source SSL and certificate-processing libraries. Web applications written for custom application servers that require the manipulation of X.509 certificates and proxies require extra tweaking. Most conflicts are the result of the JCE used by the security provider. The code provided in the companion CD-ROM has been tested in Apache Tomcat and the IBM WebSphere platforms.

8.4.1 Creating Proxies from Default Certificates Within a Web Application

We will start by writing a simple Java server page (JSP) to create a Globus Credential, also known as proxy (see Listing 8.8).

LISTING 8.8 Using proxy.jsp JSP File to Create a Globus Credential

```
<!DOCTYPE HTML PUBLIC "-//W3C//DTD HTML 4.01 Transitional//EN">
  <HTML>
  <HEAD>
  <% @page
  language = "java"
contentType = "text/html; charset=ISO-8859-1"
import = "java.util.Properties,
  java.io.*,
  java.security.cert.*,
  org.globus.gsi.*,
  org.globus.gsi.bc.*,
  org.apache.log4j.*"
  %>

  <%!
  /* Sub to create a Grid proxy certificate */
  public synchronized GlobusCredential gridProxyInit(
    InputStream inUserCert, /* certificate */
    InputStream inUserKey, /* Encrypted key */

    String pwd, /* passphrase used to encrypt the key */
    int bits, /* cert strength (512, 1024, etc....) */
```

```
    int hours /* lifetime in hours */
  )
  throws IOException, java.security.GeneralSecurityException {
  // Load cert & key from inout streams
  X509Certificate userCert = CertUtil.loadCertificate(inUserCert);
  OpenSSLKey key = new BouncyCastleOpenSSLKey(inUserKey);

  System.out.println(
    "gridProxyInit: User Cert="
    + userCert
    + " User key encrypted="
    + key.isEncrypted());

  if (key.isEncrypted()) {
    try {
      key.decrypt(pwd);
    }
    catch (java.security.GeneralSecurityException e) {
      throw new java.security.GeneralSecurityException(
        "Wrong password or other security error");
    }
  }
  System.out.println(
    "gridProxyInit: User Priv key : " + key.getPrivateKey());

  java.security.PrivateKey userKey = key.getPrivateKey();

  BouncyCastleCertProcessingFactory factory =
    BouncyCastleCertProcessingFactory.getDefault();

  return factory.createCredential(
    new X509Certificate[] {userCert},
    userKey,
    bits,
    hours * 3600,
    GSIConstants.GSI_2_PROXY,
    (org.globus.gsi.X509ExtensionSet)null);

}

%>
  <%
  Logger.getRootLogger().setLevel(Level.DEBUG);
```

```
String action = (request.getParameter("ACTION") != null)
  ? request.getParameter("ACTION") : "INIT";
String pwd = request.getParameter("txtPWD");
String bits = request.getParameter("ST");
String hours = request.getParameter("LIFETIME");

String Msg = request.getParameter("MSG");

String subject = "N/A"; // proxy subject (O=Grid,OU=Globus,CN=...)
String issuer = "N/A";
String strength = "N/A"; // proxy strength (512, 1024)
String sTimeLeft = "N/A"; // proxy time left (hours)

// is the proxy ready?
boolean proxyReady = false;

// Init
if (!action.equalsIgnoreCase("INIT")) {
}

try {
  if (action.equalsIgnoreCase("CREATE")) {

    // Load User certificate & key from the CoG
    // properties file located in
    // $USER_HOME/.globus/cog.properties
    String path = System.getProperty("user.home")
      + "/.globus/cog.properties";

    org.globus.common.CoGProperties props =
      new org.globus.common.CoGProperties();

    props.load(path);

    // get the user cert & key from cog.properties
    String certPath = props.getProperty("usercert");
    String keyPath = props.getProperty("userkey");

    System.out.println(
      "test-proxy.jsp::CREATE  pwd="
      + pwd
      + " bits="
      + bits
      + " hours="
      + hours);
```

```
    // create a globus cred. Certs read from def locs
    InputStream inCert = new FileInputStream(certPath);
    InputStream inKey = new FileInputStream(keyPath);

    int stren = Integer.parseInt(bits);
    int life = Integer.parseInt(hours);

    // create globus proxy
    GlobusCredential cred =
      gridProxyInit(inCert, inKey, pwd, stren, life);

    // get proxy information to be displayed
    subject = cred.getSubject();
    issuer = cred.getIssuer();
    strength = new Integer(cred.getStrength())
      .toString();
    sTimeLeft = org.globus.util.Util
      .formatTimeSec(cred.getTimeLeft());

    // save proxy in def location
    ByteArrayOutputStream bos
      = new ByteArrayOutputStream();

    cred.save(bos);

    proxyReady = true;
    Msg = "Proxy created.";

  }
}
catch (Exception e) {
  e.printStackTrace();
  response.sendRedirect("proxy.jsp?MSG=GridProxyInit+Error:"
                        + e.getMessage());
}
%>

  <META http -
  equiv = "Content-Type"content = "text/html; charset=ISO-8859-1">
  <META name = "GENERATOR"content = "IBM WebSphere Studio">
  <META http - equiv = "Content-Style-Type"content = "text/css">
  <
  LINK href = "../../theme/Master.css"rel = "stylesheet"type =
"text/css">
```

```
  <TITLE>Proxy.jsp </TITLE>
  <STYLE>
  TABLE, legend {

  font - family : Verdana, Arial;
  font - size : 12px;
}
  </STYLE>
  <SCRIPT LANGUAGE = javascript>
  <!--
  var proxyReady = <%= proxyReady % >;

function OnLoad() {
  var f = document.F1;
  if (document.all && proxyReady) {
    f.btnCreate.disabled = true;
    f.txtPWD.disabled = true;
  }
}

function showMsg(msg) {
  window.status = msg;
}

// fires when create btn is pressed
function Proxy_OnSubmit() {
  var action = "?ACTION=CREATE";
  var f = document.F1;

  if (f.txtPWD.value == "") {
    alert("All fields are required");
    f.txtCN.focus();
    return false;
  }

  showMsg("Working. Please wait...");
  if (document.all) {
    document.F1.btnCreate.disabled = true; // IE only
  }

  document.F1.action = action;
  document.F1.submit(); // submit
}
```

```
//-->
</SCRIPT>

  </HEAD>
  <BODY onload = "OnLoad()">

  <H1>Grid Proxy Init </H1>
  <B>Certificates
  will be loaded from default locations </B>

  <hr>
  <% if (Msg != null) {
   % >
    <br >
    <font color = red > <%= Msg % > </font >
    <%
}
 % >

  <
  FORM method = "POST"name = "F1"onsubmit = "return Proxy_OnSubmit()">

  <FIELDSET> <LEGEND>Proxy Options </LEGEND>
  <TABLE width = "100%">
  <tr class = "smallfont">
  <TD class = "smallfont">Lifetime</TD>
  <TD class = "smallfont">
  <INPUT type = "radio"name = "LIFETIME"value = "12"checked = "true">
  12h
  <INPUT type = "radio"name = "LIFETIME"value = "24">24h
  <INPUT type = "radio"name = "LIFETIME"value = "168">1week
  <INPUT type = "radio"name = "LIFETIME"value = "720">1month</TD>
  </tr>
  <tr class = "smallfont">
  <TD class = "smallfont">Strength</TD>
  <TD class = "smallfont">
  <INPUT type = "radio"name = "ST"value = "512"checked = "true">512
  <INPUT type = "radio"name = "ST"value = "1024">1024
  <INPUT type = "radio"name = "ST"value = "2048">2048
  <INPUT type = "radio"name = "ST"value = "4096">4096
  </TD>
  </tr>
  </TABLE>
  </FIELDSET>
```

```
<TABLE width = "100%">
<TR>
<td class = "smallfont">Pass Phrase</td>
<td class = "smallfont"><INPUT name = "txtPWD"type = "password"
maxlength = "20"></td>
</TR>
<TR>
<TD> & nbsp; </TD>
<td><INPUT name = "btnCreate"type = "submit"value = "Create"align =
"right">
& nbsp; & nbsp; </td>
</TR>
</TABLE>

<FIELDSET>
<LEGEND> Proxy Info</LEGEND>
<TABLE width = "100%">
<TR class = "smallfont">
<td class = "smallfont">CN</td>
<td class = "smallfont">
<font color = red></font>
</td>
</TR>
<TR>
<td class = "smallfont">Subject</td>
<td class = "smallfont"><%= subject % >
</td>
</TR>
<TR>
<td class = "smallfont">Issuer</td>
<td class = "smallfont"><%= issuer % >
</td>
</TR>
<TR>
<td class = "smallfont">Time left</td>
<td class = "smallfont"><%= sTimeLeft % >
</td>
</TR>
<TR>
<td class = "smallfont">Strength</td>
<td class = "smallfont"><%= strength % >
</td>
</TR>
</TABLE>
```

```
</FIELDSET>
<br>
</FORM>
</BODY>
</HTML>
```

To successfully run this JSP file in your favorite JSP container, make sure the following Java archive file (JAR) files are in your WEB-INF/lib folder: `cog-jglobus.jar`, `cryptix-ans1.jar`, `cryptix32.jar`, `jce-jdk13-117.jar`, `jgss.jar`, `log4j-core.jar` and `puretls.jar`. All these files are included on the GT3 distribution. Your local certificates must be configured also as shown in the following section.

8.4.2 Configuring Local Certificates for Testing

You must configure local certificates to be used by this JSP file or the Java CoG kit for that matter. The file `cog.properties` must be present under your home `.globus` folder. Thus, if you are logged in to your win32 system as "Administrator," then you must create:

```
C:\Documents and Settings\Administrator\.globus\cog.properties
```

Sample contents of this file are shown in listing 8.9.

LISTING 8.9 `cog.properties` Sample File

```
#Tue Aug 26 11:46:58 EDT 2003
usercert=C\:\\Documents and
Settings\\Administrator\\.globus\\usercert.pem
userkey=C\:\\Documents and
Settings\\Administrator\\.globus\\userkey.pem
proxy=C\:\\DOCUME~1\\ADMINI~1\\LOCALS~1\\Temp\\x509up_u_vladimir
cacert=C\:\\Documents and
Settings\\Administrator\\.globus\\simpleCA\\cacert.pem
```

This file will be setup automatically if you download and install the Java Cog kit from the Globus Web site. A user certificate and private key are required also. Once you have all the pieces in place. This JSP file will look something like Figure 8.7 in your Web browser.

The output of this JSP will look something like Figure 8.8.

This software provides functionality for grid proxy creation within a Web application. The following section demonstrates the same technique for certificates and private keys.

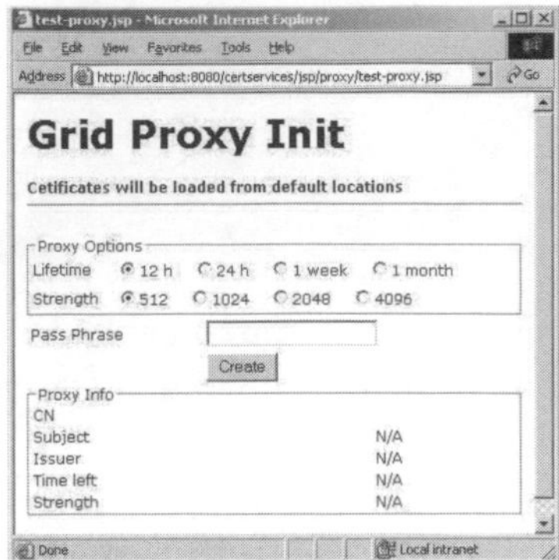

FIGURE 8.7 Proxy init test.

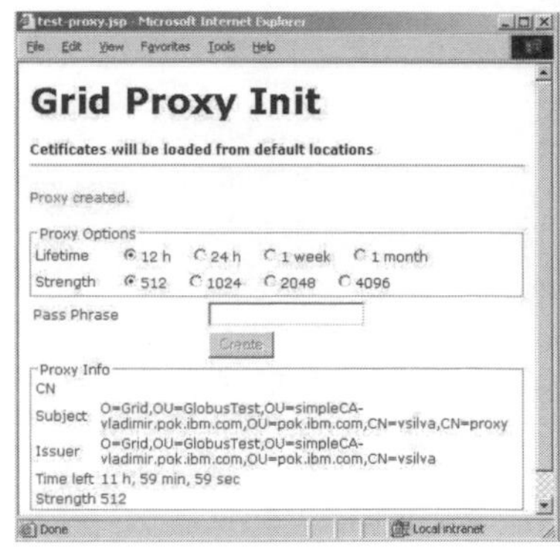

FIGURE 8.8 Creating a Globus credential.

8.4.3 Creating Certificates and Private Keys

Let us look at JSP code used to create a certificate and private key pair (see Listing 8.10).

LISTING 8.10 Using the `certkey.jsp` JSP File to Create a Certificate and Private Key

```
<!DOCTYPE HTML PUBLIC "-//W3C//DTD HTML 4.01 Transitional//EN">

  <HTML>
  <HEAD>
  <% @page language="java" contentType="text/html; charset=ISO-8859-1"
import="java.util.*,
  java.io.*,
  java.security.*,
  java.security.cert.*,
  org.globus.gsi.*,
  org.globus.gsi.bc.*,
  org.apache.log4j.*,
  COM.claymoresystems.cert.*,
  cryptix.util.mime.*"
  %>

  <%!
  /*
   * Write bytes into a PEM string
   */
  public static String writePEM(byte[] bytes, String hdr, String ftr)
  throws IOException
{
```

```
    ByteArrayOutputStream bos=new ByteArrayOutputStream();
    Base64OutputStream b64os=new Base64OutputStream(bos);
    b64os.write(bytes);
    b64os.flush();
    b64os.close();

    ByteArrayInputStream bis=new ByteArrayInputStream(bos.toByteArray());
    InputStreamReader irr=new InputStreamReader(bis);
    BufferedReader r=new BufferedReader(irr);

    StringBuffer buff=new StringBuffer();
    String line;
    buff.append(hdr);

    while ( (line=r.readLine()) != null) {
      buff.append(line + "\n");
    }
    buff.append(ftr);
    return buff.toString();

  }

  /* Create an X509 Name used for cert creation */
  private static X509Name makeCertDN(String subject) throws Exception {
    Vector tdn=new Vector();
    Vector elems=new Vector();
    StringTokenizer st=new StringTokenizer(subject, ",");

    for (; st.hasMoreTokens(); ) {
      String s=st.nextToken(); // [key=value]
      if (s.indexOf("=") == -1) {
        throw new Exception(
          "Invalid subject format: "
          + subject
          + " Offending value: "
          + s);
      }

      String key=s.substring(0, s.indexOf("=")).trim();
      String val=s.substring(s.indexOf("=") + 1).trim();

      if (val == null || val.equals("")) {
        throw new Exception(
          "Invalid subject format: "
```

```
            + subject
            + " Offending value: "
            + s);
      }

      String[] temp={
        key, val};
      tdn.addElement(temp);
    }

    // COM.claymoresystems.cert (puretls.jar)
    return CertRequest.makeSimpleDN(tdn);
  }

  /* Create a self signed Cert and key */
  public void generateSelfSignedCertAndKey
    (
      String subject, /* Example: c=us,o=ibm,ou=it,cn=John Doe */
      int bits,
      /* cert strength   512, 1024, etc */
      String Pwd, /* key passphrase */
      StringWriter swKey, /* OUT: encrypted key */
      StringWriter swCert /* OUT: PEM encoded cert */
    )

    throws NoSuchAlgorithmException, Exception {
    X509Name _subject=makeCertDN(subject);

    // Generate A Cert RQ
    // buffer for the key PEM
    BufferedWriter bw=new BufferedWriter(swKey);

    KeyPair kp=CertRequest.generateKey("RSA", bits, Pwd, bw, true);

    // certs are valid for 1 year: 31536000 secs
    byte[] certBytes=CertRequest
      .makeSelfSignedCert(kp, _subject, 31536000);

    BufferedWriter bw1=new BufferedWriter(swCert);

    // encode cert in PEM format
    String _certPEM =
      writePEM(
        certBytes,
```

```
      "-----BEGIN CERTIFICATE-----\n",
      "-----END CERTIFICATE-----\n");
  bw1.write(_certPEM);
  bw1.close();
}

%>

  <%
  org.apache.log4j.Logger.getRootLogger()
  .setLevel(org.apache.log4j.Level.DEBUG);

String action=(request.getParameter("ACTION") != null)
  ? request.getParameter("ACTION") : "INIT";
String Msg=request.getParameter("MSG");

// private key & cer pem(s)
String keyPEM=null;
String certPEM=null;

try {

  String msg="";

  if (action.equalsIgnoreCase("GENERATE")) {
    String cn=request.getParameter("txtCN");
    String org=request.getParameter("txtORG");
    String ou=request.getParameter("txtOU");
    String pwd=request.getParameter("txtPWD");

    String subject="O=" + org
      + "," + "OU=" + ou + ",CN=" + cn;
    System.out.println("Gen certs. Subject: " + subject);

    // cert PEM
    StringWriter swCert=new StringWriter();

    // priv key PEM
    StringWriter swKey=new StringWriter();

    generateSelfSignedCertAndKey(subject, 1024
                             , pwd, swKey, swCert);

    // Private key
    keyPEM=swKey.toString();
```

```
      // cert
      certPEM=swCert.toString();
    }

  }
  catch (Exception e0) {
    response.sendRedirect(
      "certkey.jsp?MSG=Error+installing+certs:"
      + e0.getMessage()
      );

  }
  %>

    <META http -
    equiv="Content-Type"content="text/html; charset=ISO-8859-1">
    <META name="GENERATOR"content="IBM WebSphere Studio">
    <META http - equiv="Content-Style-Type"content="text/css">

    <TITLE>setup - gsi.jsp </TITLE>

    <SCRIPT LANGUAGE=javascript>
    <!--
    function showMsg(msg) {
    window.status=msg;
  }

  function OnLoad() {
    document.F1.txtCN.focus();
    showMsg("Done");
  }

  // fires when create btn is pressed
  function OnSubmit() {
    var f=document.F1;

    if (f.txtCN.value == ""
        || f.txtPWD.value == "" || f.txtOU.value == "") {
      alert("All fields are required");
      f.txtCN.focus();
      return false;
    }
```

```
  showMsg("Working. Please wait...");
  if (document.all) {
    document.F1.btnCreate.disabled=true; // IE only
  }

  document.F1.submit(); // submit
}
//-->
</SCRIPT>

  </HEAD>
  <BODY onload="OnLoad()">

  <H1>Setup Certificate / Private key </H1>

  <hr>

  <% if (Msg != null) {
   % >
    <br > <font color=red > <%= Msg % > </font > <br >
    <%
}
 %>

  <B>All fields are required </B>

  <form name="F1" method="POST" action="?ACTION=GENERATE"
  onsubmit =  "return OnSubmit()">

  <TABLE width="100%"class="smallfont">
  <tr>
  <td> Common Name</td>
  <td width="40%">
  <INPUT type="text"
  name="txtCN" size="20"maxlength="50">
  </td>
  <TD> Enter your name or email</TD>
  </tr>
  <tr>
  <td> Organizational Unit</td>
  <td>
  <INPUT type="text"
  name="txtOU"size="20"maxlength="50">
  </td>
```

```
<TD class="smallfont"></TD>
</tr>
<tr>
<td> Organization</td>
<td>
<INPUT type="text"
name="txtORG"size="20"maxlength="50">
</td>
<TD class="smallfont">Organization</TD>
</tr>
<tr>
<td> Pass phrase</td>
<td>
<INPUT type="password"
name="txtPWD"size="20"maxlength="50">
</td>
<TD class="smallfont">
Password used to encrypt the private key</TD>
</tr>
</TABLE>

<hr>

<INPUT name="btnCreate"type="submit"name="Submit"value =
"Create Certs">
</form>

<% if (certPEM != null || keyPEM != null) {
 % >
  <h1 > Certificate </h1 >
  <TEXTAREA rows="10"cols="80" > <%= certPEM % > </TEXTAREA >
  <h1 > Key </h1 >
  <TEXTAREA rows="10"cols="80" > <%= keyPEM % > </TEXTAREA >
  <%
}
%>

</BODY>
</HTML>
```

On your Web browser, this code will look like Figure 8.9.

FIGURE 8.9 X.509 certificate and private key generation within a Web application.

8.4.4 Troubleshooting: Security Provider Problems

When attempting to create a certificate/private key set, the following exception may be thrown by your application server:

```
java.lang.InternalError:
java.security.NoSuchAlgorithmException:
class configured for Cipher:
com.ibm.crypto.provider.DESedeCipher
is not a subclass of xjava.security.Cipher
    at COM.claymoresystems.crypto
.PEMData.writePEMObject(PEMData.java:172)
    at COM.claymoresystems.crypto
.EAYEncryptedPrivateKey.writePrivateKey
  (EAYEncryptedPrivateKey.java:83)
    at COM.claymoresystems.cert
.CertRequest.generateKey(CertRequest.java:102)
    at jsp.article._test_2D_creds_jsp_0
.generateSelfSignedCertAndKey(_test_2D_creds_jsp_0.java:108)
    at jsp.article._test_2D_creds_jsp_0.
_jspService(_test_2D_creds_jsp_0.java:210)
```

The message class configured for Cipher: `com.ibm.crypto.provider.DESede Cipher` is not a subclass of `xjava.security. Cipher` indicates that IBM's JCE is used as the default cryptography provider by the Web container. The security provider should be `Cryptix/Bouncy-Castle`. This exception is thrown when decrypting a private key with certain application servers such as IBM WebSphere because of security provider collisions between the application server and the Java CoG kits. A solution to this conflict is described in the Hosting Environments section of Chapter 7.

8.5 SUMMARY

Security is at the foundation of grid computing. A good and efficient security model provides for enhanced authentication and communication over computer networks. This chapter presented the following security-related topics:

- An overview of the Grid Security Infrastructure (GSI)
- An explanation of the basics of digital certificates with a set of programs for certificate, key, and grid proxy generation and signature
- A sample Web-based application for certificate manipulation very similar in functionality to a certificate authority (CA), along with command-line tools and installation transcripts for two popular application servers: Tomcat and WebSphere
- Integration of the Globus Toolkit security libraries and other OGSA hosting environments along with common error messages and troubleshooting

REFERENCES

[CogKit01] Gregor von Laszewski, Ian Foster, Jarek Gawor, and Peter Lane, "A Java Commodity Grid Kit," *Concurrency and Computation: Practice and Experience,* vol. 13, no. 8–9, pp. 643–662, 2001. Available online at *http:/www.cogkit.org/.*

[GridPhysiology02] Ian Foster, Carl Kesselman, Jeffrey Nick, and Steven Tuecke, "The Physiology of the Grid: An Open Grid Services Architecture for Distributed Systems Integration." Globus Project, Available online 2002 at *http://www-unix.globus.org/ogsa/docs/alpha/physiology.pdf.*

[GSIGlobus03] Overview of the Grid Security Infrastructure. Globus Project and Globus Toolkit are trademarks held by the University of Chicago. Available online 2004 at *http://www-unix.globus.org/security/overview.html.*

[GSS-API93] RFC 1508—Generic Security Service Application Program Interface. Accessed online September 1993 at *http://www.faqs.org/rfcs/rfc1508.html.*

[X509Pki99] R. Housley, W. Ford, W. Polk, and D. Solo, Network Working Group RFC2459. Internet X.509 Public Key Infrastructure. Available January 1999 online at *http://www.ietf.org/rfc/rfc2459.txt.*

9 Resource Management

In This Chapter

- Web Services GRAM Architecture (GT3)
- Pre–Web Services GRAM Architecture (GT2)
- Summary
- References

This chapter includes information on the following topics:

- An overview of the Globus Resource Allocation Manager (GRAM) Architecture for GT3
- Description of the Resource Scripting Language (RSL) used for job submission
- Description of the Master Managed Job Factory Service (MMJFS) including installation, configuration, and troubleshooting
- Custom GRAM client program for MMJFS with security features
- Performance evaluation tests of various MMJFS clients provided by Globus
- Pre–Web Services GRAM Architecture (GT2) for job submission
- Java programs for job submission on GT2

All code shown is this chapter is available on the companion CD-ROM.

9.1 WEB SERVICES GRAM ARCHITECTURE (GT3)

The Globus Resource Allocation Manager (GRAM) is at the core of the Globus remote program execution infrastructure. It allows you to run jobs remotely, using a set of Web Service Description Language (WSDL) client interfaces for submitting, monitoring, and terminating a job. A job request is written in the RSL and processed by the Managed Job Service (MJS). MJS and RSL together are also known as the Master Managed Job Factory Service (MMJFS).

GRAM on GT3 has been divided in two big containers: the Master Hosting Environment (MHE), and the User Hosting Environment (UHE). The MHE is in charge of authorizing the GRAM request against the grid-map file and starting or pinging the UHE. The MHE then uses a redirector to forward the request to the UHE process, which in turn creates an MJS. The MJS submits the job into the back-end scheduling system. Both environments interact in a typical GRAM request (see Figure 9.1) [WSGramGuide04].

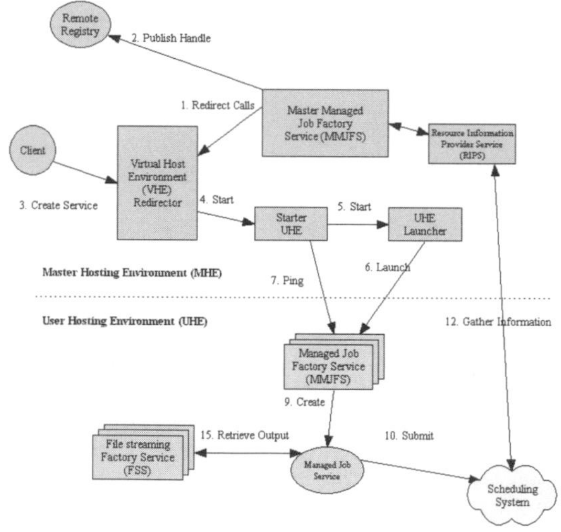

FIGURE 9.1 Workflow of a typical WS-GRAM request.

1. The Master is configured to use the Redirector to redirect calls to it and to use the Starter UHE module when there is not a running UHE for the user. A `createService` call on the Master uses the Redirector to invoke the Starter UHE module and start a UHE.
2. The Master publishes its handle to a remote registry (optional).
3. A client submits a `createService` request that is received by the Redirector.

4. The Redirector calls the Starter UHE class, which authorizes the request via the grid-map file to determine the local username and port to be used and constructs a target URL.
5. The Redirector attempts to forward the call to the target URL. If it is unable to forward the call because the UHE is not up, the Launch UHE module is invoked.
6. The Launch UHE creates a new UHE process under the authenticated user's local user id (uid).
7. The Starter UHE waits for the UHE to be started (ping loop), then returns the target URL to the Redirector.
8. The Redirector forwards the `createService` call to the MJFS unmodified, and mutual authentication/authorization can take place.
9. MMJFS creates a new MJS.
10. MJS submits the job into a back-end scheduling system.
11. Subsequent calls to the MJS from the client will be redirected through the Redirector.
12. The Resource Information Provider Service (RIPS) gathers data from the local scheduling system such as filesystem info, host info, and so on.
13. `FindServiceData` requests to the Master will forward service information SDE to the MMJFS of the requestor's UHE.
14. To stream `stdout/stderr` back to the client, the MJS creates two File Stream Factory Services (FSFS), one for `stdout` and one for `stderr`.
15. The MJS then creates the File Stream Services (FSS) instances as specified in the job request.
16. The Grid Resource Information Manager (GRIM) handler is run in the UHE to create a user host certificate. The user host certificate is used for mutual authentication between the MJS service and the client.

One of the main reasons behind a Master and User hosting environments is fault tolerance. If a GRAM request crashes the UHE for any given reason, the MHE will be able to restart the process the next time a request comes along. There will be a UHE process for each local user on the grid-map file but only one MHE instance.

9.1.1 Fault Tolerance

Fault tolerance is achieved by using several background container handlers. Among the most important are the following:

UHERestartHandler: Runs once when the MHE is started. It attempts to restart any previously started UHE. There will be a UHE process for each entry in grim-port-type.xml

UHESweeperTask: This runs every two hours in the MHE and is responsible for restarting crashed UHEs and updating files when the UHE is shutting down.

UHEActivityTask: This runs on the UHE and monitors activity, updating admin services accordingly.

9.1.2 Resource Specification Language (RSL)

The RSL now supports a brand new XML Schema as well as the previous 2.2.X format [CzajkowskiFoster99]. Two equivalent RSL representations for an `echo` job request in GT2 and GT3 are shown in Listing 9.1 and Listing 9.2.

LISTING 9.1 Echo RSL Request in GT2

```
&((executable=/bin/echo)
(directory="/bin")
(arguments="Hello World")
(stdin=/dev/null)
(stdout="stdout")
(stderr="stderr")
(count=1)
)
```

LISTING 9.2 Echo RSL Request in GT3

```
<?xml version="1.0" encoding="UTF-8"?>
<rsl:rsl
    xmlns:rsl="http://www.globus.org/namespaces/2004/02/rsl"
    xmlns:enum="http://www.globus.org/namespaces/2004/02/rsl/enum"
    xmlns:gram="http://www.globus.org/namespaces/2004/02/rsl/gram"
    xmlns:xsi="http://www.w3.org/2001/XMLSchema-instance"
    xsi:schemaLocation="
           http://www.globus.org/namespaces/2004/02/rsl
           C:/GridBookSource/ogsa-3.2.1/schema/base/gram/rsl.xsd
           http://www.globus.org/namespaces/2004/02/rsl/gram
           C:/GridBookSource/ogsa-3.2.1/schema/base/gram/gram_rsl.xsd">
    <gram:job>
        <gram:executable>
                <rsl:path>
                        <rsl:stringElement value="/bin/echo" />
                </rsl:path>
        </gram:executable>
        <gram:directory>
                <rsl:path>
                        <rsl:stringElement value="/tmp" />
```

```
        </rsl:path>
</gram:directory>
<gram:arguments>
        <rsl:stringArray>
                <rsl:string>
                      <rsl:stringElement value="Hello World" />
                </rsl:string>
        </rsl:stringArray>
</gram:arguments>

<gram:stdin>
        <rsl:path>
                <rsl:stringElement value="/dev/null" />
        </rsl:path>
</gram:stdin>
<gram:stdout>
        <rsl:pathArray>
                <rsl:path>
                        <rsl:substitutionRef name="HOME" />
                        <rsl:stringElement value="./stdout" />
                </rsl:path>
        </rsl:pathArray>
</gram:stdout>
<gram:stderr>
        <rsl:pathArray>
                <rsl:path>
                        <rsl:substitutionRef name="HOME" />
                        <rsl:stringElement value="./stderr" />
                </rsl:path>
        </rsl:pathArray>
</gram:stderr>
<gram:count>
        <rsl:integer value="1" />
</gram:count>
<gram:jobType>
        <enum:enumeration>
                <enum:enumerationValue>
                        <enum:multiple />
                </enum:enumerationValue>
        </enum:enumeration>
</gram:jobType>
<gram:gramMyJobType>
        <enum:enumeration>
                <enum:enumerationValue>
                        <enum:collective />
```

```
                        </enum:enumerationValue>
                </enum:enumeration>
        </gram:gramMyJobType>
        <gram:dryRun>
                <rsl:boolean value="false" />
        </gram:dryRun>
    </gram:job>
</rsl:rsl>
```

A full description of the new RSL XML Schema can be fount at [GramRSL04].

9.1.3 MMJFS Configuration

MMJFS configuration can be difficult for beginners. The following sections describe the basic steps to configure this service for GT3.

9.1.3.1 Testing your MMJFS Installation

After carefully following the installation transcript provided by Globus, we are ready to test our MMJFS installation by running the `managed-job-globusrun` script provided. It is assumed that host and user certificates have already been set up and the container is up and running.

Use the following command such to send an MMJFS test request:

```
$ source $GLOBUS_LOCATION/etc/globus-user-env.{sh,csh}
$ grid-proxy-init
$ GLOBUS_LOCATION/bin/managed-job-globusrun
  -factory
  http://`hostname`:8080/ogsa/services/base/gram/
  MasterForkManagedJobFactoryService
  -file $GLOBUS_LOCATION/etc/test.xml -personal –o
```

Some output should be displayed in your terminal. If you get a stack trace of errors, here are some tips for identifying the cause:

- Monitor the UHE log file for the user that is submitting the GRAM request. The file is located in `$HOME/.globus/uhe-[HOSTNAME]/log`.
- Monitor the container `stdout` terminal for messages.
- Enable `log4j` messages by editing the file `$GLOBUS_LOCATION/log4j.properties`. Specifically change the following lines:

```
log4j.rootCategory=WARN, CONSOLE
```

should be changed to

```
  log4j.rootCategory=INFO, CONSOLE
```

```
log4j.appender.CONSOLE.Threshold=WARN
```
should be changed to
```
log4j.appender.CONSOLE.Threshold=INFO
```

See the troubleshooting section later in this chapter if you run into trouble. Also, the Globus Web site provides a more complete installation guide and FAQ, which are good sources of information, along with the forums from the Globus Web site.

9.1.3.2 Scheduler Installation

If you have a job scheduler such as OpenPBS, LSF or Condor, run the following commands to set them up:

```
$ gpt-build scheduler-[name]-3.2-src_bundle.tar.gz gcc32dbg
$ gpt-postinstall
```

The scheduler interface files can be found in the folder `$GLOBUS_LOCATION/lib/perl/Globus/GRAM/JobManager/[scheduler].pm`. Edit this file if you need to adjust scheduler options such as cluster type, paths, job submission parameters, and so on.

9.1.4 Troubleshooting

This section presents some of the problems you might find when configuring MMJFS on a Red Hat Linux 8.x system running on VMWare workstation 4.x.

9.1.4.1 Authentication Failed Messages

Message:

```
init_sec_context.c:251: gss_init_sec_context:
 Mutual authentication failed:
The target name
(/O=Grid/OU=GlobusTest/
  OU=simpleCA.ibm.com/CN=host/vm-vlad-lap.pok.ibm.com)
in the context, and the target name
(/CN=host/localhost.localdomain) passed to the function
 do not match (error code 7)
```

Possible cause: The hostname used to create your host cert *hostcert.pem* is invalid. This happens when the hostname of the machine changes for some reason. Globus strongly recommends using static IP addresses for your hosts.

9.1.4.2 Connection Timeout Messages

Message:

```
Service is not up - Connection timeout
Error: error submitting job request:
```

```
Could not connect to job manager
[Root error message: ;
 nested exception is:
    java.net.SocketTimeoutException: Read timed out]
```

Possible causes:

1. Invalid path to the Java Virtual Machine (JVM) in `GLOBUS_LOCATION/bin/launch-uhe.sh`.
2. `OPTIONS` environment variable not set.
3. In slow systems, the very first connection sometimes times out before the MHE can start the UHE, otherwise the second and successive submission should work (assuming that MMJFS has been properly setup).

Solution:

1. Check the JVM path on `$GLOBUS_LOCATION/bin/launch-uhe.sh`
2. Set the environment variable
   `OPTIONS=-Dorg.globus.ogsa.client.timeout=180000 -Djava.net.preferIPv4Stack=true`

9.1.4.3 Unknown Policy Errors

Message:

```
Error processing message
org.globus.gsi.proxy.ProxyPathValidatorException:
Unknown policy: 1.3.6.1.4.1.3536.1.1.1.7
```

Possible cause:

1. File `grim-port-type.xml` not properly configured

Solution:

1. For each user in your grid, there must be an entry in the `grid-map` file and `grim-port-type.xml` files. See the earlier MMJFS configuration links for more details.

9.1.4.4 Defective Credential Errors

Message:

On the server:

```
Defective credential detected
[Root error message: Host authorization failure.
Expected target:
 '/CN=host/vm-rhl8-1.ibm.com'.
Target returned:
 '/O=Grid/OU=GlobusTest
```

```
   /OU=simpleCA-vm-rhl8-2.ibm.com
   /CN=host/vm-rhl8-2.ibm.com/CN=501']
```

On the client:

```
Error: error submitting job request: Could not connect to job manager
[Root error message: java.lang.Exception: Service is not up]
```

Possible cause: Client and host certificates do not match or were not signed by the same Certificate Authority (CA). (By looking at the hostnames, we see that the names do not match: `vm-rhl8-1.ibm.com` versus `vm-rhl8-2.ibm.com`

Solution: Re-create the host certificate by issuing the commands:

- Create a cert request (As root):
  ```
  grid-cert-request -host [HOST_NAME]
  ```
- Sign the new request. This step requires the Globus SimpleCA Certificate Authority package.
  ```
  grid-ca-sign -dir [SIMPLE CA HOME]
   -in /etc/grid-security/hostcert_request.pem
   -out /etc/grid-security/hostcert.pem
  ```

Verification tips:

- To verify a host certificate identity, run the `grid-cert-info` script. The Common Name (CN) part of the output should match the name of the host.
  ```
  grid-cert-info
   -file /etc/grid-security/hostcert.pem
   -subject
    /O=Grid/OU=GlobusTest
  /OU=simpleCA-vm-rhl8-2.ibm.com
  /CN=host/vm-rhl8-1.ibm.com
  ```
- Resubmit the MMJFS test:
  ```
  $GLOBUS_LOCATION/bin/managed-job-globusrun
  -factory http://[HOSTNAME]:8080/ogsa/services
    /base/gram/MasterForkManagedJobFactoryService
  -file
    $GLOBUS_LOCATION/schema/base/gram/examples/test.xml -o
  ```

Globus recommends installing the toolkit as a nonroot user (i.e., globus). `ProxyPathValidatorException` errors can occurs when testing MMJFS submissions as user "globus." To test your MMJFS installation, we recommend that a user different from Globus or root be used.

The following are sample grid security configuration files used by MMJFS and commonly found under `/etc/grid-security`:

`Grid-map` file:

```
"/O=Grid/OU=GlobusTest
  /OU=simpleCA-vm-vlad-lap.pok.ibm.com/CN=vsilva" vsilva
```

```
"/O=Grid/OU=GlobusTest
  /OU=simpleCA-vm-vlad-lap.pok.ibm.com/CN=globus" globus
"/C=GB/ST=Berkshire/O=ACME/OU=IT/CN=John Doe" jdoe
```

Grim-port-type.xml:

```
<authorized_port_types>
<port_type username="vsilva">
  http://www.globus.org/namespaces
  /managed_job/managed_job/ManagedJobPortType
</port_type>
<port_type username="globus">
  http://www.globus.org/namespaces
 /managed_job/managed_job/ManagedJobPortType
</port_type>
</authorized_port_types>
```

For this configuration both users, `vsilva` and `globus`, are authorized to run GT3 GRAM jobs. User `jdoe` will be able to run GT2 GRAM requests only.

9.1.5 A Custom GRAM Client for MMJFS

The next section describes a custom GRAM client for GT3 that can be run from the command line or included in a Web application or servlet. The libraries required to run this code can be found in your `GLOBUS_LOCATION/lib` folder, and should be included in your project classpath, specifically `mjs.jar`, `mmjfs.jar`, and `filestreaming.jar`.

There are remarkable similarities with GRAM 2.x. Consider the Listing 9.3.

LISTING 9.3 `CustomGRAMClient.java`, a Custom GRAM Client for MMJFS

```
package grid;

/**
 * <p>Title: Custom GRAM client for GT3.x</p>
 * <p>Description: </p>
 * @author Vladimir Silva
 * @version 1.0
 */
import java.io.*;
import java.net.URL;

import org.globus.io.gass.server.*;
import org.globus.gram.GramException;

import org.globus.ogsa.impl.base.gram.client.*;
```

```
import org.globus.ogsa.base.gram.types.JobStateType;
import org.globus.ogsa.impl.security.authentication.Constants;
import org.globus.ogsa.impl.security.authorization.Authorization;
import org.globus.ogsa.impl.security.authorization.HostAuthorization;
import
org.globus.ogsa.impl.security.authorization.IdentityAuthorization;
import org.globus.ogsa.impl.security.authorization.SelfAuthorization;

import org.apache.commons.logging.Log;
import org.apache.commons.logging.LogFactory;

/**
 * Custom GRAM client Java program
 */
public class CustomGRAMClient
    implements
    GramJobListener, // listen for job status messages
    JobOutputListener { // listen for job output from GASS server
  private String _USAGE = "-factory <URL> -file <RSL file>" +
      "[options] " +
      "\nOptions:" +
      "\n\t-help    Help" +
      "\n\t-auth    Authorization: " +
      "[host,self,(identity)e.g. /ou=ACME/o=globus/cn=John Doe" +
      "\n\t-o        Redirect output from the GASS server " +
      "\n\t-sec     'sig' for XML signature 'enc' for XML encryption" +
      "\n\t-b       'batch' mode. Mutually exclusive with -o" +
      "\n\t-quiet   No verbose messages";

  /**
   * The variable name to use in input RSL when referring to the URL
   * of the local GASS server, if started.
   */
  public static final String GLOBUSRUN_GASS_URL =
      "GLOBUSRUN_GASS_URL";

  private static Log logger =
      LogFactory.getLog(GlobusRun.class.getName());
  boolean quiet = false;
  private boolean done = false;
  private GassServer gassServer;
  private GramJob job;
```

```
// Output received from the GASS server
StringBuffer _jobOutput = new StringBuffer("");

// Cmd line arguments
private Authorization _authorization =
    SelfAuthorization.getInstance();
private Integer _xmlSecurity = Constants.SIGNATURE;

// Redirect output from the GASS server.
// batch and output redirection flags are mutually exclusive
private boolean _redirOutput = true;
private boolean _batch = false;

private int _gassOptions = 0;
private int _timeout = GramJob.DEFAULT_TIMEOUT;

private String _factory; // MJFS service factory URL
private String _rslString; // RSL file path
```

One of the basic differences with a GT2 GRAM client is the location of the client classes. For GT3, the package `org.globus.ogsa` contains the required code. The packages `org.globus.io.gass` and `org.globus.gram` are provided by the Java Commodity Grid (CoG) kit and apply to both versions.

9.1.6 Listening for Job Status Updates and Job Output

The way a GT3 client listens for job status and output is identical to that of GRAM2. The following interfaces provide for job status updates (see Listing 9.3.1):

`GramJobListener:` Implement this interface to listen for GRAM job status updates:

```
public void statusChanged(GramJob job)
```

`JobOutputListener:` Implement this interface to receive output from the Globus Access to Second Storage (GASS) server:

```
public void outputChanged(String output)
```

Fires when the output changes

```
public void outputClosed()
```

Fires when the output is closed by the server

LISTING 9.3.1 Job Status and Output Callbacks

```
/**
 * Callback as a GramJobListener.
 * Will not be called in batch mode.
 */
public void statusChanged(GramJob job) {
    String stringStatus = job.getStatusAsString();
    if (!quiet) {
        System.out.println("== Status Notification ==");
        System.out.println("Status: " + stringStatus);
        System.out.println("==================");
    }

    synchronized (this) {
        if (stringStatus.equals(JobStateType._Done)
            || stringStatus.equals(JobStateType._Failed))
  {
            this.done = true;
            notifyAll();
        }
    }
}

/**
 * It is called whenever the job's output
 * has been updated.
 *
 * @param output new output
 */
public void outputChanged(String output) {
    _jobOutput.append(output);
}

/**
 * It is called whenever job finished
 * and no more output will be generated.
 */
public void outputClosed() {
    //System.out.println("outputClosed");
}
```

9.1.7 The GASS Server

Globus Access to Second Storage (GASS) runs on the GRAM client and negotiates data transfers with the remote service. For GT2, that would be the Globus gatekeeper, and for GT3, the MJS service. The GASS server is required if the client is to receive output from the server. Of course, this doesn't apply on *batch mode* submissions.

9.1.7.1 Starting the GASS Server

```
gassServer = new GassServer();
gassServer.registerDefaultDeactivator();
```

9.1.7.2 Receiving Output from GASS

In GT2:

```
JobOutputStream stdoutStream =newJobOutputStream(this);
JobOutputStream stderrStream =newJobOutputStream(this);

String jobid = String.valueOf(System.currentTimeMillis());

gassServer.registerJobOutputStream("err-"+jobid,stderrStream);
gassServer.registerJobOutputStream("out-"+jobid,stdoutStream);
```

In GT3:

```
JobOutputStream stdoutStream = newJobOutputStream(this);
JobOutputStream stderrStream = newJobOutputStream(this);

//registeroutputlisteners
gassServer.registerJobOutputStream("err",stderrStream);
gassServer.registerJobOutputStream("out",stdoutStream);
```

9.1.8 RSL Submission

After you start the GASS server, the GRAM submission can proceed. An RSL XML string is required for this step, as shown in Listing 9.4.

LISTING 9.4 MMJFS GRAM Job Submission

```
/**
 * Return the output from the GRAM job submission
 */
public String getJobOutput() { return _jobOutput.toString(); }

/**
```

```
 * Constructor
 */
public CustomGRAMClient(String[] args) throws Exception {
    if ( parseArgs(args) )
        submitRSL(_factory, _rslString, _authorization
                  , _xmlSecurity, _batch
                  , _gassOptions, _redirOutput, _timeout);
}

/**
 * GRAM Submission sub
 * @param factoryUrl: URL of the MJS factory
 * @param rslString: RSL string as XML
 * @param authorization: Host, Self or Identity
 * @param xmlSecurity: sig for signature, enc for encryption
 * @param batchMode: Batch submission (will not wait for job)
 * @param gassOptions: GASS server options (I?O enable, disable, etc)
 * @param redirOutput: Redirect output to the client (non batch)
 * @param timeout: Job timeout in millis
 */
void submitRSL(String factoryUrl,
               String rslString,
               Authorization authorization,
               Integer xmlSecurity,
               boolean batchMode,
               int gassOptions,
               boolean redirOutput,
               int timeout) throws Exception {

    _batch = batchMode;
    //In multi-job, -batch is not allowed. Dryrun is.

    if (batchMode) {
        _verbose("Warning: Will not wait for job completion," +
               " and will not destroy job service.");
    }

    this.job = new GramJob(rslString);
    job.setTimeOut(timeout);

    job.setAuthorization(authorization);
    job.setMessageProtectionType(xmlSecurity);

    //now must ensure JVM will exit if uncaught exception:
    try {
```

```
        this.startGASSserver(gassOptions);

        //check isSubstitutionReferenced?
        //move XML string building to GramJobAttributes
        //or JobAttributesImpl
        String xmlValue = "<rsl:urlElement value=\"" +
            gassServer.getURL() + "\"/>";
        job.setSubstitutionDefinition(GLOBUSRUN_GASS_URL,
                                      xmlValue);
        //check isSubstitutionDefined

        if (redirOutput) {
            //add output path to GASS redirection
            _verbose("Adding output path to GASS redirection");
            job.addStdoutPath(GLOBUSRUN_GASS_URL, "/dev/stdout");
            job.addStderrPath(GLOBUSRUN_GASS_URL, "/dev/stderr");
            //TODO factor into GASSServer.STDOUT|STDERR...
        }

        processJob(job, factoryUrl, _batch);
    }
    catch (Exception e) {
        logger.error("Caught exception: ", e);
        throw
            new Exception
             ("submitRSL: Caught exception: " + e.getMessage());
    }
}

/**
 * processJob Send the actual GRAM request
 */
private void processJob(GramJob job, String factoryUrl, boolean batch)
    throws GramException
{

    try {
        logger.debug("Factory URL " + factoryUrl);
        job.request(new URL(factoryUrl), batch);
    }
    catch (Exception e) {
        logger
.error("Exception while submitting the job request: ", e);
        throw new GramException("error submitting job request: "
```

```
                                + e.getMessage());
    }

    if (batch) {
        _verbose("MJS WITH HANDLE: "
                  + job.getHandle());
        _jobOutput.append(job.getHandle());
    }
    else {
        job.addListener(this);
    }

    try {
        logger.debug("Starting job");
        job.start(); //leave this free to interrupt?
    }
    catch (GramException ge) {
        logger.error("Error starting job", ge);
        throw new GramException("Error starting job: "
                                + ge.getMessage());
    }

    logger.debug("Job has started.");

    if (!batch) {
        _verbose("WAITING FOR JOB TO FINISH");
        synchronized (this) {
            while (!this.done) {
                try {
                    wait();
                }
                catch (InterruptedException ie) {
                    logger.error(
                      "Interrupted waiting for job to finish", ie);
                }
            }
        }
        if (this.job.getStatusAsString()
.equals(JobStateType._Failed)) {
            throw
                new GramException("Job Fault detected: "
                                  + this.job.getFault());
        }
    }
```

```
        // GRAM submission complete. Cleanup: Stop GASS server
        cleanup();
    }
```

Listing 9.5 starts the GASS server and initializes the job output callbacks.

LISTING 9.5 Starting the MMJFS GASS Server

```
    /**
     * Start the GASS Server
     * Used to transfer data between MJFS and GRAM client
     */
    private void startGASSserver(int gassOptions) {
        logger.debug("Starting Gass server.");
        try {
            gassServer = new GassServer();
            if (gassOptions != 0) {
                gassServer.setOptions(gassOptions);

            }
            gassServer.registerDefaultDeactivator();

            // Listen for GASS stdout/stderr output
            initJobOutListeners();

        }
        catch (Exception e) {
            logger.error("Exception while starting the GASS server: ", e);
        }
        _verbose(gassServer.toString());
    }

    /*
     * Init Job Output listeners
     */
    private void initJobOutListeners() throws Exception {
        // job output vars
        JobOutputStream stdoutStream = new JobOutputStream(this);
        JobOutputStream stderrStream = new JobOutputStream(this);
        /* GT2
        String jobid = String.valueOf(System.currentTimeMillis());
        gassServer.registerJobOutputStream("err-" + jobid, stderrStream);
        gassServer.registerJobOutputStream("out-" + jobid, stdoutStream);
        */
```

```
        // register output listeners
        gassServer.registerJobOutputStream("err", stderrStream);
        gassServer.registerJobOutputStream("out", stdoutStream);

        _verbose("initJobOutListeners. Registered out listeners.");
        return;
    }

    /**
     * Cleanup: Shut down GASS server
     */
    private void cleanup() {
        if (gassServer != null) {
            gassServer.shutdown();
        }
    }
```

9.1.9 Security

It is important for custom clients to handle OGSA features such as authorization and XML security. Authorization can be one of host, self, or identity. XML security defines the way XML is encrypted: signature or XML encryption.

- Example for setting authorization:

  ```
  Authorization authorization = SelfAuthorization.getInstance();
        GramJob job = new GramJob(…);
        job.setAuthorization(authorization);
  ```

- XML security:

  ```
  …
  Integer xmlSecurity = Constants.SIGNATURE;
  …
  job.setMessageProtectionType(xmlSecurity);
  ```

The program is finally complete with the main subroutines shown in Listing 9.6.

LISTING 9.6 Command-Line Parsing and Main Subroutines

```
    /**
     * Parse command line args
     */
    private boolean parseArgs(String[] args) throws Exception
    {
        if ( args.length == 0 ) {
```

```
            System.err.println(_USAGE);
            return false;
        }
        for (int i = 0; i < args.length; i++) {
            if ( args[i].equalsIgnoreCase("-help") )  {
                System.err.println(_USAGE);
                return false;
            }

            /* factory URL */
            if ( args[i].equalsIgnoreCase("-factory") )
                _factory = args[++i];
            else if ( args[i].equalsIgnoreCase("-file") )
                _rslString =  readFile(args[++i]);
            else if ( args[i].equalsIgnoreCase("-o") ) {
                _redirOutput = true;
                _batch = false;
            }

            /* submission mode: batch, non batch */
            else if ( args[i].equalsIgnoreCase("-b") ) {
                _redirOutput = false;
                _batch = true;
            }

            /* Security options */
            else if ( args[i].equalsIgnoreCase("-sec")) {
                if ( args[++i].equalsIgnoreCase("sig") )
                    _xmlSecurity = Constants.SIGNATURE;
                else if ( args[i].equalsIgnoreCase("enc") )
                    _xmlSecurity = Constants.ENCRYPTION;
                else
                    throw
                        new Exception("Invalid xml security arg:"
    + args[i]);
            }

            /* Authorization */
            else if (args[i].equalsIgnoreCase("-auth") ){
                if ( args[++i].equalsIgnoreCase("host") )
                    _authorization = HostAuthorization.getInstance();
                else if ( args[i].equalsIgnoreCase("self") )
                    _authorization = SelfAuthorization.getInstance();
                else
```

```
                _authorization = new IdentityAuthorization(args[i]);
            }

            /* Others */
            else if (args[i].equalsIgnoreCase("-quiet") ){
                quiet = true;
            }
            else
                throw new Exception("Invalid arg:" + args[i]);
        }
        return true;
    }

    /*
     * Utility subs
     */
    private static String readFile(String path)
          throws IOException, FileNotFoundException
    {
        RandomAccessFile f = new java.io.RandomAccessFile(path, "r");
        byte[] data = new byte[ (int) f.length()];
        f.readFully(data);
        return new String(data);
    }

    private void _verbose(String text) {
        if ( ! quiet )
            System.out.println(this.getClass().getName() + ": " + text);
    }

    /**
     * Main sub
     */
    public static void main(String[] args) {
        org.apache.log4j.Logger.getRootLogger()
            .setLevel(org.apache.log4j.Level.WARN);

        try {
            CustomGRAMClient gram = new CustomGRAMClient(args);
            System.out.println(gram.getJobOutput());
        }
        catch (Exception ex) {
            ex.printStackTrace();
        }
    }
```

A sample run of this program will produce the following output:

```
# The OGSA environment should be set properly
# RSL XML runs the remote command: echo Hello World

java -Djava.endorsed.dirs=C:\ogsa-3.0\endorsed
 -Dorg.globus.ogsa.server.webroot=C:\ogsa-3.0
 -Dorg.globus.ogsa.client.timeout=180000
 -Djava.net.preferIPv4Stack=true
grid.CustomGRAMClient
 -factory
 http://192.168.220.128:8080/ogsa
 /services/base/gram/MasterForkManagedJobFactoryService
 -file rsl\echo.xml  -o

grid.CustomGRAMClient: initJobOutListeners.
Registered out listeners.
grid.CustomGRAMClient:
 GassServer:
  https://192.168.184.1:1052 options (r:+ w:+ so:+ se:+ rc:-)

grid.CustomGRAMClient: Adding output path to GASS redirection
grid.CustomGRAMClient: WAITING FOR JOB TO FINISH
========== Status Notification ==========
Status: Done
=========================================
Hello World
```

9.1.10 MMJFS Performance

Figure 9.2 presents a simple performance evaluation for a single GRAM job submission test against some of the GRAM clients available from Globus. The clients used are GT2 globus-run (C-client), Java CoG GRAM 2.x and OGSA GlobusRun GRAM (MJS). This test was run on an IBM ThinkPad T21 for both client and server. The server runs in RHL 8.x using VMWare workstation 4.x.

MJS has a performance disadvantage compared with its GT2 counterparts. If your job will run for a long time, such as hours or weeks maybe, then a few seconds difference becomes irrelevant. On the other hand, if you need quick response times, then you may want to consider running the GT2-C. CERN has an interesting set of GT3 performance benchmarks that may be of interest to you [CERNGT3Perf].

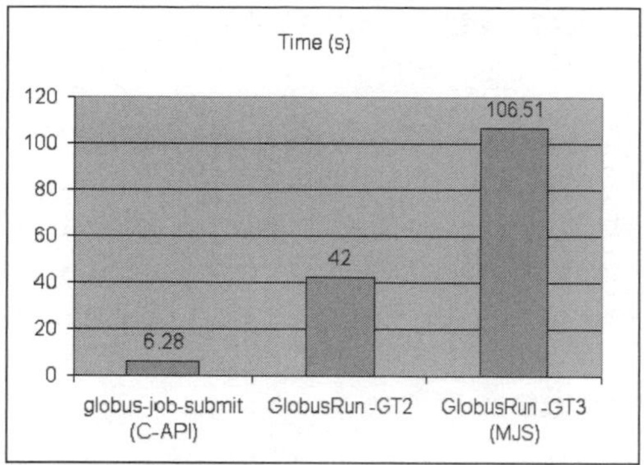

FIGURE 9.2 Performance evaluations of different GRAM clients.

9.2 PRE–WEB ERVICES GRAM ARCHITECTURE (GT2)

The code implemented in this chapter is based on the Java CoG, which combines Java technology with grid computing to develop advanced grid services and access to basic Globus resources. Other CoG implementations include CORBA, Practical Extraction and Report Language (PERL), and Python.

9.2.1 Jobs in GT2

In Globus terminology, a job is a binary executable or command to be run in a remote resource (machine). For this job to run, the remote server must have the Globus Toolkit installed. This remote server is also referred to as a "contact" or "gatekeeper." Currently, toolkit implementations exist for all major flavors of Unix and Linux. An example of a job string would be "/bin/ls," which will produce a listing of the current working directory (similar to the "dir" command in windows).

9.2.2 Job Submission Modes

When a job is submitted to a remote gatekeeper (server) for execution, it can run in two different modes: batch and nonbatch. When a job runs in batch mode, the remote submission call will return immediately with a job ID string. Job IDs use the following format: *https://server.com:39374/15621/1021382777/*. This job ID can later be used to obtain the output of the call using standard Globus Toolkit commands. In nonbatch job submission, the client will wait for the remote gatekeeper to follow through with the execution and return the output. Batch mode submission is useful for jobs that take a long time, such as process-intensive computations.

9.2.3 Resource Specification Language (RSL)

RSL provides a common interchange language to describe resources. The various components of the Globus Resource Management architecture manipulate RSL strings to perform their management functions in cooperation with the other components in the system. An example of an RSL string would be *& (executable = /bin/ls) (directory=/bin)(arguments=-l)*. This RSL string will produce a long listing of the current working directory in a Unix-like system.

9.2.4 Security Infrastructure

The Globus Toolkit uses the Grid Security Infrastructure (GSI) for enabling secure authentication and communication over an open network. GSI provides a number of useful services for grids, including mutual authentication and single sign-on.

GSI is based on public key encryption, X.509 certificates, and the Secure Sockets Layer (SSL) communication protocol. Extensions to these standards have been added for single sign-on and delegation. The Globus Toolkit implementation of the GSI adheres to the Generic Security Service API (GSS-API), which is a standard API for security systems promoted by the Internet Engineering Task Force (IETF).

For this chapter implementation, a guest certificate has been set up for clients to access grid resources. The system administrator of that remote machine can then control access to those resources. It is assumed that the Java CoG kit has been installed on the client and a user certificate has been requested and set up properly.

9.2.5 A Java Program for Job Submission on GT2

The program shown in Listing 9.7 implements a minimal job submission method. Make sure the Java CoG kit libraries are in your classpath to compile properly. User certificates are required for authentication.

The implementation begins by creating a Java class to encapsulate a GRAM Job. This class will be used to submit a job request against a machine also known as *gatekeeper* in either batch or nonbatch mode. Output will be returned on completion.

LISTING 9.7 A Java Program for GRAM2 Job Submission

```
package globus.services;

import org.globus.security.*;
import org.globus.gram.*;
import org.globus.io.gass.server.*;
import org.globus.util.deactivator.Deactivator;

/**
```

```
 * Java CoG Job submission class
 */
public class GridJob
    implements GramJobListener, JobOutputListener
{

  // GASS Server: required to get job output
  private GassServer m_gassServer;

  // URL of the GASS server
  private String m_gassURL = null;

  // GRAM JOB to be executed
  private GramJob m_job = null;

  // job output
  private String m_jobOutput = "";

  // Submission modes:
  // true: do not wait for output
  // false: non-batch, wait for output.
  private boolean m_batch = false;

  // host where job will run
  private String m_remoteHost = null;

  // Globus proxy used for authentication against gatekeeper
  private GlobusProxy m_proxy = null;

// Job output variables:
// Used for non-batch mode jobs to receive output from
// gatekeeper through the GASS server

  private JobOutputStream m_stdoutStream = null;
  private JobOutputStream m_stderrStream = null;

// Globus job id on the form:
// https://server.com:39374/15621/1021382777/
  private String m_jobid = null;

  /**
   * Constructor
   * @param Contact String remote host
   * @param batch boolean submission mode
```

```
 */
public GridJob(String Contact, boolean batch) {
  m_remoteHost = Contact; // remote host
  m_batch = batch; // submission mode
}
```

Note the interfaces implemented: `GramJobListener` and `JobOutputListener`. The `GramJobListener` interface is required if our class is to wait for job status. Job status can be one of `PENDING`, `ACTIVE`, `DONE`, `FAILED`, `SUSPENDED`, or `UNSUBMITTED`. The `JobOutputListener` interface is required for the actual job output notifications.

The constructor of this class takes two arguments: a "Contact" or remote host where the job will run and a Boolean value representing the submission mode: true=batch, false=nonbatch. Batch means "do not wait for output." In this mode, the GRAM request will return immediately with a unique job ID that can be used later on to retrieve that output. Batching is useful for long-lived jobs (jobs that take hours or even days). If the request is to take a short time (seconds or minutes), set the batch flag to false (nonbatch).

9.2.6 Listening for Job Output

Globus uses the *GASS* service to listen for output. For this output to be transferred back and forth between client and server, the code shown in Listing 9.8 can be used.

LISTING 9.8 Starting the GASS Server for Output Transfer

```
/**
 * Start the Globus GASS Server. Used to get the output from the server
 * back to the client.
 */
private boolean startGassServer(GlobusProxy proxy) {
  if (m_gassServer != null) {
    return true;
  }
  try {
    m_gassServer = new GassServer(proxy, 0);
    m_gassURL = m_gassServer.getURL();
  }
  catch (Exception e) {
    System.err.println("gass server failed to start!");
    e.printStackTrace();
    return false;
  }
  m_gassServer.registerDefaultDeactivator();
  return true;
```

```
}

/**
 * Init job out listeners for non-batch mode jobs.
 */
private void initJobOutListeners() throws Exception {
  if (m_stdoutStream != null) {
    return;
  }

  // job output vars
  m_stdoutStream = new JobOutputStream(this);
  m_stderrStream = new JobOutputStream(this);
  m_jobid = String.valueOf(System.currentTimeMillis());

  // register output listeners
  m_gassServer.registerJobOutputStream(
"err-" + m_jobid, m_stderrStream);
  m_gassServer.registerJobOutputStream(
"out-" + m_jobid, m_stdoutStream);
  return;
}
```

A GASS server must be started before sending the GRAM request. The `initJobOutListeners` method is used to register `stdout/stderr` streams so that the output can be received from the GRAM protocol. For this to work, an ID value is generated using `System.currentTimeMillis()`, and the streams are registered with the GASS server using that value (see Listing 9.9).

9.2.7 Handling Received Output

The `GramJobListener` and `JobOutputListener` interfaces implemented by our class require several methods to be implemented to handle output sent by the server (see Table 9.1).

TABLE 9.1 `GramJobListener` and `JobOutputListener` Events

Method	Description
`public void statusChanged (GramJob job)`	This method is used to notify the implementer when the status of a job has changed.
`public void outputChanged (String output)`	Called whenever the job's output is updated.
`public void outputClosed()`	Called whenever job is finished and no more output will be generated.

LISTING 9.9 Output Events Fired Though the GASS Protocol in GT2

```
/**
* This method is used to notify the implementer when the status of a
* GramJob has changed.
*
* @param job The GramJob whose status has changed.
*/
public void statusChanged(GramJob job) {
    try {
           if ( job.getStatus() == GramJob.STATUS_DONE )
           {
               // notify waiting thread when job ready
               m_jobOutput = "Job sent. url=" + job.getIDAsString();

               // if notify enabled return URL as output
               synchronized(this) {
                       notify();
               }
       }
    }
    catch (Exception ex) {
       System.out.println("statusChanged Error:" + ex.getMessage());
    }
 }

/**
* It is called whenever the job's output
* has been updated.
*
* @param output new output
*/
```

```
public void outputChanged(String output) {
   m_jobOutput += output;
}

/**
* It is called whenever job finished
* and no more output will be generated.
*/
public void outputClosed() {
}
```

Note the synchronization mechanism implemented by `statusChanged`. When the job completes execution (status equals `DONE`), a notification is sent to the job execution thread to return. We will see in the actual request implementation that, if the submission fires in nonbatch mode, the current thread must wait for the gatekeeper to complete and return the output back to the client. This scheme is recommended for jobs that take a short time to complete. If your job is to be run for hours or days, use a "batch" mode.

9.2.8 Sending the GRAM Job Request

The main part of the GRAM request is implemented in Listing 9.10. The steps required for job submission include the following:

- Loading a proxy. The `GlobusProxy` class provides a convenient method: `GlobusProxy.getDefaultUserProxy()`. Note that the Java CoG kit and user certificates must be set up properly.
- Starting the GASS server.
- Setting up job output listeners for the client to receive output and error streams.
- Formatting the RSL string properly according to the submission mode.
- Sending the actual GRAM job request and waiting for output (if nonbatch).

The Java CoG kit must be installed properly and the user certificates set up correctly or the proxy load call will fail, throwing an exception. A host certificate must be installed also in the remote gatekeeper.

LISTING 9.10 A GRAM Request in GT2

```
public synchronized String GlobusRun(String RSL) {
  try {
    // load default Globus proxy. Java CoG kit must be installed
    // and a user certificate setup properly
    m_proxy = GlobusProxy.getDefaultUserProxy();
```

```
// Start GASS server
if (!startGassServer(m_proxy)) {
  throw new Exception("Unable to stat GASS server.");
}

// setup Job Output listeners
initJobOutListeners();

System.out.println("proxy Issuer=" + m_proxy.getIssuer()
                   + "\nsubject=" + m_proxy.getSubject()
                   + "Strength=" + m_proxy.getStrength()
                   + " Gass: " + m_gassServer.toString());

// Append GASS URL to job String so we can get some output back
String newRSL = null;

// if non-batch, then get some output back
if (!m_batch) {
  newRSL = "&" + RSL.substring(0, RSL.indexOf('&')) +
      "(rsl_substitution=(GLOBUSRUN_GASS_URL " + m_gassURL + "))" +
      RSL.substring(RSL.indexOf('&') + 1, RSL.length()) +
      "(stdout=$(GLOBUSRUN_GASS_URL)/dev/stdout-" + m_jobid + ")" +
      "(stderr=$(GLOBUSRUN_GASS_URL)/dev/stderr-" + m_jobid + ")";
}
else {
  // format batching RSL so output can be retrieved
  // later on using any GTK commands
  newRSL = RSL +
      "(stdout=x-gass-cache://$(GLOBUS_GRAM_JOB_CONTACT) )" +
      "stdout anExtraTag)" +
      "(stderr=x-gass-cache://$(GLOBUS_GRAM_JOB_CONTACT)” )" +
      "stderr anExtraTag)";
}

m_job = new GramJob(newRSL);

// Load a GSI proxy.
// CoG kit and user credentials must be installed and set
// up properly
m_job.setCredentials(m_proxy);

// if non-batch then listen for output
if (!m_batch) {
  m_job.addListener(this);
```

```
        }

        System.out.println("Sending job request to: " + m_remoteHost);
        m_job.request(m_remoteHost, m_batch, false);

        // Wait for job to complete
        if (!m_batch) {
          synchronized (this) {
            try {
              wait();
            }
            catch (InterruptedException e) {}
          }
        }
        else {
          // do not wait for job. Return immediately
          m_jobOutput = "Job sent. url=" + m_job.getIDAsString();
        }
      }
      catch (Exception ex) {
        if (m_gassServer != null) {
          // unregister from gass server
          m_gassServer.unregisterJobOutputStream("err-" + m_jobid);
          m_gassServer.unregisterJobOutputStream("out-" + m_jobid);
        }
        m_jobOutput = "Error submitting job: " + ex.getClass() + ":" +
            ex.getMessage();
      }

      // cleanup
      Deactivator.deactivateAll();
      return m_jobOutput;
    }
```

This method is implemented as synchronized for thread safety. Also, if the request is to be sent in nonbatch mode, the running thread must wait for the server to complete execution and return the output. When the job completes, a `statusChanged` event will fire, setting the status to `DONE`. At this point, the running thread will notify waiting threads to proceed with execution returning the output back to the client.

9.2.9 Job Submission Test

Finally, the last step is to write a test subroutine for the GRAM2 client class. Listing 9.11 submits a test request for a date command on a remote GT2 host.

LISTING 9.11 GRAM2 Submission Test

```
/**
 * GRAM2 submission test
 * @param args String[]
 */
public static void main(String[] args) {
      // GRAM request test
      // run /bin/date on myserver.mygrid.com
      String RSL = "& (executable = /bin/date)(directory=/bin)";

      GridJob Job1 = new GridJob("myserver.mygrid.com", false);

      // wait for job to complete and display output
      String jobOut = Job1.GlobusRun(RSL);
      System.out.println(jobOut);
}
```

Note the RSL string *& (executable = /bin/ls)(directory=/bin)(arguments=-l)*. It contains the actual job arguments to be executed on the remote server. These arguments can be changed to represent any executable or program present on the server. The output of this program should be as shown in Listing 9.12.

LISTING 9.12 GT2 GRAM Request Output

```
proxy Issuer=CN=BlueGrid Guest,OU=Guest_Project,O=BlueGrid,O=IBM
subject=CN=proxy,CN=BlueGrid Guest,OU=Guest_Project,O=BlueGrid,O=IBM
Strength=512 Gass: GassServer: https://9.45.188.210:4294 options
  (r:+ w:+ so:+ se:+ rc:-)
GASS URL: https://9.45.188.210:4294
Sending job request to: 9.45.124.126

The current date is: Mon 02/07/2005
```

This code demonstrates the GRAM 2 Java API for job submission using the CoG Kit. It can be easily enhanced into a Web service or servlet. Such a service has the advantage of allowing clients to access grid resources without requiring the grid API libraries to be installed in the client. Furthermore, clients can be written in any computer language that supports the Simple Object Access Protocol (SOAP), such as Java, Visual Basic, HTML, and so on. Currently, there are efforts to develop an open grid services infrastructure by the Globus project.

9.3 SUMMARY

Resource allocation is at the core of the Globus remote program execution infrastructure. It allows you to run jobs remotely, using a set of WSDL client interfaces for submitting, monitoring, and terminating a job. This chapter introduced the following resource allocation topics:

- An overview of the GRAM architecture
- A description of grid services for job submission, including installation, configuration, and troubleshooting
- Sample programs for resource management and security
- Performance evaluation tests of various MMJFS clients provided by Globus
- Pre-Web Services GRAM Architecture (GT2) for job submission
- Sample programs for GT2 job submission

REFERENCES

[CERNGT3Perf] CERN GT3 performance benchmarks. Available online at *http://lcg.web.cern.ch/LCG/PEB/GTA/GTA_OGSA/DummyService.*

[CzajkowskiFoster99] K. Czajkowski, Ian Foster, and Carl Kesselman. "Resource Co-Allocation in Computational Grids." *Proceedings of the Eighth IEEE International Symposium on High Performance Distributed Computing (HPDC-8)*, pp. 219–228, 1999.

[GramRSL04] Resource Management for the Globus Toolkit. University of Chicago. Accessed March 2004 at *http://www-fp.globus.org/toolkit/resource-management.html.*

[WSGramGuide04] *WS GRAM: Developer's Guide.* The Globus project. University of Chicago. Accessed online July 2004 at *http://www-unix.globus.org/toolkit/docs/3.2/gram/ws/developer/architecture.html.*

10 Data Management

In This Chapter

- GridFTP
- Transferring Files Using Multiple Protocols
- Summary
- References

This chapter describes the basics of data transfer on grid environments using the GridFTP APIs provided by the Java Commodity Grid (CoG) Kit 1.2 and the Globus Toolkit. The source code for all programs can be found in the companion CD-ROM of this book.

This chapter includes information on the following topics:

- An overview of the GridFTP protocol for remote file transfer
- A sample Java program for connecting to the GridFTP server, performing single, multiple, or parallel transfers
- Common mistakes and error messages seen when working with GridFTP and troubleshooting tips for those errors
- Transferring files using other grid protocols such Globus Access to Secondary Storage (GASS)

10.1 GRIDFTP

GridFTP is a high-performance file transfer protocol designed specifically for grid environments. The following sections describe GridFTP features along with source code.

10.1.1 Overview

Computational grids provide the infrastructure for powerful new tools for investigation, including desktop computing, smart instruments, collaboration, and distributed computing. The Globus Project is currently engaged in defining and developing a persistent data grid with the following capabilities [ReliableDataTransfer04]:

- High-performance, secure, robust data transfer mechanisms
- A set of tools for creating and manipulating replicas of large datasets
- A mechanism for maintaining a catalog of dataset replicas

GridFTP is a high-performance, secure, reliable data transfer protocol optimized for high-bandwidth wide-area networks. The GridFTP protocol is based on FTP, the popular Internet file transfer protocol [ReliableDataTransfer04]. This protocol and family of tools were born from a realization that the grid environment needed a fast, secure, efficient, and reliable transport mechanism. According to Allcock and colleagues [GridDataManagement02], large decentralized computational grids require a robust transport mechanism with the following features:

- **Parallel data transfer:** Multiple TCP streams to improve bandwidth over using a single TCP stream. Parallel data transfer is supported through FTP command extensions and data channel extensions.
- **Grid Security Infrastructure (GSI) and Kerberos authentication support:** User-controlled settings of various levels of data integrity and confidentiality. This feature provides a robust and flexible authentication, integrity, and confidentiality mechanism for transferring files.
- **Third-party control of data transfer:** Support for managing large data sets for large distributed communities. This provides third-party control of transfers between storage servers.
- **Striped data transfer:** Capabilities to partition data across multiple servers to improve aggregate bandwidth. GridFTP supports striped data transfers through extensions defined in the Grid Forum draft.
- **Partial file transfer:** New FTP commands to support transfers of regions of a file, unlike standard FTP that requires the application to transfer the entire file.
- **Reliable data transfer:** Fault recovery methods for handling transient network failures and server outages and for restarting failed transfers.

- **Manual control of TCP buffer size:** Support for achieving maximum bandwidth with TCP/IP.
- **Integrated instrumentation:** Support for returning restart and performance markers.

10.1.2 Connecting to a GridFTP Server

The Java program in Listing 10.1 implements a basic GridFTP transfer to the local filesystem.

LISTING 10.1 GridFTP.java, a Client Program to Transfer Files via GridFTP

```
package grid.ftp;

import java.io.*;

import org.globus.ftp.*;
import org.globus.ftp.exception.*;
import org.globus.gsi.*;
import org.globus.gsi.gssapi.*;
import org.ietf.jgss.GSSCredential;

import java.util.*;
import org.apache.log4j.Logger;
import org.apache.log4j.Level;

import java.security.cert.X509Certificate;

/**
 * GridFTP: Transfer files via the GridFTP protocol
 * run grid-proxy-init before running this program
 *
 * Both client and server must have each other CA certificates
 * for mutual authentication to work
 */
public class GridFTP
{
    private static Logger logger =
            Logger.getLogger(GridFTP.class.getName());

    // Protocol client,  provided by he Cog API
    private GridFTPClient client = null;

    // default port
    private static int GRIDFTP_PORT = 2811;
```

```
/**
  * Constructor
  * @param host remote GridFTP host
  * @param port remote GridFTP port (default is 2811)
  */
public GridFTP(String host, int port)
    throws ServerException, IOException
{
        client = new GridFTPClient(host, port);

        /**
         * Authenticate using the default credentials.
         * Requires GSI to be configured properly on the client.
         * Including user cert/key pair and CA certificates
         *
         * Note: You should run grid-proxy-init before running this
         * program
         */
        client.authenticate(null);
}
```

The Globus Toolkit uses the standard Apache log4j package from *http://jakarta.apache.org/log4j/docs/* to display log messages by defining a static logger:

```
private static Logger logger =
Logger.getLogger(MyGridFTP.class.getName());
```

This package is very popular among Java programmers and can be very helpful when debugging your classes. The class constructor takes the hostname and port as arguments and authenticates against the server using GSI credentials.

This class works only with the Globus Toolkit 2.2 or later. GSI changed significantly after version 2.0. To ensure that you use the correct version of the Java Commodity Grid (CoG) Kit, look at Table 12.1 for a summary of the main GSI changes from Java CoG Kit 0.9.13 to the current version, Java CoG Kit 1.2:

The functionality of the `org.globus.security.GlobusProxy` class is largely replaced by the `org.globus.gsi.GlobusCredential` class. However, Globus recommends not using the `org.globus.gsi.GlobusCredential` class because it is a representation of Public Key Infrastructure (PKI) credentials that are specific to one security protocol. Instead, Globus recommends using the Generic Security Service (GSS) abstractions as much as possible.

TABLE 12.1 Summary of Changes in the API Provided by the Java CoG Kit

Deprecated packages	Replaced by
`org.globus.security`	`org.ietf.jgss`
`org.globus.io.ftp`	`org.globus.ftp`
`org.globus.mds.MDS`	Obsolete: Globus recommends the use of JNDI with an LDAP provider or Netscape Directory SDK to access MDS directly.

10.1.3 Converting Legacy Proxies to GSS Credentials

If you are porting applications from GT2 to GT3, you may need to convert legacy proxies known as `GSI_2_PROXY` to `GSSCredentials` to authenticate to the GridFTP server in some cases. The code snippet from Listing 10.2 shows how to do this conversion:

```
GlobusCredential globusCred = new GlobusCredential(...);
GSSCredential  cred = new GlobusGSSCredentialImpl(globusCred,
GSSCredential.DEFAULT_LIFETIME);
```

For legacy proxies (level2), the second argument must be one of the following: `DEFAULT_LIFETIME`, `INITIATE_AND_ACCEPT`, or `INITIATE_ONLY`. Otherwise, you may see the following exception: *Authentication failed [Root error message: Defective credential error]. Root exception is Defective credential error. (Mechanism level: Invalid credential usage.)*

10.1.4 Transferring Data

The code in Listing 10.2 implements a single file transfer through GridFTP.

LISTING 10.2 Single GridFTP Transfer

```
/**
 * Transfer a file from a remote host
 * @param remoteFile Remote file. It must exist in the server
 * @param localFile Where should the remote file be stored?
 * @param transferType FTP transfer type. One of:
 *     GridFTPSession.ASCII
 *     GridFTPSession.BINARY
 */
```

```
public void download(String remoteFile
, String localFile, int transferType)

    throws ServerException, ClientException, IOException

{
  // remote file size
  long size = client.getSize(remoteFile);

  // check if remote file exists
  // if not an exception will be thrown...
  if (client.exists(remoteFile)) {
    client.setType(transferType);

    /** required to transfer multiple files **/
    client.setLocalPassive();
    client.setActive();

    final FileOutputStream fos = new FileOutputStream(localFile);

    // get the file, use the DataSink interface to write incoming data
    // Implement this interface to provide your own ways
    // of storing data.
    // It must be thread safe; in parallel transfer mode several
    // streams may attempt to write.
    client.get(remoteFile, new DataSink() {
public synchronized void write(Buffer buffer)
throws IOException
{
System.err.println(
"received " + buffer.getLength() + " bytes");

fos.write(buffer.getBuffer());
}

public void close() throws IOException {
// close File output streams
fos.flush();
fos.close();
};
    }, null);

    // transfer ok
    logger.info(
```

```
                "Successfully transferred: "
                        + remoteFile
                        + " to "
                        + localFile
                        + " size: "
                        + size);

    } else {
            System.err.println(remoteFile + " doesn't exist");
    }
}
```

The interface `DataSink` is useful for writing the incoming data. Implement it to provide your own ways of storing data. *Note:* The code must be thread safe. In parallel transfer mode, several streams may attempt to write to the interface.

10.1.5 Transferring Multiple Files

Transferring multiple files requires the client to set the transfer mode to passive for the listening side and to active for the sending side. It is not enough to use multiple get calls because the data channel is automatically closed after each transfer. For each get call, the client side is receiving data (Passive) and the remote host is sending (Active). Before each `get` call, issue the following line of code:

```
client.setLocalPassive();
client.setActive();
```

Before each `put` operation, the inverse is required:

```
client.setLocalActive();
client.setPassive();.
```

10.1.6 Parallel Transfers

At first glance, a parallel transfer may sound as though the client is capable of transferring multiple files from multiple servers in Kazaa or Morpheus style. In reality, however, parallel transfer means simply that multiple streams will be opened to transfer the same file from the same server. For two-party transfers, GridFTP will only add overhead in single processor machines [ReliableDataTransfer04]. In any case, the client will transfer multiple copies of the same file without any slicing whatsoever, although it may increase performance if you have a multiprocessor system.

In case of two-party transfer, parallelism should be carefully chosen. The advantage of having multiple streams has mostly to do with low-level TCP procedures and is also related to the TCP window size. Using twice the number of parallel streams will not necessarily produce twice the performance. Actually, from a certain point, you will experience a decrease in performance. Current implementation of the FTP package handles each data pathway in a separate thread, so unless your machine has multiple CPUs, you only add computing overhead by increasing parallelism [ReliableDataTransfer04].

A parallel transfer requires extended mode. Furthermore, the transfer type must be image, and the data sink/source must support random data access and be thread safe. Multiple threads may write to it. See Listing 10.3 for a method that implements a parallel *get* call:

LISTING 10.3 Parallel Transfer

```
/**
 * Transfer a file in parallel:
 * Useful if you have a multiprocessor system.
 * Note: Not to be confused with file slicing transfers like Kazaa!
 * In reality, it opens 2 parallel transfer streams to the
 * same remote file.
 * Requires transfer type IMAGE and transfer mode EBLOCK
 */
public void parallelDownload(String remoteFile, String localFile)
    throws ServerException, ClientException
    , FileNotFoundException, IOException
{
  // check if remote file exists
  // if not an exception will be thrown by the server
  if (client.exists(remoteFile)) {
    // transfer type must be IMAGE for parallel...
    client.setType(GridFTPSession.TYPE_IMAGE);

    /** extended mode is required by parallel transfers **/
    client.setMode(GridFTPSession.MODE_EBLOCK);

    /** required to transfer multiple files **/
    client.setLocalPassive();
    client.setActive();

    /** set parallelism **/
    // Number of parallel streams to be opened
    client.setOptions(new RetrieveOptions(2));

    // get file, use the DataSink interface to write incoming data
    // Implement it to provide your own ways of storing data.
```

```
        // It must be thread safe; in parallel transfer
        // mode several streams may attempt to write.
        DataSink sink =
            new FileRandomIO(new RandomAccessFile(localFile, "rw"));

        long size = client.getSize(remoteFile);
        client.extendedGet(remoteFile, size, sink, null);

        // transfer ok
        logger.info(
            "Successfully transferred: "
            + remoteFile
            + " to "
            + localFile
            + " size: "
            + size);
      }
      else {
        System.err.println(remoteFile + " doesn't exist");
      }
    }
```

10.1.7 Testing the Transfer

To test the remote file transfer, use Listing 10.4.

LISTING 10.4 Testing the Transfer

```
    /**
     * Cleanup FTP connection & certs
     */
    public void close() throws ServerException, IOException {
            client.close();
    }

    /**
    * Simple test
    */
    public static void main(String[] args)
    {
        /**
         * This line is very useful for debugging errors.
         * It displays log4j debug messages including
         * server information
         */
```

```
        Logger.getRoot().setLevel(Level.INFO);

        /**
         * Simple GridFTP Transfer test
         */

        // remote files
        String rf1 = "/tmp/testfile1.txt";
        String rf2 = "/tmp/testfile2.txt";

        String host = "myhost.mygrid.com";

        // local files
        String lf1 = "c:\\temp\\testfile1.txt";
        String lf2 = "c:\\temp\\testfile2.txt";

        int TRANSFER_TYPE = GridFTPSession.TYPE_ASCII;

        try {

            GridFTP myGridFTP = new GridFTP(host, GridFTP.GRIDFTP_PORT);

            // regular transfer test
            myGridFTP.download(rf1, lf1, TRANSFER_TYPE);
            myGridFTP.download(rf2, lf2, TRANSFER_TYPE);

            // parallel transfer test
            myGridFTP.parallelDownload(rf1, lf1);
            myGridFTP.parallelDownload(rf2, lf2);

            myGridFTP.close();

        } catch (Exception e) {
                System.err.println(e);
        }
    }
```

The log4j tool is useful both for debugging and for monitoring the FTP transfer:

- For basic messages, use `Logger.getRoot().setLevel(Level.INFO)`.
- For extended information, use `Logger.getRoot().setLevel(Level.DEBUG)`.

An INFO level execution of this class renders the following sample output:

```
    [main] INFO test.MyGridFTP - subject : O = IBM, O = intraGrid,
    OU = Guest Project, CN = intraGrid Guest, CN = limited proxy

    issuer : O = IBM, O = intraGrid, OU = Guest Project, CN = intraGrid
Guest
    strength : 512bits
    timeleft : 31568251sec
    proxy type : limited legacy globus proxy

    [main] INFO vanilla.FTPControlChannel - Control channel received :
    220dhcp126.adtech.internet.ibm.com GridFTP Server 1.5GSSAPI type
Globus /
    GSI wu - 2.6.2 (gcc32dbg, 1032298778 - 28) ready.
    [main] INFO vanilla.FTPControlChannel - Control channel sending :
    AUTH GSSAPI

    [main] INFO vanilla.FTPControlChannel - Control channel received :
334Using authentication type GSSAPI; ADAT must follow
    [main] INFO auth.HostAuthorization - Authorization : HOST
    [main] INFO vanilla.FTPControlChannel - Control channel received :
    235GSSAPI Authentication succeeded
    [main] INFO vanilla.FTPControlChannel - Control channel sending :
USER :
    globus - mapping :

    [main] INFO vanilla.FTPControlChannel - Control channel received :
    331GSSAPI user / O = IBM / O = intraGrid / OU = Guest Project /
    CN = intraGrid Guest is authorized as ig_guest
    [main] INFO vanilla.FTPControlChannel - Control channel sending :
    PASS dummy

    [main] INFO vanilla.FTPControlChannel - Control channel received :
    230User ig_guest logged in.
    [main] INFO vanilla.FTPControlChannel - Control channel sending :
    SIZE / home / intraGrid / ig_guest / .shared_files / libuser.conf

    [main] INFO vanilla.FTPControlChannel - Control channel received :
2132378
    [main] INFO vanilla.FTPControlChannel - Control channel sending :
    SIZE / home / intraGrid / ig_guest / .shared_files / libuser.conf

    [main] INFO vanilla.FTPControlChannel - Control channel received :
2132378
```

```
    [main] INFO vanilla.FTPControlChannel - Control channel sending :
TYPE A

    [main] INFO vanilla.FTPControlChannel - Control channel received :
    200Type set to A.
    [main] INFO vanilla.FTPControlChannel - Control channel sending :
PASV

    [main] INFO vanilla.FTPControlChannel - Control channel received :
    227Entering Passive Mode(9, 45, 124, 126, 164, 7)
    [main] INFO vanilla.FTPControlChannel - Control channel sending :
    RETR / home / intraGrid / ig_guest / .shared_files / libuser.conf

    [Thread - 0] INFO auth.SelfAuthorization - Authorization : SELF
    received 2048bytes
    received 330bytes
    [Thread - 1] INFO vanilla.FTPControlChannel - Control channel
received :
    150Opening ASCII mode data connection.
    [Thread - 1] INFO vanilla.FTPControlChannel - Control channel
received :
    226Transfer complete.

    [main] INFO test.MyGridFTP - Successfully transferred :
    /home /intraGrid/ig_guest/.shared_files/libuser.conf to d :
    \temp \libuser.conf size : 2378
    [main] INFO vanilla.FTPControlChannel - Control channel sending :
QUIT

    [main] INFO vanilla.FTPControlChannel - Control channel received :
    221 - You have transferred 0bytes in 1files.

    221 - Total traffic for this session was 6260bytes in 1transfers.
    221 -
    Thank you for using the FTP service on
dhcp126.adtech.internet.ibm.com.
    221Goodbye.

    [main] INFO vanilla.FTPControlChannel - Control channel sending :
QUIT
```

Useful information in the preceding sample output includes the version of the GridFTP server. In this particular case, it is GridFTP Server 1.5 GSSAPI type Globus/GSI wu-2.6.2 (gcc32dbg, 1032298778-28).

10.1.8 Troubleshooting

Most of the problems in writing this code relates to dealing with legacy proxies and converting them to `GSSCredentials`. Take a careful look at the constructor of this class to make sure you understand the conversion process. Also ensure that you are running the correct versions of the Globus Toolkit and the GridFTP servers. Older versions (before 1.5) are not enabled for GSSAPI.

Also make sure your client-side Java libraries, provided by the CoG kit, are properly configured in your class path. A set of user certificates is also required to connect through GSI.

10.1.8.1 Runtime or Defective Credential Errors

Defective credentials indicate a problem with your client and server certificates. The following tips should be kept in mind when you run the code in this chapter:

- Make sure your Java environment is setup properly. This is done by setting the environment variable `GLOBUS_LOCATION` to the install directory, and running the Java environment configuration script `$GLOBUS_LOCATION/etc/globus-dev-env.{csh,sh}`.
- A GSI proxy should be generated first on the client by running the command `grid-proxy-init`.

10.1.8.2 Authentication Failed Errors

If you run into an authentication failed error, here are some tips that can help you fix them:

- For mutual authentication to succeed, both client and server require a user certificate, private key, and CA certificate to be properly configured. On the client, the path to these files is described in the file `cog.properites` found in the user's home directory `$HOME/.globus` (in Unix systems). See, for example, Listing 10.5.

LISTING 10.5 Sample Client GSI Configuration File `cog.properties`

```
#Java CoG Kit Configuration File
#Wed Feb 02 11:15:41 EST 2005
usercert=C\:\\Documents and Settings
\\Administrator\\.globus\\usercert.pem
userkey=C\:\\Documents and Settings
\\Administrator\\.globus\\userkey.pem
proxy=C\:\\DOCUME~1\\vsilva
\\LOCALS~1\\Temp\\x509up_u_vsilva
```

```
cacert=C\:\\Documents and Settings\\
Administrator\\.globus\\CA\\9d8d5dcd.0,
C\:\\Documents and Settings\\
Administrator\\.globus\\certificates\\c8af9b73.0
ip=9.42.87.139
```

- Mutual authentication requires that both client and server trust each other. This means that either all certificates must be signed by the same CA, or both CA certificates be installed in the client and server. This is very important and a source of many problems for developers and system administrators.

10.2 TRANSFERRING FILES USING MULTIPLE PROTOCOLS

If your organization requires transferring data using multiple protocols, the CoG API provides everything you need to make these transfer types a snap. The package `org.globus.io.urlcopy` provides a set of interfaces for transferring files using multiple grid protocols including GASS, GridFTP, HTTPS, and HTTP. The transfers are performed using URLs of the form:

```
PROTOCOL://HOST:PORT/FILE
```

For example to transfer a file between two GridFTP servers:

Source URL: gsiftp://host1:2811/c:/temp/file.xml
Destination URL: gsiftp://host2:2811/c:/temp/file.xml

Or, to perform a third-party transfer from a GASS server to a GridFTP server:

Source URL: https://host1:3154/c:/temp/file.xml
Destination URL: gsiftp://host2:2811/tmp/file.xml

A program to perform these types of transfers in GT 3.2.x is simple (see Listing 10.6).

LISTING 10.6 URLCopy.java, a Program to Transfer Data Using Multiple Protocols

```
package grid.datatransfer;

import java.net.MalformedURLException;

import org.apache.log4j.Level;
```

```
import org.apache.log4j.Logger;

import org.globus.io.urlcopy.*;
import org.globus.util.*;
import org.globus.gsi.gssapi.auth.IdentityAuthorization;

/**
 * Sample program for data transfer using multiple protocols:
 *  GASS - Globus Access to Secondary Storage
 *  GridFTP - A high-performance, secure, reliable data
 *          transfer protocol optimized for high-bandwidth
 *          wide-area networks.
 *
 * @author Vladimir Silva
 */
public class URLCopy
        implements UrlCopyListener
{
    long transferredBytes;

    // UrlCopyListener Interface methods
    // fires multiple times
    public void transfer(long transferredBytes, long totalBytes)
    {
            this.transferredBytes += transferredBytes;
    }

    // fires if a transfer error occurs
    public void transferError(Exception e) {
            System.err.println("transferError:" + e);
    }

    // fires when transfer is complete
    public void transferCompleted() {
            System.out.println("transferCompleted: bytes"
                    + transferredBytes);
    }

    /**
     * A method to transfer data between machines
     * @param fromURL Source URL. For example:
     *              https://localhost:3154/c:/temp/foo.xml (for GASS)
     *              gsiftp://localhost:2811/c:/temp/foo.xml (GridFTP)
     * @param toURL Destination URL.
```

```
 * @param subject Certificate subject or NULL to use default
 * @param thirdParty Third party transfer (GsiFTP only)
 * @param dcau Data Channel
 */
void transferData (String fromURL, String toURL
        , String subject, boolean thirdParty, boolean dcau)

        throws MalformedURLException, UrlCopyException
{
        GlobusURL from= new GlobusURL(fromURL);
        GlobusURL to  = new GlobusURL(toURL);
        UrlCopy uc          = new UrlCopy();

        // ftp only options: thirdParty, dcau

        uc.setSourceUrl(from);
        uc.setDestinationUrl(to);
        uc.setUseThirdPartyCopy(thirdParty);
        uc.setDCAU(dcau);

        // set Authorization - subject if any
        if ( subject != null && ! subject.equals("") ) {
                uc.setSourceAuthorization(
                       new IdentityAuthorization(subject));
                uc.setDestinationAuthorization(
                       new IdentityAuthorization(subject));
        }


        // fire transfer thread
        uc.addUrlCopyListener(this);
        uc.run();

}

/* for test purposes only */
public static void main(String[] args) {
    try {
      Logger.getRootLogger().setLevel(Level.INFO);

      /**
       * Test #1: GASS server transfer test between
       * 2 instances running in the same host
       */
```

```
            String fromURL = "https://localhost:3154/c:/temp/foo.xml";
            String toURL   = "https://localhost:3155/c:/temp/foo1.xml";

            // cert subject. Set to null to use the default
            String subject = null;

            // GridFTP only options
            boolean thirdp = false;
            boolean dcau   = false;

            // fire transfer
            URLCopy transClient = new URLCopy();
            transClient.transferData(fromURL, toURL
                                    , subject, thirdp, dcau);

            /**
             * Other transfer samples.
             * Third party transfer between  2 FTP servers
             *             (from) gsiftp://host1:2811/c:/temp/foo.xml
             *             (to) gsiftp://host2:2811/c:/temp/foo.xml
             *
             * GASS to FTP transfer
             *             (from)
https://localhost:3154/c:/temp/foo.xml
             *             (to) gsiftp://host1:2811/c:/temp/foo.xml
             */

        } catch (Exception e) {
                System.err.println(e);
        }
    }
}
```

10.3 SUMMARY

GridFTP is a secure, reliable data transfer protocol optimized for high-performance networks based on FTP, the popular Internet protocol. This chapter has provided a developer's overview of GridFTP features with sample programs based on the Java Cog Kit API provided by the Globus Toolkit. GridFTP is the foundation of data management services, which constitute the second pillar of the Grid Services Architecture. The third major pillar, Information Services, is discussed in the next chapter.

REFERENCES

[GridDataManagement02] B. Allcock, J. Bester, J. Bresnahan, A. L. Chervenak, I. Foster, C. Kesselman, S. Meder, V. Nefedova, D. Quesnal, and S. Tuecke. "Data Management and Transfer in High Performance Computational Grid Environments." *Parallel Computing Journal, 28*(5), May 2002, pp. 749–771.

[ReliableDataTransfer04] W. E. Allcock, I. Foster, and R. Madduri. "Reliable Data Transport: A Critical Service for the Grid." Building Service Based Grids Workshop, Global Grid Forum 11, June 2004.

11 Information Services

In This Chapter

- WS Information Services (MDS3)
- Querying Default Data Providers
- Custom MDS3 Data Providers
- Pre-WS Information Services (MDS2)
- Summary
- References

Information Services are also known as Monitoring and Discovery Services (MDS). MDS provides information for resource discovery, selection, and optimization. It can be used by applications or virtual organizations (VO) to obtain a general overview of the capabilities and services provided by a computational grid. Globus has divided MDS into pre–Web Services (MDS2) and WS Information Services (MDS3) [InfoServices01]. This chapter provides information on the following topics:

- Information Services for GT3, also known as MDS3, includes the Information Model, Data Collection, Aggregation, Queries, and Security.
- Sample programs to query the default data providers.
- A real-world application of a custom information provider for GT3: an Information Provider for remote schedulers using the SSH protocol. Supported schedulers are OpenPBS, Condor, and SGE.

- Sample programs for pre-WS Information Services (MDS2), including step-by-step implementation, installation, configuration, and troubleshooting.
- A custom MDS2 client program for the Java language.

11.1 WS INFORMATION SERVICES (MDS3)

MDS3 is implemented as a set of grid services. Grid services can be classified into two big groups: *Persistent* if they outlive the process that created them or *transient* if otherwise. Services are identified by one or more instances and express their state via Service Data Elements (SDE) [MDSGuide03].

11.1.1 Information Model

The model used by MDS is based on mechanisms provided by Open Grid Services Architecture (OGSA), such as:

Factories: Objects that create service instances. They return a GSH and maintain service data elements.

Grid Service Handle (GSH): A unique identifier for a service. A GSH must be converted to a GSR before the service can be used.

Grid Service Reference (GSR): Includes the GSH and binding information for transport protocol and data encoding format.

Registry Services: A repository for GSHs. Services can register their GSHs for service discovery.

Notification Services: Used by client subscription to send asynchronous messages between services.

11.1.2 Data Collection

Resource information is collected via *service data providers*. Providers are external programs that generate *service data* dynamically. Some providers are part of the core Globus Toolkit or they can be implemented by developers. Data providers can be connected to service instances [InfoServices01].

11.1.3 Aggregation

Service data generated by providers or delivered from other grid services can be presented in different *aggregate data views*. Notification or subscription mechanisms can then be applied to service data by command or GUI clients [InfoServices01].

11.1.4 Queries

MDS3 provides a standard, extensible query interface to service data elements. Queries can be executed by SDE name or by using a more complex language like XPath or XQuery. Good XPath or XQuery specification and tutorials are available online [XQuery01, XPath01, XPath02].

Client Subscription: Clients may subscribe to index services to receive specific messages defined by arbitrary values or linked to service data elements. Subscriptions are handled via the `NotificationSource` interface, which provides asynchronous delivery of notification messages.

Query modes: Queries can be executed in a simple synchronous pull fashion (`FindServiceData`) or in an asynchronous response-push (notification subscription).

Index Services can be combined in a variety of topologies to build VOs by combining data aggregation, service group, and data provider components.

11.1.5 User Interfaces

GT3 provides two types of user interfaces to query Information Services: The Service browser GUI (see Figures 11.1 and 11.2) and a set of command-line query tools: `ogsi-find-service-data-by-name`, `ogsi-find-service-data-by-xpath`.

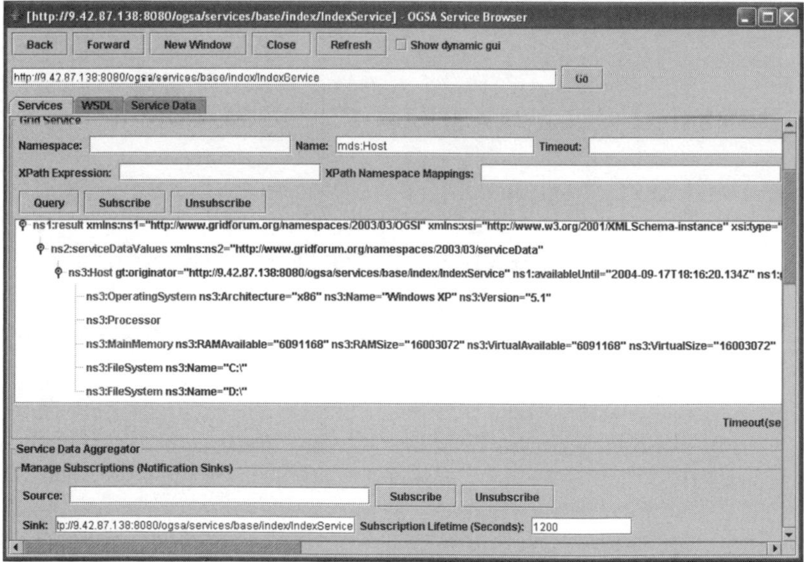

FIGURE 11.1 Service Data Browser showing a query against the `SystemInformation` data provider.

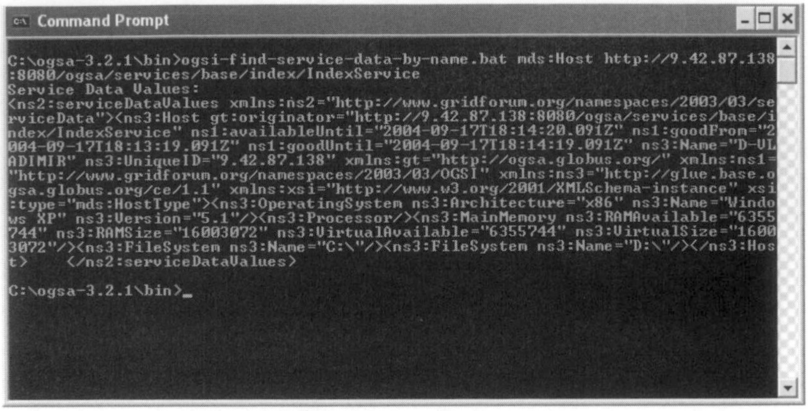

```
Command Prompt
C:\ogsa-3.2.1\bin>ogsi-find-service-data-by-name.bat mds:Host http://9.42.87.138
:8080/ogsa/services/base/index/IndexService
Service Data Values:
<ns2:serviceDataValues xmlns:ns2="http://www.gridforum.org/namespaces/2003/03/se
rviceData"><ns3:Host gt:originator="http://9.42.87.138:8080/ogsa/services/base/i
ndex/IndexService" ns1:availableUntil="2004-09-17T18:14:20.091Z" ns1:goodFrom="2
004-09-17T18:13:19.091Z" ns1:goodUntil="2004-09-17T18:14:19.091Z" ns3:Name="D-VL
ADIMIR" ns3:UniqueID="9.42.87.138" xmlns:gt="http://ogsa.globus.org/" xmlns:ns1=
"http://www.gridforum.org/namespaces/2003/03/OGSI" xmlns:ns3="http://glue.base.o
gsa.globus.org/ce/1.1" xmlns:xsi="http://www.w3.org/2001/XMLSchema-instance" xsi
:type="mds:HostType"><ns3:OperatingSystem ns3:Architecture="x86" ns3:Name="Windo
ws XP" ns3:Version="5.1"/><ns3:Processor/><ns3:MainMemory ns3:RAMAvailable="6355
744" ns3:RAMSize="16003072" ns3:VirtualAvailable="6355744" ns3:VirtualSize="1600
3072"/><ns3:FileSystem ns3:Name="C:\"/><ns3:FileSystem ns3:Name="D:\"/></ns3:Hos
t>    </ns2:serviceDataValues>

C:\ogsa-3.2.1\bin>_
```

FIGURE 11.2 Command-line query tool.

11.1.6 Security

The index service is compatible with Grid Security Infrastructure (GSI). GSI provides a *single sign-on* authentication service and it is built on open standards such as X.509 and proxy certificates. GSI implements *message-level* and *transport-level* security and sits on top of a Secure Sockets Layer/Transport Layer Security (SSL/TLS) library. GSI defines protocols for mutual authentication, credential delegation, proxy signing, message protection, and authorization. *By default, security is not enabled on index services* [GridSecurity98].

11.2 QUERYING DEFAULT DATA PROVIDERS

Several default data providers are available to the Index Service:

`SimpleSystemInformation`: A Java-based provider for CPU count, memory statistics, OS type, and logical disk volumes.

`HostScriptProvider`: A provider capable of running shell scripts in Unix-like systems.

The following transcript demonstrates the use of the `SystemInformation` data provider:

11.2.1 Enable the `ServiceDataProvider` and `DataAggregation` in the Service Browser GUI

Edit the file `$GLOBUS_LOCATION/client-gui-config.xml` to add the following panels:

```
<panel portType="ServiceDataProviderExecutionPortType"
class="org.globus.ogsa.gui.ProviderExecutionPortTypePanel"/>
<panel portType="DataAggregationPortType"
class="org.globus.ogsa.gui.AggregatorPortTypePanel"/>
```

11.2.2 Test the Default `SystemInformation` Service Data Provider via the OGSA Service Browser GUI

1. Start the OGSA container: `ant startContainer`.
2. Start service browser: `ant gui`.
3. Create an index service instance:
   a. Double-click the index service from the service group list.
   b. Select `SystemInformation` from the *Service Data Providers* list in the *Provider Execution* panel.
   c. In the *New* `ServiceData` *from Provider* section, enter a refresh frequency and click *Create.*
   d. In the Grid Service query panel in the *Name* textbox, enter `mds:Host` or `Host` and click Query. System information XML is displayed (see Figures 11.1 and 11.3).

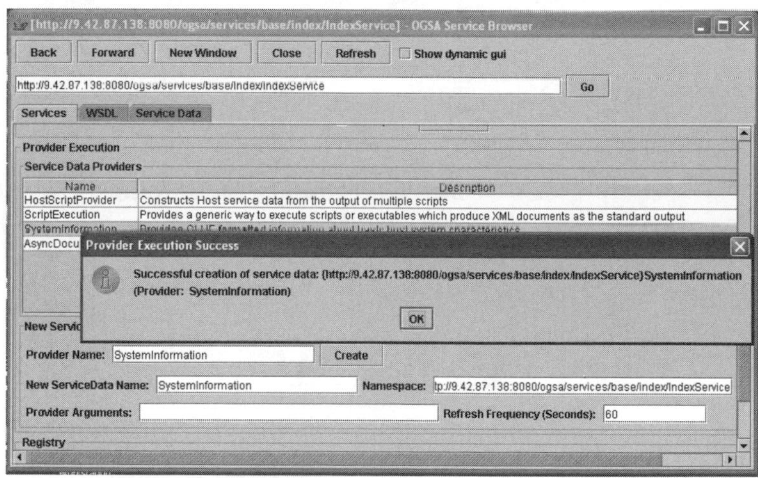

FIGURE 11.3 A default System Information provider.

4. Queries can be run using the command-line tools (see Listing 11.1). For example, to query for system information, use the following:

```
C:\ogsa-3.2.1\bin>ogsi-find-service-data-by-name
 mds:Host
 http://9.42.87.138:8080/ogsa/services/base/index/IndexService
```

LISTING 11.1 Querying for Service Information Using MDS3 Command-Line Tools

```
<ns2:serviceDataValues
  xmlns:ns2="http://www.gridforum.org/namespaces/2003/03/serviceData">
  <ns3:Host
    gt:originator="http://host:8080/ogsa/services/base/index/
IndexService"
    ns1:availableUntil="2004-09-17T15:19:49.616Z"
    ns1:goodFrom="2 004-09-17T15:18:48.616Z"
    ns1:goodUntil="2004-09-17T15:19:48.616Z" ns3:Name="D-VLADIMIR"
    ns3:UniqueID="9.42.87.138" xmlns:gt="http://ogsa.globus.org/"
    xmlns:ns1="http://www.gridforum.org/namespaces/2003/03/OGSI"
    xmlns:ns3="http://glue.base.o gsa.globus.org/ce/1.1"
    xmlns:xsi="http://www.w3.org/2001/XMLSchema-instance"
    xsi:type="mds:HostType">
    <ns3:OperatingSystem ns3:Architecture="x86" ns3:Name="Windows XP"
      ns3:Version="5.1" />
    <ns3:Processor />
    <ns3:MainMemory ns3:RAMAvailable="1341 3984"
      ns3:RAMSize="27734016" ns3:VirtualAvailable="13413984"
      ns3:VirtualSize="27 734016" />
    <ns3:FileSystem ns3:Name="C:\" />
    <ns3:FileSystem ns3:Name="D:\" />
  </ns3:Host>
</ns2:serviceDataValues>
```

The Service Data Provider configuration file is located in `$GLOBUS_LOCATION/etc/index-service-config.xml`. *This file should contain configuration for the* `SimpleSystemInformationProvider`.

11.3 CUSTOM MDS3 DATA PROVIDERS

The following sections describe custom information providers that could be used to obtain information about the status of the resources on a grid, such as host information, resource availability, network status, and others.

11.3.1 GT 3.2 Core Data Providers

Core data providers are available out of the box and provide resource information such as OS Type, number of CPUs, and amount of RAM. They also provide simple shell execution capabilities (see Table 11.1).

TABLE 11.1 Core Data Providers in GT3

Provider Name	Description
`SimpleSystemInformationProvider`	Provides information about the host: CPU, memory, OS, and disk volumes
`HostScriptProvider`	A set of Unix shell scripts to provide host resource information
`ScriptExecutionProvider`	A provider to execute shell scripts
`AsyncDocumentProvider`	An asynchronous utility to read an XML periodically; implements the `AsyncDataProvider` interface

11.3.2 Provider Interfaces

Provider interfaces allow developers to use MDS services on GT3. For example, a custom information provider can query for system information or display an overall view of the status of a grid within a VO. MDS3 interfaces are classified as follows:

`SimpleDataProvider:` This is the basic interface all providers must implement. It produces output in XML format. This interface defines the following methods:

```
// Returns the display name of the provider.
String getName();

// Returns a description of the provider's functionality.
String getDescription();

// If the provider has a set of default arguments,
// they can be retrieved with this function.
String getDefaultArgs();

// The provider should return a string representation
// of the current error, if any.
String getErrorString();

// Triggers the execution of the provider in order
// to update the provider's internal state,
// sending the output to the specified OutputStream.
void run(String args, java.io.OutputStream outStream);
```

`DOMDataProvider`: Inherits from `SimpleDataProvider` and produces XML output. It is useful for providers that return XML. This interface is defined as

```
public interface DOMDataProvider
 extends SimpleDataProvider
{
    public org.w3c.dom.Document run(String args)
}
```

`AsyncDataProvider`: This provides an asynchronous version of `SimpleDataProvider`. It takes a callback name and a valid `ServiceDataProviderDocumentCallback` object as arguments. This interface defines the following methods:

```
// Triggers the asynchronous execution of the provider,
// which will call the callbackName method on the specified
// ServiceDataProviderDocumentCallback object.
// Context is defined by the calling thread.
void run(String args,
             String callbackName,
             ServiceDataProviderDocumentCallback callback,
             Object context) throws Exception;

// Signals the provider to shut down, cease data callbacks,
// and free any associated resources.
void terminate() throws Exception;

// Retrieve the current state
int getState();
```

11.3.3 The Simplest Case

The easiest and fastest way to create an MDS3 information provider is to write a shell script and use the `ScriptExecution` provider to run it. The shell script should dump well-formatted XML output. Consider the simple shell script (in Listing 11.2) to query for host system information.

LISTING 11.2 Server Script to Emit System Information for MDS3

```
#!/bin/bash

# Globals
prefix="rips"

# Emit system information
emit_sysinfo () {
```

```
  # uname -a
  echo "<$prefix:sysinfo xmlns:$prefix=\
    "http://www.globus.org/namespaces/2003/04/rips\">"
  uname -a | awk '{ \
    prefix="rips";
    print "\t<"prefix":os>"$1"</"prefix":os>";
    print "\t<"prefix":host>"$2"</"prefix":host>";
    print "\t<"prefix":kernel>"$3"</"prefix":kernel>";
  }'
  uptime | awk -F, '{
    prefix="rips";
    print "\t<"prefix":uptime>"$1"</"prefix":uptime>";
    print "\t<"prefix":users>"$2"</"prefix":users>";
    print "\t<"prefix":userload>"$3"</"prefix":userload>";
    print "\t<"prefix":sysload>"$4"</"prefix":sysload>";
    print "\t<"prefix":kernelload>"$5"</"prefix":kernelload>";
  }'

  echo "</$prefix:sysinfo>"
}

#
# Main
#
emit_sysinfo
```

A run of this script from the command line will produce the following output:

```
$ /tmp/sysinfo.sh
<rips:sysinfo
xmlns:rips="http://www.globus.org/namespaces/2003/04/rips">
        <rips:os>Linux</rips:os>
        <rips:host>vm-rhl8.ibm.com</rips:host>
        <rips:kernel>2.4.18-14</rips:kernel>
        <rips:uptime>  2:23pm  up  6:22</rips:uptime>
        <rips:users>  1 user</rips:users>
        <rips:userload>  load average: 1.04</rips:userload>
        <rips:sysload> 0.53</rips:sysload>
        <rips:kernelload> 0.43</rips:kernelload>
</rips:sysinfo>
```

To use this information provider is simple:

1. Start your service browser GUI. Make sure the GUI has been configured to display the information provider panels. (See earlier.)

2. Start the index service by double-clicking it from the Service Group Entry list in your browser.
3. Scroll down to the Provider Execution panel and select `ScriptExectution`.
4. In the New Service data from the Provider panel, enter the path to the script in the Arguments text box (see Figure 11.4), then click Create.

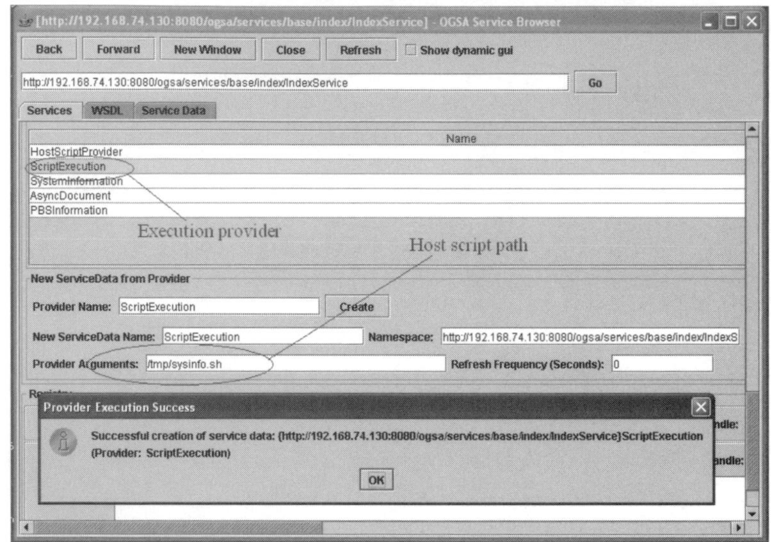

FIGURE 11.4 Creating a `ScriptExecution` MDS3 provider.

5. You should be able to query the service data by entering the name of the root node XML in the query *Name* (see Figure 11.5)

11.3.4 The Real World: An MDS3 Information Provider for Remote Schedulers Using SSH

It is time to create our first information service for MDS3. For this implementation, we have chosen a *Remote Cluster Information Provider*. The rationale for this service is simple: a service to query node, queue, and job information from many disparate schedulers remotely. Supported schedulers include OpenPBS, Condor, and Sun Grid Engine SGE). This provider has many advantages over the default Globus providers:

1. Supports many simultaneous schedulers: *Condor 6.6.6, OpenPBS & SGE 6.x*
2. Can be run from any GT3 container, such as Windows, Unix
3. Can be easily extended to support new schedulers

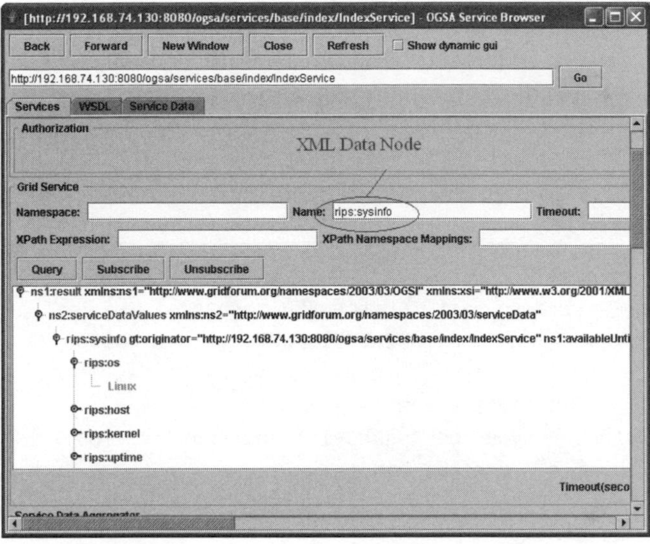

FIGURE 11.5 Querying information from the provider.

The only requirement is that the remote server must have a Secure Shell (SSH) daemon running.

11.3.4.1 Provider Architecture

The Remote Cluster Information Provider uses an SSH client API to send node, queue, and job requests to a given scheduler. This information, in turn, is translated into XML and sent back to the index service. Clients can then use the standard query mechanisms to access that information. Scheduler is kept in an XML configuration file that is the only argument to the provider (see Figure 11.6).

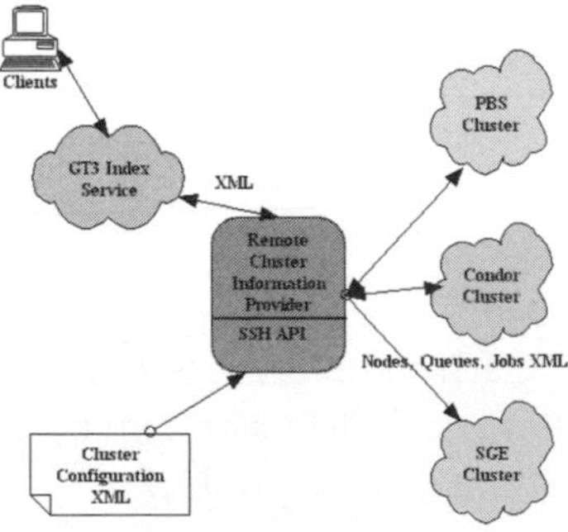

FIGURE 11.6 MDS provider architecture.

11.3.4.2 Configuration File

Server connection information such as protocol, hostname, port, and so on is kept in an XML configuration file. The protocols supported are SSH 1.5 /2; authentication methods can be by password or RSA private keys.

LISTING 11.3 clusters.xml MDS3 Remote Cluster Information Provider Sample Configuration File

```
<clusters>
  <!-- Time to wait for the SSH thread(s) -->
  <param name="SSH_THREAD_TIMEOUT" value="60000" />

  <!-- PBS cluster sample -->
  <cluster type="pbs" sshurl="ssh2:root@192.168.74.130"
    bindir="/usr/pbs/bin/">
    <auth type="passwd" encrypted="false">2p2dkdt</auth>
  </cluster>

  <!-- A Condor cluster using an ssh2 protocol & passwd
  authentication -->
  <cluster type="condor" sshurl="ssh2:root@192.168.74.130"
    bindir="/opt/condor-6.6.6/bin/">
    <auth type="passwd" encrypted="false">2p2dkdt</auth>
  </cluster>

  <!-- An SGE cluster using an ssh1 protocol & rsa authentication -->
  <!-- SGE requires the SGE_ROOT env var -->
  <cluster type="sge" sshurl="ssh1:root@192.168.74.129"
    bindir="/opt/sge6/bin/lx24-x86/">
    <env var="SGE_ROOT" value="/opt/sge6" />
    <auth type="rsa" encrypted="false" algorithm="DES3"
      privatekey="C:\\rsakeys\\identity">
      2p2dkdt
    </auth>
  </cluster>
</clusters>
```

11.3.4.3 UML Class Diagram

The provider design is fairly simple. An SSH thread is fired for each cluster in the configuration file, then a set of parsers are run on the returned output to grab node, queue, and job information (see Figure 11.7).

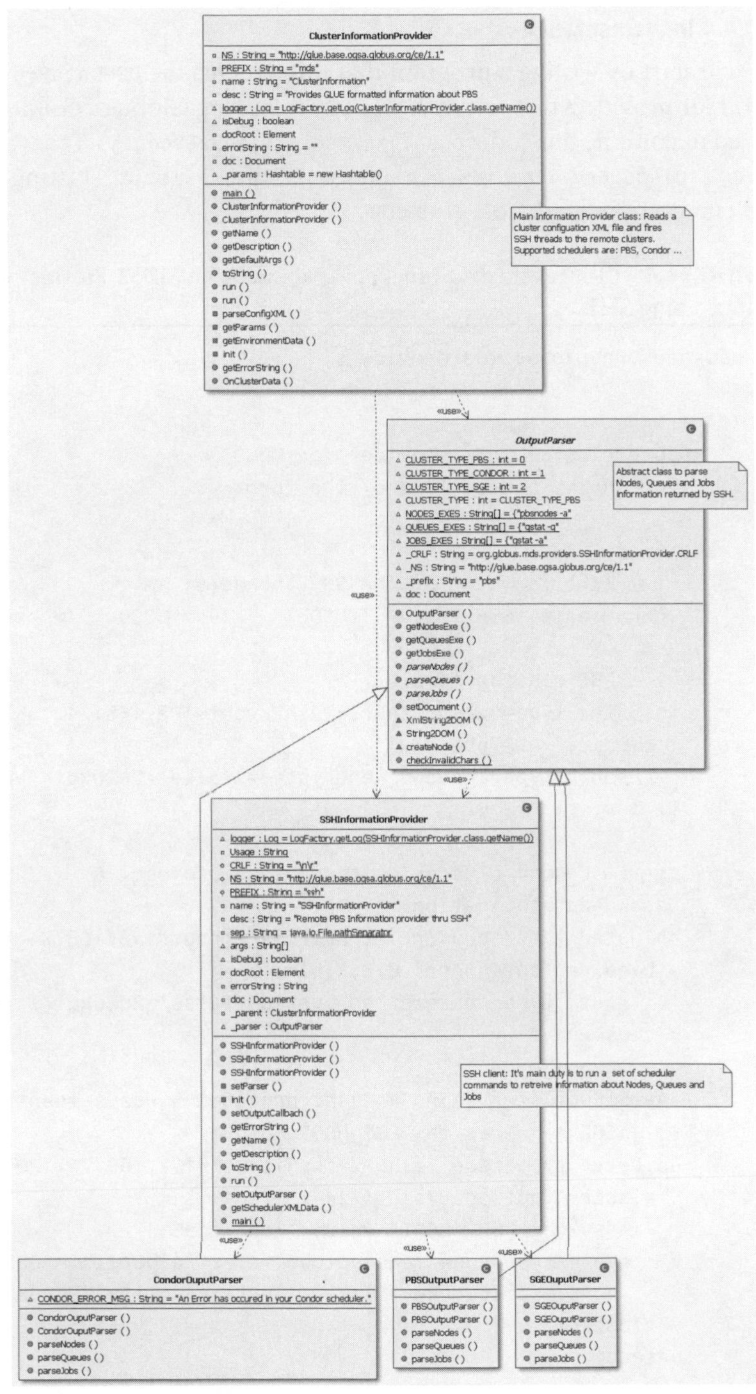

FIGURE 11.7 MDS provider UML diagram.

11.3.4.4 Implementation

We will start by writing a program that implements the `DOMDataProvider` interface, useful for providers that return XML. The following Globus Toolkit libraries are required to compile this code: `ogsa.jar`, `wsdl4j.jar`, `xerces.jar`, `common-logging.jar`, `commons-discovery.jar`, `mds-providers.jar` and `axis.jar`. Listing 11.4 shows the implementation for remote clusters.

LISTING 11.4 `ClusterInformationProvider.java`, **an MDS3 Provider for Remote Clusters Using SSH**

```
package org.globus.mds.providers;

/**
 * Remote cluster info provider for MDS3
 * Given an XML config file of the form:
 *
 <clusters>
     <!-- Time to wait for the SSH thread(s) -->
     <param name="SSH_THREAD_TIMEOUT" value="60000" />

     <!-- PBS cluster sample -->
     <cluster type="pbs" sshurl="ssh2:root@192.168.74.130"
       bindir="/usr/pbs/bin/">
         <auth type="passwd" encrypted="false">2p2dkdt</auth>
     </cluster>

     <!-- A Condor cluster using an ssh2 protocol &
     passwd authentication  -->
     <cluster type="condor" sshurl="ssh2:root@192.168.74.130"
       bindir="/opt/condor-6.6.6/bin/">
         <auth type="passwd" encrypted="false">2p2dkdt</auth>
     </cluster>

 <!-- An SGE cluster using an ssh1 protocol & rsa authentication -->
     <!-- SGE requires the SGE_ROOT env var -->
     <cluster type="sge" sshurl="ssh1:root@192.168.74.129"
       bindir="/opt/sge6/bin/lx24-x86/">
         <env var="SGE_ROOT" value="/opt/sge6" />
         <auth type="rsa" encrypted="false" algorithm="DES3"
                 privatekey="C:\\rsakeys\\identity">2p2dkdt</auth>
     </cluster>
 </clusters>
 *
 * Query remote clusters for Queue, Node & Job Info using
```

```
 * SSH (ver 1 or 2)
 * SSH authentication can be password or RSA key based.
 *
 * Supported cluster types are: PBS, Condor , SGE
 *
 * @author Vladimir Silva
 *
 */

import org.w3c.dom.Element;
import org.w3c.dom.Document;
import org.w3c.dom.NamedNodeMap;
import org.w3c.dom.Node;
import org.w3c.dom.NodeList;

import org.globus.mds.providers.parsers.CondorOuputParser;
import org.globus.mds.providers.parsers.OutputParser;
import org.globus.mds.providers.parsers.PBSOutputParser;
import org.globus.mds.providers.parsers.SGEOuputParser;
import org.globus.ogsa.utils.XmlFactory;

import com.ibm.wsdl.util.xml.DOM2Writer;

import org.apache.commons.logging.Log;
import org.apache.commons.logging.LogFactory;

import java.io.File;
import java.io.OutputStream;
import java.net.InetAddress;
import java.util.Arrays;
import java.util.Hashtable;
import java.util.List;
import java.util.ArrayList;

import org.globus.ogsa.impl.base.providers.servicedata.
  DOMDataProvider;

public class ClusterInformationProvider
  implements DOMDataProvider {
  private static String NS =
    "http://www.globus.org/namespaces/2003/04/rips";
  private static String PREFIX = "rips";

  private final String name = "ClusterInformation";
```

```
private final String desc =
  "Provides GLUE formatted information about PBS," +
  "Condor or SGE remote clusters thru SSH.";

static Log logger =
  LogFactory.getLog(ClusterInformationProvider.class.getName());
boolean isDebug;

// XML return vars
private Document doc;
private Element docRoot;
private String errorString = "";

// Config XML params: <param .... />
Hashtable _params = new Hashtable();

/**
 * Main sub
 * @param args
 */
public static void main(String args[]) {
  try {
    ClusterInformationProvider sysInfo =
      new ClusterInformationProvider();
    String argstr = "";
    if (args.length != 0) {
      for (int i = 0; i < args.length; i++) {
        argstr += args[i] + " ";
      }
    }
    else {
      argstr = sysInfo.getDefaultArgs();
    }
    sysInfo.run(argstr, System.out);
  }
  catch (Exception e) {
    //System.err.println(e);
    e.printStackTrace();
  }
}

/**
 * Creates a new instance of ClusterInformationProvider
 * @param namespacePrefix Example: rips, pbs, condor, sge ,etc.
```

```
 * @param namespaceURI
 */
public ClusterInformationProvider(
  String namespacePrefix,
  String namespaceURI) throws Exception {
  PREFIX = namespacePrefix;
  NS = namespaceURI;

  this.doc = XmlFactory.newDocument();
  init();
}

/** Creates a new instance of SystemInformationProvider */
public ClusterInformationProvider() throws Exception {
  this.doc = XmlFactory.newDocument();
  init();
}

// DOMDataProvider Interface methods
public String getName() {
  return this.name;
}

public String getDescription() {
  return this.desc;
}

public String getDefaultArgs() {
  return "clusters.xml";
}

public String toString() {
  return DOM2Writer.nodeToString(this.doc);
}

/**
 * Main provider sub: Load config XML & fire SSH threads
 * @param args Path to the xml config
 */
public void run(String args, OutputStream outStream) throws
  Exception {
  try {
    logger.info(
      "Remote Cluster Info Provider has started. Config file:"
```

```
        + args);

      // Get the cluster xml config file
      Document d = XmlFactory.newDocument(args);
      processConfigXML(d);

      // Print output
      outStream.write(DOM2Writer.nodeToString(this.doc).getBytes());

      if (this.isDebug) {
        logger.debug(DOM2Writer.nodeToString(this.doc));
      }
    }
    catch (Exception e) {
      //System.err.println(e);
      e.printStackTrace();
    }
  }

  /**
   * Main provider sub: Load config XML & fire SSH threads
   * @param args Path to the xml config
   */
  public Document run(String args) throws Exception {
    try {
      logger.info(
        "Remote Cluster Info Provider has started. Config file:"
        + args);

      Document d = XmlFactory.newDocument(args);
      processConfigXML(d);

      if (isDebug) {
        logger.debug(DOM2Writer.nodeToString(this.doc));
      }
    }
    catch (Exception e) {
      // Send error back as XML
      logger.error(e);
      docRoot.appendChild(doc.createCDATASection(e.toString()));
    }
    return this.doc;
  }
```

```
/**
 * Parse cluster config XML & fire SSH Scheduler threads
 * @param d Config XML doc
 */
private void processConfigXML(Document d) throws Exception {
  NodeList clusters = d.getElementsByTagName("cluster");
  Element e, auth;

  String clusterType; // cluster type
  String sshURL; // SSH connect string
  String binDir; // location of cluster binaries

  String passwd; // ssh host pwd or passphrase if auth == rsa
  String authType; // ssh auth type: passwd | rsa
  String privKey; // priv key path if auth == rsa
  String encrypted; // TODO: not implemented

  // Get params values from config XML
  getParams(d.getElementsByTagName("param"));

  // SSH Schedule shell
  SSHInformationProvider shell;

  // Provider args
  String[] args;

  // Number of running  threads
  int threadCount = 0;

  for (int i = 0; i < clusters.getLength(); i++) {
    e = (Element) clusters.item(i);
    auth = (Element) e.getElementsByTagName("auth").item(0);
    args = new String[7];

    clusterType = e.getAttribute("type");
    // cluster type=pbs,condor,sge
    encrypted = auth.getAttribute("encrypted"); // pwd encrypted?

    sshURL = args[0] = e.getAttribute("sshurl");
    authType = args[2] = auth.getAttribute("type");
    passwd = args[3] = auth.getFirstChild().getNodeValue();
    privKey = args[4] = auth.getAttribute("privatekey");
    binDir = args[5] = e.getAttribute("bindir");
```

```
// cluster type
args[1] = clusterType;

// Environment from XML env tag.
// Example: "export SGE_ROOT=/opt/sge6"
args[6] = getEnvironmentData(e.getElementsByTagName("env"));

//System.out.println(DOM2Writer.nodeToString(e));
if (authType.equalsIgnoreCase("passwd")) {
  privKey = args[4] = "NULL";
}

logger.debug(
  "parseConfigXML CLUSTER type:" + clusterType
  + " SSH Host:" + sshURL
  + " bin:" + binDir
  + " auth=" + authType
  + " pwd:" + passwd
  + " pk:" + privKey
  + " enc:" + encrypted);

// Pwd encryption not implemented yet.
if (encrypted.equalsIgnoreCase("true")) {
  logger.info(
    "Encryption not implemented for cluster type: "
    + clusterType
    + " SSH: "
    + sshURL);
}
else {
  logger.info(
    "Firing SSH Thread for cluster type:"
    + clusterType
    + " Arguments:"
    + Arrays.asList(args));

  // create an SSH shell and run Nodes,
  // Queues, Job executables defined in OutputParser
  shell = new
    SSHInformationProvider(clusterType, NS, args, doc);
  shell.setOutputCallbach(this);

  // Start the SSH provider thread
  new Thread(shell).start();
```

```
        threadCount++;
      }
    }

    // wait for all running threads
    for (int i = 0; i < threadCount; i++) {
      synchronized (this) {
        wait(
          Long.parseLong(
            _params.get("SSH_THREAD_TIMEOUT").toString()));
      }
    }
    logger.info("Received Cluster DOM\n"
                + DOM2Writer.nodeToString(doc));
  }

  /* get params from config xml <param name="key" value="val" /> */
  private void getParams(NodeList params) {
    for (int i = 0; i < params.getLength(); i++) {
      Element e = (Element) params.item(i);
      _params.put(e.getAttribute("name"), e.getAttribute("value"));
    }
  }

  /**
   * Add environment string to executable from cluster config XML
   * Example: "/bin/date;export GLOBUS_LOCATION=/opt/gt3,..."
   */
  private String getEnvironmentData(NodeList envNodes) throws
    Exception {
    StringBuffer buff = new StringBuffer("");

    Element e;
    e = (Element) envNodes.item(0);

    if (e != null) {
      buff.append("export " + e.getAttribute("var")
                  + "="
                  + OutputParser
                  .checkInvalidChars(e.getAttribute("value")));
    }

    for (int i = 1; i < envNodes.getLength(); i++) {
      e = (Element) envNodes.item(i);
```

```
        buff.append(";"
                    + "export " + e.getAttribute("var")
                    + "="
                    + OutputParser
                    .checkInvalidChars(e.getAttribute("value")));
      }
      return buff.toString();
    }

    /*
     * XML doc initialization
     */
    private void init() throws Exception {
      // internal objects
      this.isDebug = logger.isDebugEnabled();

      // init document structure
      this.docRoot = this.doc.createElementNS(NS, PREFIX
                                    + ":" + "Cluster");
      this.doc.appendChild(this.docRoot);

      // def params init
      _params.put("SSH_THREAD_TIMEOUT", "60000");
    }

    /**
     * The provider should return a string representation
     * of the current error, if any
     */
    public String getErrorString() {
      return this.errorString;
    }

    /**
     * SSH Data Provider callback.
     * Fires when the SSH data provider sends XML data
     * @param xmlDoc
     */
    public synchronized void OnClusterData(Document xmlDoc) {
      // Notify waiting threads
      notify();
    }
  }
```

11.3.4.5 SSH Provider API

This program (Listing 11.5) encapsulates a thread used to do the actual work of connecting to the remote server and querying the required information. It uses an SSH client shell compatible with SSH protocol 1.5 and 2. The authentication mechanisms can be password or RSA keys.

LISTING 11.5 `SSHInformationProvider.java` SSH1-2 Client API

```
package org.globus.mds.providers;

import org.w3c.dom.Element;
import org.w3c.dom.Document;

import org.globus.mds.providers.parsers.*;

import org.globus.ogsa.utils.XmlFactory;
import com.ibm.wsdl.util.xml.DOM2Writer;

import org.apache.commons.logging.Log;
import org.apache.commons.logging.LogFactory;

import java.io.File;
import java.io.OutputStream;
import java.net.InetAddress;
import java.util.Arrays;
import java.util.Vector;

import org.globus.ogsa.impl.base.providers.servicedata.
  DOMDataProvider;
import ssh.tools.SecureShell;

/**
 * A program to query for Node, Que & Job from Schedulers
 * thru SSH. Returns a GT3 Index Service compatible XML
 * Example SSH Arguments
 *  -url [SSHURL] -auth [passwd|rsa] -pwd [PWD] -pk [RSA_KEY]
 * Example SSH URL: [ssh2:]root@192.168.74.130[:22]
 * @author Vladimir Silva
 */
public class SSHInformationProvider
  implements Runnable {
  static Log logger =
    LogFactory.getLog(SSHInformationProvider.class.getName());
```

```
public static final String CRLF = "\n\r";
public static String PREFIX = "rips";
private final String name = "SSHInformationProvider";

public static String NS
  = "http://www.globus.org/namespaces/2003/04/rips";

private static final String sep = java.io.File.pathSeparator;

// program arguments
String[] args;
boolean isDebug;

private Element docRoot;
private String errorString;
private Document doc;

// Caller Cluster provider
private ClusterInformationProvider _parent;

// Object used to parse output
OutputParser _parser;
String _clusterType;

/**
 * Creates a new instance of SystemInformationProvider
 * @param clusterType pbs, sge or condor
 * @param namespaceURI
 * @param args SSH Arguments.
 * Example
 *   -url [SSHURL] -auth [passwd|rsa] -pwd [PWD] -pk [RSA_KEY]
 *   Example SSH URL: [ssh2:]root@192.168.74.130[:22]
 */
public SSHInformationProvider(String clusterType,
                              String namespaceURI, String[] args,
                              Document doc)
  throws Exception
{
  _clusterType = clusterType;
  NS = namespaceURI;

  this.doc = doc;
  this.args = args;
  init();
```

```
  setParser(clusterType);
}

/**
 * Adjust to a given parser: pbs, condor or sge are supported
 * @param clusterType String
 * @throws Exception
 */
private void setParser(String clusterType) throws Exception {
  if (clusterType.equalsIgnoreCase("pbs")) {
    setOutputParser(new PBSOutputParser(PREFIX, NS, doc));
  }
  else if (clusterType.equalsIgnoreCase("condor")) {
    setOutputParser(new CondorOuputParser(PREFIX, NS, doc));
  }
  else if (clusterType.equalsIgnoreCase("sge")) {
    setOutputParser(new SGEOuputParser(PREFIX, NS, doc));
  }
  else {
    errorString += "Unknown cluster type: " + clusterType;
    throw new Exception(errorString);
  }
}

/**
 * Initialize return XML
 * @throws Exception
 */
private void init() throws Exception {
  if (doc == null) {
    this.doc = XmlFactory.newDocument();
  }

  // internal objects
  this.isDebug = logger.isDebugEnabled();

  // init document structure
  this.docRoot = this.doc.createElementNS(NS, PREFIX
                                  + ":" + "Scheduler");
  this.docRoot.setAttributeNS(NS, "type", _clusterType);

  if (!this.doc.hasChildNodes()) {
    this.doc.appendChild(this.docRoot);
  }
```

```
  else {
    this.doc.getDocumentElement().appendChild(this.docRoot);
  }
}

/**
 * Cluster XML Data callback
 * @param p
 */
public void setOutputCallbach(ClusterInformationProvider p) {
  _parent = p;
}

/**
 * The provider should return a string representation
 * of the current error, if any
 */
public String getErrorString() {
  return this.errorString;
}

public String getName() {
  return this.name;
}

public String toString() {
  return DOM2Writer.nodeToString(this.doc);
}

/**
 * Main Thread sub:
 * Fires an SSH shell command batches for Nodes, Queues & Jobs
 */
public void run() {
  try {
    getSchedulerXMLData();

    if (_parent != null) {
      _parent.OnClusterData(doc);
    }

  }
  catch (Exception e) {
    // Send error back as XML
```

```
      Element elem = doc.createElementNS(NS, PREFIX + ":Error");
      elem.setAttribute("src", getName());
      elem.appendChild(doc.createCDATASection(e.toString()));

      docRoot.appendChild(elem);

      // send doc to parent callback
      if (_parent != null) {
        _parent.OnClusterData(doc);
      }

      //e.printStackTrace();
      logger.error("SSH Arguments: "
                   + Arrays.asList(args) + " Error:" + e);
    }
  }

  /* Set the object used to parse the result data */
  public void setOutputParser(OutputParser p) {
    _parser = p;
  }

  /**
   * Main logic
   */
  public Document getSchedulerXMLData() throws Exception {

    String sshUrl = args[0];
    String clusterType = args[1];
    String authType = args[2];
    String passwd = args[3];
    String privKey = args[4];
    String binDir = args[5];
    String env = "";

    if (args.length > 6) {
      env = args[6];
    }

    // Simple Check for script injection.
    // Example: rm -F /*;/usr/pbs/bin/)
     OutputParser.checkInvalidChars(binDir);

    logger.debug("getSchedulerXMLData: SSH Host=" + sshUrl
```

```
            + " auth:" + authType
            + " pwd:" + passwd + " pk: " + privKey
            + " bin:" + binDir + " Env:" + env
            + " Cluster type: " + clusterType);

String[] args1 = {
  "-url", sshUrl, "-auth", authType, "-pwd", passwd, "-pk",
  privKey};

SecureShell shell = new SecureShell(args1);

// Append the hostname to the XML docRoot element
docRoot.setAttributeNS(NS, "host", shell.getHostName());

// connect to remote host thru SSH
shell.connect();

// Run a command batch consisting of:
// [ENV STR];{BIN-DIR/EXECUTABLE}
// commands contains the cmd batch
Vector commands = new Vector();
String cmdPrefix = (!env.equals("")) ? env + ";" : "";

// Add executables. There must be 3 executables
// Nodes info exe
commands.add(cmdPrefix + binDir + _parser.getNodesExe());

// Queues info executable
commands.add(cmdPrefix + binDir + _parser.getQueuesExe());

// Jobs info exe
commands.add(cmdPrefix + binDir + _parser.getJobsExe());

logger.debug("getSchedulerXMLData: Remote SSH Command vector="
            + commands);

java.util.Vector outV = shell.runCommandBatch(commands);

shell.disconnect();

_parser.setDocument(this.doc);

docRoot.appendChild(_parser.parseNodes(outV.get(0).toString()));
docRoot.appendChild(_parser.parseQueues(outV.get(1).toString()));
```

```
        docRoot.appendChild(_parser.parseJobs(outV.get(2).toString()));

        //
        logger.debug("getSchedulerXMLData Got XML:\n" +
                DOM2Writer.nodeToString(this.doc));

        return this.doc;
    }
}
```

11.3.4.6 Parsing the Output

Output parsing is done through an abstract class `OuputParser` (see Listing 11.6) and a series of parser subclasses for each supported cluster type (see Figure 11.1). These classes encapsulate information of the cluster types such as the executables required to query for the required information, parsing rules, and so on.

LISTING 11.6 `OuputParser.java` Abstract Class for Scheduler Node, Queue and Job Information

```
/*
 * Created on Sep 20, 2004
 *
 */
package org.globus.mds.providers.parsers;

import java.io.ByteArrayInputStream;

import org.globus.ogsa.utils.XmlFactory;
import org.w3c.dom.Element;
import org.w3c.dom.Document;
import org.w3c.dom.Text;

/**
 * Remote Cluster Information Provider for MDS3
 * Query remote clusters for Queue, Node & Job data
 * using SSH (ver 1 or 2).
 *
 * SSH authentication can be password or RSA key based.
 * Supported cluster types are: PBS, Condor 6.6.6 , SGE 6.x
 *
 * @author Vladimir Silva
 */
public abstract class OutputParser {
```

```
static final int CLUSTER_TYPE_PBS = 0;
static final int CLUSTER_TYPE_CONDOR = 1;
static final int CLUSTER_TYPE_SGE = 2;

int CLUSTER_TYPE = CLUSTER_TYPE_PBS;

/**
 * Executables used to query Node, Que & Job Info
 * for PBS, CONDOR and SGE
 * Example (PBS) pbsnodes -a
 *         (CONDOR) condor_status -xml | sed -e 's/<!DOCTYPE.*>//'
 */
static final String[] NODES_EXES = {
  "pbsnodes -a"
  , "condor_status -xml | sed -e 's/<!DOCTYPE.*>//'"
  , "qhost"};

static final String[] QUEUES_EXES = {
  "qstat -q"
  , "condor_q -xml | sed -e 's/--.*\\w//' -e 's/<!DOCTYPE.*>//'"
  , "qstat -F -xml"};

static final String[] JOBS_EXES = {
  "qstat -a"
  , "condor_q -xml | sed -e 's/--.*\\w//' -e 's/<!DOCTYPE.*>//'"
  , "qstat -xml"};

// XML output vars
String _CRLF = org.globus.mds.providers.SSHInformationProvider.CRLF;
String _NS = "http://www.globus.org/namespaces/2003/04/rips";
String _prefix = "rips";

Document doc;

public OutputParser(int type) {
  CLUSTER_TYPE = type;
}

public String getNodesExe() throws Exception {
  return NODES_EXES[CLUSTER_TYPE];
}

public String getQueuesExe() throws Exception {
  return QUEUES_EXES[CLUSTER_TYPE];
```

```
}

public String getJobsExe() throws Exception {
  return JOBS_EXES[CLUSTER_TYPE];
}

public abstract Element parseNodes(String data);

public abstract Element parseQueues(String data);

public abstract Element parseJobs(String data);

public void setDocument(Document doc) {
  this.doc = doc;
}

/* String to DOM Element */
Element XmlString2DOM(String xml) {
  Document d = null;
  try {
    d = XmlFactory.newDocument(
      new BytcArrayInputStream(xml.getBytes()));
  }
  catch (Exception e) {
    Element ex = doc.createElementNS(_NS, _prefix + ":Nodes");
    ex.appendChild(doc.createCDATASection(e.toString()));
    return ex;
  }
  // import the xml argument into the current DOM doc
  return (Element) doc.importNode(d.getDocumentElement(), true);
}

/* Standard error node: Used to return error msgs */
Element createErrorNode(String source, String text) {
  Element e = String2DOM("Error", text);
  e.setAttributeNS(_NS, "src", source);
  return e;
}

/* Convert a text message into a DOM element */
Element String2DOM(String nodeName, String text) {
  Element e = doc.createElementNS(_NS, nodeName);
  e.appendChild(doc.createCDATASection(text));
  return e;
```

```
    }

    /**
     * Create a DOM Node given a name value pair
     * @param nodeName
     * @param value
     * @return
     */
    Element createNode(String nodeName, String value) {
      // no need to prepend a prefix. nodeName already includes it
      Element e = doc.createElementNS(_NS, nodeName);
      Text t = doc.createTextNode(value);
      e.appendChild(t);
      return e;
    }

    /* Sub to prevent script injection in env vars or bin dirs */
    static public String checkInvalidChars(String value) throws
      Exception {
      if (value.indexOf(";") > 0) {
        throw new Exception("Invalid characters detected in: "
                            + value);
      }
      return value;
    }
  }
```

11.3.4.7 Portable Batch System (PBS) Output Parser Program

The main function of this program is to convert the output from the PBS `qstat` command returned by SSH into an XML Document Object Model (DOM) document as shown in Listing 11.7.

LISTING 11.7 `PBSOutputParser.java`, a Program to Parse PBS Scheduler Information

```
package org.globus.mds.providers.parsers;

import java.util.StringTokenizer;

import org.globus.mds.providers.*;
import org.w3c.dom.Element;
import org.w3c.dom.Document;

import org.w3c.dom.Text;
import org.globus.ogsa.utils.XmlFactory;
```

```
import com.ibm.wsdl.util.xml.DOM2Writer;

/**
 * Remote Cluster Information Provider for MDS3
 * Query remote clusters for Queue, Node & Job Info using SSH (ver 1 or
2)
 * SSH authentication can be password or RSA key based.
 * Supported cluster types are: PBS, Condor 6.6.6 , SGE 6.x
 *
 * Sample call of this program:
 *
    // SSH CN args
    String[] args1 = {"-url"
        , "ssh2:root@192.168.74.130", "-pwd", "2p2dkdt"};

    ssh.tools.SecureShell shell = new ssh.tools.SecureShell(args1);
    shell.connect();

    // Query for some remote PBS info Thru SSH
    java.util.Vector v = new java.util.Vector();

    // 3 commands
    v.add("/usr/pbs/bin/pbsnodes -a");
    v.add("/usr/pbs/bin/qstat -q");
    v.add("/usr/pbs/bin/qstat -a");

    java.util.Vector outV = shell.runCommandBatch(v);
    shell.disconnect();

    // Parse PBS output
    PBSOutputParser p = new PBSOutputParser(
            org.globus.ogsa.utils.XmlFactory.newDocument());

    // out from CMD #1
    System.out.println(DOM2Writer.nodeToString(
            p.parseNodes(outV.get(0).toString())));
    //out CMD #2
    System.out.println(DOM2Writer.nodeToString(
            p.parseQueues(outV.get(1).toString())));
    // out CMD #3
    System.out.println(DOM2Writer.nodeToString(
            p.parseJobs(outV.get(2).toString())));

 * @author Vladimir Silva
```

```
 */
public class PBSOutputParser
  extends OutputParser {

  public PBSOutputParser(Document doc) throws Exception {
    super(OutputParser.CLUSTER_TYPE_PBS);
    this.doc = doc;
  }

  public PBSOutputParser(String prefix, String ns, Document doc)
    throws  Exception
  {
    super(OutputParser.CLUSTER_TYPE_PBS);
    this.doc = doc;
    _prefix = prefix;
    _NS = ns;
  }

  /**
   * Parse output from the command:
   * [globus@vm-rhl8 etc]$pbsnodes -a
   vm-rhl8.ibm.com
   state = free
   np = 1
   ntype = cluster
   * @param data command output
   * @return An XML representation of node info
   */
  public Element parseNodes(String data) {
    StringTokenizer st = new StringTokenizer(data, _CRLF);
    int numToks = st.countTokens();
    boolean close = false;

    Element nodes = doc.createElementNS(_NS, _prefix + ":Nodes");
    Element node = null;

    if (data.indexOf("state") > 0) {
      StringTokenizer st1;

      for (int i = 0; i < numToks; i++) {
        String tok = st.nextToken();

        if (tok.startsWith("\t") || tok.startsWith("  ")) {
          st1 = new StringTokenizer(tok, "=");
```

```
        if (st1.countTokens() > 1) {
          node.setAttributeNS(_NS, st1.nextToken().trim(),
                              st1.nextToken().trim());
        }
      }
      else {
        node = doc.createElementNS(_NS, _prefix + ":Node");
        node.setAttributeNS(_NS, "name", tok);
        nodes.appendChild(node);
      }
    }
  }
  return nodes;
}

/**
 * Parse PBS command: qstat -q
 server: vm-rhl8

 Queue            Memory CPU Time Walltime Node Run Que Lm  State
 ---------------- ------ -------- -------- ---- --- --- --  -----
 workq              --      --       --     --    2   0 --   E R
 work1              --      --       --     --    2   0 --   E R
                                               --- ---
                                                 2   0
 * @param data
 * @return an XML representation of Queue information
 */
public Element parseQueues(String data) {
  StringTokenizer st = new StringTokenizer(data, _CRLF);
  int numToks = st.countTokens();

  Element queues = doc.createElementNS(_NS, _prefix + ":Queues");
  Element queue = null;

  if (numToks > 2) {
    // skip headers
    for (int i = 0; i < 3; i++) {
      st.nextToken();
    }

    // num queues = num of lines minus 2 total lines
    int numQueues = st.countTokens() - 2;
```

```
    for (int i = 0; i < numQueues; i++) {
      String qLine = st.nextToken();

      StringTokenizer st1 = new StringTokenizer(qLine, " ");
      int size = st1.countTokens();
      //System.out.println("q num toks=" + size);

      // extract data from line:
      // workq      --       --        --      --    2   0 --   E R
      if (size >= 9) {
        queue = doc.createElementNS(_NS, _prefix + ":Queue");
        queues.appendChild(queue);

        queue.setAttributeNS(_NS, "name", st1.nextToken());
        queue.appendChild(createNode(_prefix + ":maxJobMemory",
                                     st1.nextToken().trim()));
        queue.appendChild(createNode(_prefix + ":maxCPUtime",
                                     st1.nextToken().trim()));
        queue.appendChild(createNode(_prefix + ":maxWalltime",
                                     st1.nextToken().trim()));
        queue.appendChild(createNode(_prefix + ":maxReqNodes",
                                     st1.nextToken().trim()));
        queue.appendChild(createNode(_prefix + ":numRunningJobs",
                                     st1.nextToken().trim()));
        queue.appendChild(createNode(_prefix + ":numJobsInQueue",
                                     st1.nextToken().trim()));
        queue.appendChild(createNode(_prefix + ":numMaxConcurrJobs",
                                     st1.nextToken().trim()));
        queue.appendChild(createNode(_prefix + ":queueStatus",
                                     st1.nextToken().trim()));
      }
    }
  }
  return queues;
}

/**
 * Parse Job output of the form
                                                     Req'd  Req'd   Elap
 Job ID          Username Queue    Jobname    SessID NDS  TSK  Memory
 --------------- -------- -------- ---------- ------ ---  ---  ------
 4.vm-rhl8.ibm.c globus   workq    STDIN        1828  --   --      --

 * @param data
```

```
 * @return an XML representation of Job Information
 */
public Element parseJobs(String data) {
  StringTokenizer st = new StringTokenizer(data, _CRLF);
  int numToks = st.countTokens();

  Element jobs = doc.createElementNS(_NS, _prefix + ":Jobs");
  Element job = null;

  if (numToks > 1) {
    // skip headers
    for (int i = 0; i < 4; i++) {
      st.nextToken();
    }

    // num queues = num of lines
    int numJobs = st.countTokens();

    for (int i = 0; i < numJobs; i++) {
      String jLine = st.nextToken();
      StringTokenizer st1 = new StringTokenizer(jLine, " ");

      int size = st1.countTokens();

      // extract data from line:
      // 4.host globus  workq STDIN  1828  --  --     --  -- R  --
      if (size >= 11) {
        job = doc.createElementNS(_NS, _prefix + ":Job");
        jobs.appendChild(job);

        job.appendChild(createNode(_prefix + ":jobID"
                                   , st1.nextToken().trim()));
        job.appendChild(createNode(_prefix + ":userName",
                                   st1.nextToken().trim()));
        job.appendChild(createNode(_prefix + ":Queue"
                                   , st1.nextToken().trim()));
        job.appendChild(createNode(_prefix + ":jobName"
                                   , st1.nextToken().trim()));
        job.appendChild(createNode(_prefix + ":sessID"
                                   , st1.nextToken().trim()));
        job.appendChild(createNode(_prefix + ":NDS"
                                   , st1.nextToken().trim()));
        job.appendChild(createNode(_prefix + ":TSK"
                                   , st1.nextToken().trim()));
```

```
                job.appendChild(createNode(_prefix + ":reqMem"
                                              , st1.nextToken().trim()));
                job.appendChild(createNode(_prefix + ":reqTime"
                                              , st1.nextToken().trim()));
                job.appendChild(createNode(_prefix + ":status"
                                              , st1.nextToken().trim()));
                job.appendChild(createNode(_prefix + ":elapsedTime"
                                              , st1.nextToken().trim()));
            }
        }
    }
    return jobs;
  }
}
```

11.3.4.8 Condor Output Parser

The Condor scheduler 6.6.6 is already XML aware, so you can query information in XML format already (see Listing 11.8).

LISTING 11.8 `CondorOutputParser.java`, a Program to Parse Condor Scheduler Information

```
package org.globus.mds.providers.parsers;

import java.io.ByteArrayInputStream;
import java.util.StringTokenizer;

import org.globus.mds.providers.*;
import org.w3c.dom.Element;
import org.w3c.dom.Document;
import org.w3c.dom.Text;
import org.globus.ogsa.utils.XmlFactory;
import com.ibm.wsdl.util.xml.DOM2Writer;

/**
 * Program to parse the output from the Condor Scheduler 6.6.6
 * The scheduler is already XML enabled so there is not much to do.
 * Data from the following cmds is sent to this program:
 * Nodes: $CONDOR_BIN/condor_status -xml | sed -e 's/<!DOCTYPE.*>//'
 * Queues: Already return by cmd bellow
 * Jobs: condor_q -xml | sed -e 's/--.*\\w//' -e 's/<!DOCTYPE.*>//'
 *
 * @author Vladimir Silva
 */
```

```
public class CondorOuputParser
    extends OutputParser {
  // the SSH is unable to capture server stderr msgs
  // thus use our own
  static final String CONDOR_ERROR_MSG =
      "An Error has occurred in your Condor scheduler.";

  /**
   * Condor output parser
   * @param doc DOM document that should contain the parsed output
   * @throws Exception
   */
  public CondorOuputParser(Document doc) throws Exception {
    super(OutputParser.CLUSTER_TYPE_CONDOR);
    this.doc = doc;
  }

  /**
   * Condor output parser
   * @param prefix
   * @param ns
   * @throws Exception
   */
  public CondorOuputParser(String prefix, String ns, Document doc)
      throws Exception
  {
    super(OutputParser.CLUSTER_TYPE_CONDOR);
    this.doc = doc;
    _prefix = prefix;
    _NS = ns;
  }

  /**
   * Convert the following SSH command into an XML DOM
   * $CONDOR_BIN/condor_status -xml | sed -e 's/<!DOCTYPE.*>//'
   */
  public Element parseNodes(String data) {
    // data  is xml so send it back
    if (data.equals("")) {
      return createErrorNode("CondorOutputParser", CONDOR_ERROR_MSG);
    }
    else {
      return XmlString2DOM(data);
    }
```

```
    }

    /**
     * No queues cmd in condor so return an empty xml element
     */
    public Element parseQueues(String data) {
      if (data.equals("")) {
        return createErrorNode("CondorOutputParser", CONDOR_ERROR_MSG);
      }
      else {
        return doc.createElementNS(_NS, _prefix + ":Queues");
      }
    }

    /**
     * Convert the following SSH command into an XML DOM
     * condor_q -xml | sed -e 's/--.*\\w//' -e 's/<!DOCTYPE.*>//'
     */
    public Element parseJobs(String data) {
      // Condor Jobs cmd already return xml so send it back
      if (data.equals("")) {
        return createErrorNode("CondorOutputParser", CONDOR_ERROR_MSG);
      }
      else {
        return XmlString2DOM(data);
      }
    }
  }
```

11.3.4.9 Integration with Other Schedulers

This provider can be easily enhanced to support other schedulers just by changing the abstract class `OuputParser` to include the required shell commands and implement a parser for the new scheduler.

11.3.4.10 Provider Installation

The final step in this project is to deploy the provider to your OGSA container. This is just a matter of dropping the project libraries: `ssh.jar` and `myprovider.jar` into the `$GLOBUS_LOCATION/lib` directory of the OGSA container and creating a `clusters.xml` configuration file with your custom scheduler parameters. The provider can be started from the services browser GUI as shown at the beginning of this chapter. Once the provider is started, queries can be run (see Figure 11.8). The file `$GLOBUS_LOCATION/etc/index.-service-config.xml` (Listing 11.9) must be updated to include the new provider.

LISTING 11.9 Index Service Configuration File

```
<installedProviders>
  <providerEntry
    class="org.globus.ogsa.impl.base.providers.servicedata.impl
        .SimpleSystemInformationProvider" />
  <providerEntry
    class="org.globus.ogsa.impl.base.providers.servicedata.impl
        .AsyncDocumentProvider" />
  <providerEntry
    class="org.globus.ogsa.impl.base.providers.servicedata.impl
        .ScriptExecutionProvider" />
  <providerEntry
    class="org.globus.ogsa.impl.base.providers.servicedata.impl
      .HostScriptProvider" />

  <!– Remote Cluster Information Provider entry -->
  <providerEntry
      class="org.globus.mds.providers.ClusterInformationProvider" />
</installedProviders>
```

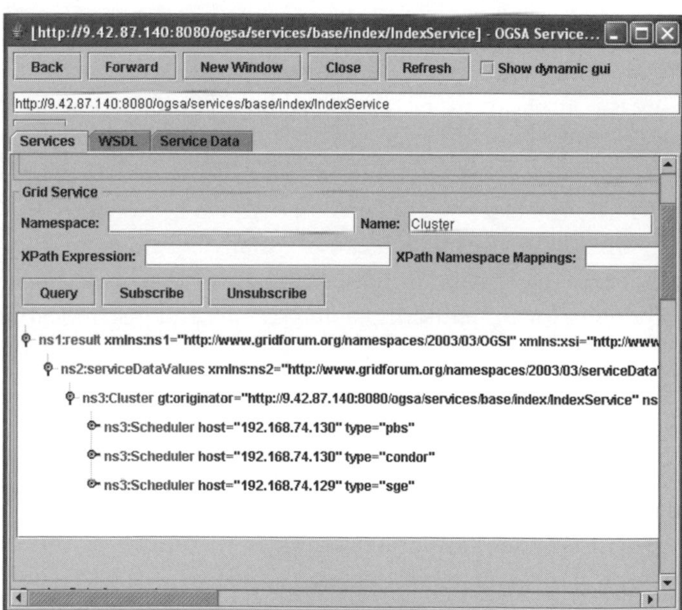

FIGURE 11.8 Remote cluster MDS provider test.

11.4 PRE-WS INFORMATION SERVICES (MDS2)

In a computational grid, information is a critical resource, and gathering this information is a vital activity. The information services component of the Globus Toolkit, the MDS2, gathers information about grid resources by means of the *Grid Resource Information Service* (GRIS) and the *Grid Index Information Service* (GIIS).

The MDS component of the Globus Toolkit uses an extensible framework for managing static and dynamic information about the status of a computational grid and all its components: networks, computer nodes, storage systems, and instruments. The benefits of MDS include the following:

- Access to static and dynamic information about system components
- Uniform, flexible access to information
- Access to multiple information sources
- A basis for configuration and adaptation in heterogeneous, dynamic environments
- Decentralized maintenance

You can use MDS to answer the following questions about the status of your grid:

- What resources are available?
- What is the state of the computational grid?
- How can applications be optimized based on the configuration of the underlying system?

MDS uses the Lightweight Directory Access Protocol (LDAP) as the interface to this information. However, you can use many commercial or open source software components to implement the basic features of MDS, including establishing connections, querying for contents, displaying results, and disconnecting from the server.

11.4.1 Architecture: GRIS and GIIS

MDS provides ways to discover properties of the machines, computers, and networks in your grid such as the number of processors available at the moment, the bandwidth provided, and the storage type (tape or disk). Using an LDAP server, MDS provides middleware information in a common interface to put a unifying picture on top of disparate resources.

The GRIS provides a uniform means to query resources on a computational grid including current configuration, capabilities, and status. The GRIS is a distributed information service that can answer queries about a particular resource by directing the query to an information provider deployed as part of the Globus services on a grid resource. Examples of information provided by this service include host identity (operating systems and versions) as well as more dynamic information (CPU and memory availability).

The GIIS combines arbitrary GRIS services to provide exploring and searching capabilities by grid applications. Within a coherent image of the computational grid, GIIS provides the means to identify resources of particular interest, such as the availability of computational resources, storage, data, and networks (see Figure 11.9).

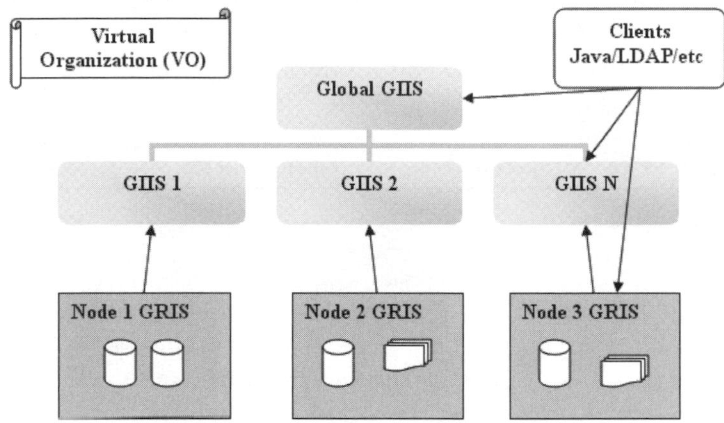

FIGURE 11.9 Information Services model within a VO.

11.4.2 Implementing a Grid Information Provider for MDS2

The following sections describe the steps required to implement an information provider for MDS2, which is compatible with Globus versions 2 or earlier.

11.4.2.1 Overview

The MDS2 is the Information Services component of the Globus Toolkit versions 2 or earlier MDS2 is maintained for compatibility with older versions of the toolkit and provides grid legacy information such as the resources that are available and the state of the computational grid. This information may include properties of the machines, computers, and networks in your grid, such as the number of processors available, CPU load, network interfaces, filesystem information, bandwidth, storage devices, and memory. MDS2 architecture is significantly different from MDS3 as it uses the LDAP to provide middleware information in a common interface. MDS2 includes two components: the *GRIS* and the *GIIS*. With the MDS2, you can publish information about almost anything in your grid.

11.4.2.2 LDAP Configuration

In writing an implementation, you should aim to have each GRIS on the grid publish information about shared files on each resource and machine available. You can then use the *Java Commodity Grid (CoG)* Kit API to search for downloadable files in an application that resembles the music and file sharing application, Morpheus. Finally, you can use GridFTP to download and upload files on the remote resources.

For this sample implementation, the code has been tested on Red Hat Linux 7.3 systems running the Globus Toolkit 2.2. It is not guaranteed to work on other platforms or toolkit versions. A good starting point is to look at the LDAP configuration file that MDS uses. This file, located in `$GLOBUS_LOCATION/etc/grid-info-slapd.conf`, as shown in Listing 11.10.

LISTING 11.10 MDS-LDAP Daemon Configuration File, `grid-info-slapd.conf`

```
schemacheck off

include         /opt/globus/etc/openldap/schema/core.schema
include         /opt/globus/etc/grid-info-resource.schema
...
pidfile         /opt/globus/var/resourceslapd.pid
argsfile        /opt/globus/var/resourceslapd.args

modulepath      /opt/globus/libexec/openldap/gcc32pthr
moduleload      libback_ldif.la
moduleload      libback_giis.la
...
```

The `schemacheck off` line indicates that an LDAP schema is not required for the provider. However, if your grid requires schema checks, you must create a custom LDAP schema for use with your custom provider.

11.4.2.3 Creating a Custom LDAP Schema

The first step in writing an MDS provider is to write a schema file and include this file in the `grid-info-slapd.conf` file under the `$GLOBUS_LOCATION/etc` directory. Writing the schema file can be difficult and time-consuming, and one mistake can render your MDS unusable. Therefore, you should take great care with this step of the process. Listing 11.11 provides a sample.

LISTING 11.11 A Custom LDAP Schema to Publish Shared File Information

```
attributetype ( 1.3.6.1.4.1.3536.2.6.3536.3.0.123.1
    NAME 'Mds-File-name'
    DESC 'File Name'
    EQUALITY caseIgnoreMatch
    ORDERING caseIgnoreOrderingMatch
    SUBSTR caseIgnoreSubstringsMatch
    SYNTAX 1.3.6.1.4.1.1466.115.121.1.44
    SINGLE-VALUE
 )

attributetype ( 1.3.6.1.4.1.3536.2.6.3536.3.0.123.2
    NAME 'Mds-File-location'
    DESC 'File Location'
    EQUALITY caseIgnoreMatch
    ORDERING caseIgnoreOrderingMatch
    SUBSTR caseIgnoreSubstringsMatch
    SYNTAX 1.3.6.1.4.1.1466.115.121.1.44
    SINGLE-VALUE
 )

attributetype ( 1.3.6.1.4.1.3536.2.6.3536.3.0.123.3
    NAME 'Mds-File-size'
    DESC 'File Size(bytes)'
    EQUALITY caseIgnoreMatch
    ORDERING caseIgnoreOrderingMatch
    SUBSTR caseIgnoreSubstringsMatch
    SYNTAX 1.3.6.1.4.1.1466.115.121.1.44
    SINGLE-VALUE
 )

objectclass ( 1.3.6.1.4.1.3536.2.6.3536.3.0.123
    NAME 'MdsDataGrid'
    SUP 'Mds'
    STRUCTURAL
    MUST ( Mds-File-name $ Mds-File-location $ Mds-File-size )
 )
```

To include this schema, add the following line to `grid-info-slapd.conf`:

```
include /opt/globus/etc/grid-info-resource.schema
```

Each attribute to be published must include an *object ID (OID)*. All attributes are in turn grouped in an `objectclass`. As the developer of the provider, you must define all OIDs and must follow a registered format. Globus has registered the following OIDs with IANA Private Enterprise Numbers:

1.3.6.1.4.1.3536.*	Globus OID subspace
1.3.6.1.4.1.3536.2.*	Globus Info Services OID subspace
1.3.6.1.4.1.3536.2.6.*	MDS2 OID subspace

Information to be published by this provider includes the file name, the location (to be used by GridFTP for download), and the file size. Once the schema is ready, the next step is to modify the `grid-info-resource-ldif.conf` file.

11.4.2.4 Modifying the grid-info-resource-ldif.conf File

The `grid-info-resource-ldif.conf` file describes how the information provider will be called and what it should emit. This file, located in `$GLOBUS_LOCATION/etc`, is presented in the Listing 11.12.

LISTING 11.12 The `grid-info-resource-ldif.conf` File

```
# generate shared file info every 5 min
#
dn: Mds-Software-deployment=DataGrid, Mds-Host-hn=myhost.com,
    Mds-Vo-name=local,  o=grid
objectclass: GlobusTop
objectclass: GlobusActiveObject
objectclass: GlobusActiveSearch
type: exec
path: /opt/globus/libexec
base: grid-info-fileshare

# args
args: -devclassobj -devobjs
  -dn Mds-Host-hn=myhost.com,Mds-Vo-name=local,o=grid
  -validto-secs 60 -keepto-secs 900
# end args

cachetime: 300
timelimit: 20
#sizelimit: 20
```

This file must use the following format:

Distinguished name (Dn)	Where the Object Lives in the Directory Information Tree (DIT)
objectclass: `GlobusTop`	
objectclass: `GlobusActiveObject`	
objectclass: `GlobusActiveSearch`	
type: `exec`	These lines are required.
`Path`	Path to the information provider program.
`Base`	Name of the information provider program.
`Args`	Arguments to be passed to the information provider program.
`Cachetime`	In seconds, how long GRIS will consider the data to not be stale.
`Timelimit`	In seconds, how long the GRIS should wait for the information provider to return data before giving up on it.
`Sizelimit`	Max number of LDIF objects to be read from the output of the information provider.

11.4.2.5 Writing the Information Provider Program

The next step in developing the custom MDS provider is to write a program (such as the one presented in Listing 11.13) that will emit the information you want to publish. You can use any language and can pass any arguments that you need. The only requirements are the following:

- The I/O interface of the program must be callable by the UNIX system calls `fork` and `exec` in the LDAP main process (`slapd`).
- The data returned must match the LDAP schema described in the LDAP Data Interchange Format (LDIF) internet document (RFC 2849).

LISTING 11.13 MDS Information Provider Shell Script Program

```
#!/bin/sh -f

# default libexecdir used to bootstrap scripts
libexecdir=${GLOBUS_LOCATION}/libexec
```

```
# load GRIS common code and initialization
. ${libexecdir}/grid-info-common


####################################################

# Globals
USERS_HOME_DIR=/home
GRID_MAP_FILE="/etc/grid-security/grid-mapfile"
#

#
# Modified Globus sub to work with my stuff
#
emit_timestamps ()
{
cat <<EOF
${_line_class_av}Mds-validfrom: ${_mds_validfrom}\n
${_line_class_av}Mds-validto: ${_mds_validto}\n
${_line_class_av}Mds-keepto: ${_mds_keepto}\n
EOF
}

#
# Display Top DN info
#
emit_datagrid_dn() {

# Display output
cat <<EOF
${_line_class_dn}dn: Mds-Software-deployment=DataGrid,${_suffix}
${_line_class_oc}objectclass: Mds
${_line_class_oc}objectclass: MdsDataGrid
`emit_mds_object_timestamps`
EOF

}

#
# Emit file info by reading /etc/grid-security/grid-mapfile
# grabbing user names and reading files under the users home/.data_grid
#
emit_file_info() {
    # TODO: remove duplicates from: $grid_map_users
```

```
    grid_map_users=`cat ${GRID_MAP_FILE} | awk -F\" '{print $3}'`

    # debug
    # echo $grid_map_users

    for user in $grid_map_users; do

    # Any files in home dir?
    if [ "`ls -l $USERS_HOME_DIR/$user/.data_grid`" != "total 0" ]
    then
      # For each user print: file name, location & size
      # of each file under $HOME/.data-grid
      _cmd="ls -l $USERS_HOME_DIR/$user/.data_grid |
         awk '{ if (length >10) print \"dn: Mds-File-name=\" \$9
         \", Mds-Software-deployment=DataGrid,$1\",
          \"\n${_line_class_oc}objectclass: Mds\",
            \"\n${_line_class_oc}objectclass: MdsDataGrid\",
            \"\n${_line_class_av}Mds-File-name:\" \$9,
            \"\n${_line_class_av}Mds-File-location: ",
                "$USERS_HOME_DIR/$user/.data_grid\",
            \"\n${_line_class_av}Mds-File-size:\" \$5,
            \"\n`emit_timestamps`\" }' | sed 's/ //' " #

            eval $_cmd
        fi
    done
}


#
# MAIN
# Required: globus stuff
probe_mds_object_timestamps

# emit Parent DN
emit_datagrid_dn
echo ""

# emit file info
emit_file_info "${_suffix}"
```

11.4.2.6 Running the Information Provider Program

You can run this program from the command line by issuing a command such as the following:

```
./grid-info-fileshare -devclassobj -devobjs -dn Mds-Host-
hn=[HOSTNAME],Mds-Vo-name=local,o=grid -validto-secs 60 -keepto-secs
900
```

The output should look like this:

```
dn: Mds-Software-deployment=DataGrid
 , Mds-Software-deployment=DataGrid,
Mds-Host-hn=dhcp126.adtech.internet.ibm.com
 , Mds-Vo-name=local,  o=grid
objectclass: Mds
objectclass: MdsDataGrid
Mds-validfrom: 20030222183857Z
Mds-validto: 20030222183857Z
Mds-keepto: 20030222183857Z

dn:Mds-File-name=gram_job_mgr_12725.log
 , Mds-Software-deployment=DataGrid,
Mds-Software-deployment=DataGrid
 , Mds-Host-hn=dhcp126.adtech.internet.ibm.com,
Mds-Vo-name=local,  o=grid
objectclass:Mds
objectclass:MdsDataGrid
Mds-File-name:gram_job_mgr_12725.log
Mds-File-location:/home/bg_guest/.data_grid
Mds-File-size:6537
Mds-validfrom:20030222183733Z
Mds-validto: 20030222183733Z
Mds-keepto: 20030222183733Z

dn:Mds-File-name=gram_job_mgr_12738.log
 , Mds-Software-deployment=DataGrid,
Mds-Software-deployment=DataGrid
 , Mds-Host-hn=dhcp126.adtech.internet.ibm.com,
Mds-Vo-name=local,  o=grid
objectclass:Mds
objectclass:MdsDataGrid
Mds-File-name:gram_job_mgr_12738.log
Mds-File-location:/home/bg_guest/.data_grid
Mds-File-size:2996
Mds-validfrom:20030222183733Z
Mds-validto: 20030222183733Z
Mds-keepto: 20030222183733Z
```

11.4.2.7 Information Provider Installation

Now it is time to test the custom MDS information provider. Restart the Globus service on a Red Hat Linux 7.3 system with the following commands:

1. `service globus stop`
2. `service globus start`

Use the installation script in Listing 11.14 to modify and copy the required files to the proper locations.

LISTING 11.14 Provider Installation Script

```
#!/bin/sh
# Only root can run this stuff...
if [ "`whoami`" != root ];then
        echo "You need to be root to execute."
        exit 1;
fi

# GLOBUS_LOCATION must be defined
if [ -z "$GLOBUS_LOCATION" ]; then
        echo "Environment variable 'GLOBUS_LOCATION' is not set."
        exit 1
fi

GLOBUS_LOCATION_SED=`echo $GLOBUS_LOCATION | sed -e 's/\//\\\\\//g'`

#
# Copy files to globus/etc and /libexec directories
#
cp -f ./grid-info-fileshare ${GLOBUS_LOCATION}/libexec

HOSTNAME=`hostname`

# Modify resources.ldif to take into account the new reporter.
# Remove old config if present.
echo "Modifying ${GLOBUS_LOCATION}/etc/grid-info-resource-ldif.conf"

TOT=
 `more ${GLOBUS_LOCATION}/etc/grid-info-resource-ldif.conf | wc -l `

NUM=`grep -n "## INTRAGRID FILE REPORTER ##"
        ${GLOBUS_LOCATION}/etc/grid-info-resource-ldif.conf
        | tail -1 | sed -e 's/:.*//'`
```

```
if [ "$NUM" != "" ]; then
      NUM=`expr $NUM - 1`

      NUM2=`grep -n "## INTRAGRID FILE REPORTER END ##"
        ${GLOBUS_LOCATION}/etc/grid-info-resource-ldif.conf
        | tail -1 | sed -e 's/:.*//' `

      NUM2=`expr $TOT - $NUM2`

      head -$NUM ${GLOBUS_LOCATION}/etc/grid-info-resource-ldif.conf
          > top
      tail -$NUM2 ${GLOBUS_LOCATION}/etc/grid-info-resource-ldif.conf
          > bottom

      cat top  ./resource-ldif-fileshare.conf bottom |
      sed -e 's/_-GLOBUS_LOCATION-_/'    $GLOBUS_LOCATION_SED'/' | \
              sed -e 's/_-HOSTNAME-_/'$HOSTNAME'/' > \
              ${GLOBUS_LOCATION}/etc/grid-info-resource-ldif.conf

      rm -rf top bottom
else
    cat ./resource-ldif-fileshare.conf
        |  sed -e 's/_-GLOBUS_LOCATION-_/' \
        $GLOBUS_LOCATION_SED'/'
        |  sed -e 's/_-HOSTNAME-_/'$HOSTNAME'/' >> \
        ${GLOBUS_LOCATION}/etc/grid-info-resource-ldif.conf

fi

#
# SETUP CODE
#

# Globals
USERS_HOME_DIR=/home
GRID_MAP_FILE="/etc/grid-security/grid-mapfile"

#
setup_homedirs() {
    #
    grid_map_users=`cat ${GRID_MAP_FILE} | awk -F\" '{print $3}'`

    for user in ${grid_map_users}; do
        if [ -d $USERS_HOME_DIR/$user/.data_grid ]
        then
            echo "$USERS_HOME_DIR/$user/.data_grid already exists."
```

```
        else
            cmd1=`mkdir $USERS_HOME_DIR/$user/.data_grid`
            cmd2=`chown $user:$user $USERS_HOME_DIR/$user/.data_grid`
            # echo $cmd1 $cmd2
        fi
    done
}

# Create ~$user/.data_grid dirs for each user to store shared files
echo "$0: Setting up default shared directories..."
setup_homedirs


echo "$0: Done."
```

11.4.2.8 Troubleshooting Tips

If the LDAP server fails to start after you make configuration changes, check all the schemas defined in the `grid-info-slapd.conf` file for OID collisions. If the `schemacheck off` line is present, you do not need to include the schema in the configuration file. Note that this code has been tested only on Red Hat Linux 7.3 servers running Globus Toolkit 2.2.

11.4.3 Custom MDS2 Clients

The Java CoG Kit provides a Java API to query both GRIS and GIIS services on your grid. The program in Listing 11.15 demonstrates a simple client capable of submitting queries against MDS2 using this API.

LISTING 11.15 `MDSService.java`, a Custom Client for MDS2

```
package ord.globus.services.mds2;

import org.globus.mds.*;
import java.util.Hashtable;
import java.util.Enumeration;

/**
 * A Sample Program to query information from the MDS2 service
 */
public class MDSService {
  // Default MDS server parameters.
  // Change to fit your Global MDS server values
  private final String _MDS_SERVER = "giis.myvo.com";
  private final String _MDS_BASE_DN = "Mds-Vo-name=VO_NAME,o=grid";
```

```
// Our Grid uses port 2135. Default globus MDS port is 391
private final String _MDS_PORT = "2135";
private MDS _mds = null;

/**
 * Constructors
 * @param _MDS_SERVER LDAP Host
 * @param _MDS_PORT LDAP port
 * @param _MDS_BASE_DN LDAP search Dn (Distinguished name)
 */
public MDSService() {
  _mds = new MDS(_MDS_SERVER, _MDS_PORT, _MDS_BASE_DN);
}

public MDSService(String host, String port, String baseDN) {
  _mds = new MDS(host, port, baseDN);
}

/**
 * This method performs the actual MDS search.
 * @param filter search filter to be used.
 * Example: (objectClass=*)
 */
public String HostInfoLookup(String filter) {
  try {
    // Attributes to be returned by the search
    String[] attribs = null;
    _mds.connect();

    // The MDS pkg returns a Multi-valued hashtable
    Hashtable t = _mds.search(filter, attribs
                          , _mds.SUBTREE_SCOPE);
    _mds.disconnect();

    return "<mds>\n"
      + buildStatusXML(false, this.getClass()
                    + "HostLookup", "ok")
      + "\n<data>\n" + ht2XML(t)
      + "</data>\n</mds>";
  }
  catch (Exception ex) {
    ex.printStackTrace();
    return "<mds>" +
      buildStatusXML(true, this.getClass().getName(),
```

```
                    ex.getMessage()) + "</mds>";
  }
}

/*
 * Return xml is composed by a status tag
 */
private String buildStatusXML(boolean bError, String source,
                              String desc) {
  String XML = "<status>\n\t"
    + "<error>" + bError
    + "</error>\n\t<source>" + source
    + "</source>\n\t" +
    "<desc>" + desc + "</desc>\n</status>";
  return XML;
}

/**
 * Convert an MDS Search HashTable (Multi-valued) to XML
 */
private String ht2XML(Hashtable t) throws Exception {
  Enumeration e = t.elements();

  // MDS result is a multi-val hash table
  MDSResult mvRecord = null;

  // Hash table key is a dn
  String dn = "";

  StringBuffer xml = new StringBuffer();

  // Convert an MDS2 result multi-valued hash table
  // into XML
  for (Enumeration dnEnum = t.keys(); dnEnum.hasMoreElements(); )
  {
    mvRecord = (MDSResult) e.nextElement();
    dn = (String) dnEnum.nextElement();

    if (mvRecord.size() > 0) {
      xml.append("\t<record dn=\""
                 + dn.replace('"', ' ').trim()
                 + "\">\n\t");
```

```
            Enumeration recKeys = mvRecord.keys();
            String sKey = "";

            for (int i = 0; i < mvRecord.size(); i++) {
              sKey = (String) recKeys.nextElement();
              xml.append("\t<" + sKey + ">"
                         + mvRecord.getValueAt(sKey, 0)
                         + "</" + sKey + ">\n\t");
            }
            xml.append("</record>\n");
          }
        }
        return xml.toString();
      }

      /**
       * For testing purposes only
       */
      public static void main(String[] args) {
        String baseDN = "Mds-Vo-name=AKgrid,o=grid";
        String host = "host.mygrid.com";

        // Query a GRIS machine
        MDSService mds = new MDSService(host, "2135", baseDN);
        String xml = mds.HostInfoLookup("(objectclass=*)");

        System.out.println("GRIS output\n" + xml);
      }
    }
```

The `org.globus.mds` package supports connecting to an MDS server, querying for contents, printing the results of a query, and disconnecting from the server. It provides an intermediate application layer that you can easily adapt to different LDAP client libraries such as Java Naming and Directory Interface (JNDI), Netscape SDK, and Microsoft SDK. The current release is based on JNDI.

11.4.3.1 Calling the MDS Constructor

The first step in using this Java class is to establish a connection (that is, call the MDS constructor) by issuing the following line of code:

```
MDS mds = new MDS("www.globus.org", "389", "o=Globus, c=US");
```

The parameters of this class are the name of the MDS server, the port number (389 by default), and the distinguished name or base directory. LDAP queries conduct searches on the base directory (DN). The default is o=Globus, c=US. *Note:* Your grid may use a different setup.

11.4.3.2 Opening Connections and Searching

After you have called the MDS constructor, the next step before searching is to open a connection using the `connect()` method of the MDS class. Then you are ready to search with a call such as the following:

```
result = mds.search("(objectClass=*)", MDS.ONELEVEL_SCOPE);
```

The filter (`objectClass=*`) means "get all data." Another parameter specifies the search scope (`ONELEVEL` searches the current DN level, while `SUBTREE` descends the directory structure).

11.4.3.3 Translating the Search Results to an XML String

The result of the `search()` method of the MDS class is a hash table of type `org.globus.common.MVHashtable` wrapped around the `MDSResult` class. It is basically a hash table of multivalued hash tables. The client translates the results from the MDS from the hash table into an XML string that other processes can easily understand.

The value of the host and the value of the base DN determine whether a query runs against the GRIS or the GIIS. The `org.globus.mds` package provides several constructors to manipulate these arguments. A run of this program will produce the output shown in Listing 11.16.

LISTING 11.16 MDS2 Client Sample Output

```
<mds>
<status>
  <error>false</error>
  <source>
    class com.ibm.globus.services.mds.MDSServiceHostLookup
  </source>
  <desc>ok</desc>
</status>
<data>
  <record dn="Mds-Device-name=/usr,Mds-Device-Group-name=filesystems,
  Mds-Host-hn=mdev1.raleigh.ibm.com , Mds-Vo-name=AKgrid,o=grid">
    <objectClass>MdsDevice</objectClass>
    <Mds-Device-name>/usr</Mds-Device-name>
    <Mds-keepto>20030212112509Z</Mds-keepto>
    <Mds-validto>20030212112509Z</Mds-validto>
    <Mds-Fs-freeMB>15592</Mds-Fs-freeMB>
```

```
    <Mds-validfrom>20030212111009Z</Mds-validfrom>
    <Mds-Fs-sizeMB>17078</Mds-Fs-sizeMB>
    <Mds-Fs-mount>/usr</Mds-Fs-mount>
  </record>
  <record dn="Mds-Device-name=eth0,Mds-Device-Group-name=networks,
  Mds-Host-hn=mdev6.raleigh.ibm.com, Mds-Vo-name=AKgrid,o=grid">
    <objectClass>MdsDevice</objectClass>
    <Mds-Device-name>eth0</Mds-Device-name>
    <Mds-Net-addr>10.30.10.15</Mds-Net-addr>
    <Mds-keepto>20030212151853Z</Mds-keepto>
    <Mds-Net-netaddr>10.30.0.0/16</Mds-Net-netaddr>
    <Mds-validto>20030212151853Z</Mds-validto>
    <Mds-Net-name>eth0</Mds-Net-name>
   <Mds-validfrom>20030212150353Z</Mds-validfrom>
  </record>
</data>
</mds>

GIIS output
<mds>
<status>
  <error>false</error>
  <source>class
com.ibm.globus.services.mds.MDSServiceHostLookup</source>
  <desc>ok</desc>
</status>
<data>
  <record dn="Pool-info=ISE Server System Grid Computing - hyperion,
  Mds-Vo-name=POOL-CONTACT,o=grid">
    <intraGrid-Pool-name>
      ISE Server System Grid Computing - hyperion
    </intraGrid-Pool-name>
    <Mds-Host-hn>hyperion.fscjapan.ibm.com</Mds-Host-hn>
    <objectClass>intraGrid</objectClass>
    <intraGrid-Pool-administrator>trent@jp.ibm.com
    </intraGrid-Pool-administrator>
    <Mds-Vo-name>
      ISE Server System Grid Computing - hyperion
    </Mds-Vo-name>
    <Mds-Service-Ldap-suffix>
      Mds-Vo-name=ISE Server System Grid Computing -
      hyperion, o=grid
    </Mds-Service-Ldap-suffix>
    <intraGrid-Pool-localGIIS>
```

```
        hyperion.fscjapan.ibm.com
      </intraGrid-Pool-localGIIS>
      <Mds-Service-port>2135</Mds-Service-port>
      <intraGrid-Geo-location>
        CHIBA CITY-CHIBA, 12, Japan (140.11,35.59)
      </intraGrid-Geo-location>
    </record>
  </data>
  </mds>
```

This output provides a great deal of information about the machines, networks, filesystems, and pools of resources as well as a mechanism for identifying resources of particular interest. Because MDS is built on top of LDAP, you can use any LDAP browsing tool to explore the machines on your grid. There are many free tools available for such a task.

11.5 SUMMARY

Information Services, also known as Monitoring and Discovery Services (MDS), provide resource discovery, selection, and optimization. They can be used by applications to obtain a general overview of the capabilities and services provided by a computational grid. The Globus Toolkit MDS offers the means of combining services to provide a coherent system image that grid applications can explore or search. This chapter has presented a set of Java programs to easily query and discover information in your organization's grid. A set of enhanced tools are provided by Globus to develop applications that use MDS as well as other services. Those tools are described in Chapter 12.

REFERENCES

[GridSecurity98] Ian Foster, Carl Kesselman, G. Tsudik, and S. Tuecke. "A Security Architecture for Computational Grids." Proceedings of the 5th ACM Conference on Computer and Communications Security Conference, pp. 83–92, 1998.

[InfoServices01] K. Czajkowski, S. Fitzgerald, Ian Foster, and Carl Kesselman. "Grid Information Services for Distributed Resource Sharing." Proceedings of the Tenth IEEE International Symposium on High-Performance Distributed Computing (HPDC-10), IEEE Press, August 2001.

[MDSGuide03] The Globus Alliance. Information Services (MDS) Documentation. *http://www-unix.globus.org/toolkit/docs/3.2/infosvcs/.*

[XPath01] XPath Specification: Available online at *http://www.w3.org/TR/xpath.html.*

[XPath02] XPath Tutorial: Available online at *http://www.zvon.org/xxl/XPathTutorial/General/examples.html.*

[XQuery01] XQuery Specification: Available online at *http://www.w3.org/TR/xquery//.*

12 Commodity Grid Kits (CoGs)

In This Chapter

- Overview
- Language Bindings
- Java
- Other Language Bindings
- Summary

This chapter includes information on the following topics:

- An overview of the different language bindings for the Java Commodity Grid Kit (CoG), including the basic services it provides and the security libraries it uses.
- Sample programs for self-signed certificate and key generation including grid proxy certificates.
- Sample programs for the data management services provided including file transfer code, testing scripts, common error messages, and troubleshooting tips.
- A basic overview of other language bindings such as Python and Practical Extraction and Report Language (PERL).

All code is available from the companion CD-ROM.

12.1 OVERVIEW

Commodity frameworks are designed to provide service reusability. The integration of commodity and Grid service technologies aims to enhance the functionality, maintenance, and deployment of Grid Services. Building on this philosophy, the Argonne National Laboratory (ARNL), provides a set of CoGs that include a set of simple application programming interfaces (APIs) for grid service management. These kits include several language bindings such as Java, Python, and PERL.

12.2 LANGUAGE BINDINGS

The most used CoG kit is written in Java. As a matter of fact, the Java CoG kit is distributed as an integral part of the Globus Toolkit 3.x. Other important language bindings include Python and PERL. The following compatibility matrix describes each language binding and its compatibility with the different versions of the Globus Toolkit. It can help you decide which CoG kit to use depending on your Globus or operating system version:

TABLE 12.1 CoG Kits Compatibility Matrix

Language	OS	Relevant Interfaces	Globus Toolkit Compatibility
Java	Unix Windows	**Resource Management** Globus Resource Allocation Manager (GRAM) 1.5 client GRAM Server **Data Management** GridFTP Globus Access to Secondary Storage (GASS) **Security** Grid Security Infrastructure (GSI)	3.x, 4.x
Python (pyGlobus)	Unix	Implemented as a set of wrappers to the Globus Toolkit 2 and 3 versions. It requires a Globus installation plus additional configuration bundles, such as GT3.2 all-source bundle.	2.x, 3.x

→

Language	OS	Relevant Interfaces	Globus Toolkit Compatibility
PERL (GridPort 2)	Unix	**Resource Management** GRAM 1.5 client Data Management GridFTP GASS Security Grid Security Infrastructure (GSI)	2.2.x

12.3 JAVA

At the time of this writing, the stable release is version 1.2 for use with the Globus Toolkit 2 and 3. For the upcoming release of GT4, versioning numbering has been synchronized for both packages; thus, all code shown throughout this chapter has been written for GT2 or GT3 and Java CoG 1.2.

12.3.1 Installation Requirements and Configuration

An installation is the first step to be performed for a proper operation. It ensures the client APIs exist in the local machine with the right configuration. The two basic installation requirements are a Java Development Kit and Apache Ant (for development purposes). For download and installation instructions, follow the *Java CoG Kit User Manual* [JavaCoGManual03].

12.3.2 Basic Java CoG Services

The Java CoG Kit provides a complete API implementation for managing grid services. Among the most important packages are the following:

`org.globus.security`: A partial implementation of the GSI.

`org.globus.gram`: A full implementation of the GRAM client and Server APIs for resource management

`org.globus.io.gass`: A pure Java implementation of the GASS client and server for transferring files via HTTPS.

`org.globus.io.ftp`: Provides a client API for accessing and transferring files from GSI-enabled FTP servers.

Other services include the General-purpose Architecture for Reservation and Allocation (GARA), a mechanism to allow advanced and immediate reservations for quality of service , Gatekeeper services, Information Services through the Monitoring and Discovery Service (MDS) and `MyProxy` client API for grid proxy management.

12.3.3 Security

The GSI is built on top of the Internet X.509 Public Key Certificate and certificate revocation list (CRL) Profile standards. This API provides a standard way to access all the attributes of an X.509 certificate through the use of Java Cryptography Extensions (JCE).

X.509 certificates are widely used to support authentication and other functionality in Internet security systems. Examples of such systems are the following:

- Privacy Enhanced Mail (PEM)
- Transport Layer Security (TLS)
- Secure Electronic Transactions (SET)

Certificates are usually managed by certificate authorities (CAs). CAs provide services for creating certificates in the X.509 standard and then digitally signing them. A CA is basically a trusted third party. It makes introductions between entities that have no direct knowledge of each other. CA certificates can be signed by themselves, or by other CAs also known as root CAs.

The structure of an X.509 certificate as described by ISO/IEC and ANSI X9 uses the Abstract Syntax Notation number One (ASN.1) format:

```
Certificate  ::=  SEQUENCE  {
    tbsCertificate       TBSCertificate,
    signatureAlgorithm   AlgorithmIdentifier,
    signature            BIT STRING  }
```

A `tbsCertificate` as described by ASN.1 consists of the following:

```
TBSCertificate  ::=  SEQUENCE  {
    version         [0]  EXPLICIT Version DEFAULT v1,
    serialNumber         CertificateSerialNumber,
    signature            AlgorithmIdentifier,
    issuer               Name,
    validity             Validity,
    subject              Name,
    subjectPublicKeyInfo SubjectPublicKeyInfo,
    issuerUniqueID  [1]  IMPLICIT UniqueIdentifier OPTIONAL,
                         -- If present, version must be v2 or v3
    subjectUniqueID [2]  IMPLICIT UniqueIdentifier OPTIONAL,
```

```
                         -- If present, version must be v2 or v3
    extensions      [3]  EXPLICIT Extensions OPTIONAL
                         -- If present, version must be v3
    }
```

Certificates should be instantiated through a *certificate factory*. Globus relieves the developer from most of the burden of creating X.509 certificates through the cryptography extensions. For a more in-depth overview of X.509 certificates and grid proxies, read Chapter 8.

12.3.3.1 CoG Configuration File

The configuration file for the CoG kit can be found in `$USER_HOME/.globus/cog.properties` where `$USER_HOME` represents the user's home directory. For example,

- C:\Documents and Settings\Administrator\.globus (for Windows systems)
- /home/vsilva/.globus (for Red Hat Linux)

This configuration file contains important information about the locations of four pieces of information required by GSI:

- Location of the user certificate
- Location of the encrypted private key
- Location of the generated user proxy
- Location of the CA (Trusted) certificate(s)

A typical configuration file may look something like this:

```
#Java CoG Kit Configuration File
#Thu Oct 21 09:51:57 EDT 2004
usercert=C\:\\Documents and Settings\\vsilva\\.globus\\usercert.pem
userkey=C\:\\Documents and Settings\\vsilva\\.globus\\userkey.pem
proxy=C\:\\DOCUME~1\\vsilva\\LOCALS~1\\Temp\\x509up_u_vsilva
cacert=C\:\\Documents and Settings\\vsilva\\.globus\\CA\\9d8d5dcd.0
```

12.3.3.2 Security Libraries

To be able to create or manipulate certificates, a set of security libraries is required to be in your compilation classpath. These libraries are distributed as part of the Globus Toolkit:

Cryptography extensions: As of GT 3.x, Globus uses the open source cryptography extensions provided by The Legion of the Bouncy Castle *http://www.bouncycastle.org/*, as well as a Java-only implementation of the SSLv3 and TLSv1 standards provided by *Cryptix* and *Claymore Systems.*

```
Cryptix*.jar
puretls.jar
jce-jdk-xxx.jar
```

CoG API:

```
cog-jglobus.jar
```

Logging: Used for message debugging

```
log4j-xxx.jar
```

GSI: implementations of the General Security Services (GSS) API

`jgss.jar`
`j2ee.jar` (not part of the OGSA distribution)

12.3.3.3 Proxy and User Certificate Generation

The Java CoG kit provides a complete set of APIs for proxy, user, and CA certificate manipulation, as shown in the following code sections.

Listing 12.1 demonstrates a technique used to generate a grid proxy certificate given user-specific information.

LISTING 12.1 Generating a Proxy Certificate

```
/* for logging */
private static Logger logger = Logger.getLogger(GridProxy.class.get-
Name());

/* Cog kit properties */
private CoGProperties props = CoGProperties.getDefault();

/**
 * Generate a Globus Proxy certificate
 * @param inUserCert User certificate input stream
 * @param inUserKey Private Key input stream
 * @param pwd Private key decryption pass phrase
```

```
 * @param bits Proxy strength in bits (512, 1024, etc)
 * @param hours Proxy life time in hours (12 recommended)
 * @return a Globus Credential object
 * @throws IOException
 * @throws java.security.GeneralSecurityException
 */
public synchronized GlobusCredential gridProxyInit(
        InputStream inUserCert,
        InputStream inUserKey,
        String pwd,
        int bits,
        int hours)
        throws IOException, java.security.GeneralSecurityException
{
        X509Certificate userCert =
CertUtil.loadCertificate(inUserCert);
        OpenSSLKey key = new BouncyCastleOpenSSLKey(inUserKey);

        logger.debug(
                "gridProxyInit: User Cert:\n"
                        + userCert
                        + "\nUser key encrypted="
                        + key.isEncrypted());

        /* decrypt the private key with the passphrase */
        if (key.isEncrypted()) {
                try {
                    key.decrypt(pwd);
                } catch (java.security.GeneralSecurityException e) {
                    throw new java.security.GeneralSecurityException(
                            "Wrong password or other security error");
                }
        }

        /* proxy generation */
        java.security.PrivateKey userKey = key.getPrivateKey();

        BouncyCastleCertProcessingFactory factory =
                BouncyCastleCertProcessingFactory.getDefault();

        return factory.createCredential(
                new X509Certificate[] { userCert },
                userKey,
                bits,
```

```
                hours * 3600,
                GSIConstants.GSI_2_PROXY,
                (org.globus.gsi.X509ExtensionSet) null);

}
```

The code in Listing 12.1 can be used to create a grid proxy with default credentials. This information is read from the CoG configuration file (`cog.properties`), as shown in Listing 12.2.

LISTING 12.2 Creating a Proxy Certificate Using Default Values

```
/**
 * Create a Globus proxy using the default values
 * from $HOME/.globus/cog.properties
 * @param passphrase Private key decryption passphrase
 * @throws FileNotFoundException
 * @throws IOException
  * @throws GeneralSecurityException
*/
public void gridProxyInitDefault(String passphrase) throws
    FileNotFoundException, IOException, GeneralSecurityException
{
  int bits = 1024;
  int hours = 12;

  InputStream inCert = new FileInputStream(props.getUserCertFile());
  InputStream inKey = new FileInputStream(props.getUserKeyFile());

  // create globus proxy
  GlobusCredential cred = gridProxyInit(inCert,
inKey, passphrase, bits, hours);

  logger.debug(cred);

  // save proxy in default location
  logger.info("Saving proxy as: " + props.getProxyFile());

  OutputStream bos = new FileOutputStream(props.getProxyFile());
  cred.save(bos);
}
```

Another useful functionality provided by this API includes the ability to display certificate attribute information, such as subject, issuer, strength, or lifetime (see Listing 12.3).

LISTING 12.3 Displaying Default Certificate Information

```
/**
 * Display information from the default proxy
 * @throws GlobusCredentialException
 */
public void gridProxyInfoDefault() throws GlobusCredentialException {
  ProxyInfo(props.getProxyFile());
}

/**
 * Display proxy information
 * @param file Full path to the globus proxy
 * @throws GlobusCredentialException
 */
public void ProxyInfo (String file) throws GlobusCredentialException {
  GlobusCredential cred = new GlobusCredential(file);

  System.out.println("Subject:" + cred.getSubject()
+ "\nIssuer: " + cred.getIssuer()
      + "\nStrength: " +
          new Integer(cred.getStrength()).toString()
+ "\nTime left: "
+ org.globus.util.Util.formatTimeSec(cred.getTimeLeft())
);
}
```

12.3.3.4 User and Self-Signed Certificates

Depending on the needs of your virtual organization (VO), you may find yourself in need of creating user or CA certificates. The Java COG kit provides capabilities for you to create your own CA or manage user and host certificates within your organization. For example, a self-signed certificate may require the following parameters:

- A certificate subject of the form: O=ACME,OU=Information Technology, CN=John Doe
- A password used to encrypt the private key
- Certificate strength in bits (512, 1024, etc.…)

Such a certificate can be easily created (see Listing 12.4).

LISTING 12.4 Creating a Self-Signed Certificate

```
/**
 * Create a self-signed  (CA) certificate and encrypted private key
 * @param subject String of the form
 *  O=ACME,OU=Information Technology,CN=Vladimir Silva
 * @param bits Certificate strength in bits (512, 1024, ...)
 * @param Pwd Passphrase used to encrypt the private key
 * @param swKey Buffer for the encrypted key
 * @param swCert Buffer for the certificate
 */
public void generateSelfSignedCertAndKey(String subject, int bits,
                                          String Pwd,
                                          StringWriter swKey,
                                          StringWriter swCert)
  throws
  NoSuchAlgorithmException, Exception {
  X509Name _subject = makeCertDN(subject);

  logger.debug("generateSelfSignedCertAndKey Cert subject: "
             + _subject.getNameString() + " Strength="
             + bits
             + " Pwd=" + Pwd);

  // Buffer for the encrypted key
  BufferedWriter bw = new BufferedWriter(swKey);

  // Start by generating an RSA key pair
  KeyPair kp = CertRequest.generateKey("RSA", bits, Pwd, bw, true);

  // certs validity is set for 1 year: 31536000 secs
  byte[] certBytes =
    CertRequest.makeSelfSignedCert(kp, _subject, 31536000);

  // Encode cert bytes in PEM format and store it in the certificate
  // buffer
  BufferedWriter bw1 = new BufferedWriter(swCert);
  String _certPEM = writePEM(certBytes,
                          "-----BEGIN CERTIFICATE-----\n",
                          "-----END CERTIFICATE-----\n");
  bw1.write(_certPEM);
  bw1.close();
}
```

This method requires two utility subroutines. The first one (`writePEM`) is used to encode the certificate raw bytes in the PEM format. A second method (`makeCertDN`) is used to split the certificate subject in a format that is understandable by the cryptography extensions also known as an X.509Name (see Listing 12.5).

LISTING 12.5 Encoding a Certificate in Privacy Enhanced Mail (PEM) Format

```
/**
 * Encode Certificate bytes in the Privacy Enhanced Message (PEM)
 * format
 * @param bytes Certificate bytes to encode
 * @param hdr Certificate header: -----BEGIN CERTIFICATE-----
 * @param ftr Footer: -----END CERTIFICATE-----
 * @return PEM encoded string
 * @throws IOException
 */
public static String writePEM(byte[] bytes, String hdr, String ftr)
  throws IOException
{
  ByteArrayOutputStream bos = new ByteArrayOutputStream();
  Base64OutputStream b64os = new Base64OutputStream(bos);

  b64os.write(bytes);
  b64os.flush();
  b64os.close();

  ByteArrayInputStream bis =
    new ByteArrayInputStream(bos.toByteArray());
  InputStreamReader irr =
    new InputStreamReader(bis);
  BufferedReader r =
    new BufferedReader(irr);

  StringBuffer buff = new StringBuffer();
  String line;
  buff.append(hdr);

  while ( (line = r.readLine()) != null) {
    buff.append(line + "\n");
  }
  buff.append(ftr);
  return buff.toString();

}
```

```
/**
 * Create an X509 Distinguished  Name (DN) used for cert creation
 * @param subject Certificate subject string.
 *  Example: O=ACME,OU=Information Technology,CN=Vladimir Silva
 * @return X509Name
 */
private static X509Name makeCertDN(String subject)
  throws Exception
{
  Vector tdn = new Vector();
  Vector elems = new Vector();

  StringTokenizer st = new StringTokenizer(subject, ",");

  // The string of the form: O=ACME,OU=...,CN=...
  // must be converted into a Vector of String[2] arrays
  // containing (key,value) pairs
  for (; st.hasMoreTokens(); ) {
    // (key=value) pairs
    String s = st.nextToken();

    if (s.indexOf("=") == -1) {
      throw new Exception("Invalid subject format: "
                          + subject
                          + " Offending value: " + s);
    }

    String key = s.substring(0, s.indexOf("=")).trim();
    String val = s.substring(s.indexOf("=") + 1).trim();

    if (val == null || val.equals("")) {
      throw new Exception("Invalid subject format: "
                          + subject + " Offending value: "
                          + s);
    }

    String[] temp = {
        key, val};
    tdn.addElement(temp);
  }
  // COM.claymoresystems.cert (puretls.jar)
  return CertRequest.makeSimpleDN(tdn);
}
```

As demonstrated in the previous sections, the Java CoG Kit provides powerful security features for certificate and proxy manipulation. Appendix A includes an implementation of Web-based CA that can be used to satisfy the security needs of your organization.

12.3.4 Resource Management

For a complete overview of the GRAM APIs, including source code, read Chapter 9.

12.3.5 Data Management

Data management in the Globus Toolkit is built on two basic protocols:

- GridFTP: Also known as GsiFTP. A high-performance, secure, reliable data transfer protocol optimized for high-bandwidth wide-area networks.
- Globus Access to Secondary storage (GASS): A protocol for single file transfers via HTTPS.

Transferring files across multiples machines is a snap using the Java CoG Kit APIs (see Listing 12.6).

LISTING 12.6 Transferring Files Across Multiple Machines Using GridFTP

```
package data.management;

import java.net.MalformedURLException;
import org.apache.log4j.Level;
import org.apache.log4j.Logger;
import org.globus.io.urlcopy.*;
import org.globus.util.*;
import org.globus.gsi.gssapi.auth.IdentityAuthorization;

/**
 * Sample program for transferring data using the
 *  GASS - Globus Access to Secondary Storage
 *  GridFTP - A high-performance, secure, reliable data
 *  transfer protocol optimized for high-bandwidth wide-area
 *   networks.
 * protocols
 */
public class DataTransfer
  implements UrlCopyListener
{
```

```
long transferredBytes;

// UrlCopyListener Interface methods
// fires multiple times
public void transfer(long transferedBytes, long totalBytes) {
  this.transferedBytes += transferedBytes;
}

// fires if a transfer error occurs
public void transferError(Exception e) {
  System.err.println("transferError:" + e);
}

// fires when transfer
public void transferCompleted() {
  System.out.println("transferCompleted: bytes"
                     + transferedBytes);
}

/**
 * A method to transfer data between machines
 * @param fromURL Source URL. For example:
 *  https://localhost:3154/c:/temp/foo.xml (for GASS)
 *  gsiftp://localhost:2811/c:/temp/foo.xml (GridFTP)
 * @param toURL Destination URL.
 * @param subject Certificate subject or NULL to use defaults
 * @param thirdParty Third party transfer (GFTP only)
 * @param dcau Data Channel
 */
void transferData(String fromURL, String toURL, String subject,
                  boolean thirdParty, boolean dcau)
  throws MalformedURLException, UrlCopyException
{
  GlobusURL from = new GlobusURL(fromURL);
  GlobusURL to = new GlobusURL(toURL);
  UrlCopy uc = new UrlCopy();

  // ftp options: thirdparty, dcau

  uc.setSourceUrl(from);
  uc.setDestinationUrl(to);
  uc.setUseThirdPartyCopy(thirdParty);
  uc.setDCAU(dcau);
```

```
    // set Authorization - subject
    if (subject != null && !subject.equals("")) {
      uc.setSourceAuthorization(new IdentityAuthorization(subject));
      uc.setDestinationAuthorization(new IdentityAuthorization(
        subject));
    }

    // fire transfer thread
    uc.addUrlCopyListener(this);
    uc.run();

  }

  /* for test purposes only */
  public static void main(String[] args) {
    try {
      Logger.getRootLogger().setLevel(Level.INFO);

      String fromURL = "https://localhost:3154/c:/temp/foo.xml";
      String toURL = "https://localhost:3155/c:/temp/foo1.xml";
      String subject = null;

      // GridFTP only options
      boolean thirdp = false;
      boolean dcau = false;

      DataTransfer data = new DataTransfer();
      data.transferData(fromURL, toURL, subject, thirdp, dcau);

    }
    catch (Exception e) {
      System.err.println(e);
    }
  }
}
```

12.3.5.1 Transfer Tests

An easy transfer test can be performed by using the GASS protocol in the following manner:

1. Generate a grid proxy: `grid-proxy-init`

```
Your identity:
O=Grid,OU=GlobusTest
 ,OU=simpleCA-vm-rhl8-2.ibm.com,OU=ibm.com
 ,CN= globusEnter GRID pass phrase for this identity: 2p2dkdt
Creating proxy, please wait...
Proxy verify OK
Your proxy is valid until Thu Jan 06 02:54:10 EST 2005
```

2. Start two instances of the GASS server:

```
c:\> globus-gass-server.bat
https://9.42.87.130:3154

c:\> globus-gass-server.bat
https://9.42.87.130:3155
```

3. Run a transfer with the following parameters:

```
String fromURL = "https://localhost:3154/c:/temp/foo.xml";
String toURL   = "https://localhost:3155/c:/temp/foo1.xml";
```

4. The output should look like this:

```
[main] INFO  gssapi.GlobusGSSManagerImpl - Getting default credential
[main] INFO auth.SelfAuthorization - Authorization: SELF
[main] INFO urlcopy.UrlCopy - Source size: 890
[main] INFO gssapi.GlobusGSSManagerImpl - Getting default credential
[main] INFO  auth.SelfAuthorization  - Authorization: SELF
transferCompleted: bytes 890
```

12.3.6 Data Transfer Troubleshooting

12.3.6.1 Class Not Found Errors

A message such as the following is very common when dealing with data management:

```
java.lang.NoClassDefFoundError:
javax/security/auth/Subject
 at org.globus.gsi.jaas.GlobusSubject
 .getSubject(GlobusSubject.java:33)
 at org.globus.gsi.jaas
 .JaasSubject.getCurrentSubject(JaasSubject.java:100)
 at org.globus.gsi.gssapi
```

```
.GlobusGSSManagerImpl.createCredential
 (GlobusGSSManagerImpl.java:91)
```

The most common cause for this error is missing one or more of the required libraries in your Java classpath. Make sure all the libraries mentioned in the previous sections are included.

12.3.6.2 Defective Credential Errors

These types of errors are produced when the GSI certificates have not been properly installed or a grid proxy has not been created. For example, the following error text indicates that the proxy file has not been created in the client system.

```
org.globus.io.urlcopy.UrlCopyException:
 UrlCopy transfer failed.
[Root error message:
 Security error
  [Root error message:
   Defective credential error.
  [Root error message:
   Proxy file (C:\DOCUME~1\vsilva\LOCALS~1\Temp\x509up_u_vsilva)
   not found.]]]
```

To fix these errors, make sure the client has a user certificate, encrypted private key, and CA (trusted) certificate installed properly; and the full path to those files is included in the `cog.properties` configuration file.

12.4 OTHER LANGUAGE BINDINGS

There are bindings to the Globus toolkit APIs from two popular Unix scripting languages: Python and Perl. This bindings support version 2.x of the toolkit only, although there are projects out there to support the latest OGSA and WSRF standards.

12.4.1 Python

If you are a Python and grid developer enthusiast, then pyGlobus is for you. pyGlobus is a set of wrappers to the Globus Toolkit executables provided by the Computational Research Division at Lawrence Berkeley National Laboratory (LBNL) [pyGlobus]. The goals of this project are as follows:

- Provide an object-oriented interface to the Globus toolkit.

- Provide a high-performance set of wrappers as close to the underlying C code as possible.
- Make the Globus Toolkit as natural to use from Python as possible.

pyGlobus is useful for portal development in Unix environments. Although it is important to have variety in regards to interfaces for grid development, Java has quickly become the platform to use for any kind of middle tier development. Thus, if your goal is to learn about grid portal development, you should seriously consider the Java language as a development platform. Chapter 4 covers many of the topics related to this subject.

12.4.2 PERL

Yet another grid interface for Unix portal development, PERL is a very popular language among systems administrators providing a robust way to program Web applications. This commodity kit is also known as GridPort and consists of a collection of technologies for science portals on computational grids [GridPort]. It is currently used by the National Partnership for Advanced Computational Infrastructure (NPACI) to provide the following:

- Information about computational resources
- Job submission and control
- File and directory manipulation and transfer

It is not the goal of this book to provide samples or code about the PERL or Python grid bindings. Nevertheless, following are some script comparisons between the C API and PERL for resource and data management:

12.4.2.1 Resource Management

C-command line: The following script will submit a date command to the backend job manager Portable Batch System [PBS]) running on host `acme`:

```
globus-job-run acme.host.com/jobmanager-pbs -np 16 /bin/date
```

GridPort script: Here is the equivalent GridPort PERL script:

```
$job = Cog::Globus::Job->new (
 contact=>'acme.host.com/jobmanager-pbs',
 executable=>'/bin/date',
 cpus=>'16'
 );

 $job->submit();
 print $job->get_stdout();
```

12.4.2.2 Data Management

C-command line: The following command will transfer two files located in the `/user` filesystem using the GridFTP protocol:

```
globus-url-copy gsiftp://host1.acme.edu/user/big.file
gsiftp://host2.acme.edu/user/bigcopy.file
```

GridPort script: An equivalent PERL script:

```
use Cog::Globus::URLCopy;
@output = Cog::Globus::URLCopy::copy(
 source_url=>'gsiftp://host1.acme.edu/user/big.file',
 dest_url  =>'gsiftp://host2.acme.edu/user/bigcopy.file'
             );

#
# Returns: @output. If all goes well, this array will be undef.
# Else, an array with the server error messages in it.
if(defined(@output)) {
 # Print server errors...
 foreach(@output) print;
}
```

GridPort and pyGlobus are APIs for Unix-style systems that give portal developers access to grid functionality such as secure user authentication, job submission/management, and file transfer. Although currently used in the development of science portals, they leverage standard, portable technologies to provide grid services that can be incorporated into your VOs.

12.5 SUMMARY

The code shown in this chapter will get you started with the basic services provided by the Java CoG Kit within your organization or computational grid. Those services include security management policies for X.509 certificates and private keys, and data management interfaces for data transfer, including GridFTP, GASS, and others.

For a more in-depth overview of GridFTP and other data transfer protocols, read Chapter 10.

REFERENCES

[GridPort] The Grid Portal Toolkit. Available online at *https://gridport.npaci.edu/.*

[JavaCoG01] Gregor von Laszewski, Ian Foster, Jarek Gawor, and Peter Lane, "A Java Commodity Grid Kit," *Concurrency and Computation: Practice and Experience, 13*(8–9), pp. 643–662. Available online at *http:/www.cogkit.org/*, 2001.

[JavaCoGManual03] Gregor von Laszewski, Beulah Alunkal, Kaizar Amin , Jarek Gawor, Mihael Hategan, Sandeep Nijsure. *The Java CoG Kit User Manual Draft Version 1.1.* ANL/MCS-TM-259 Revisions March 14, 2003. Available online at *http://www-unix.globus.org/cog/manual-user.pdf,* July 18, 2003.

[pyGlobus] Python Globus. Lawrence Berkeley National Laboratory, Computational Research Division. Available online at *http://dsd.lbl.gov/gtg/projects/pyGlobus/.*

13 Web Services Resource Framework (WSRF)

In This Chapter

This chapter includes information on the following topics:

- An overview of the Web Services Resource Framework (WSRF), which is the latest specification in Web Services technology. This section covers stateless versus stateful services, and the WS-Resource construct.
- The integration of WSRF with the Open Grid Services Infrastructure (OGSI) framework.
- A description of the WSRF normative specifications: WS-ResourceProperties, WS-Addressing, WS-Resource Lifecycle, WS-ServiceGroup, WS-BaseFaults, and WS-Notification.
- An overview of the upcoming Globus Toolkit 4, the latest and most advanced grid middleware software available today.
- A sample grid service for WSRF in the topic of large integer factorization, which is very common in asymmetric cryptography.

ON THE CD

Complete code listings can be found in the companion CD-ROM.

13.1 UNDERSTANDING WSRF

To understand how WSRF can provide stateful services, we must first understand Web Services and define their state in a standard manner. A Web service is a software component that's capable of machine-to-machine interaction with a network address described in Web Service Description Language (WSDL). Service interaction is described using Simple Object Access Protocol (SOAP) messages, typically composed by an XML serialization using a transport protocol such as HTTP or other Web standards [StatefulWebServices04].

The concept of a *service-oriented architecture* (SOA) has emerged to define a distributed system where Web Services coordinate by sending messages. Web Services are *stateless;* they exchange messages with no access or use of information not contained in the input message.

13.1.1 Stateless versus Stateful Services

A stateful service is a service that has access to, or manipulates, logical stateful resources through the propagation of execution context in headers on message exchanges. In general, a *stateless* service enhances reliability and scalability. (For example, after a failure, a service can be restarted without concern of previous interactions. New service instances can be created or destroyed in response to the system load.) Thus, *stateless* services are considered a good practice by the Web Services community [StatefulWebServices04].

However, there are situations where a *stateful* service (a service that manipulates stateful resources based on message exchanges) may be desirable. Such scenarios involve interoperability among services. Thus, it is important to standardize the patterns by which state is represented, to facilitate the construction of interoperable services [StatefulWebServices04].

13.1.2 WS-Resource

A WS-Resource is defined as an entity composed by a *Web Service* and a *stateful resource.* A stateful resource can be used in the Web Service message exchanges. WS-Resources can be created and destroyed, and their state can be queried or modified via message exchanges.

WS-Resource has four characteristics that are very important in software engineering, known as the *ACID* properties. Most of these properties are described in the Web Services Atomic Transaction specification [WS-AtomicTransaction]:

- **Atomicity:** Stateful resource updates within a transactional unit are made in an *all-or-nothing* fashion.
- **Consistency:** Stateful resources should always be in a consistent state even after failures.
- **Isolation:** Updates to stateful resources should be isolated within a given transactional work unit.
- **Durability:** It provides for the permanence of stateful resource updates made under the transactional unit of work.

13.1.2.1 Stateful Resource

A stateful resource can be defined as a component that has three characteristics:

1. It is composed by *state* data defined in XML format.
2. It has a life cycle.
3. It can be manipulated by one or more Web Services.

Some examples of stateful resources are files, java objects, or rows in a database. Stateful resources can be compound (e.g., contain other resources), and their instances can be created or destroyed via *service factories*. A stateful resource instance should be identified by an identity or *resource identifier*; moreover, applications using a resource may assign additional identities or *aliases* [StatefulWebServices04].

Relationships between Web Services and stateful resources are defined through the concept of a *resource pattern*. A resource pattern defines the mechanisms that associate a stateful resource with the message exchanges of a Web Service. This relationship can be static if a resource is associated with a service when deployed or dynamic if the resource is associated at the message exchange. Resource patterns are implemented using standards such as XML, WSDL, and *WS-Addressing*.

13.2 WSRF AND OGSI

WSRF and OGSI are the latest attempts for a standardization of grid services. They are being evaluated carefully by the Web Services community. The following sections describe their advantages and disadvantages.

13.2.1 OGSI Evolution

OGSI jumped to center stage to address the needs of applications in distributed environments such as the following:

- A framework for creating, addressing, inspecting, and managing the lifetime of stateful services on grid environments
- Mechanisms to deal with service creation and discovery
- The need for controlled, fault tolerant, and secure management of state

By relying on open specifications like WSDL and XML Schema, OGSI introduced new concepts into the Web Services world: instances, common metadata and inspection, asynchronous notification, instance references, collections of service instances, and service state.

To accomplish these goals, OGSI has enhanced Web Services with extensions such as the following:

- Support for WSDL 2.0 extensions
- WSDL extensions for representing, querying, and updating service data
- Grid service handle and grid service reference constructs
- Fault information through WSDL fault messages
- A set of operations for creating and destroying grid services
- Mechanisms asynchronous notifications

This remarkable work has created an aura of competition and compatibility issues between Web Services and OGSI and the need for a brand new specification to address the common ground of these two important emerging technologies [OGSA2WSRF04].

13.2.2 From OGSI to WSRF

In July 2003, the OGSI specification was released to address the need for stateful Grid services. OGSI defines interfaces for creating, addressing, inspecting, and managing the lifetime of stateful grid services. A grid service as defined by OGSI is a Web Service that implements a specific set of interfaces and behaviors. Through the use of extended WSDL and XML Schema definitions, OGSI introduces the following [OGSA2WSRF04]:

- Stateful Web Service instances
- Common service metadata and inspection
- Service asynchronous notification
- Collections of service instances
- Service state data

At the same time, the Web Services world has evolved significantly; specifically, a number of new specifications that overlap ideas expressed by OGSI. For example:

WS-Addressing: This provides transport neutral mechanisms to address Web Services through XML elements (service endpoints) within the messages.

WS-MetaDataExchange: This provides mechanisms for obtaining information about a published service, including WSDL description, XML Schema, and policy information.

This overlap has prompted the OGSI community for an integration effort with those Web Service specifications rather than maintaining a redundant specification with the same functionality. The integration of the OGSI and the Web Services community is based on the following critiques about OGSI [StatefulWebServices04]:

- *Too bulky:* Not a clean separation to support incremental adoption. For example, event notification and metadata should be partitioned to support flexible composition. This issue is addressed by two new specifications: WS-Resource and WS-Notification.
- *Compatibility with existing Web Services and XML tooling:* By extending the WSDL 1.1 `portType` definition, OGSI has made it tough for Web Service developers to use standard XML Schema mechanisms such as the Java API for XML-based Remote Procedure Calls (JAX-RPC). WSRF tackles this problem by using standard XML Schema and `portType` *annotations* to associate this XML information model of the resource with Web Service operations, thus preserving compatibility with WSDL 1.1.
- *Too object oriented:* OGSI couples Web Services and resource state as a single entity. The Web Service community argues, *Web Services do not have state or instances.* WSRF addresses this problem by making a clear distinction between the *service* and the stateful entities acted upon. WSRF defines the means by which a Web Service and a stateful resource are composed through the concept of *implied resource pattern.*
- *WSDL 2.0 compatibility:* Delays in the WSDL 2.0 specification made it difficult to support the OGSI WSDL extensions with existing Web Services runtimes.

13.3 WSRF NORMATIVE SPECIFICATIONS

WSRF is composed by five specifications that describe the way stateful resources interact with each other.

13.3.1 WS-ResourceProperties

WS-Resource property defines the constructs by which the state of a WS-Resource can be manipulated through the Web Service interface. A *resource property* maps to an individual component of the resource *state*. WS-ResourceProperties describes WS-Resources by associating stateful resources and Web Services. It also defines methods to retrieve, change, and delete visible properties of a WS-Resource.

13.3.1.1 Properties Document

It is a view or projection of the actual state of the WS-Resource. The WS-Resource properties document is expressed as an XML Schema declaration within a namespace, comprising a set of references to XML declarations of the individual resource properties. The following is an example of a WS-Resource properties document named `ResourceExample` with two property references: `prop1`, `prop2`

```
<xs:schema targetNamespace="http://example.com/ResourceExample"
  xmlns:tns="http://example.com/ResourceExample"
  xmlns:xs="http://www.w3.org/2001/XMLSchema"
  ...>

  <xs:element name="prop1" type=… />
  <xs:element name="prop2" type=… />

  <xs:element name="ResourceExample">
    <xs:complexType>
      <xs:sequence>
        <xs:element ref="tns:prop1" />
        <xs:element ref="tns:prop2" />
      </xs:sequence>
    </xs:complexType>
  </xs:element>

</xs:schema>
```

The WS-Resource properties document declaration is associated with the WSDL `portType` definition via the use of the `ResourceProperties` attribute thus enabling service requestors to retrieve resource properties from the Web Service description:

```
<wsdl:definitions>

 <!-- Web service description file (WSDL) -->
 <!-- Web service stuff -->
```

```
<wsdl:portType name="SomePortTypeName"
 wsrp:ResourceProperties="tns:ResourceExample" >

<operation name="...

</wsdl:portType>
```

13.3.1.2 Property Composition

In WSDL 1.1, Web Service interfaces have been designed to be compassable. This means that simple interfaces can be aggregated to compose more complex ones. In the same fashion, WS-Resource properties can be aggregated by referencing additional declarations using the `xs:ref` attribute

```
<xs:element name="ResourcePropsExample">
  <xs:complexType>
   <xs:sequence>
    <!-- some properties ... -->
    <xs:element ref="ns:AggregatedResourceProperty"
     xmlns:ns= ... />
   </xs:sequence>
  </xs:complexTypc>
</xs:element>
```

13.3.1.3 Accessing Property Values

Resource property values can be read, modified, and queried by exchanging messages between the Web Service client and server. For example, a "`get`" operation will retrieve the value of a resource property, and a "`set`" operation will modify the value. The WS-ResourceProperties specification provides more details on these operations [WS-ResourceProperties].

The following message exchange represents a "`get`" operation for property `prop1:Client "get" request:`

```
<soap:Envelope>
    <soap:Header>
      <tns:resourceID>MY_RESOURCE_ID</tns:resourceID>
    </soap:Header>

    <soap:Body>
      <wsrp:GetMultipleResourceProperty>
        <wsrp:ResourceProperty>tns:prop1</wsrp:ResourceProperty>
      </wsrp:GetMultipleResourceProperty>
```

```
    </soap:Body>
</soap:Envelope>
```

Server response:

```
<soap:Envelope>
 <soap:Body>
   <wsrp:GetMultipleResourcePropertyResponse>
    <prop1>Hello World</prop1>
   </wsrp:GetMultipleResourcePropertyResponse>
 </soap:Body>
</soap:Envelope>
```

13.3.2 WS-Addressing

WS-Addressing is a construct used to standardize an *endpoint reference* (see Listing 13.1). An endpoint reference represents the address of a Web-Service deployed over a network endpoint. It is represented as an XML serialization usually returned by a Web Service request to create a new resource. An endpoint reference may contain, besides the Web Service address, metadata such as service description and reference properties.

LISTING 13.1 WS-Addressing Endpoint Reference

```
<wsa:EndpointReference>
  <!-- Web Service address over a network endpoint -->
  <wsa:Address>
   http://helloworld.com/myWebService
  </wsa:Address>

  <!-- Meta Data -->
  <!-- Endpoint reference properties -->
  <wsa:ReferenceProperties>
   <tns:resourceID> ID-12345 </tns:resourceID>
  </wsa:ReferenceProperties>
</wsa:EndpointReference>
```

The use of endpoint references is demonstrated in the Figures 13.1 and 13.2, depicting the message exchange for the creation of a Web Service called Large Integer Factorization (LIF) service.

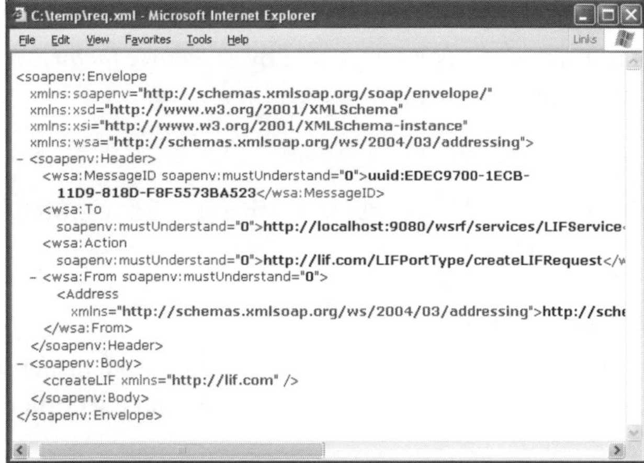

FIGURE 13.1 Web Service creation SOAP request.

FIGURE 13.2 Web Service creation SOAP responses.

13.3.3 WS-Resource Lifecycle

A lifecycle is defined as the period between a WS-Resource creation and destruction that takes into account the following:

13.3.3.1 Creation

Stateful resources are usually created by a *resource factory*. A *creation* call returns an endpoint reference to the new stateful resource.

13.3.3.2 Destruction

Destruction defines the means by which a stateful resource is destroyed and system resources are reclaimed.

13.3.3.3 Resource Identifier

Stateful resources must have at least one *resource identifier*. It is returned as part of the endpoint reference and can be made available to other Web Services in a distributed system.

13.3.4 WS-ServiceGroup

WS-ServiceGroup is used to organize collections of WS-Resources to build registries or to build services that can perform collective operations. The WS-ServiceGroup defines the means for managing heterogeneous collections of Web Services. A WS-ServiceGroup uses memberships, rules, constraints, and classifications to define groups. A group is a collection of members that meets some constraints defined using resource properties [WS-ServiceGroup].

13.3.5 WS-BaseFaults

WS-BaseFaults defines a consistent way for dealing with faults generated by operations within a Web Service. This specification is used by all of the other WS-Resource framework specifications for fault reporting related to WS-Resource use.

13.3.6 WS-Notification

This is a separate family of specifications that enable publish and subscribe (pub/sub) interactions among Web Services. WS-Notification defines interfaces that clients use to subscribe to topics of interest, and receive notifications asynchronously, for example, changes to a resource property value.

WS-Notification consists of the following members [WS-Notification]:

13.3.6.1 WS-BaseNotification

This defines mechanisms that allow a subscriber to register to receive notifications from a producer.

13.3.6.2 WS-Topics

This defines a hierarchical organization of notification messages that subscribers can understand and subscribe to. Topics use an XML representation and can be further decomposed in child topics. They are usually prefixed by a namespace much like XML is.

13.3.6.3 WS-BrokeredNotification

This defines the interface to a Notification Broker that manages subscriptions in the system.

13.3.7 WS-Resource Security

Security is defined via the WS-Policy and WS-SecurityPolicy specifications, which are part of the Web Services security roadmap. They state the set of policies used to secure message exchanges between clients and Web Services.

13.4 GT4 AND WSRF: STATEFUL SERVICES FOR GRID ENVIRONMENTS

The following sections describe the new features of the upcoming version of the Globus Toolkit as well as a sample WSRF service.

13.4.1 Overview

The Globus Toolkit 4 (GT4) (31 Jan 2005) features a new implementation of the WSRF and the Web Services Notification (WSN) [OASIS-WSNotification] standards. GT4 provides an API for building stateful Web Services targeted to distributed heterogeneous computing environments [OASIS-WSRF].

The purpose of this chapter is to provide a description of the new standards used by GT4 with a real-world example to get you started modeling stateful services for your organization.

13.4.2 Newcomers: WS-Components

Among the new Web Services components in GT4 are:

13.4.2.1 WS Authentication Authorization

WS Authentication Authorization replaces Grid Security Infrastructure (GSI) and it is subdivided into *Message-Level Security* and *Authorization Framework*. Message-level security implements two standards: WS-Security and WS-SecureConversation. These standards provide SOAP message encryption, integrity, and replay protection.

The Authorization Framework component is designed to handle many authorization schemas such as grid-mapfile, access control lists (ACL), and custom authorization handlers via the SAML protocol [OASIS-WSRF].

13.4.2.2 WS Core

WS Core is an implementation of two brand-new standards: WSRF and WSN. Other new features include an Apache Tomcat–based JNDI registry, HTTP/1.1 client server support, a resolver service for URI to WS-Addressing conversion, and others [GT4StatusPlan].

13.4.2.3 C WS Core

Hey! Here is something C programmers will appreciate. GT4 features a basic toolset in C for creating WSRF-enabled Web Services and clients conforming to WS-Resource and WS-Notification. The most exiting features of this C core include the following:

- A standalone service container
- API for embedding services in a C application
- Resource API for managing resources from within a service
- HTTP/1.1 client & server support
- Generation of pure C stubs (blocking or asynchronous) directly from WSDL schemas
- Dynamically loadable operation providers and service modules based on the new extension API

13.4.3 Old Protocols, New Faces

All the well-known GT3 protocols—WS-GRAM for resource management, RFT for data management, and MDS for information services—have been redesigned to use WSRF. The security protocol GSI is now called WS Authentication Authorization. The following compatibility matrix outlines the basic features and compatibility issues of the major protocols of the Globus Toolkit upcoming release. More information can be found in Status and Plans for the Globus Toolkit [GT4Status-Plan], and shown in Table 13.1.

TABLE 13.1 WSRF/OGSA Comparison Matrix

Service	**Protocol**	**Features**	**Backward Compatibility**
Data Transfer	Reliable File Transfer (RFT)	1. Controls and monitors third-party file transfers using GridFTP 2. Exponential back-off 3. Transfer all or none 4. Parallel streams 5. TCP buffer size 6. Recursive directory transfer	Not backward compatible with OGSI (GT3.2).
Resource Management	WS-GRAM	1. Improved job performance: concurrency, throughput, latency 2. Improved reliability/recovery 3. Support for mpich-g2 jobs including: a. multijob submission b. processes coordination in a job c. subjob coordination in a multijob	The protocol has been changed to be WSRF compliant. There is no backward compatibility between this version and previous versions.
Information Services	MDS4	Index Service: 1. Based on WSRF rather than OGSI 2. Xindice support has been removed 3. Persistent configuration of aggregations has been refactored Brand new services: 1. Trigger Service 2. Aggregator 3. Archive Service	Incompatible with the GT3.2 index service as the service has been remodeled to use WSRF instead of OGSI.

13.5 SERVICE EXAMPLE: A WSRF LARGE INTEGER FACTORIZATION (LIF) SERVICE

Current cryptographic methods such as Secure Sockets Layer (SSL) and others rely on the mathematical property that factoring very large numbers requires significant computing power. It has been proven mathematically that given current computational resources, it will take many years for an individual to find the factors (numbers that multiplied by themselves give the original number) of a very large number. The security of cryptosystems such as RSA relies on the difficulty of factoring integers. There have been successful factorizations of large numbers including the factoring of a 129-digit RSA modulus. Currently, RSA moduli of 512 bits, or about 155 digits would be feasible to factor and, in fact, have been factored. In August 1999, a team including Arjen Lenstra and Peter Montgomery factored a 512-bit RSA modulus using the Number Field Sieve in 8400 (8400 millions of instructions per second (MIPS) years [QuadSieve01]. Current estimates say that a 768-bit modulus will be good until 2004, so for short-term or personal use, such a key size is adequate. For corporate use, a 1024-bit modula is suggested, and a 2048-bit modulus is suggested for much more permanent usage. These suggestions take into account possible advances in factoring techniques and for processor speed increases [QuadSieve01].

The first WSRF-enabled Web Service implements a large integer factorization algorithm using a quadratic sieve. This is a popular topic among cryptographers, given that most of today's secure communications are based in the difficulty of factorizing large integers (e.g., 100+ digits). The mathematical background and rationale for this example can be found in Chapter 8.

13.5.1 Web Service Description (WSDL) File

The interface to any Web Service is described in WSDL. WSDL allows you to define the operations exposed by a Web Service as well as the network endpoints required to reach it. This particular service exposes an operation called *factor* that takes a string argument and returns a string result (see Listing 13.2).

LISTING 13.2 Large Integer Factorization Web Service Description File

```
<?xml version="1.0" encoding="UTF-8"?>
<definitions
  name="LIF"
  targetNamespace="http://lif.com"
  xmlns:tns="http://lif.com"
  xmlns:wsa="http://schemas.xmlsoap.org/ws/2004/03/addressing"
  xmlns="http://schemas.xmlsoap.org/wsdl/"
```

```
  xmlns:gtwsdl=
  "http://www.globus.org/namespaces/2004/01/GTWSDLExtensions"
  xmlns:wsdl="http://schemas.xmlsoap.org/wsdl/"
  xmlns:xsd="http://www.w3.org/2001/XMLSchema">

  <!-- LIF (Large Integer Factorization) Web Service description file -
->
  <wsdl:import
    location="../../../wsrf/properties/WS-ResourceProperties.wsdl" />

  <wsdl:import
    location="../../../wsrf/lifetime/WS-ResourceLifetime.wsdl" />

  <wsdl:import
    location="../../../wsrf/notification/WS-BaseN.wsdl" />

  <types>
    <xsd:schema
      targetNamespace="http://lif.com"
      xmlns:tns="http://lif.com"
      xmlns:xsd="http://www.w3.org/2001/XMLSchema">

      <xsd:import
        namespace="http://schemas.xmlsoap.org/ws/2004/03/addressing"
        schemaLocation="../../../ws/addressing/WS-Addressing.xsd" />

      <xsd:element name="createLIF">
        <xsd:complexType />
      </xsd:element>

      <xsd:element name="createLIFResponse">
        <xsd:complexType>
          <xsd:sequence>
            <xsd:element ref="wsa:EndpointReference" />
          </xsd:sequence>
        </xsd:complexType>
      </xsd:element>

      <xsd:element
        name="factor"
        type="xsd:string" />
      <xsd:element
        name="factorResponse"
        type="xsd:string" />
```

```
    <xsd:element
      name="Value"
      type="xsd:int" />

    <xsd:element name="LIFRP">
      <xsd:complexType>
        <xsd:sequence>
          <xsd:element
            ref="tns:Value"
            minOccurs="1"
            maxOccurs="1" />
        </xsd:sequence>
      </xsd:complexType>
    </xsd:element>

  </xsd:schema>
</types>

<message name="CreateLIFRequest">
  <part
    name="request"
    element="tns:createLIF" />
</message>
<message name="CreateLIFResponse">
  <part
    name="response"
    element="tns:createLIFResponse" />
</message>

<!-- factor operation input/output arguments -->
<!-- Input is a string argument-->
<message name="FactorInputMessage">
  <part
    name="parameters"
    element="tns:factor" />
</message>
<!-- Output is a string value -->
<message name="FactorOutputMessage">
  <part
    name="parameters"
    element="tns:factorResponse" />
</message>

<portType
```

```
    name="LIFPortType"
    gtwsdl:implements="wsntw:NotificationProducer
                       wsrlw:ImmediateResourceTermination
                       wsrlw:ScheduledResourceTermination"
    wsrp:ResourceProperties="tns:LIFRP">

    <!-- Operation invoked when creating the web service -->
    <operation name="createLIF">
      <input message="tns:CreateLIFRequest" />
      <output message="tns:CreateLIFResponse" />
    </operation>

    <!-- Factorization operation
    <operation name="factor">
      <input message="tns:FactorInputMessage" />
      <output message="tns:FactorOutputMessage" />
    </operation>
  </portType>
</definitions>
```

13.5.2 Resource Implementation

Resources within WSRF services are used to maintain state across service calls through message exchanges between a client and a Web Service. Listing 13.3 uses LIF to store the result of a factorization operation.

LISTING 13.3 WSRF Stateful Resource Implementation Sample

```
/**
 * Large Integer Factorization (LIF) WSRF Service
 * Description: A WSRF Service for large integer factorization
 *
 * @author Vladimir Silva
 */
package org.globus.wsrf.samples.lif;

import java.util.Calendar;

import javax.xml.namespace.QName;

import org.globus.wsrf.ResourceIdentifier;
import org.globus.wsrf.ResourceProperties;
import org.globus.wsrf.ResourceProperty;
import org.globus.wsrf.ResourcePropertySet;
```

```
import org.globus.wsrf.Topic;
import org.globus.wsrf.TopicList;
import org.globus.wsrf.TopicListAccessor;
import org.globus.wsrf.ResourceLifetime;
import org.globus.wsrf.WSRFConstants;
import org.globus.wsrf.impl.ReflectionResourceProperty;
import org.globus.wsrf.impl.ResourcePropertyTopic;
import org.globus.wsrf.impl.SimpleResourcePropertySet;
import org.globus.wsrf.impl.SimpleTopicList;
import org.globus.wsrf.impl.SimpleTopic;
import org.globus.wsrf.impl.SimpleResourceProperty;

/**
 * LIF Resource Implementation
 * A LIF resource is used to save the value of a specific factorization
 */
public class LIF
    implements
    ResourceLifetime,
    ResourceIdentifier,
    ResourceProperties,
    TopicListAccessor {

  public static final QName KEY =
new QName("http://lif.com", "LIFKey");
  public static final QName RP_SET =
new QName("http://lif.com", "LIF");
  public static final QName VALUE =
new QName("http://lif.com", "Value");

  private ResourcePropertySet propSet;
  private TopicList topicList;

  protected Calendar terminationTime = null;
  protected Object key;
  protected ResourceProperty value;

  /**
   * initialize Resource
   * @param key
   */
  protected void initialize(Object key) {
    this.key = key;
    this.propSet = new SimpleResourcePropertySet(RP_SET);
```

```
  this.topicList = new SimpleTopicList(this);
  ResourceProperty prop = null;

  try {
    this.value =
        new ResourcePropertyTopic(new SimpleResourceProperty(VALUE));
    this.propSet.add(this.value);
    this.topicList.addTopic( (Topic)this.value);
    this.value.add(new String());

    prop =
        new ReflectionResourceProperty(
            WSRFConstants.TERMINATION_TIME,
            this);
    this.propSet.add(prop);
    this.topicList.addTopic(
        new SimpleTopic(WSRFConstants.TERMINATION_TOPIC));

    prop =
        new ReflectionResourceProperty(
            WSRFConstants.CURRENT_TIME,
            this);
    this.propSet.add(prop);
  }
  catch (Exception e) {
    throw new RuntimeException(e.getMessage());
  }
}

public ResourcePropertySet getResourcePropertySet() {
  return this.propSet;
}

public TopicList getTopicList() {
  return this.topicList;
}

/*
 * Methods to get or set the value of the resource
 */
public String getValue(int idx) {
  return ( (String)this.value.get(idx));
}
```

```
    public void setValue(String value) {
      this.value.set(0, value);
    }

    /**
     * Called when a new LIF resource is created.
     *
     * @return the resource key
     */
    public Object create() throws Exception {
      // just an example, might be a file already...
      this.key = new Integer(hashCode());
      initialize(key);
      return key;
    }

    public Object getID() {
      return this.key;
    }

    /* Service Lifetime Management methods
     *  (non-Javadoc)
     */
    public void setTerminationTime(Calendar time) {
      this.terminationTime = time;
    }

    /*
     *  (non-Javadoc)
     * @see org.globus.wsrf.ResourceLifetime#getTerminationTime()
     */
    public Calendar getTerminationTime() {
      return this.terminationTime;
    }

    public Calendar getCurrentTime() {
      return Calendar.getInstance();
    }
  }
```

13.5.3 Service Implementation

The service implementation contains the operations exposed by the Web Service to the outside world. In this particular example, two operations are exposed (see Listing 13.4)

- `createLIF`: This fires when an instance of the Web Service is created. Its main talk is to create a stateful resource identified by a *resource key*, and an *endpoint reference*, which is returned in the response message.
- `Factor`: This operation is used to factorize the large integer using a quadratic sieve and uses a stateful resource to store its result.

LISTING 13.4 Service Implementation

```
package org.globus.wsrf.samples.lif;

import java.rmi.RemoteException;
import org.apache.axis.message.addressing.EndpointReferenceType;

import org.globus.wsrf.ResourceContext;
import org.globus.wsrf.ResourceKey;
import org.globus.wsrf.utils.AddressingUtils;

import com.lif._createLIF;
import com.lif._createLIFResponse;

import javax.math.factorization.Factorizer;
import java.math.BigInteger;

/**
 * Large Integer Factorization (LIF) WSRF Service
 * Description: A WSRF Service for large integer factorization
 *
 * Service Implementation
 * @author Vladimir Silva
 */
public class LIFService {
  ResourceKey key = null;

  /**
   * OPERATION1: Fires when the webservice is created.
   * Creates a stateful resource (identified by a key)
   * and endpoint reference (EPR) which is returned
   * @param request
```

```
     * @return Response object containing an endpoint reference (EPR)
     * @throws RemoteException
     */
    public _createLIFResponse createLIF(_createLIF request) throws
        RemoteException
  {
      ResourceContext ctx = null;
      LIFHome home = null;

      /*
       * Create a Resource...
       */
      try {
        ctx = ResourceContext.getResourceContext();
        home = (LIFHome) ctx.getResourceHome();
        key = home.create();
      }
      catch (RemoteException e) {
        throw e;
      }
      catch (Exception e) {
        throw new RemoteException("", e);
      }

      /*
       * Add an endpoint reference to the response
       */
      EndpointReferenceType epr = null;
      try {
        epr = AddressingUtils.createEndpointReference(ctx, key);
      }
      catch (Exception e) {
        throw new RemoteException("", e);
      }

      _createLIFResponse response = new _createLIFResponse();
      response.setEndpointReference(epr);

      return response;
    }

    /**
     * OPERATION2: Find factors operation
     * @param largeInteger Large prime/integer string to be factored
```

```
   * @return Result of the form: f1^p1 * f2^p2 ... fn^pn
   * @throws RemoteException
   */
  public String factor(String largeInteger) throws RemoteException {
    /*
     * Retrieve resource
     */
    Object resource = null;
    try {
      resource = ResourceContext.getResourceContext().getResource();
    }
    catch (RemoteException e) {
      throw e;
    }
    catch (Exception e) {
      throw new RemoteException("", e);
    }
    LIF lif = (LIF) resource;

    /*
     * Use a quadratic sieve to find factors
     */
    Factorizer f;
    try {
      // Factorize number, Timeout = 10 secs, verbose = false
      f = new Factorizer(new BigInteger(largeInteger), 10, false);
      f.factor();
    }
    catch (Exception ex) {
      throw new RemoteException("Factorizer", ex);
    }

    // save factors within the LIF resource
    lif.setValue(f.factorsAsString());
    return f.factorsAsString();
  }
}
```

13.5.4 Service Client

The final step in the implementation process is to write a service client to invoke the service. Globus provides APIs to deal with most of the low-level work. The sequence of steps required to invoke a service operation are simple:

1. Obtain a service address locator:

```
LIFServiceAddressingLocator locator = new LIFServiceAddressing-
Locator();
```

2. Obtain an endpoint reference (EPR) and a `port` to invoke the desired Web Service operation:

```
EndpointReferenceType endpoint =
 new EndpointReferenceType();
endpoint.setAddress(
 new Address(
  "http://localhost:8080/wdrf/services/MyService")
 );
LIFPortType port = locator.getLIFPortTypePort(endpoint);
```

3. Invoke the desired operation. For example, the following creates an instance of the `LIF` service:

```
_createLIFResponse createResponse = port.createLIF(new
_createLIF());
endpoint = createResponse.getEndpointReference();
```

The complete process is shown in Listing 13.5

LISTING 13.5 Web Service Client Program

```
package org.globus.wsrf.samples.lif.client;

/**
 * <p>Title: LIF (Large Integer Factorization) WSRF Service</p>
 * <p>Description: Large Integer Factorization service for GT4</p>
 * <p>Copyright: Copyright (c) 2004</p>
 * <p>Company: </p>
 * @author Vladimir Silva
 * @version 1.0
 */

import java.util.List;

import org.apache.axis.message.addressing.Address;
import org.apache.axis.message.addressing.EndpointReferenceType;
import org.globus.wsrf.NotificationConsumerManager;
```

```
import com.lif.LIFPortType;
import com.lif._createLIF;
import com.lif._createLIFResponse;
import com.lif.service.LIFServiceAddressingLocator;

import org.oasis.wsrf.lifetime._Destroy;

import javax.xml.rpc.Stub;
import org.globus.wsrf.impl.security.authentication.Constants;
import org.globus.wsrf.impl.security.authorization.SelfAuthorization;

import org.globus.wsrf.client.BaseClient;
import org.apache.commons.cli.ParseException;
import org.apache.commons.cli.CommandLine;

/**
 * Large Integer Factorization (LIF) WSRF Service
 * Description: A WSRF Service for large integer factorization
 *
 * This class is used to create a resource which will be used
 * to save the result of a given factorization
 *
 * @author Vladimir Silva
 */
public class FactorClient
    extends BaseClient {
  public static void main(String[] args) {
    FactorClient client = new FactorClient();

    // client takes 1 arg : large integer
    client.setCustomUsage("<large integer>");

    LIFServiceAddressingLocator locator =
        new LIFServiceAddressingLocator();

    // Client Security descriptor file
    // Uses GSI Secure Conversation, signature
    // without delegation, self authz.
    String CLIENT_DESC =
        "org/globus/wsrf/samples/lif/client/client-security-
config.xml";

    NotificationConsumerManager consumer = null;
```

```
    // large number to factor
    String largeInt;

    try {
      // Parse arguments: 1 arg => large number
      CommandLine line = client.parse(args);
      List options = line.getArgList();

      if (options == null || options.isEmpty()) {
        throw new ParseException("Expected large integer argument");
      }

      // get number to factor from cmd line
      largeInt = (String) options.get(0);

      // Service URL
      String servURL = line.getOptionValue("s");

      if (servURL == null) {
        servURL = "http://localhost:8080/wsrf/services/LIFService";
      }

      // Use security? (Use security if the Service URL contains
      // Secure e.g., SecureLIFService
      boolean secure = (servURL.indexOf("Secure") > 0) ? true : false;

      // STEP1: Obtain a SOAP endpoint reference (EPR)
      // Contains the service URL & metadata
// such as resource properties)
      EndpointReferenceType endpoint = new EndpointReferenceType();
      endpoint.setAddress(new Address(servURL));

      // STEP2: Obtain a Port (using the EPR)
      // to create a web service instance
      LIFPortType port = locator.getLIFPortTypePort(endpoint);

      if (secure) {
        ( (Stub) port)._setProperty(
            Constants.CLIENT_DESCRIPTOR_FILE,
            CLIENT_DESC);
      }

      // Create lif (Large Integer factorizer) resource
      // Returns the EPR of the new instance
```

```
        _createLIFResponse createResponse =
            port.createLIF(new _createLIF());

        endpoint = createResponse.getEndpointReference();

        // STEP3: Use the new EPR to obtain a second Port
        // used to factor the number
        LIFPortType factorPort = locator.getLIFPortTypePort(endpoint);

        if (secure) {
          // Secure message
          ( (Stub) factorPort)._setProperty(
              Constants.GSI_SEC_MSG,
              Constants.SIGNATURE);
          ( (Stub) factorPort)._setProperty(
              Constants.AUTHORIZATION,
              new SelfAuthorization());
        }

        // Show factorization result
        System.out.println(largeInt + "=" +
                           factorPort.factor(largeInt));

        // STEP3: Use the EPR to obtain a third port
        // to destroy the service
        LIFPortType destroyPort = locator.getLIFPortTypePort(endpoint);

        if (secure) {
          ( (Stub) destroyPort)._setProperty(
              Constants.CLIENT_DESCRIPTOR_FILE,
              CLIENT_DESC);
        }

        // Destroy the lif resource
        destroyPort.destroy(new _Destroy());

      }
      catch (Exception e) {
        e.printStackTrace();
      }
    }
  }
```

13.5.5 Enabling Security

If you want enable security in your service, you must perform a sequence of extra steps and files. For example, in the previous service security–enabled versions of the resource class and service, implementation files must be written. A security configuration XML file for the service is also required, plus the client program must be enabled for security, too. For the sake of simplicity, secure services will be explored in future work. However, the source code provided includes the security-enabled files.

13.5.6 Build and Deployment

Globus has made service compilation and deployment a snap by using an extremely useful set of `ant` scripts. Thus, packaging and deploying a service (provided that you have the right files) is just a matter of running the following:

To `deploy` (within the project directory):

```
set GLOBUS_LOCATION=[WSRF_CONTAINER_LOCATION]
ant deploy
```

To `undeploy`:

```
ant undeploy
```

13.5.7 Runtime Test

Once the service has been successfully deployed, start the WSRF container and run the service by executing within the `$GLOBUS_LOCATION/bin directory: lif-client -s http://localhost:8080/wsrf/services/LIFService` [number] (see Figure 13.3)

```
Command Prompt
C:\GridBookSource\wsrf-3.9.2\bin>lif-client.bat -s http://localhost:8080/wsrf/se
rvices/LIFService 556158012756522140970101270050308458769458529626977
0    [main] WARN  org.apache.axis.utils.JavaUtils  - Unable to find required cla
sses (javax.activation.DataHandler and javax.mail.internet.MimeMultipart). Attac
hment support is disabled.
556158012756522140970101270050308458769458529626977=449818591141 * 1236405128000
1208707758462283541191843977
C:\GridBookSource\wsrf-3.9.2\bin>_
```

FIGURE 13.3 Sample test output for the LIF WSRF service.

13.6 SUMMARY

In July 2003, the OGSI specification was released to address the need for stateful grid services. OGSI defines interfaces for creating, addressing, inspecting, and managing the lifetime of stateful grid services. WSRF is a brand new specification on grid computing that evolved from the critiques of the Web Services community against OGSI. It improves on OGSI by making use of the latest standards and focusing on interoperability. WSRF has been designed for Atomicity, Consistency, Isolation, and Durability (ACID). This chapter has provided the foundation for writing WSRF services using a step-by-step, practical example.

REFERENCES

[GT4StatusPlan]77. Status and Plans for the Globus Toolkit 4.0 (GT4). Available online at *http://www-unix.globus.org/toolkit/docs/4.0/.*

[OGSA2WSRF04] Karl Czajkowski, Don Ferguson, Ian Foster, Jeff Frey, Steve Graham, Tom Maguire, David Snelling, Steve Tuecke . *From Open Grid Services Infrastructure to WSResource Framework: Refactoring & Evolution.* Version 1.1 3/05/2004. Copyright Fujitsu Limited, International Business Machines Corporation, and the University of Chicago 2003, 2004. All Rights Reserved. Available online at *http://www.chinagrid.net/dvnews/upload/2005_04/05040200359561.pdf.*

[OASIS-WSRF] OASIS Web Services Resource Framework Technical Committee. *http://www.oasis-open.org/committees/tc_home.php?wg_abbrev=wsrf.*

[OASIS-WSNotification] OASIS Web Services Notification. Available online at *http://www.oasis-open.org/committees/tc_home.php?wg_abbrev=wsn.*

[QuadSieve01] Eric Landquist. "The Quadratic Sieve Factoring Algorithm, Cryptographic Algorithms." December 14, 2001.

[StatefulWebServices04] Ian Foster, Jeffrey Frey, Steve Graham, Steve Tuecke, Karl Czajkowski, Don Ferguson, Frank Leymann, Martin Nally, Igor Sedukhin, David Snelling, Tony Storey, William Vambenepe, Sanjiva Weerawarana. *Modeling Stateful Resources with Web Services.* Copyright Computer Associates International, Inc., Fujitsu Limited, Hewlett-Packard Development Company, International Business Machines Corporation, and the University of Chicago 2003, 2004. Available online at *http://www-128.ibm.com/developerworks/library/ws-resource/ws-modelingresources.pdf.*

[WS-AtomicTransaction] Available online at *http://www.ibm.com/developerworks/webservices/library/ws-atomtran/.*

[WS-ResourceProperties] This specification describes how elements of publicly visible properties of a resource can be described, retrieved, changed, and deleted. Available online at *http://www-106.ibm.com/developerworks/library/ws-resource/ws-resourceproperties.pdf.*

[WS-ServiceGroup] At the time of this writing, this specification was still a work in progress.

[WS-Notification] WS-Notification whitepaper and family of specifications: (WS-BaseNotification, WS-Topics and WSBrokeredNotification). Available online at *http://www-106.ibm.com/developerworks/library/ws-pubsub/WS-PubSub.pdf.*

Part IV

The Message Passing Interface (MPI) Standard

In this part, we look at a comprehensive study of the following topics:

The Message Passing Interface Standard: Includes a comprehensive guide of basic MPI concepts such as procedures, arguments, data types, opaque objects, processes, error handling, point-to-point communication, communicators, and process topologies along with source code examples.

MPI Standard 2.0: Chapter 15 shows changes since version 1, such as deprecated names and functions, process management, resource control, new data types, and miscellaneous features. The chapter also includes descriptions of MPI-IO for parallel file operations with sample code. Common parallel algorithms are explained for prime integer generation, sparse matrix multiplication, and others.

MPICH2: This is a portable implementation of MPI by the Argonne National Lab widely used by the research community. Chapter 16 includes an overview of MPICH and installation transcripts. The chapter also demonstrates a parallel implementation of a sieve algorithm used to factorize large integers, which are the basis of cryptosystems such as RSA. A section of MPICH and WS-GRAM integration is included with a GT3 compatible scheduler interface to MPICH along with transcripts and sample tests.

14 An Introduction to the MPI Standard

In This Chapter

- Overview
- Procedures and Arguments
- Data Types
- Processes
- Error Handling
- Platform Independence
- Point-to-Point Communication
- Collective Communication
- Groups, Contexts, and Communicators
- Process Topologies
- Summary
- References

MPI provides an interface to write portable message-passing programs in FORTRAN 77 and C designed for running on parallel machines. The MPI standardization effort involved many organizations mainly from the United States and Europe. Most of the major vendors of high-end computers were involved in MPI, along with researchers from universities, government laboratories, and the software industry. MPI has been influenced by work at the IBM T. J. Watson Research Center [CommLibaries92], Intel, and nCUBE with important contributions from Chimp [CHIMP91], Parallel Virtual Machine [PVM93], Portable Instrumented Communication Library [PICL91] and others. This chapter includes information on the following topics:

- An overview of MPI
- Explanations of MPI syntax constructs such as procedures and arguments, data types, processes, and error handling

- Platform independence
- Point-to-point communication including messages, communication modes, buffering, blocking versus nonblocking communication, probe and cancel, derived data types, and pack/unpack
- Collective communication operations
- Miscellaneous group and communicator examples
- Process topologies

14.1 OVERVIEW

MPI is a standard for writing message-passing programs that provides portability and ease of use with a clearly defined base set of routines. MPI is a basic concept of processes communicating through messages. Message passing is a paradigm used mostly on parallel machines, especially those with distributed memory. Message passing systems can be efficient and portable as demonstrated by many vendors' implementations. *System memory* is used to buffer and store internal representation of various MPI objects such as *groups, communicators, data types,* and so on.

MPI has the following characteristics [MPIStandard97]:

- MPI provides efficient communication and application programming interface to avoid memory-to-memory copying and allow overlap of computation and communication.
- MPI can be can be used in heterogeneous environments.
- MPI provides a reliable communication interface: the user need not cope with communication failures. Such failures are dealt with by the underlying communication subsystem.
- MPI is portable and can be implemented on many vendors' platforms, with no significant changes.
- The MPI interface is language independent and designed for thread safety. MPI provides many features that can improve performance on scalable parallel computers with specialized interprocessor communication hardware.

The standard features include the following:

- Point-to-point communication
- Collective operations
- Process groups
- Communication contexts
- Process topologies
- Bindings for FORTRAN 77 and C

- Environmental management and inquiry
- Profiling interface

Because of time constraints imposed in finishing the standard, the standard does not specify the following:

- Explicit shared-memory operations
- Operations that require more operating system support than is currently standard; for example, interrupt-driven receives, remote execution, or active messages
- Program construction tools
- Debugging facilities
- Explicit support for threads
- Support for task management
- I/O functions

Features not included can be offered as extensions by specific implementations.

14.2 PROCEDURES AND ARGUMENTS

Procedures in MPI may be *blocking* (synchronous) if they block execution or non-blocking (asynchronous) if they return before the operation completes. Procedures may be *local* to the current process or *nonlocal* if they are required to be executed by another process or *collective* if all processes in a group need to execute the procedure. MPI procedures are specified using a language-independent notation. Arguments can be IN, OUT, or INOUT. IN arguments can only be used by the procedure; OUT arguments may be updated; INOUT can be both used and updated [MPIStandard97].

14.3 DATA TYPES

Basic data types are classified as opaque objects, arrays, constants, unions, and others.

14.3.1 Opaque Objects

Opaque objects are data structures that hide their size and shape from the user. They are accessed via *handles* that exist in the user space. Handles are sent to MPI procedures that operate on opaque objects as well as on assignments and comparisons. This design hides the internal representation used for MPI data structures, thus allowing similar calls in many languages such as C or FORTRAN [MPIStandard97].

Opaque objects are allocated and deallocated by specific system calls and their handle values do not change with a few exceptions such as commits and frees. An opaque object and its handle are specific only to the process where created and cannot be transferred to another. MPI provides predefined opaque objects and static handles that may not be destroyed.

The separation of handles in user space and objects in system space allows space reclaiming and efficient deallocation and scope control. Objects are *marked* for deallocation when they are out of scope, and this persists until all operations are complete [MPIStandard97].

14.3.2 Arrays and Constants

Arrays in MPI include an additional argument for its length. All named constants, with the exception of `MPI_BOTTOM` in FORTRAN, can be used in initialization expressions or assignments. These constants do not change values during execution. Opaque objects accessed by constant handles do not change value between MPI initialization (`MPI_INIT`) and MPI completion (`MPI_FINALIZE`) [MPIStandard97].

14.3.3 Other Data Types

MPI supports other data types such as *unions,* also known as *choices.* Distinct calls to the same routine may pass by reference actual arguments of different types. *Address* arguments represent an absolute address in the calling program. The data type of such argument is an integer of the size needed to hold any valid address in the execution environment [MPIStandard97].

14.4 PROCESSES

Processes are autonomous when executing their own code, which may or may not be identical. They communicate via calls to MPI communication primitives. Typically, each process executes in its own address space, although shared-memory implementations of MPI are possible. A process can be sequential, or can be multithreaded, with threads possibly executing concurrently. MPI has been designed to be thread safe by avoiding the use of implicit state. MPI uses reentrant calls; blocking calls only block the invoking thread allowing the scheduling of another [MPIStandard97].

14.5 ERROR HANDLING

Messages in MPI are reliable. They do not need to be checked for transmission errors, time-outs, or other error conditions. Messages are guaranteed to be received correctly, in other words, MPI does not provide mechanisms for dealing with failures in the communication system. MPI itself provides no mechanisms for handling processor failures. Almost all MPI calls return a code that indicates successful completion of the operation. Whenever possible, MPI calls return an error code if an error occurred during the call [MPIStandard97].

14.6 PLATFORM INDEPENDENCE

The intent of MPI to be thread and signal safe has a number of side effects. For example, on Unix systems, catchable signals must not cause an MPI routine to behave differently than it would have in the absence of the signal. A second effect is that a signal handler that performs MPI calls must not interfere with the operation of MPI. For example, an MPI operation that occurs within a signal handler must not cause erroneous behavior [MPIStandard97].

MPI programs require that language primitives (such as date and write in FORTRAN and `printf` in ANSI C) that are executed after `MPI_INIT` and before `MPI_FINALIZE` operate independently and that their completion is independent of the action of other processes in an MPI program. For example, the following program is expected to complete in ANSI C, assuming that I/O is available at the executing nodes [ANLMPI01].

```
int rank;
MPI_Init( argc, argv );
MPI_Comm_rank( MPI_COMM_WORLD, &rank );
if (rank == 0) printf( "Starting program\n" );
MPI_Finalize();
```

14.7 POINT-TO-POINT COMMUNICATION

Sending and receiving of messages by processes is done through point-to-point operations send and receive. Their use is illustrated in Listing 14.1.

LISTING 14.1 Point-to-Point Communication in MPI

```
#include "mpi.h"

void main( int argc, char ** argv )
{
    char message[20];
    int rank;
    MPI_Status status;

    /* MPI Initialization */
    MPI_Init( &argc, &argv );

    /**
     * MPI_COMM_WORLD is a handle to an object that represents
     * all processes
     * available at start-up time and allows operations to communicate
     * with any of them.
     * rank returns the current process number.
     */
    MPI_Comm_rank( MPI_COMM_WORLD, &rank );

    if (rank == 0)     /* code for process zero */
    {
        strcpy(message, "Hello, world!");

        /* Send the string "message" of type char MPI_CHAR */
        /* to process 1, Tag the message with value (99) */
        MPI_Send(message, strlen(message)
                 , MPI_CHAR, 1, 99, MPI_COMM_WORLD);
    }
    else  /* code for process one */
    {
        /* Receive a message of type char from process 0 (rank == 0) */
        MPI_Recv(message, 20
, MPI_CHAR, 0, 99, MPI_COMM_WORLD, &status);
        printf("received :%s:\n", message);
    }

    /* shut down MPI */
    MPI_Finalize();
}
```

In this example, process zero (rank = 0) sends a message to process one using the *send* operation `MPI_Send`. The operation specifies a send buffer in the sender memory from which the message data is taken. The location, size, and type of the send buffer are specified by the first three parameters of the send operation. The message sent will contain the 13 characters of this variable. In addition, the send operation associates an envelope with the message. This envelope specifies the message destination and contains distinguishing information that can be used by the *receive* operation to select a particular message. The last three parameters of the send operation specify the envelope for the message sent.

Process one (rank = 1) receives this message with the *receive* operation `MPI_Recv`. The message to be received is selected according to the value of its envelope, and the message data is stored into the receive buffer. In Listing 14.1, the receive buffer consists of the storage containing the string message in the memory of process one. The first three parameters of the receive operation specify the location, size, and type of the receive buffer. The next three parameters are used for selecting the incoming message. The last parameter is used to return information on the message just received.

14.7.1 Message Data Type Conversions

MPI cannot assume that a communication call has information on the data type of variables in the communication buffer; this information must be supplied by an explicit argument. The data part of the message consists of a sequence of values of a specific type. The basic data types correspond to the basic data types of the host language. MPI specifies the message length in terms of number of elements, rather than number of bytes. This allows for machine independence. Table 14.1 maps C primitive data types with MPI data types [ANLMPI01].

TABLE 14.1 MPI/C Data Type Mappings

MPI	C
MPI_CHAR	Signed char
MPI_SHORT	Signed short int
MPI_INT	Signed int
MPI_LONG	Signed long int
MPI_UNSIGNED_CHAR	Unsigned char
MPI_UNSIGNED_SHORT	Unsigned short int
MPI_UNSIGNED	Unsigned int
MPI_UNSIGNED_LONG	Unsigned long int

→

MPI_FLOAT	Float
MPI_DOUBLE	Double
MPI_LONG_DOUBLE	Long double
MPI_BYTE	
MPI_PACKED	

The types MPI_BYTE and MPI_PACKED do not correspond to a C data type. MPI_BYTE (8 bits) is different from a traditional character. Different machines may use more than one byte to represent characters. On the other hand, a byte has the same binary value on all machines. is explained in the section "Pack/Unpack" later in this chapter.

14.7.2 Message Envelopes

In addition to the data part, messages carry information that can be used to distinguish messages and selectively receive them. This information consists of a fixed number of fields, known as the *message envelope*. The message source is implicitly determined by the identity of the message sender. The other fields are specified by arguments in the send operation [MPIStandard97].

For example, the syntax of the blocking send operation is as follows:

```
MPI_SEND(buf, count, datatype, dest, tag, comm)
```

Where:

IN buf*:* The initial address of send buffer (choice).

IN count*:* The number of elements in send buffer (nonnegative integer).

IN datatype*:* A data type of each send buffer element (handle).

IN dest*:* The message destination—rank of destination (integer).

IN tag*:* A message tag (integer): This integer can be used by the program to distinguish different types of messages.

IN comm*:* A Communicator (handle): Specifies the communicator that is used for the send operation.

In C:

```
int MPI_Send(void* buf, int count, MPI_Datatype datatype, int dest, int
tag, MPI_Comm comm)
```

The syntax of the blocking *receive* is as follows:

```
MPI_RECV (buf, count, datatype, source, tag, comm, status)
```

Where:

`OUT buf`*:* Initial address of receive buffer (choice): Storage containing count consecutive elements of the type specified by data type.

`IN count`*:* Number of elements in receive buffer (integer).

`IN datatype`*:* Data type of each receive buffer element (handle).

`IN source`*:* Rank of source (integer).

`IN tag`*:* Message tag (integer).

`IN comm`*:* A communicator (handle).

`OUT status`*:* A status object (status).

In C:

```
int MPI_Recv(void* buf, int count, MPI_Datatype datatype, int source,
int tag, MPI_Comm comm, MPI_Status *status)
```

Note that a receive operation may accept messages from an arbitrary sender, whereas a send operation must specify a unique receiver. This matches a push communication mechanism, where data transfer is affected by the sender rather than a pull mechanism, where a transfer is affected by the receiver.

14.7.3 Data Type Matching and Conversion

MPI messages consist of three steps. First, data is pulled out of the send buffer and a message is assembled. Second, the message is transferred from sender to receiver. Third, data is pulled from the incoming message and disassembled into the receive buffer.

Type matching has to be observed at each of these three phases. The type specified by the send operation has to match the type specified by the receive operation, and the type of each variable in the receive buffer has to match the type specified for that entry by the receive operation. That is, `MPI_INTEGER` matches `MPI_INTEGER`, `MPI_REAL` matches `MPI_REAL`, and so on. There is one exception to this rule: `MPI_PACKED` can match any other type [MPIStandard97].

A program that fails to observe these three rules is erroneous.

By design, MPI supports parallel computations across heterogeneous environments. Communication in a heterogeneous environment may require *data conversions* for a given type. MPI requires that a representation conversion be performed when a typed value is transferred across environments that use different representations for the data type. Such conversion is expected to preserve integer, logical, character, or floating-point values [MPIStandard97].

14.7.4 Communication Modes

MPI calls can use several communication modes [ANLMPI01]:

Blocking: The call does not return until the message data and envelope have been safely stored away so that the sender is free to access and overwrite the send buffer. The message might be copied directly into the matching receive buffer, or it might be copied into a temporary system buffer.

Standard: In this mode, the MPI decides whether outgoing messages will be buffered. MPI may buffer outgoing messages. In such a case, the send call may complete before a matching receive is invoked. On the other hand, buffer space may be unavailable, or MPI may choose not to buffer outgoing messages for performance reasons. In this case, the send call will not complete until a matching receive has been posted, and the data has been moved to the receiver.

Nonlocal: In nonlocal mode, successful completion of send operations may depend on the occurrence of a matching receives. The standard mode send is nonlocal.

Three additional communication modes include the following:

Buffered: A buffered mode send operation can be started whether or not a matching receive has been posted and may complete before a matching receive is posted. However, unlike the standard send, this operation is *local*, and its completion does not depend on the occurrence of a matching receive.

Synchronous: A send can be started whether or not a matching receive was posted. However, the send will complete successfully only if a matching receive is posted, and the receive operation has started to receive the message sent by the synchronous send.

Ready: A send may be started only if the matching receive is already posted. Otherwise, the operation is erroneous and its outcome is undefined. On some systems, this allows the removal of a handshake operation that is otherwise required and results in improved performance.

14.7.5 Buffering

The sender does buffering in MPI by attaching the buffer in the user's memory to be used for outgoing messages:

```
int MPI_Buffer_attach( void* buffer, int size)
```

To detach the buffer currently associated with MPI, use the following:

```
int MPI_Buffer_detach( void* buffer_addr, int* size)
```

The call returns the address and the size of the detached buffer. This operation will block until all messages currently in the buffer have been transmitted. Upon return of this function, the user may reuse or deallocate the space taken by the buffer. For example, consider the following calls to attach and detach buffers:

```
#define BUFFSIZE 10000
int size
char *buff;

MPI_Buffer_attach( malloc(BUFFSIZE), BUFFSIZE);

/* A buffer of 10000 bytes can now be used by MPI_Bsend */
MPI_Buffer_detach( &buff, &size);

/* Buffer size reduced to zero */
MPI_Buffer_attach( buff, size);

/* Buffer of 10000 bytes available again */
```

14.7.6 Nonblocking Communication

MPI uses nonblocking calls to improve performance on many systems by overlapping communication and computation. A send operation is started by a *send start* call, but does not complete it. The send start call will return before the message was copied out of the send buffer. A separate *send complete* call is needed to verify that the data has been copied out of the send buffer [ANLMPI01].

Nonblocking *send start* calls can use the same four modes as blocking sends: standard, buffered, synchronous, and ready. These carry the same meaning. *Nonblocking sends* can be matched with *blocking receives*, and viceversa. The message-passing model implies that communication is initiated by the sender. The communication will generally have lower overhead if a *receive* is already posted when the sender initiates the communication. However, a *receive* operation can complete only after the matching *send* has occurred. The use of nonblocking *receives* allows one to achieve lower communication overheads without blocking the receiver while it waits for the *send* [MPIStandard97].

Completion: The completion of a send operation indicates that the sender is now free to update the locations in the send buffer. It does not indicate that the message has been received. In *synchronous mode*, the completion of the *send* operation indicates that a matching *receive* was initiated, and that the message will eventually be received. Nonblocking communication completes by calling the functions `MPI_Wait` and `MPI_Test`, as shown in the following pseudocode:

```
MPI_Comm_Rank(comm, rank, ierr);

if (rank == 0) {
    MPI_ISend (arry[1], 10, MPI_REAL, 1, tag, comm, request, ierr);

    /**** do some computation to mask latency ****/
    MPI_Wait(request, status, ierr)
}
else {
    MPI_IRecv(arry[1], 15, MPI_REAL, 0, tag, comm, request, ierr);

    /**** do some computation to mask latency ****/
    MPI_Wait(request, status, ierr);
}
```

14.7.7 Probe and Cancel

Incoming operations can be checked without receiving them (`MPI_PROBE`, `MPI_IPROBE`). This allows the client to make decisions based on the information returned. To free resources tied up by *send* or *receive* operations, `MPI_CANCEL` can be used for cleanup purposes. Listing 14.2 demonstrates probing techniques.

LISTING 14.2 `Probe` and `Cancel` Techniques

```
#include "mpi.h"

void main( int argc, char ** argv )
{
    int i = 128;
    foat f = 3.14.16;

    int rank;
    int dest, tag;

    MPI_Status status;

    /* MPI Initialization */
    MPI_Init( &argc, &argv );
```

```
    /**
     * MPI_COMM_WORLD is a handle to an object that represents all
     * processes available at start-up time, and allows operations
     * to communicate with any of them.
     * rank returns the current process number.
     */    MPI_Comm_rank( MPI_COMM_WORLD, &rank );

    /* Process zero */
    if (rank == 0)
    {
        /* Send 1 integer to process #2 Tag(0) */
        dest      = 2;
        tag       = 0;
        MPI_Send(i, 1, MPI_INTEGER, dest, tag, MPI_COMM_WORLD) ;
    }

    /Process 1*/
    else if (rank == 1)
    {
        /* Send 1 float value to process #2 Tag(0) */
        dest      = 2;
        tag       = 0;
        MPI_Send(f, 1, MPI_FLOAT, dest, tag, MPI_COMM_WORLD);
    }
    else
    {
        tag = 0;

        for ( int j = 0 ; j < 2 ; j++ )
        {
            /* Probe from any source a message with tag (0)  */
            MPI_Probe(MPI_ANY_SOURCE, tag, MPI_COMM_WORLD, status);

            if ( status.MPI_SOURCE == 0)
                    /* Receive an int from process 0 */
                    MPI_Recv(i, 1, MPI_INTEGER, 0, 0, status);
            else
                    /* Receive a float from process 1 */
                    MPI_Recv(f, 1, MPI_REAL, 1, 0, status) ;
        }
    }
}
```

14.7.8 Derived Data Types

MPI allows passing of messages that contain values with different data types such as a structure of objects of various shapes and sizes or array sections. To achieve this goal in a platform independent manner, MPI requires the definition of a communication buffer that mimics the structure or array section in question. These *complex* types are created through opaque objects called *general data types* that specify a sequence of basic data types and a sequence of byte *displacements*.

The set of basic types and displacements $\{(type_0, disp_0),\ldots,(type_n, disp_n)\}$ is called a *type map*. The set of all types without displacements is called the *type signature*. This type map, together with a base address *buf*, specifies a communication buffer where the i-th entry is at address $buf + disp_i$ and has type $type_i$. General data types can be used in all send and receive operations [ANLMPI01].

Data type construction can be done by concatenation of n copies of the original type in blocks of size *(extent)* in *contiguous* locations (`MPI_TYPE_CONTIGUOUS`) or by replication of a data type into locations that consist of equally spaced blocks (`MPI_TYPE_VECTOR`). Each block is obtained by concatenating the same number of copies of the old data type. The spacing between blocks is a multiple of the extent of the old data type [MPIStandard97].

Elements in the general data type can be indexed using a location relative to the initial buffer address or they can be addressed from the start of the address space (*absolute*) using the `MPI_BOTTOM` constant. MPI designers recommend caution when using absolute addresses because of how address management is implemented in different platforms [MPIStandard97].

Before using general data types in an operation, they must be committed (`MPI_TYPE_COMMIT`). When they are no longer used, they should be freed with a call to `MPI_TYPE_FREE` [MPIStandard97].

14.7.8.1 Derived Data Types Examples

The following examples illustrate the basic use of derived data types in MPI.

LISTING 14.3 Derived Data Types

```
/* A Point in the Cartesian table */
struct Point {
    int x;
    int y;
}

/* array of 1000 points */
struct Point    points[1000];
```

```
int i, dest, rank;
MPI_Comm comm;

/* build datatype describing structure */
MPI_Datatype PointType;
MPI_Datatype type[2] = {MPI_INT, MPI_INT};

/* An array for each block size */
int          blocklen[2] = {1, 1};

/* An array for displacements */
MPI_Aint     disp[2];
int          base;

/* compute displacements of structure components */

MPI_Address( points, disp);
MPI_Address( points[0].y, disp+1);
base = disp[0];

for (i=0; i <3; i++)
   disp[i] -= base;

/* Build the General data type */
MPI_Type_struct( 2, blocklen, disp, type, &PointType);

/* Send the entire array */
MPI_Type_commit( &PointType);
MPI_Send( points, 1000, PointType, dest, tag, comm);

/* Send the entire array */
/* Using an Absolute address */

MPI_Type_commit( &PointType);
MPI_Send( MPI_BOTTOM, 1000, PointType, dest, tag, comm);
```

14.7.9 Pack/Unpack

Pack/unpack provide functions for sending noncontiguous data (i.e., data that is not an array) in a continuous buffer. Derived data types may also be included. Listing 14.4 packs two integers and sends them across the node ring.

LISTING 14.4 Pack/Unpack Example

```
/* Pack/Unpack example          */
/* Pack 2 integers and send them */
/* to all processes in the group */
int i, j;

/* position of the integers in the packed array */
int position;

/* array used to receive both ints */
int a[2];

/* packed buffer */
char buff[1000];

...

MPI_Comm_rank(MPI_COMM_WORLD, &myrank);

/ * Sender */
if (myrank == 0) {
    /* Pack 2 integers into a buffer array */
    position = 0;
    MPI_Pack(&i, 1, MPI_INT, buff, 1000, &position, MPI_COMM_WORLD);
    MPI_Pack(&j, 1, MPI_INT, buff, 1000, &position, MPI_COMM_WORLD);

    /* Send the packed buffer */
    MPI_Send( buff, position, MPI_PACKED, 1, 0, MPI_COMM_WORLD);
}

/* Receiver */
else
{
    /* Receive 2 integers into the array (a) from process 0 */
    MPI_Recv( a, 2, MPI_INT, 0, 0, MPI_COMM_WORLD)
}
```

14.8 COLLECTIVE COMMUNICATION

Collective communication in MPI involves a group of processes. Several methods of collective communication have been defined.

14.8.1 Barrier Synchronization (MPI_BARRIER)

MPI_BARRIER blocks the caller process until all group members have entered the call.

14.8.2 Broadcast (MPI_BCAST)

MPI_BCAST is used to broadcast a message from the process with a sender rank to all processes of the group, itself included, and using the same arguments. On return, the contents of the sender communication buffer have been copied to all processes.

```
int array[10];
int root=0;

/*  Broadcast 10 ints from process 0
to every process in the group. */
MPI_Bcast( array, 10, MPI_INT, root, MPI_COMM_WORLD);
```

14.8.3 Gather (MPI_GATHER)

Messages sent by the group processes are concatenated in rank order, and the resulting message is received by the root process as if by a call to MPI_RECV. General and derived data types are allowed for both send and receive as shown in the following example:

```
/* MPI_Gather Example: Gather an array of 100 integers */
/* from multiple processes */

/* number of active processes */
int gsize;

/* send buffer */
int sendarray[100];

/* root process */
int root = 0;

/* current process number */
int myrank;

/* receive buffer */
int *rbuf;

MPI_Comm_rank(MPI_COMM_WORLD, &myrank);
```

```
if ( myrank == root)
{
    MPI_Comm_size ( comm, &gsize);
    rbuf = (int *) malloc (gsize * 100 * sizeof(int) );
}

MPI_Gather( sendarray, 100, MPI_INT
            , rbuf, 100, MPI_INT
            , root, MPI_COMM_WORLD);
```

14.8.4 Scatter (MPI_SCATTER)

MPI_SCATTER is the inverse operation to MPI_GATHER. The root sends a message buffer with MPI_SEND. This message is split into n equal segments; the i-th segment is sent to the i-th process in the group. The send buffer is ignored for all nonroot processes. Note that the amount of data sent must equal the amount received between each process and the root as shown in the following example:

```
/* MPI_Scatter Example:Scatter an array of 100 integers */
/* across multiple processes    */
/* Get the number of Processes  */
int gsize;

int root;
int rbuf[100];

MPI_Comm_size (MPI_COMM_WORLD, &gsize);

/* An array of 100 ints */
int *sendbuf = (int *) malloc ( gsize * 100 * sizeof(int) );

/**
* Scatter the array across all proceses
* All arguments to the function are significant on process root
* On the sub processes, only arguments:
     * recvbuf (rbuf),
     * recvcount (100),
     * recvtype (MPI_INT),
     *root and comm are significant
    **/
    MPI_Scatter( sendbuf, 100, MPI_INT
                 , rbuf, 100, MPI_INT, root, comm);
```

14.8.5 Gather-to-All (MPI_ALLGATHER)

MPI_ALLGATHER works as MPI_GATHER does, but all processes receive the result, instead of just the root. It is as if all processes executed n calls to MPI_GATHER, as shown in the following code:

```
/**
 * All-gather version MPI_GATHER.
 * gather 100 integers from every process in the group
 * to every process.
 */
int gsize;
int sendarray[100];
int *rbuf;

MPI_Comm_size (MPI_COMM_WORLD, &gsize);

/* Allocate space for the receive buffer */
rbuf = (int *) malloc (gsize * 100 * sizeof(int));

/*  After the call,
 every process has the group-wide concatenation
 of the sets of data. */
MPI_Allgather (sendarray, 100, MPI_INT
                , rbuf, 100, MPI_INT, MPI_COMM_WORLD);
```

14.8.6 All to All (MPI_ALLTOALL)

MPI_ALLTOALL sends a buffer to a given number of elements on each process using the same data type, and messages are gathered to sequential storage. It is an extension of MPI_ALLGATHER where each process sends distinct data to each receiver.

14.8.7 Global Reduction

Global reduction performs operations such as SUM, MIN, MAX, AND, OR, and so on across the members of a group through MPI_REDUCE. MPI_REDUCE combines the elements provided in the input buffer of each process in the group, using the given operation, and returns the combined value in the output buffer of the process with rank root. Reduction operations can be predefined or user defined [MPIStandard97]:

Predefined operations are shown in Table 14.2.

TABLE 14.2 Predefined MPI Operations

Operation	Meaning	Data type
MPI_MAX, MPI_MIN	Maximum, Minimum (FORTRAN/C)	Integer, floating point
MPI_SUM, MPI_PROD or derived (complex) FORTRAN/C	Sum, Product	Integer, floating point
MPI_LAND, MPI_LOR, MPI_LXOR	Logical AND, OR, XOR C integer, Logical	
MPI_BAND, MPI_BOR, MPI_BXOR integer, byte	Bitwise AND, OR, XOR	C integer, FORTRAN

User-defined operations can be created with MPI_OP_CREATE, which binds a user-defined global operation to a handle that can subsequently be used in collective communications operations.

User-defined functions must use the ANSI C prototype:

```
typedef void MPI_User_function
( void *invec, void *inoutvec, int *len, MPI_Datatype *datatype);
```

For example, Listing 14.5 computes the product of an array of complex numbers in C.

LISTING 14.5 Global Reduction

```
typedef struct
{
    double r;
    double i;
} Complex;

/* User defined complex product function */

void ComplexProd ( Complex *in, Complex *inout
                   , int *len, MPI_Datatype *dptr )
{
int i; Complex c;

/* loop thru the complex array (in) of size (len) */
```

```
for (i=0; i < *len; ++i)
{
    c.r = inout->r * in->r - inout->i * in->i;
    c.i = inout->r * in->i + inout->i * in->r;

    /* assign the product to the out buffer (inout)
     *inout = c;

    /* next complex element */
     in++;
     inout++;
    }
}

/* Main stuff goes here...*/

/* Each process has an array of 100 Complexes */
 Complex a[100], result[100];

/* User defined operation */
 MPI_Op CxOp;

/* User defined (derived) type */
 MPI_Datatype ctype;

/* Define the MPI Derived Type: 2 doubles */
 MPI_Type_contiguous( 2, MPI_DOUBLE, &ctype );
 MPI_Type_commit( &ctype );

/* Create the user defined operation */
MPI_Op_create( ComplexProd, True, &CxOp );

/**
 * Combine the elements provided in the input buffer of
 * each process in the group, and return the combined value
 * in the output buffer of the process with rank root.
 */
 MPI_Reduce( a, result, 100, ctype, CxOp, root, comm );
/**
 * At this point, the answer, which consists of 100 Complexes,
 * resides on process root
 */
```

14.8.8 Reduce Scatter (MPI_REDUCE_SCATTER)

MPI_REDUCE_SCATTER is a variant of the reduce operations where the result is scattered to all processes in the group on return. It is equivalent to a MPI_REDUCE followed by MPI_SCATTERV [MPIStandard97].

14.8.9 Scan

MPI_SCAN performs a prefix reduction on data within a group. The operation returns, in the receive buffer of the process with rank *i*, the reduction of the values in the send buffers of processes with ranks *[0,...,i]*. It supports the same operations, types, and buffers as MPI_REDUCE does, [MPIStandard97].

14.8.10 Avoiding Deadlocks

Collective communications must be invoked so that deadlocks will not occur, whether they are synchronizing or not.

Deadlock example:
Two broadcast operations in reverse order will cause a deadlock if synchronizing:
Process A:

```
MPI_Bcast(buf1, count, type, 0, comm);
MPI_Bcast(buf2, count, type, 1, comm);
break;
```

Process B (reverse broadcast):

```
MPI_Bcast(buf2, count, type, 1, comm);
MPI_Bcast(buf1, count, type, 0, comm);
```

Collective operations must be executed in the same order within all group members.

14.8.11 Cyclic Dependencies

Cyclic dependences in synchronous broadcasts will cause deadlocks, thus must be avoided. For example:

```
switch(rank)
{
    case 0:
    /* Process 0 broadcasts to process 2 */
       MPI_Bcast(buf2, count, type, 2, comm2);
       break;
```

```
    case 1:
    /* Process 1 broadcasts to process 0 */
       MPI_Bcast(buf2, count, type, 0, comm0);
       break;

    case 2:
    /* Process 2 broadcasts to process 1 */
        MPI_Bcast(buf2, count, type, 1, comm1);
        break;
}
```

The cyclic dependency 0-2-1-0 will cause a deadlock if synchronous operations are used.

14.9 GROUPS, CONTEXTS, AND COMMUNICATORS

Communicators in MPI are used to support communication operations based on the following [Feitelson99]:

Contexts: These provide *universes* of message passing in MPI. A *context* is similar to a tag that differentiates messages managed by the system. They are designed to insulate internal or external communications.

Groups: A group is an ordered collection of processes, each with a rank used for sending and receiving. Groups define a scope for process names in point-to-point communication and the scope of collective operations. They also define the participants in the communication.

Virtual topologies: These define special mappings of the ranks in a group to and from a topology.

Attribute caching: This mechanism allows one to associate new attributes with communicators. Attributes are used by users to enhance communicators further, and by MPI to implement communicator functions.

MPI defines two kinds of communicators: *intracommunicators* for operations within a single group of processes, and *intercommunicators*, for point-to-point communication between two groups of processes. Intracommunicators are the most common. Intracommunicators contain an instance of a group, contexts for both point-to-point and collective communication, and the ability to include virtual topology and other attributes [SkjellumLeung99].

14.9.1 Predefined Communicators

The following are the predefined communicators in MPI:

- `MPI_COMM_WORLD`: Includes all processes the local process can communicate with after initialization. It may simultaneously have different values in different processes.
- `MPI_COMM_SELF`: Includes only the process itself.
- `MPI_COMM_NULL`: Used for invalid communicator handles.

14.9.2 Miscellaneous Group and Communicator Examples

The code in Listing 14.6 describes the basic usage of communicators for message exchange among processes.

LISTING 14.6 Group and Communicator Examples

```
/**
 * Example 1: print the current process number and size
 * of the MPI ring
 */
void main(int argc, char **argv)
{
    int rank, size;

    /* MPI Initialization */
    MPI_Init ( &argc, &argv );

    /* Obtain the rank of the current process */
    MPI_Comm_rank (MPI_COMM_WORLD, &rank);

    /* Obtain the number of processes in the MPI_COMM_WORLD */
    /* channel */
    MPI_Comm_size (MPI_COMM_WORLD, &size);


    printf ("Process %d size %d\n", rank, size);
    MPI_Finalize();
}

/**
 * Example 2: illustrates how a group consisting of all
 * but the (0) process is created.
 * A communicator is formed (COMMSLAVE) for that new group.
```

```
 * The new communicator is used in a collective call
 * in the MPI_COMM_WORLD context.
 * This example illustrates insulation between
 * MPI_COMM_WORLD and COMMSLAVE
 */
void main(int argc, char **argv)
{
    int me, count, count2;
    void *send_buf, *recv_buf, *send_buf2, *recv_buf2;

    MPI_Group MPI_GROUP_WORLD, grprem;
    MPI_Comm COMM_SLAVE;

    /* rank of the root process */
    static int ranks[] = {0};

    MPI_Init(&argc, &argv);

    MPI_Comm_group(MPI_COMM_WORLD, &MPI_GROUP_WORLD);

    /* rank of the local process*/
    MPI_Comm_rank(MPI_COMM_WORLD, &me);

    /* Exclude the root process (0) from the group COMM_SLAVE */
    MPI_Group_excl(MPI_GROUP_WORLD, 1, ranks, &grprem);

    /* Create the communicator COMM_SLAVE */
    MPI_Comm_create(MPI_COMM_WORLD, grprem, &COMM_SLAVE);

    if( me != 0)
    {
      /* Compute on slave using the communicator COMM_SLAVE */
      /* ... */
      MPI_Reduce(send_buf,recv_buff, count
                 , MPI_INT, MPI_SUM, 1, COMM_SLAVE);
      /* ... */
    }

    /* Compute on MPI_COMM_WORLD communicator */
    /* MPI_COMM_WORLD is insulated from COMM_SLAVE */
    /* Process (0) falls through immediately to this reduce, */
    /*  others do later */
    MPI_Reduce(send_buf2, recv_buff2, count2
               , MPI_INT, MPI_SUM, 0, MPI_COMM_WORLD);
```

```
        MPI_Comm_free(&commslave);
        MPI_Group_free(&MPI_GROUP_WORLD);
        MPI_Group_free(&grprem);
        MPI_Finalize();
}
```

14.9.3 Intracommunicators versus Intercommunicators

All point-to-point communication discussed thus far involved communication between processes that are members of the same group. This type of communication is called *intracommunication*. However, many applications may require different process and groups to communicate in a pipeline or a more general module graph. In these applications, the most natural way for a process to specify a target process is by the rank of the target process within the target group [Feitelson99].

This type of communication is called *intercommunication*. An intercommunication is a point-to-point communication between processes in different groups. Intercommunication has the following characteristics:

- All intercommunicator constructors are blocking and require that the local and remote groups be disjoint to avoid deadlock.
- The syntax of point-to-point communication is the same for both inter- and intracommunication.
- A target process is addressed by its rank in the remote group for sends and receives.
- Intercommunicator cannot be used in collective communication.

14.10 PROCESS TOPOLOGIES

A topology is an extra, optional attribute that can be given to an *intra-communicator*. It provides a convenient naming mechanism for the processes of a group and mapping the processes onto hardware. Topologies cannot be added to *intercommunicators*.

14.10.1 Overview

MPI defines a *group* as a collection of n processes. Processes are arranged in a linear ranking from 0 to n-1. In many parallel applications, however, a linear ranking of processes does not adequately reflect the logical communication pattern, for example, processes arranged in topological patterns such as a two-dimensional grid. Ultimately, logical process arrangement is described by a general graph and is called a *virtual topology* [MPIStandard97].

14.10.2 Virtual Topologies

In MPI, the communication pattern of a set of processes is represented by a general graph. The nodes stand for the processes, and the edges connect processes that communicate with each other. This is sufficient for all applications. However, in applications that use ring-like topologies or n-dimensional grids (Cartesian) a general graph topology would be inconvenient for efficiency reasons [MPIStandard97].

For such applications, MPI provides a Cartesian topology, which is defined by an n-dimensional grid of coordinates (processes). Thus, for a 2x2 Cartesian grid, processes are ranked as follows:

Coordinate	rank
(0,0)	0
(0,1)	1
(1,0)	2
(1,1)	3

14.11 SUMMARY

MPI is a standard for writing message-passing programs that provides portability and ease of use with a clearly defined base set of routines. MPI provides an interface to write portable message-passing programs in FORTRAN 77 and C designed for running on parallel machines. Message passing systems can be efficient and portable as demonstrated by many vendors' implementations. This chapter has provided the foundation for the MPI framework as a prelude to several practical examples covered in the next chapter, MPI Standard 2.0.

REFERENCES

[ANLMPI01] ANL Mathematics and Computer Science. "The Message Passing Interface (MPI) standard." Available online at *http://www-unix.mcs.anl.gov/mpi/*.

[CHIMP91] Edinburgh Parallel Computing Centre, University of Edinburgh. "CHIMP Concepts," June 1991.

[CommLibaries92] V. Bala, S. Kipnis, L. Rudolph, and Marc Snir. *Designing Efficient, Scalable, and Portable Collective Communication Libraries.* Technical report, IBM T. J. Watson Research Center, October 1992. Preprint.

[Feitelson99] D. Feitelson. "Communicators: Object-based Multiparty Interactions for Parallel Programming." Technical Report 91-12, Dept. Computer Science. The Hebrew University of Jerusalem, November 1991.

[MPIStandard97] The Message Passing Interface (MPI) standard. Copyright© 1995, 1996, 1997 University of Tennessee, Knoxville, Tennessee. Permission to copy without fee all or part of this material is granted provided the University of Tennessee copyright notice and the title of this document appears, and notice is given that copying is by permission of the University of Tennessee. Available online at *http://www.mpi-forum.org/docs/mpi-11-html/mpi-report.html.*

[PICL91] G. A. Geist, M. T. Heath, B. W. Peyton, and P. H. Worley. *A User's Guide to PICL: A Portable Instrumented Communication Library.* Technical Report TM-11616, Oak Ridge National Laboratory, October 1990.

[PVM93] J. Dongarra, A. Geist, R. Manchek, and V. Sunderam. Integrated PVM Framework Supports Heterogeneous Network Computing. *Computers in Physics, 7*(2),—166–175, April 1993.

[SkjellumLeung99] A. Skjellum and A. Leung. "Zipcode: A Portable Multicomputer Communication Library Atop the Reactive Kernel." In D. W. Walker and Q. F. Stout, editors, *Proceedings of the Fifth Distributed Memory Concurrent Computing Conference,* pages 767–776. IEEE Press, 1990.

15 MPI Standard 2.0

In This Chapter

- Overview
- Changes Since Version 1
- Miscellaneous Enhancements
- MPI Examples: Common Parallel
- Summary
- References

This chapter provides information on the following topics:

- Overview of the MPI standard 2.0
- A description of the changes since version 1
- Miscellaneous enhancements such as the new MPI-2 process model, and memory allocation
- Practical MPI examples such as parallel algorithms for prime generation and sparse matrix multiplication

All code listings shown are available in the companion CD-ROM.

15.1 OVERVIEW

MPI-2 functionality is a set of corrections and extensions to the original MPI Standard released in March 1995. This effort has focused in the following areas [MPIStandard97]:

- Further corrections and clarifications for the MPI-1.1 standard
- Additions such as new data-type constructors, language interoperability, and so on.
- New functionality including dynamic processes, one-sided communication, parallel I/O, and so forth.
- Bindings for FORTRAN 90 and C++

15.2 CHANGES SINCE VERSION 1

The following sections describe extension to the MPI 1.1 standard focusing in miscellaneous topics, process creation and management, one-sided communications, extended collective operations, external interfaces, I/O, and additional language bindings.

15.2.1 Deprecated Names and Functions

Many functions in MPI-1 have been deprecated. For example:, MPI-1 FORTRAN bindings that have address arguments of type `INTEGER` are inconsistent with the C binding. Another example is the MPI-1 predefined data types `MPI_UB` and `MPI_LB`. They are deprecated because their use is awkward and error prone, and have been replaced by the MPI-2 subroutine `MPI_TYPE_CREATE_RESIZED`, which provides a more convenient mechanism to achieve the same effect.

The following is a list of all the deprecated constructs in MPI-2 [MPIStandard97]:

Deprecated	MPI-2 Replacement
MPI_ADDRESS	MPI_GET_ADDRESS
MPI_TYPE_HINDEXED	MPI_TYPE_CREATE_HINDEXED
MPI_TYPE_HVECTOR	MPI_TYPE_CREATE_HVECTOR
MPI_TYPE_STRUCT	MPI_TYPE_CREATE_STRUCT
MPI_TYPE_EXTENT	MPI_TYPE_GET_EXTENT
MPI_TYPE_UB	MPI_TYPE_GET_EXTENT
MPI_TYPE_LB	MPI_TYPE_GET_EXTENT
MPI_LB	MPI_TYPE_CREATE_RESIZED
MPI_UB	MPI_TYPE_CREATE_RESIZED

MPI_ERRHANDLER_CREATE	MPI_COMM_CREATE_ERRHANDLER
MPI_ERRHANDLER_GET	MPI_COMM_GET_ERRHANDLER
MPI_ERRHANDLER_SET	MPI_COMM_SET_ERRHANDLER
MPI_Handler_function	MPI_Comm_errhandler_fn
MPI_KEYVAL_CREATE	MPI_COMM_CREATE_KEYVAL
MPI_KEYVAL_FREE	MPI_COMM_FREE_KEYVAL
MPI_DUP_FN	MPI_COMM_DUP_FN
MPI_NULL_COPY_FN	MPI_COMM_NULL_COPY_FN
MPI_NULL_DELETE_FN	MPI_COMM_NULL_DELETE_FN
MPI_Copy_function	MPI_Comm_copy_attr_function
COPY_FUNCTION	COMM_COPY_ATTR_FN
MPI_Delete_function	MPI_Comm_delete_attr_function
DELETE_FUNCTION	COMM_DELETE_ATTR_FN
MPI_ATTR_DELETE	MPI_COMM_DELETE_ATTR
MPI_ATTR_GET	MPI_COMM_GET_ATTR
MPI_ATTR_PUT	MPI_COMM_SET_ATTR

15.2.2 Processes

A program in MPI consists of a set of autonomous processes, in a multiple-instruction multiple-data (MIMD) style. The processes communicate via calls to MPI communication primitives. Typically, each process executes in its own address space, although shared-memory implementations of MPI are possible [MPIStandard97].

15.3 MISCELLANEOUS ENHANCEMENTS

The following sections describe enhancements to the process model and memory allocation architecture in MPI2.

15.3.1 The MPI-2 Process Model

In MPI-1, the process startup command is given by the following:

```
mpirun <mpirun arguments> <program> <program arguments>
```

MPI-2 recommends, but does not require, `mpiexec`, which provides greater flexibility and portability, particularly for network and heterogeneous implementations. MIPI-2 suggests the following as the new way to start a process with an initial MPI_COMM_WORLD whose group contains <numprocs> processes:

```
mpiexec -n <numprocs> <program>
```

15.3.2 Process Management and Resource Control

MPI-2 introduces a new, dynamic process management model. Unlike MPI-1 where applications are static, no processes can be added to or deleted from an application after it has been started. This new model allows for process creation and management after an MPI application has been started.

An example where process management would be useful is certain message passing applications such as task farms, serial applications with parallel modules, and problems that require a runtime manipulation of the number of processes to be started. It will also help migration of Parallel Virtual Machine (PVM) applications, which include capabilities for process and resource management [ANLMPI01].

On the other hand, the MPI Forum decided not to address resource control in MPI-2 mostly because of portability issues. Resource control can encompass a wide range of abilities such as the following: adding and deleting nodes from a virtual machine, reserving and scheduling resources, managing compute partitions, and so forth. MPI-2 assumes that resource control is provided externally by computer vendors, or by third-party software [MPIStandard97].

15.3.3 Memory Allocation

MPI-2 provides support for message-passing and remote-memory access (RMA) operations that are faster when accessing specially allocated memory (memory shared by processes in a group on SMP processors). The use of such memory for message passing or RMA is not mandatory, and this memory can be used without restrictions as any other dynamically allocated memory. The C prototypes for this functionality are as follows:

```
int MPI_Alloc_mem(MPI_Aint size, MPI_Info info, void *baseptr)
void MPI::Free_mem(void *base)
```

15.3.4 New Predefined Data Types

New data types are as follows:

Wide Characters: MPI-2 adds support for international character sets such as Unicode with a new data type, `MPI_WCHAR`.

Signed Characters and Reductions: MPI-2 has created the new predefined data type `MPI_SIGNED_CHAR` to allow reductions on signed or unsigned chars. Unlike MPI-1, these reductions could be useful, particularly in image-processing applications where pixel values are often represented as "unsigned char."

Unsigned long long type: The ISO C9X committee has included *long long* and *unsigned long long* as standard C types, so a new optional MPI type, `MPI_UNSIGNED_LONG_LONG` in C has been added.

15.3.5 MPI-IO

MPI-IO was developed by IBM's Watson Laboratory to provide parallel I/O support for MPI. In 1996, MPI-IO was adopted by NASA and incorporated into the MPI-2 standard. MPI-IO was quickly accepted for the following reasons [ANLMPI01]:

- It provides a clean simple interface reminiscent of MPI calls.
- Writing MPI files is similar to sending MPI messages and reading MPI files is similar to receiving MPI messages.
- MPI-IO embraces the versatility and flexibility of MPI data types and takes this concept one step further in defining MPI file views.
- MPI-IO supports reads and writes in normal blocking or asynchronous non-blocking modes.
- It supports the concept of collective operations. Processes can access MPI files individually or all at the same time.

Opening a File

```
MPI_File fh;

int rc = MPI_File_open(
  MPI_COMM_WORLD
  /* Communicator */
  , filename /* File name */
  , MPI_MODE_RDONLY /* Open mode: read, write, etc. */
  , MPI_INFO_NULL
  , & fh); /* File handle */

/* check for error */
if (rc != MPI_SUCCESS) {
  printf("IO ERROR: %s\n", MPI_Get_ErrorString(rc));
  MPI_Abort(MPI_COMM_WORLD, rc);
}
```

File Size and Seek

```
MPI_Offset fileSize, offset; /* long long */
MPI_status status;

MPI_File_get_size(fh, & fileSize); /* get file size */

/* seek file at the right offset */
MPI_File_seek(fh, offset, MPI_SEEK_SET);
```

Reading from a File

```
MPI_File_read(fh /* File handle MPI_file */
              , readBuffer /* Data buffer: char * */
              , numBytes /* # of bytes to read */
              , MPI_BYTE /* type of data */
              , & status); /* Operation status (MPI_Status) */
```

Writing to a File

```
MPI_File_write(fh /* file handle */ << < Author Query :
               please change tab characters in this code to the
               appropriate number of spaces >>>
               , dataArray /* array to be written */
               , arraySize /* # of elements in array */
               , MPI_INT /* array element type */
               , & status); /* operation status (MPI_Status) */
```

Closing a File

```
    /* close file */
    MPI_File_close (&fh);
```

15.3.6 File Views

File views can be used to skip headers on files or to access files that contain a sequence of data to be accessed in different patterns. Separate views, each using a different displacement and file type, can be used to access each segment. For example:

```
View #1:   [_ _ _ _ _ _ _ ...]
View #2:   [__  __  __  __   ...]

File structure: [header _ _ _ _ _ _ ...  ...     __ __ __ __ __ ... ]
                        ?                        ?
                        View 1 displacement      View 2 displacement
```

15.4 MPI EXAMPLES: COMMON PARALLEL ALGORITHMS

The following examples demonstrate common techniques used in parallel algorithms, specifically, solving a smaller case of the same problem to speed the solution of the full problem. A good parallel algorithm time complexity should be close to the time for a good sequential algorithm that solves the same problem. Without this condition, we cannot hope to speed up the parallel algorithm over the sequential one. Parallel algorithms are referred to as *work-efficient* relative to a sequential algorithm if their work is within a constant factor of the time of the sequential algorithm [ACMParallel96].

15.4.1 Prime Generation—The Sieve of Eratosthenes

The sieve of Eratosthenes is the most common sequential algorithm for finding primes. The algorithm returns an array in which the *i-th* position is set to true if i is a prime and to false otherwise. The algorithm works by initializing the array A to `TRUE` and then setting to `FALSE` all multiples of each prime it finds. It starts with the first prime, 2, and works up to `sqrt(n)`. The algorithm only needs go up to `sqrt(n)` since all composite numbers (nonprimes) less than *n* must have a factor less or equal to `sqrt(n)` [ACMParallel96].

The pseudocode of the algorithms is as follows:

```
1 PROCEDURE PRIMES (N)
2 Let A be an Array of length N
3 Set all but the first element of A to TRUE
4 for i = 2 to sqrt(N)
5   Begin
6       if A[i] is True
7           set all multiples of i up to N to FALSE
8   End
9 End
```

If line 7 is implemented by looping over the multiples, then the algorithm can be shown to take *O(n log log n)* time and the constant is small. The sieve of Eratosthenes is not theoretically the best algorithm for finding primes, but it is close and it is a good candidate for a parallel implementation.

15.4.1.1 MPI Implementation

The algorithm in Listing 15.1 demonstrates basic MPI techniques such as MPI initialization, communicators, and array reductions. The implementation is based on the pseudocode from the previous sections.

LISTING 15.1 `mpi_eratosthenes.c` MPI Implementation of the Sieve of Eratosthenes

```
/**
 Sieve of Eratosthenes: A basic algorithm for finding primes

Based on: Programming Parallel Algorithms.
 Communications of the ACM, 39(3), March, 1996.
 http://www-2.cs.cmu.edu/~scandal/cacm/node8.html
   #SECTION00031000000000000000

1 PROCEDURE PRIMES (N)
 2 Let A be an array of length N 3 Set all but the first
    element of A to TRUE
 4 for i = 2 to sqrt(N) 5   Begin 6         if A[i] is True
 7              set all multiples of i up to N to FALSE
 8   End 9 End

 The algorithm returns an array in which the ith position is set to
 true if i is a prime and to false otherwise. The algorithm works by
 initializing the array A to TRUE and then setting to FALSE all
 multiples of each prime it finds. It starts with the first prime, 2,
 and works its way up to sqrt(n). The algorithm only needs go up to
 sqrt(n) since all composite numbers (non-primes) less than n must
 have a factor less or equal to sqrt(n). If line 7 is implemented by
 looping over the multiples, then the algorithm can be shown to take
 O(n log log n) time and the constant is small.  @author Vladimir Silva
 @version 1.0
*/

#include <stdio.h>
#include <stdlib.h>

#include <string.h>
#include <math.h>

/* MPI stuff */
#include "mpi.h"

// process ID of the master task
#define MASTER 0
```

```
/* MPI Globals */
int taskid; // MPI process id
int numprocs; // number of parallel processes
int namelen; // size of the machine name

// machine name
char processor_name[MPI_MAX_PROCESSOR_NAME];
/* End MPI */

#define TRUE 1
#define FALSE 0

/** Initialize the sieve array */
void init( long * A, long N )
{
  long i;
  A[0] = FALSE;
  for ( i = 1; i < N; i++ )
  {
    A[i] = TRUE;
  }

}

/** Actual Sieve */
void sieve( long * A, long N )
{
  long i, j;

  for ( i = 2 + taskid; ( float )i < sqrt( N ); i += numprocs )
  {
    if ( A[i] )
    {
      // set all multiples of i up to N to FALSE
      printf( "Task [%d]: Sieving value %ld\n", taskid, i );

      for ( j = 2; ( i * j ) < N; j++ )
      {
        A[i * j] = FALSE;
      }
    }
  }
}
```

```
/** Show primes */
void printPrimes( long * A, long N )
{
  long i;
  printf( "Task [%d] Sieve of Eratosthenes: %ld primes = ",
     taskid, N );

  for ( i = 0; i < N; i++ )
  {
    if ( A[i] )
    {
      printf( "%ld ", i );
    }
  }
  printf( "\n" );
}

/** Main */
int main( int argc, char * * argv )
{
  const char * Usage = "Eratosthenes <number of primes>\n";

  long N; // Number of primes to sieve
  long * A; // Sieve array

  // for time check
  double startwtime = 0.0, endwtime;

  /** Check arguments */
  if ( argc != 2 )
  {
    if ( taskid == MASTER )
      printf( "%s", Usage );
    return -1;
  }

  // init
  N = atol( argv[1] );

  // Allocate space for the Sieve Array
  A = ( long * ) malloc( N * sizeof( long ) );

  /* * MPI Initialization */
  MPI_Init( & argc, & argv );
  MPI_Comm_size( MPI_COMM_WORLD, & numprocs );
```

```
  MPI_Comm_rank( MPI_COMM_WORLD, & taskid );
  MPI_Get_processor_name( processor_name, & namelen );

  // Only the Master prints headings

  if ( taskid == MASTER )
  {
    startwtime = MPI_Wtime();
  }


  init( A, N );
  sieve( A, N );

  // Compute an AND operation across
  // all processes in the ring
  MPI_Reduce( A, A, N, MPI_LONG, MPI_BAND, 0, MPI_COMM_WORLD );

  // Master prints primes...
  if ( taskid == MASTER )
  {
    printPrimes( A, N );
    endwtime = MPI_Wtime();
    printf( "Wall clock time = %f\n", endwtime - startwtime );
  }


  // cleanup
  free( A );

  MPI_Finalize();
  return 0;
}
```

15.4.2 Sparse Matrix Multiplication

Sparse matrices, which are common in scientific applications, are matrices in which most elements are zero. To save space and running time, it is critical to only store the nonzero elements. A standard representation of sparse matrices in sequential languages is to use an array with one element per row, each of which contains a linked-list of the nonzero values in that row along with their column number. A similar representation can be used in parallel. A sparse matrix can be represented as a sequence of rows, each of which is a sequence of (column-number, value) pairs of the nonzero values in the row [ACMParallel96]. For example, the matrix

$$A = \begin{matrix} 2.0 & -1.0 & 0 & 0 \\ -1.0 & 2.0 & -1.0 & 0 \\ 0 & -1.0 & 2.0 & -1.0 \\ 0 & 0 & -1.0 & 2.0 \end{matrix}$$

is represented in this way as:

```
A = [[(0, 2.0), (1, -1.0)]
  , [(0, -1.0), (1, 2.0), (2, -1.0)]
  , [(1, -1.0), (2, 2.0), (3, -1.0)]
  , [(2, -1.0), (3, 2.0)]]
```

Where A is a nested sequence (i.e., a vector of vectors). This representation can be used for matrices with arbitrary patterns of nonzero elements because each subsequence can be of a different size. A common operation on sparse matrices is to multiply them by a dense vector. In such an operation, the result is the dot-product of each sparse row of the matrix with the dense vector [ACMParallel96].

15.4.2.1 MPI C++ Implementation

LISTING 15.2 `mpi_sparsemat.cpp` Sparse Matrix Multiplication

```
/**
* Sparse Matrix Multiplication
*
* Based on: Programming Parallel Algorithms.
* Communications of the ACM, 39(3), March, 1996.
* http://www-2.cs.cmu.edu/~scandal/cacm/node9.html
*   #SECTION00032000000000000000
*
* Sparse matrices, which are common in scientific calculations, are
* matrices in which most elements are zero. To save space and
* time only the nonzero elements are stored. A standard representation
* of sparse matrices is to use an array with one element per row each
* of which contains a linked-list of the nonzero values in that row
* along with their column number. A sparse matrix can be represented as
* a sequence of rows, each of which is a sequence of (column-number,
* value) pairs of the nonzero values in the row. The matrix
```

```
      2.0   -1.0    0      0
A =  -1.0    2.0   -1.0    0
      0     -1.0    2.0   -1.0
      0      0     -1.0    2.0

is represented in this way as

A = [[(0, 2.0), (1, -1.0)],
     [(0, -1.0), (1, 2.0), (2, -1.0)],
     [(1, -1.0), (2, 2.0), (3, -1.0)],
     [(2, -1.0), (3, 2.0)]]

* where A is a nested sequence. This representation can be used
* for matrices with arbitrary patterns of nonzero elements since each
* subsequence can be of a different size.
*
* This algorithm represents the dot-product of each sparse row
* of the matrix with the dense vector also known as sparse matrix
* multiplication.
*
* @author Vladimir Silva
*
* This program requires the C++ Standard Template Library
* @date 11/02/2004
*/

#include <iostream>
#include <vector.h>
#include <list.h>
#include <set.h>

/* MPI stuff */
#include "mpi.h"

// process ID of the master task
#define MASTER 0
#define DEBUG 0


/* MPI Globals */
int taskid; // MPI process id
int numprocs; // number of parallel processes
int namelen; // size of the machine name
```

```
// machine name
char processor_name[MPI_MAX_PROCESSOR_NAME];
/* End MPI */



/**
* A Pair (c, v) used to represent an element in the sparse Matrix
* Where:
*     x = column number (int)
*     v = Matrix value (float)
*/
class CPair
{
  int col_num;
  float value;

public:
  CPair( int c, float v )
  {
    col_num = c;
    value = v;
  };

  int getColumn()
  {
    return col_num;
  };

  float getValue()
  {
    return value;
  };

  void setValue( float val )
  {
    value = val;
  };
};

/**
* A Row in the sparse mat is a vector of CPair(s)
```

```
*/
typedef vector < CPair > SPARSE_MAT_ROW;

/**
* The sparse matrix type is a nested Vector: A vector of vectors
* vector < vector < CPair > >
*/
typedef vector < SPARSE_MAT_ROW > SparseMat;

/** Subs to print a Sparse Matrix */
void print_pair( CPair pair )
{
  cout << "(" << pair.getColumn() << ", " << pair.getValue() << ")";
}

void print_row( SPARSE_MAT_ROW Row )
{
  cout << "[";
  for_each( Row.begin(), Row.end(), print_pair );
  cout << "] ";
}

void print_mat( const char * lbl, SparseMat M )
{
  cout << lbl << "[";
  for_each( M.begin(), M.end(), print_row );
  cout << "]" << endl;
}

void print_float_vector( const char * lbl, vector < float > v )
{
  cout << lbl;
  ostream_iterator < float > out( cout, " " );
  copy( v.begin(), v.end(), out );
}

void print_float_array( float * f, int size )
{
  int i;
  printf( "(" );
  for ( i = 0; i < size; i++ )
  {
    printf( "%.2f ", f[i] );
  }
```

```
  printf( ")" );
}

/**
* Compute the dot product of the sparse mat (M . v) in parallel by
* having each child process compute v1 = (M[i] . v) and send
* v1 to the master
*/
SparseMat dot_product( SparseMat M, vector < float > v )
{
  SparseMat MProd = M;
  int i, j, k;
  int rowsMaster = 0; // num rows the master process

  // Child(s) dot product (M[i] . v)
  float * prod;

  // loop thru rows: row(i) goes to process(n)
  for ( i = 0 + taskid; ( unsigned )i < M.size(); i += numprocs )
  {
    int min = ( M[i].size() < v.size() ) ? M[i].size() : v.size();

    // Allocate space for dot prod array
    prod = ( float * ) malloc( min * sizeof( float ) );

    // print row dot prod M(i) . v
    printf( "Task [%d]: row(%d):", taskid, i );
    print_row( M[i] );
    print_float_vector( ". (", v );
    printf( ") = " );

    // compute dot product P = M[i] . v
    for ( j = 0; j < min; j++ )
    {
      // Master uses STL, Child(s) stores
      // Xi *Yi in a temp float array
      if ( taskid == MASTER )
      {
        MProd[i] [j].
            setValue( ( float )MProd[i] [j].getValue() * v[j] );
      }
      else
        prod[j] = M[i] [j].getValue() * v[j];
    }
```

```
    // Print (dot)  M[i] . v
    if ( taskid == MASTER )
    {
      print_row( MProd[i] );
    }
    else
    {
      // child(s)
      print_float_array( prod, min );
    }
    printf( "\n" );

    // Child(s) sends size, product array of floats and
    // row number to the master
    if ( taskid != MASTER )
    {
      // Send: Prod array size
      if ( DEBUG )
      {
        printf( "Task [%d] sending row=%d, size=%d, arry=",
           taskid, i, min );
        for ( k = 0; k < min; k++ )
          printf( "%f ", prod[k] );

        printf( "\n" );
      }

      MPI_Send( & min, 1, MPI_INT, MASTER, 0, MPI_COMM_WORLD );
      MPI_Send( prod, min, MPI_FLOAT, MASTER, 0, MPI_COMM_WORLD );
      MPI_Send( & i, 1, MPI_INT, MASTER, 0, MPI_COMM_WORLD );
    }
    else
      rowsMaster++; // count rows processed by the master

    // cleanup
    free( prod );
  }

  if ( taskid == MASTER )
  {
    // Master Receives data
    // Array size
    int size, row;
    int childNum; // child number
```

```
float * rec_v; // receive data
MPI_Status status; // status

// loop thru the number of msgs sent by all childs:
// Mat size - rows processed
// by the master
for ( j = 0; ( unsigned )j < ( M.size() - rowsMaster ); j++ )
{
  childNum = j + 1; // children start from 1...

  // check the bound of the child processes [1, numprocs-1]
  if ( childNum > ( numprocs - 1 ) )
    childNum = 1;

  // receive from children...
  MPI_Recv( & size, 1, MPI_INT, childNum, 0, MPI_COMM_WORLD,
     & status );

  rec_v = ( float * ) malloc( size * sizeof( float ) );

  MPI_Recv( rec_v, size, MPI_FLOAT, childNum, 0, MPI_COMM_WORLD,
     & status );

  MPI_Recv( & row, 1, MPI_INT, childNum, 0, MPI_COMM_WORLD,
     & status );

  if ( DEBUG )
  {
    printf( "MASTER received from [%d]: row=%d, size=%d, arry=",
       childNum, row, size );

    for ( k = 0; k < size; k++ )
      printf( "%f ", rec_v[k] );

    printf( "\n" );
  }

  // Master stores data in the Sparse Mat
  for ( k = 0; k < size; k++ )
  {
    MProd[row] [k].setValue( rec_v[k] );
  }
  // cleanup
  free( rec_v );
```

```
    }
  }
  return MProd;
}


/** Main */
int main( int argc, char * * argv )
{
  SPARSE_MAT_ROW Row1, Row2, Row3, Row4;

  // for time count
  double startwtime = 0.0, endwtime;

  // row 1
  Row1.insert( Row1.end(), CPair( 0, 2.0 ) );
  Row1.insert( Row1.end(), CPair( 1, -1.0 ) );

  // row2
  Row2.insert( Row2.end(), CPair( 0, -1.0 ) );
  Row2.insert( Row2.end(), CPair( 0, 2.0 ) );
  Row2.insert( Row2.end(), CPair( 0, -1.0 ) );

  // row 3
  Row3.insert( Row3.end(), CPair( 0, -1.0 ) );
  Row3.insert( Row3.end(), CPair( 0, 2.0 ) );
  Row3.insert( Row3.end(), CPair( 0, -1.0 ) );

  // row 4
  Row4.insert( Row4.end(), CPair( 0, -1.0 ) );
  Row4.insert( Row4.end(), CPair( 0, 2.0 ) );

  SparseMat M;
  M.insert( M.end(), Row1 );
  M.insert( M.end(), Row2 );
  M.insert( M.end(), Row3 );
  M.insert( M.end(), Row4 );

  vector < float > v( 3 );
  v[0] = 2.0;
  v[1] = 1.0;
  v[2] = 0.0;

  /* * MPI Initialization */
```

```
    MPI_Init( & argc, & argv );
    MPI_Comm_size( MPI_COMM_WORLD, & numprocs );
    MPI_Comm_rank( MPI_COMM_WORLD, & taskid );
    MPI_Get_processor_name( processor_name, & namelen );

    // print Mat & vector (Master only)
    if ( taskid == MASTER )
    {
      startwtime = MPI_Wtime();

      print_mat( "M = ", M );
      print_float_vector( "v = ", v );
      cout << endl << endl;
    }

    // dot product
    SparseMat P = dot_product( M, v );

    // print P . v
    if ( taskid == MASTER )
    {
      print_mat( "\nP . v = ", P );

      endwtime = MPI_Wtime();
      printf( "Wall clock time = %f\n", endwtime - startwtime );
    }

    MPI_Finalize();
    return 0;
  }
```

15.4.3 MPI-IO: Parallel Writes and Reads

ON THE CD

The programs discussed in this section are located on the companion CD-ROM to this chapter. Compilation make files for Windows and Linux systems are also included.

15.4.3.1 Parallel Write Example: Random Integers

In MPI-IO, all processes should start by querying the size of the process pool and their own rank number within it. A process of rank 0 is assumed to be the master and parses the command line:

```
/**
* Initialize MPI
*/
MPI_Init( &argc, &argv );
```

```
MPI_Comm_rank( MPI_COMM_WORLD, &rank );
MPI_Comm_size( MPI_COMM_WORLD, &poolSize );

/* if master read cmd line, abort if error */
if ( rank == MASTER ) {
    parseCommandLine(argc, argv);
}
```

If an error occurs, the master aborts, taking every other process down with the following command:

```
MPI_Abort( MPI_COMM_WORLD, 1 );
```

Note that any open buffers should be cleaned up before aborting. On successful parsing of the command line, the master process broadcasts the following:

- The number of blocks of random integers each process will write
- The length of the file name

At this point, each child calls `malloc` to allocate enough space for the file string:

```
/* Broadcast args to children: fileName, fileNamelen, numBlocks */
MPI_Bcast (&numBlocks, 1, MPI_INT, MASTER, MPI_COMM_WORLD);
MPI_Bcast (&fileNameLen, 1, MPI_INT, MASTER, MPI_COMM_WORLD);

if ( rank != MASTER )
    fileName = (char *) malloc(fileNameLen);
```

Because the master is the only one that parsed the command line, it must broadcast the name of the file to the children:

```
MPI_Bcast (fileName, fileNameLen, MPI_CHAR, MASTER, MPI_COMM_WORLD );
printf ("[%2d]: file:%s, # Blocks:%d\n", rank, fileName, numBlocks);
```

Now each process calculates the number of random integers it is going to write and the number of bytes it will need to store all these integers in memory.

```
/**
* 1) # of integers to be written/process = # blocks * 1MB
* 2) # of bytes/process
* 3) Total # of bytes = # bytes/process * total # of processes
*/
int numIntegers     = numBlocks * BLOCK_SIZE;
```

```
int numBytes        = numIntegers * sizeof (int);
long long totBytes  = poolSize * numBytes;
```

Notice the type `long long totBytes`. This type is usually a 64-bit integer in most systems. It is used because the total number of bytes written to the file may exceed the total amount of memory available to a single process. Each process writes at a different offset (`MPI_Offset`). If `MPI_Offset` is not long enough, you will not be able to generate very large MPI files.

```
/* each process writes at a different offset: 64-bit integer */
    MPI_Offset offset   = rank * numBytes;
```

The basic instruction to open a file in MPI is as follows:

```
rc = MPI_File_open(MPI_COMM_WORLD /* communicator */
                  , fileName /* file name */
                  , MODE /* file mode */
                  , MPI_INFO_NULL
                  , fh); /* file handle */
```

The most common file open modes are as follows:

Mode	**Description**
`MPI_MODE_RDONLY`	read only
`MPI_MODE_RDWR`	read and write
`MPI_MODE_WRONLY`	write only
`MPI_MODE_CREATE`	create if it doesn't exist
`MPI_MODE_EXCL`	throw an error if a file exists already
`MPI_MODE_DELETE_ON_CLOSE`	delete on close

Having opened the file, each child should seek its respective offset:

```
MPI_File_seek ( FILE_HANDLE, offset, SEEK_MODE );
```

Where:

`FILE_HANDLE` is a handle to an `MPI_File`

offset is an `MPI_Offset` (long long type) seek position

SEEK_MODE can be any of the following:

MPI_SEEK_SET: Set the pointer to the value *offset*

MPI_SEEK_CUR :Advance the pointer to *offset* from its current position

MPI_SEEK_END: Advance to *offset* from the end of file.

Now the write operation can be performed as follows:

```
/**
* Write to the file & compute times
*/
double start = MPI_Wtime();
MPI_File_write( fh  /* file handle */
    , randInts      /* array to be written */
    , numIntegers   /* # of elements in array */
    , MPI_INT       /* array element type */
    , &status );    /* operation statusof type MPI_Status */
double finish = MPI_Wtime();

double io_time = finish - start;

/* How many elements have been written ? */
MPI_Get_count( &status, MPI_INT, &count );
```

The function MPI_Wtime() is used to capture the operation execution times (using the wall clock) , and MPI_Get_count is used to find out how many elements have actually been written to the file. The file is then finally closed with the following:

```
/* close file */
MPI_File_close (&fh);
```

The maximum IO time can be calculated by reducing the variable io_time to the maximum as shown here:

```
/* calculate the Maximum io_time among all processes */
MPI_Allreduce( &io_time /* variable to be reduced to a maximum */
    , &longestTime      /* buffer for the maximum */
    , 1                 /* size of the argument */
    , MPI_DOUBLE        /* argument type - double */
    , MPI_MAX           /* calculate the maximum */
    , MPI_COMM_WORLD ); /* communicator: send to all processes */
```

15.4.3.2 Parallel Read Example

For a read operation, the file is opened in read-only mode, and the function MPI_File_open is checked for the return type. If there is an error, a string description is extracted and execution aborts. If `MPI_File_open` succeeds, the file size is retrieved with the following:

```
MPI_File_get_size(fh  /* file handle */
    ,&totalBytes      /* # of bytes(MPI_Offset)long long */
    );
```

Depending on the length of the file and the number of processes, the last process may have to read more bytes than the number allocated to each sibling. To calculate the number of bytes for the last process, use the following:

```
/* numBytes  = bytes allocated to each process */
/* totalBytes  = size in bytes of the file */
/* poolSize= # of processes in the MPI ring */
/* maxBytes= # of bytes to be read by the last process (rank) */
maxBytes = numBytes + (totalBytes % poolSize);

...
/* rank of the last process */
int lastRank = poolSize - 1;

...
/* figure out how many bytes the current proc has to read */
/* The last process will read maxBytes, the rest numBytes */
numBytes = (rank == lastRank) ? (int) maxBytes : (int) numBytes;
```

Once the offset for each process has been calculated, all processes should seek that offset and establish a "barrier" for synchronization before starting the actual read.

```
/* seek file at the right offset */
MPI_File_seek(fh, offset, MPI_SEEK_SET);

/* wait until all processes seek to their respective offsets */
MPI_Barrier(MPI_COMM_WORLD);

MPI_File_read(fh /* file handle */
                 , readBuffer /* read buffer */
                 , numBytes /* number of bytes to read */
                 , MPI_BYTE /* buffer element type */
                 , & status); /* operation status MPI_Status */
```

The entire parallel read subroutine is implemented as follows:

```
/**
```

```
* Read a file in parallel
* @param fileName File to read (The file should contain random integers)
*/
void parallelRead (char * fileName)
{
    MPI_File fh;
    MPI_Status status;

    int rc = MPI_File_open (MPI_COMM_WORLD, fileName
            , MPI_MODE_RDONLY, MPI_INFO_NULL, &fh );

    /* if error , abort */
    if ( rc != MPI_SUCCESS ) {
        printf("\nERROR parallelRead: %s\n", MPI_Get_ErrorString(rc) );
        MPI_Abort( MPI_COMM_WORLD, rc );
    }

    /**
    * Read vars
    */
    MPI_Offset totBytes, maxBytes, offset;
    char * readBuffer;
    int numBytes, count;

    MPI_File_get_size( fh, &totBytes );  /* get file size */

    /* # of bytes read by each process */
    numBytes = totBytes/poolSize;

    /**
    * If poolSize does not divide totBytes evenly,
    * the last process will
    * have to read to the end of the file.
    */
    maxBytes     = numBytes + (totBytes % poolSize);
    int lastRank = poolSize - 1;

    printf("-- Parallel Read --\n");

    if ( maxBytes < INT_MAX )
    {
        /* figure out how many bytes the curr proc has to write */
        numBytes   = ( rank == lastRank )
? (int)maxBytes : (int)numBytes;
```

```
            readBuffer  = (char *) malloc( numBytes );
            offset      = (MPI_Offset) rank * numBytes;

            printf( "[%d] Allocated %d bytes\n", rank, numBytes );
            printf( "[%d] Total # of bytes: %lld\n", rank, totBytes );
            printf( "[%d] Offset = %lld\n", rank, offset );

            /* seek file at the right offset */
            MPI_File_seek( fh, offset, MPI_SEEK_SET );

            /* wait until all processes seek to their respective offsets */
            MPI_Barrier( MPI_COMM_WORLD );

            /* start reading in parallel */
            double start = MPI_Wtime();
            MPI_File_read( fh, readBuffer, numBytes, MPI_BYTE, &status );
            double finish = MPI_Wtime();

            /* get read count and offset */
            MPI_Get_count( &status, MPI_BYTE, &count );
            MPI_File_get_position( fh, &offset );

            printf( "[%d Read %d bytes\n", rank, count );
            printf( "[%d] Offset: %lld\n", rank, offset );

            /* print transfer rates */
            printTransRates( finish - start, totBytes);
        }
        else {
            if ( rank == MASTER )
                printf("Not enough memory for %lld bytes\n", maxBytes );
        }

        /* close file */
        MPI_File_close (&fh);
    }
```

15.5 SUMMARY

MPI-2 functionality is a set of corrections and extensions to the original MPI Standard released in March 1995. This effort is focused in the following areas:

- New data type constructors and language interoperability
- New functionality including dynamic processes, one-sided communication, and parallel I/O
- New language bindings: FORTRAN 90 and C++

This chapter has provided a comprehensive overview of these new changes and used simple examples to illustrate them. A very popular implementation of MPI2 (MPICH2) is covered in the next chapter with more powerful examples. These examples cover interesting subjects such as cryptography and large integer factorization.

REFERENCES

[ACMParallel96] "Programming Parallel Algorithms." *Communications of the ACM*, 39(3), March, 1996. Available online at *http://www-2.cs.cmu.edu/~scandal/cacm/node7.html.*

[ANLMPI01] ANL Mathematics and Computer Science. "The Message Passing Interface (MPI) standard." *http://www-unix.mcs.anl.gov/mpi/.*

[MPIStandard97] The Message Passing Interface (MPI) standard. Copyright© 1995, 1996, 1997 University of Tennessee, Knoxville, Tennessee. Permission to copy without fee all or part of this material is granted provided the University of Tennessee copyright notice and the title of this document appears, and notice is given that copying is by permission of the University of Tennessee. *http://www.mpi-forum.org/docs/mpi-11-html/mpi-report.html.*

16 MPICH2–A Portable Implementation of MPI

In This Chapter

- Overview
- Quick Start Installation Transcript
- Large Integer Factorizaion Revisited: The Number Field Sieve (NFS)
- MPICH2-WS-Gram Integration
- MPICH2-MDS3 Integration
- Summary
- References

This chapter includes information on the following topics:

- An overview of MPICH2—a portable implementation of Message Passing Interface (MPI)
- MPICH2 installation transcript along with testing and troubleshooting tips
- A practical MPI sample in large integer factorization (LIF) implementing a number field sieve (NFS)
- A practical parallel sieve algorithm in MPI along with execution times, compilation, and runtime data
- MPICH2–WS-GRAM Integration including: a scheduler interface for MPICH2 as well as MMJFS service configuration, packaging advice, testing, and troubleshooting
- MPICH2–MDS3 Integration with a sample information service script for MPICH2 as well as configuration and testing data

All code shown in this chapter is available on the companion CD-ROM.

16.1 OVERVIEW

MPICH2 is pronounced Em Pee Eye See Aych, and is a free implementation of the MPI standard available from the Argonne National Laboratory at *www.mcs.anl.gov/mpi/mpich2*. MPICH2 runs on a wide variety of systems including the following [MPICHUserGuide96]:

- Workstation networks, Beowulf clusters, individual workstations, or SMP nodes running multiple process multiple data (MPMD) programs.
- Grids through a globus2 (*www.globus.org*)–enabled implementation of MPI.
- Symmetric multiprocessors for shared-memory systems.
- Massively parallel processors (MPPs) and others by means of their own MPI implementations. Both vendors and research groups have used MPICH as the basis for their implementation.

To provide portability, MPI uses the concept of *abstract device interface* (ADI). Each ADI implementation is called a *device* [MPICHUserGuide96].

16.1.1 Language Bindings

MPICH2 supports Fortran 77, Fortran 90, and C++ languages. It has been tested in every major OS platform, including many flavors of Unix, Linux, Windows, OSX, and so forth.

16.2 QUICK START INSTALLATION TRANSCRIPT

We have prepared the following basic installation transcript run on a Red Hat Linux 8.x system under VMWare workstation 4.x. If you experience any installation problems in your platform, refer to the official installation guide [MPICHAdmin-Guide96].

16.2.1 Software Prerequisites

The following software is required to install and run MPICH on a UNIX system:

- The source file: `mpich2.tar.gz`
- A C compiler (`gcc` or other)
- A FORTRAN compiler (`g77`), if FORTRAN applications are to be used

- A C++ compiler for the C++ MPI bindings (g++ is sufficient)
- *Python 2.2* or later (for the default MPD process manager)
- PyXML and an XML parser like EXPAT (so you can use `mpiexec` with the MPD process manager)
- A Fortran 90 compiler if you enable Fortran 90; configure with `--enable-f90`.

16.2.2 Unpack the Tar File into a Temporary Directory

```
tar xfz mpich2.tar.gz
cd mpich2-0.97
```

16.2.3 Create an Installation Directory (Default Is `/usr/local/bin`)

```
mkdir /opt/mpich2
```

Share this directory with all the machines where you intend to run processes.

16.2.4 Configure MPICH2, Specifying the Installation Directory

```
./configure -prefix=/opt/mpich2
```

16.2.5 Build and Install MPICH2

```
Make
Make install
```

16.2.6 Add the bin Subdirectory of the Installation Directory to Your Path

C shell: `setenv PATH /home/you/mpich2-install:$PATH`
Bash Shell: `export PATH=/home/you/mpich2-install:$PATH`
Check that everything is OK by running the commands:

```
which mpd
which mpiexec
```

16.2.7 Test the MPICH2 Daemon Ring

MPICH2 uses a new external process manager for scalable startup of large MPI jobs. The default process manager is called MPI Process Daemon (MPD), which is a ring of daemons on the machines where you will run MPI programs.

As user root: Create the file `/etc/mpd.conf`

As a local user: Create the file `$HOME/.mpd.conf`

Inside this configuration file, place the line: `secretword=<secretword>`. This is an authentication password for all the machines on your ring.

The password must be the same for all machines or the authentication process will not work. Also, make sure the file is readable by the owner only (`chmod 600 file_name`*) or you may see the following message when booting MPI: "configuration file* `/etc/mpd.conf` *not found." A file named* `.mpd.conf` *file must be present in the user's home directory (*`/etc/mpd.conf if root`*) with read and write access only for the user, and must contain at least a line with* `secretword=<secretword>`

16.2.8 Check the Sanity of the MPD Daemon

The first sanity check consists of bringing up a ring of one MPD on the local machine, testing a command, and shutting down:

```
# mpd &
 [1] 32714
# mpdtrace
 vm-rhl8
# mpdallexit
 [1]+  Done mpd
```

16.2.9 Create an MPD Ring and Test It

On the master host, run the following:

```
# mpd &
# mpdtrace –l
    master.mydomain.com_32718
```

The number *32718* is the *port number* the master daemon is listening to.

On the rest of machines on your ring do the following:

```
#mpd –h master.mydomain.com –p 32718 &
```

This will connect each machine on your ring to the master daemon running on host `master.mydomain.com:32718`.

Verify the ring:

```
#mpdtrace
 master.mydomain.com
 host1.mydomain.com
```

```
host2.mydomain.com
```

If something goes wrong at this point, make sure the secretword in your `mpd.conf` *file is the same for all machines. An authentication failure is indicated by the following message:*

```
vm-rhl8.ibm.com_33235
 (_handle_rhs_challenge_response 864):
 INVALID msg for rhs response
 msg=:{'host': 'vm-rhl8-2.ibm.com'
   , 'cmd': 'challenge_response'
   , 'response': '\xacH\xa7\xbf;\xcb\xf9\xc6\xa9\x130I_\x07\x8bl'
   , 'port': 32872}:"
```

16.2.10 Run Simple Commands

Once the ring is up and running, try running simple commands such as the following:

```
# mpdringtest 100
time for 100 loops = 0.177493095398 seconds
```

This command is telling us how long it takes to loop 100 times through the ring.

16.2.11 Run the Sample MPI Programs

The MPICH2 distribution provides sample programs in the `examples` directory. For example:

```
# mpiexec -n 5 /opt/mpich2/examples/cpi
Process 0 of 5 is on vm-rhl8
Process 1 of 5 is on vm-rhl8
Process 2 of 5 is on vm-rhl8
Process 3 of 5 is on vm-rhl8
Process 4 of 5 is on vm-rhl8
pi is approximately 3.1415926544231230, Error is 0.0000000008333298
wall clock time = 0.023988
```

The previous program spawns five processes to run a parallel PI computation, by numerical integration, on your ring of machines. As with `mpdrun` (which is used internally by `mpiexec`), the number of processes need not match the number of hosts. The `cpi` example will tell you which hosts it is running on. By default, the processes are launched one after the other on the hosts in the MPD ring, so it is not necessary to specify hosts when running a job with `mpiexec`. At this point, you have successfully created an MPI ring capable of running parallel programs. The following section describes a real-world example.

16.3 LARGE INTEGER FACTORIZATION REVISITED: THE NUMBER FIELD SIEVE (NFS)

The General Number Field Sieve (GNFS) is an algorithm to factor integers of the form re ± s; where r and s are small positive integers. The heuristic expected execution time of GNFS is as follows [LenstraNFS]:

$$\exp((1+o(1))(\log n)^{1/2}(\log \log n)^{1/2}).$$

With $c = 2(2/3)^{2/3} \approx 1.526$

GNFS is the fastest known method for factoring large integers. Research and development of this algorithm within the past five years has facilitated factorizations of integers that were once speculated to require thousands of years of supercomputer time to accomplish. GNFS is an algorithm used specially in cryptanalysis to attempt to scramble RSA keys. In fact, GNFS was used to factor many of the RSA challenge integers [BriggsThesis98].

16.3.1 GNFS Algorithm

GNFS is a very complex algorithm that requires extensive mathematical background to understand. Briggs has a good introduction to the algorithm [BriggsThesis98], and more extensive information can be found in Lenstra and Lenstra, Montgomery, and Cohen [Lenstra93, Montgomery95, Cohen96]. Given $n = {}^{e} - s$ we select an extension degree $d \in Z_{>0}$. Given d, let k be the minimal such that $kd \geq$ e, so that $r^{kd} = sr^{kd-e}$ modulo n. Let $f(X) = X^d - c \in Z[X]$. For a reasonable choice of d a nontrivial factor of f will lead to a nontrivial factor of n, so that we may assume that f is irreducible. There is a better than 50-50 chance that this will produce a nontrivial factor of n [Lenstra93].

GNFS can be divided in five stages, as described in the following sections.

16.3.1.1 Stage1: Polynomial Selection

GNFS requires a monic, irreducible polynomial $f(x)$ of degree d with integer coefficients and which has a root m *modulo* n, where n denotes the integer to factor. No method is given for finding the optimal degree d or the coefficients of $f(x)$. In practice, however, it requires careful experimentation to select an optimal *f(x)* because the time required to factor an integer *n* can be dramatically reduced. The key is to find choices for *d, m* and *f(x)* that lead to many *(a, b)* pairs for which $a + b\theta$ and are smooth. This is currently one of the most active areas in GNFS research [LenstraNFS].

16.3.1.2 Stage2: Factor Base Creation

This stage requires a rational, algebraic factor base and a quadratic character base.

Rational factor base: The rational factor base consists of prime integers 2, 3, 5, and so on up to a particular bound, which is usually determined by experimenting with the smoothness of $a + bm$ for different (a, b) pairs.

Algebraic factor base: The algebraic factor base consists of first-degree prime ideals of $Z[\theta]$ represented as pairs *(r, p)* where *p* is a prime integer and *r* is a root of *f(x)*.

Quadratic character base: A small set of first-degree prime ideals of that $Z[\theta]$ don't occur in the algebraic factor base.

16.3.1.3 Stage 3: Sieving

Sieving uses a sieve algorithm to find pairs of integers *(a, b)* with $a + bm$ smooth over a rational factor base. Most implementations of the GNFS simply fix a value for *b* and then scan the *a* values within a range $u < a < u$ for values of $a + bm$ that are smooth. After enough smooth pairs are found, a *sparse matrix* B is constructed where a single column of the matrix corresponds to an *(a, b)* pair found in the previous stage. The entries in each column vector are determined from the factorization of $a + bm$ over the rational factor base [LenstraNFS].

16.3.1.4 Stage 4: Finding Dependencies

The *Block Lanczos* procedure is applied to the matrix B constructed in the previous stage to find dependencies among the binary vectors corresponding to the *(a, b)* pairs [Montgomery95].

16.3.1.5 Stage 5: Square Root

Square Root is used to solve the imposed condition that the product of the elements $a + bm$ corresponding to pairs in *U* be a perfect square in both Z and $Z[\theta]$. [Cohen96].

16.3.1.6 Further Information on NFS

Large integer factorization (LIF) is a complex subject that requires some advanced mathematics, especially in the fields of linear algebra and modular arithmetic. If you are looking for an in-depth study on the inner workings of the quadratic or number field sieves, Briggs [BriggsThesis98] is a good beginner's guide to the NFS. For the more technical reader, Cohen, Lenstra et al., Lenstra and Lenstra, and Montgomery [Cohen96, LenstraNFS, Lenstra93, Montgomery95] are appropriate.

ON THE CD

The CD-ROM provided with this book contains a Java implementation of the quadratic sieve, which is roughly 10,000 lines in size. Another open source algorithm studied in this book, Public Domain GNFS by Chris Monico, is 50,000 lines in size. This should give the reader an idea of the complexity of this subject.

16.3.2 Public Domain GNFS—Sieving Over a Factor Base

Many implementations of GNFS are available for download from the Web. For the implementation of a parallel sieve algorithm in MPI, we have chosen GGNFS. GGNFS is a public domain implementation of GNFS by Chris Monico, distributed under the GNU General Public License (GPL) [MonicoGNFS].

GGNFS is written in C and provides a command-line set of tools for all the NFS stages mentioned in the previous section: polynomial selection, factor base creation, sieving, dependencies, and square root.

16.3.3 Sieve Algorithm

We start the parallel sieve implementation by presenting a classic sieve algorithm as described by Briggs [BriggsThesis98]:

Let p be a fixed prime in the rational factor base F and b a fixed, positive integer. Then for any $a \in Z$ the prime p divides $a + bm$ if and only if $a + bm \equiv 0 (\text{mod } p)$. This implies that $a = -bm + kp$ for some $k \in Z$. Thus,

1. Create sieve array with a single position allocated for each $\_u < a < u$.
2. For a fixed value of b, each position in the sieve array is initialized with the appropriate value of $ln(a+bm)$.
3. For a fixed b and prime p, subtract $ln(p)$ from the array location for a = $-bm + kp$ with $k \in Z$ and $\_u < a < u$. From the elementary theory of logarithms, dividing $a + bm$ by a prime p is equivalent to $\ln(a + bm) - \ln(p)$.
4. After processing all primes in F for a fixed b, the sieve array is then scanned for values $\leq 0 = \ln(1)$. Such a position yields a value for $a \in Z$ with the value $a + bm$ very likely to be smooth. Smoothness is then tested on such $a + bm$ by performing trial division over F.

In some cases, because of the round-off errors in approximating logarithms, some $a + bm$ values will turn out to not be smooth over F. These occurrences are infrequent in practice, and are negligible compared with the savings in time by not performing divisions on a large number of $a + bm$ values.

For your convenience, Listing 16.1 shows the sieve algorithm that will be used on our parallel implementation, taken from GGNFS [MonicoGNFS].

LISTING 16.1 Sieve Algorithm from GGNFS

```
/**************************************************************/
/* clsieve.c                                                  */
/* Chris Monico, 1/7/03                                       */
/* Classical sieve for the NFS.                               */
/**************************************************************/
/* Copyright 2004, Chris Monico.                              */
/**************************************************************/
/*  This file is part of GGNFS.
*
*   GGNFS is free software; you can redistribute it and/or modify
*   it under the terms of the GNU General Public License as published
by
*   the Free Software Foundation; either version 2 of the License, or
*   (at your option) any later version.
*
*   GGNFS is distributed in the hope that it will be useful,
*   but WITHOUT ANY WARRANTY; without even the implied warranty of
*   MERCHANTABILITY or FITNESS FOR A PARTICULAR PURPOSE.  See the
*   GNU General Public License for more details.
*
*/

#include <stdio.h>
#include <stdlib.h>
#include <string.h>
#include "ggnfs.h"

#define SKIP_R_PRIMES 0
#define SKIP_A_PRIMES 0

#define VERY_SMALL_ENTRY -127

#define CHUNK_SIZE 524288
```

```
int clSieve(long *smooth_a, int maxSmooth
            , nfs_fb_t *FB, long _a0, long _a1, long b)
/*****************************************************************/
/* Sieve from (a0, b) to (a1, b). Put the smooth a's in smooth_a. */
/* That is, sieve on a - b*m, and store the values of 'a' that    */
/* give smooth values.                                            */
/* Return value: Number of relations found, or < 0 on error.      */
/*****************************************************************/
{ static int initialized=0;
  static mpz_t bm, t;
  static char    *tmp, *t2, *tStop;
  long   p, pStopIndex, residue, k;
  short int  numFound, numChunks, c;
  char  plog, ratVal, logM;
  long   i, r, g, a, a0, a1;
  int    evenB=0;

  if (!(initialized)) {
    mpz_init(bm); mpz_init(t);
    if (!(tmp = (char *)malloc((CHUNK_SIZE+1)*sizeof(char)))) {
      fprintf(stderr, "clSieve() : Memory allocation error!\n");
      return -1;
    }
    initialized=1;
  }
  if (b%2==0) evenB=1;

  numChunks = (_a1 - _a0 + 1)/CHUNK_SIZE;
  if ((_a1 - _a0 + 1)%CHUNK_SIZE)
    numChunks++;
  a0 = _a0;
  a1 = _a0 + CHUNK_SIZE-1;
  mpz_mul_si(bm, FB->m, b);
  logM = fplog_mpz(FB->m);
  numFound=0;
  tStop = tmp + CHUNK_SIZE;

  for (c=0; c<numChunks; c++) {
    /* Initialize the sieve with logs */
    ratVal = (char)(-logM - fplog(b) + FB->rfb_log_ff);
    memset(tmp, (int)ratVal, CHUNK_SIZE*sizeof(char));

    pStopIndex = 2*FB->rfb_size;
```

```
    if (!evenB) {
      for (i=2*SKIP_R_PRIMES; i<pStopIndex; i+=2) {
        p = FB->rfb[i];
        plog = FB->rfb_log[i/2];
        /*********************************************/
        /* Find the smallest (a, b) pair s.t.  a-bm */
        /* is divisible by 'p'.                     */
        /*********************************************/
        MULMOD32(residue, FB->rfb[i+1], b, p);
        k = (residue + p - (a0 % p))%p; /* Make sure 'k' is positive.
*/
        t2 = tmp+k;
        while (t2 < tStop) {
          *t2 += plog;
           t2 += p;
        }
      }
    } else {
      /* 'b' is even. We do as above, but sieving over values of 2a+1
         instead. */
      i=0;
      if (FB->rfb[0]==2) i=2;
      for ( ; i<pStopIndex; i+=2) {
        p = FB->rfb[i];
        plog = FB->rfb_log[i/2];
        /************************************************/
        /* Find the smallest (a, b) pair s.t.  2a+1-bm */
        /* is divisible by 'p'.                        */
        /************************************************/
        MULMOD32(residue, FB->rfb[i+1], b, p);
        MULMOD32(residue, p+residue-1, (p+1)/2, p);
/* Make sure 'k' is positive. */

        k = (residue + p - (a0 % p))%p;

        t2 = tmp+k;
        while (t2 < tStop) {
          *t2 += plog;
           t2 += p;
        }

      }

    }
```

```
/***** Prepare for the algebraic sieve. *****/
if (!evenB) {
  for (i=0; i<CHUNK_SIZE; i++) {
    tmp[i] =  (tmp[i] >= 0) ?
        (char)(FB->afb_log_ff - fplog_evalF(a0+i, b, FB))
        : VERY_SMALL_ENTRY;
  }
} else {
  for (i=0; i<CHUNK_SIZE; i++) {
    tmp[i] =  (tmp[i] >= 0)
        ? (char)(FB->afb_log_ff - fplog_evalF(2*(a0+i)+1, b, FB))
        : VERY_SMALL_ENTRY;
  }
}

pStopIndex = 2*FB->afb_size;
if (!evenB) {
  for (i=2*SKIP_A_PRIMES; i<pStopIndex; i+=2) {
    p = FB->afb[i];
    r = FB->afb[i+1];
    MULMOD32(residue, b, r, p);
    plog = (FB->afb_log[i/2]);
    /********************************************/
    /* Find the smallest (a, b) pair s.t.  a-br */
    /* is divisible by 'p'.                     */
    /********************************************/
    k = (p + residue - (a0%p))%p;
    t2 = tmp+k;
    while (t2 < tStop) {
      *t2 += plog;
       t2 += p;
    }
  }
} else {
  /* Again, as above, but sieving over 2a+1 instead. */
  i=0;
  while (FB->afb[i]==2) i+=2;
  for ( ; i<pStopIndex; i+=2) {
    p = FB->afb[i];
    r = FB->afb[i+1];
    MULMOD32(residue, b, r, p);
    MULMOD32(residue, p+residue-1, (p+1)/2, p);
    plog = (FB->afb_log[i/2]);
    /***********************************************/
```

```
          /* Find the smallest (a, b) pair s.t.  2a+1-br */
          /* is divisible by 'p'.                         */
          /**********************************************/
          k = (p + residue - (a0%p))%p;
          t2 = tmp+k;
          while (t2 < tStop) {
            *t2 += plog;
             t2 += p;
          }
        }
      }

      t2=tmp;
      while (t2 < tStop) {
        if (*t2 >= 0) {
          a = (evenB ? (1+2*(a0 + (t2-tmp))) : (a0+ (t2-tmp)));
          g = gcd(a, b);
          if (g*g==1)
            if (numFound < maxSmooth)
              smooth_a[numFound++] = a;
        }
        t2++;
      }
      /* Update the interval for the next pass: */
      a0 += CHUNK_SIZE;
      a1 += CHUNK_SIZE;
    }

    return numFound;
  }
```

16.3.4 LIF Execution Times

Some of the factorization times posted by Monico [MonicoGNFS] show that a significant amount of time of the overall factorization is consumed by the sieve. Thus, speeding up the sieve is the prime goal of the developers of this algorithm. Consider Table 16.1 (all times in hours).

TABLE 16.1 GNFS Sieving Times on a Single Processor Machine

Number	Digits	Sieve Time Rectangular or Lattice	Dependencies	Total
(7^135 – 26)/17189077	107	10.4	2	12.8
(2^488+1)/257	144	29	2.75	33
RSA-100	100	14.8	3.1	18
RSA-110	110	50	7.8	58
Average		26.05	3.91	

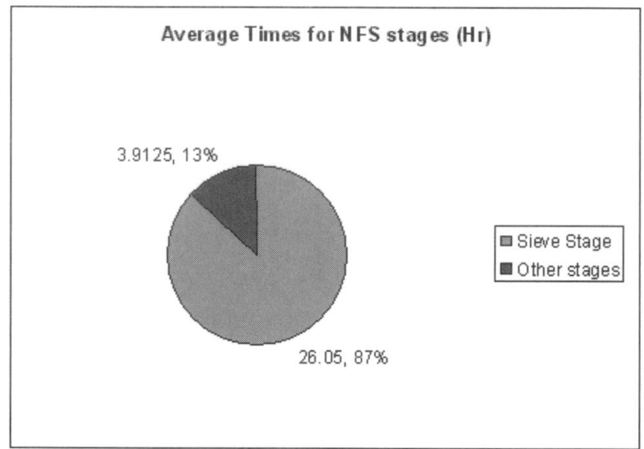

FIGURE 16.1 Average times for the various factorization stages of GGNFS.

16.3.5 Parallel Sieve Implementation in MPI

The graph from the previous section shows that the sieve consumes an average of 80% of the overall factorization time. Thus, a parallel sieve implementation significantly improves GNFS execution time.

16.3.5.1 Parallel Sieve Architecture

The parallel algorithm works by distributing the sieve range among all the processes on the MPI ring. Each task will then use the standard GGNFS sieve algorithm to compute the smooth values and send them back to the master process, which in turn, will save them to disk (See Figure 16.2).

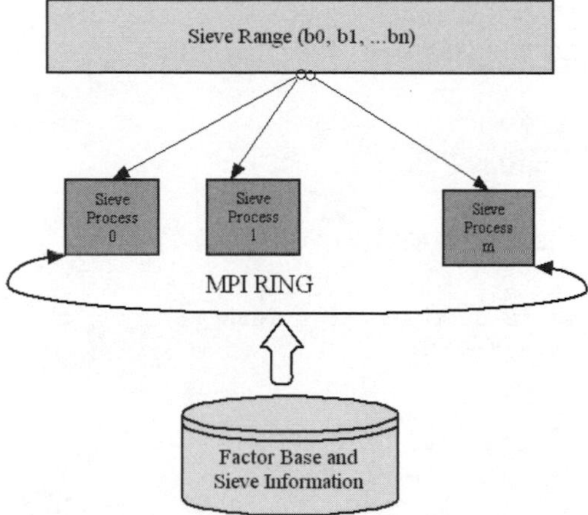

FIGURE 16.2 Parallel sieve architecture.

16.3.5.2 Implementation in C

Listing 16.2 shows an MPI adaptation from `sieve.c` available from the GGNFS source distribution [MonicoGNFS].

LISTING 16.2 `mpi_sieve.c` Parallel Sieve Program for GGNFS

```
/* mpi_sieve.c */
/* Copyright 2004, Chris Monico. */
/* MPI Modifications by: Vladimir Silva */
/**  */
/*  This file is part of GGNFS. * * GGNFS is free software; you can
redistribute it and/or modify * it under the terms of the GNU
General Public License as published by
* the Free Software Foundation; either version 2 of the License, or
* (at your option) any later version. *
*   GGNFS is distributed in the hope that it will be useful,
*   but WITHOUT ANY WARRANTY; without even the implied warranty of
*   MERCHANTABILITY or FITNESS FOR A PARTICULAR PURPOSE.  See the
*   GNU General Public License for more details. */

#include <stdio.h>
#include <stdlib.h>
#include <string.h>
#include <signal.h>
#include <time.h>
#include <gmp.h>
#include "ggnfs.h"
```

```
#define _CATCH_SIGNALS
#define DEFAULT_OUTNAME "spairs.out"

/* MPI stuff */
#include "mpi.h"

//#define SIEVE_CLASSICAL_MPI 3

// process ID of the master task
#define MASTER 0


/* end MPI */

// Debug flags
#define DEBUG 0
#define DEBUG_5(A1,A2,A3,A4,A5) if (DEBUG) printf(A1,A2,A3,A4,A5);
#define DEBUG_6(A1,A2,A3,A4,A5,A6) \
  if (DEBUG) printf(A1,A2,A3,A4,A5,A6);

#define ADJUST_FREQ 2000

#define USAGE \
   "[OPTIONS]\n"\
   "--help               : show this help and exit\n"\
   "-fb <filename>       : use factor base in file <filename>\n"\
   "-j  <filename>       : use job file <filename>"

#define START_MSG \
   "\n"\
   " ___________________________________________________________ \n"\
   "|          This is the sieve program for GGNFS.             |\n"\
   "| Version: %-15s                                  |\n"\
   "| This program is copyright 2004, Chris Monico, and subject|\n"\
   "| to the terms of the GNU General Public License version 2.|\n"\
   "|___________________________________________________________|\n"

/** Globals *** */
double startTime;
int forceStop = 0;

/* MPI Globals */
int taskid; // MPI process id
int numprocs; // number of parallel processes
```

```
int namelen; // size of the machine name

// machine name
char processor_name[MPI_MAX_PROCESSOR_NAME];

/* End MPI Globals */

/**  */
void catch_term( int sig )

/**  */
{
  printf( "Term signal caught. Doing clean shutdown..." );
  fflush( stdout );
  forceStop = 1;
}

/**  */
int parseJobFile( nfs_sieve_job_t * job, char * fName )

/**  */
{
  FILE * fp;
  char token[256], value[256], thisLine[1024];

  if ( !( fp = fopen( fName, "r" ) ) )
  {
    printf( "Error opening %s for read!\n", fName );
    return -1;
  }

  /** Set defaults. ** */
  job->type = SIEVE_UNKNOWN;
  job->rat_ff = job->alg_ff = 0;
  job->a0 = job->a1 = job->b0 = job->b1 = 0;
  job->qIndex0 = job->qIndex1 = 0;
  job->sieveArea = 0.0;
  job->RAM = 0;
  strcpy( job->outName, DEFAULT_OUTNAME );

  while ( !( feof( fp ) ) )
  {
    thisLine[0] = 0;
    fgets( thisLine, 1023, fp );
```

```
if ( ( sscanf( thisLine, "%255s %255s", token, value ) == 2 )
   && ( thisLine[0] != '#' ) )
   {
     if ( strncmp( token, "type:", 5 ) == 0 )
     {
       if ( strcmp( value, "classical" ) == 0 )
         job->type = SIEVE_CLASSICAL;
       else if ( strncmp( value, "lattice", 7 ) == 0 )
         job->type = SIEVE_LATTICE;
       else
         job->type = SIEVE_UNKNOWN;
     }
     else if ( strncmp( token, "a0:", 3 ) == 0 )
     {
       job->a0 = atol( value );
     }
     else if ( strncmp( token, "a1:", 3 ) == 0 )
     {
       job->a1 = atol( value );
     }
     else if ( strncmp( token, "b0:", 3 ) == 0 )
     {
       job->b0 = atol( value );
     }
     else if ( strncmp( token, "b1:", 3 ) == 0 )
     {
       job->b1 = atol( value );
     }
     else if ( strncmp( token, "q0:", 3 ) == 0 )
     {
       job->qIndex0 = atol( value );
     }
     else if ( strncmp( token, "q1:", 3 ) == 0 )
     {
       job->qIndex1 = atol( value );
     }
     else if ( strncmp( token, "sieveArea:", 10 ) == 0 )
     {
       job->sieveArea = atof( value );
       << < Author Query : atol ? >> >
     }
     else if ( strncmp( token, "RAM:", 3 ) == 0 )
     {
       job->RAM = atol( value );
```

```
          }
          else if ( strncmp( token, "rff:", 4 ) == 0 )
          {
            job->rat_ff = atol( value );
          }
          else if ( strncmp( token, "aff:", 4 ) == 0 )
          {
            job->alg_ff = atol( value );
          }
      }
    }
    fclose( fp );
    if ( job->type == SIEVE_UNKNOWN )
    {
      printf( "Couldn't determine sieve type!\n" );
      return -1;
    }
    return 0;
}

/*
* Report: On the status of the MPI Classic sieve process
* Arguments:
*  candidates: Size of the potentially smooth  array of longs
*  smooth_a: Array of potentially smooth
values over the Factor Basse  (FB)
*  b: The value currently sieved
*  totSmooth: Total number of candidates (MASTER + children)
* FB: Factor Base structure
*/

void Report( long candidates, long * smooth_a, long b,
   long totSmooth, nfs_fb_t * FB )
   {
     int numSmooth = 0, i = 0;
     double weight = 0.0;

     if ( rand() > RAND_MAX / 20 || DEBUG )
       return;

     for ( i = 0; i < candidates; i++ )
     {
       if ( ( isSmooth_alg( smooth_a[i], b, FB ) >= 0 )
          && ( isSmooth_rat( smooth_a[i], b, FB ) >= 0 ) )
```

```
            numSmooth++;
        }

        double smoothPerc =
           ( ( candidates > 0 ) ?
           ( double )100.0 * numSmooth / ( double )candidates : 100.0 );
        double weightedAvg =
           ( weight * weightedAvg + candidates * smoothPerc )
           / ( weight + candidates );

        weight += candidates;

        printf( "[task %d] total: %ld, b = %ld, newR: %ld
        ( % 1.3lf % % are smooth, avg = % 1.3lf )\n",
        taskid, totSmooth, b, candidates, smoothPerc, weightedAvg );
}

/* * Dump an array of longs for debugging */
void dump_LongArray( char * lbl, long * arry,
   << < Author Query : array ? If so,
   check throughout >> > long size )
   {
     int i;
     printf( "%s = [%ld", lbl, arry[0] );
     for ( i = 1; i < size; i++ )
       printf( ", %ld", arry[i] );
     printf( "]\n" );
}

/* * Save an Arry of long values to an ASCII file */
void saveArray( char * outName, long * smooth_a, int candidates,
   long sieve_val )
   {
     FILE * ofp;
     ofp = fopen( outName, "a" );
     int i;
     for ( i = 0; i < candidates; i++ )
     {
       fprintf( ofp, "%ld %ld\n", smooth_a[i], sieve_val );
     }
     fclose( ofp );
}

/**
```

```
 MPI Parallel implementation of a Classical Sieve over a factor base
 Note: The executable must be present in all machines.
 including the arguments (Factor Base, Sieve Job Information, etc)
 Arguments: J: Sieve Job information file
   (Sieve type: classic, lattice or classic_mpi, bounds, etc)
 FB: Factor Base
*/

int MPI_Classic_Sieve( nfs_sieve_job_t * J, nfs_fb_t * FB )
{
  long maxSmooth, totSmooth, * smooth_a;
  long i, a0, a1, b0, b1, b, candidates;

  /* Set up parameters. */
  FB->rfb_log_ff = J->rat_ff;
  FB->afb_log_ff = J->alg_ff;
  a0 = J->a0;
  a1 = J->a1;
  b0 = J->b0;
  b1 = J->b1;

  maxSmooth = 10000;

  int rc, // MPI return code
     mtype = 0; // MPI message type
  longsieve_count = 0; // num values sieved by each process

  // for timing
  double startWTime = 0.0, endWTime;

  // array of sieved values created by children
  long * recv_smooth_a =
     ( long * ) malloc( maxSmooth * sizeof( long ) );

  MPI_Status status;

  // Smooth values array
  smooth_a = ( long * ) malloc( maxSmooth * sizeof( long ) );


  // Only the Master prints headings
  if ( taskid == MASTER )
  {
    printf( "**MPI sieve** on a=[%ld, %ld] from b=%ld to b=%ld.\n",
```

```
        a0, a1, b0, b1 );
    printf( "Large rational prime bound : %ld\n", FB->maxP_r );
    printf( "Large algebraic prime bound: %ld\n", FB->maxP_a );
    printf( "Range [%ld, %ld] among %d processes...\n", b0,
        b1, numprocs );
}

// Total number of smooth values
totSmooth = 0;

/**  */
/* This is the main loop */
/**  */
if ( taskid == MASTER )
  startWTime = MPI_Wtime();

// currently sieved value
long sieved_val;

// loop thru sieving range [b0, b1]
for ( b = b0; ( b <= b1 ) && !( forceStop ); b += numprocs )
{
  // sieving range is split among the MASTER process and all
  // the children
  sieved_val = b + taskid;

  if ( sieved_val > b1 ) break;

  DEBUG_6( "[%d - %s] Sieving on range [%ld, %ld], b=%ld...\n",
     taskid, processor_name, b0, b1, sieved_val );

  // each process tracks how many values are sieved
  sieve_count++;

  // All tasks sieve on the value: (b + taskid)
  candidates =
     clSieve( smooth_a, maxSmooth, FB, a0, a1, sieved_val );

  // Report sieve status
  Report( candidates, smooth_a, sieved_val, totSmooth, FB );

  if ( taskid != MASTER )
  {
    // Children send sieved arry size
```

```
        // The array contents and the sieved value back to the master
        DEBUG_5( "[%d - %s] Sending %ld candidates. Sieved val=%ld\n",
           taskid, processor_name, candidates, sieved_val );

        // Send sieved array size
        rc = MPI_Send( & candidates, 1, MPI_LONG, MASTER, mtype,
           MPI_COMM_WORLD );

        // Send sieved array (1 Send only)
        rc = MPI_Send( smooth_a, candidates, MPI_LONG, MASTER, mtype,
           MPI_COMM_WORLD );

        if ( rc != MPI_SUCCESS )
          fprintf( stderr, "%d: send failure on round %d\n",
             taskid, mtype );

        // Send sieved value
        MPI_Send( & sieved_val, 1, MPI_LONG, MASTER, mtype,
           MPI_COMM_WORLD );
      }
      else
      {
        // Master must save sieved array here...
        totSmooth += candidates;

        saveArray( J->outName, smooth_a, candidates, sieved_val );
      }
    }

    // receive stuff from children
    if ( taskid == MASTER )
    {
      // Master receives sieve array size, array contents
      // and sieved  value from children
      long recv_size = 0; // sieved array size

      // Number of messages the master must receive (
      // upper bound - sieve count)
      // Each process (including the MASTER) may sieve 1 or more values
      long numMsgs = ( b0 > 0 ) ? b1 - sieve_count :
         ( b1 + abs( b0 ) ) - sieve_count;

      // Child number
      int childNum = 1;
```

```
  for ( i = 0; i < numMsgs; i++, childNum++ )
  {
    // receive data from children (1 receive only)
    if ( childNum > ( numprocs - 1 ) )
      childNum = 1;


    MPI_Recv( & recv_size, 1, MPI_LONG, childNum, mtype,
       MPI_COMM_WORLD, & status );

    // receive sieved array...
    MPI_Recv( recv_smooth_a, recv_size, MPI_LONG, childNum, mtype,
       MPI_COMM_WORLD, & status );

    // receive sieved value
    rc = MPI_Recv
       ( & sieved_val, 1, MPI_LONG, childNum, mtype,
       MPI_COMM_WORLD, & status );

    if ( rc != MPI_SUCCESS )
      fprintf( stderr, "%d: receive failure on round %d\n",
         taskid, mtype );
    else
    {
      // Save sieved  array from child here
      totSmooth += recv_size;

      saveArray( J->outName, recv_smooth_a, recv_size,
         sieved_val );
    }
  }
}

if ( taskid == MASTER )
{
  endWTime = MPI_Wtime();
  printf( "Done sieving. Wall clock time=%f \
    , Total smooth values=%ld\n",
     endWTime - startWTime, totSmooth );
}

free( smooth_a );
free( recv_smooth_a );
```

```
  return totSmooth;
}


/*
* A Parallel sieve algorithm for GGNFS using MPI (based on sieve.c)
* Author: Vladimir Silva
* Note:This parallel program requires the executable and all

* input files (factor base, sieve info file) to be present
*  in all machines!
* Also, all input files must be the same (have
the same arguments)
* or the program will not behave correctly.
*/
int main( int argC, char * args[] )
{
  char fbname[MAXFNAMESIZE], jobfile[MAXFNAMESIZE];
  int i, res;
  nfs_fb_t FB;
  nfs_sieve_job_t Job;
  double now;

  fbname[0] = jobfile[0] = 0;

  /* * MPI Initialization */

  MPI_Init( & argC, & args );
  MPI_Comm_size( MPI_COMM_WORLD, & numprocs );
  MPI_Comm_rank( MPI_COMM_WORLD, & taskid );
  MPI_Get_processor_name( processor_name, & namelen );

  // Only the Master prints a header
  if ( taskid == MASTER )
  {
    printf( START_MSG, GGNFS_VERSION );
  }

  /* Register signal handler for clean shutdowns. */
#ifdef _CATCH_SIGNALS
  signal( SIGTERM, catch_term );
  signal( SIGINT, catch_term );
  #ifndef _MSC_VER
  signal( SIGQUIT, catch_term );
```

```
  #endif
#endif

  /**  */
  /* Parse command-line args */
  /**  */
  for ( i = 1; i < argC; i++ )
  {
    if ( strcmp( args[i], "-fb" ) == 0 )
    {
      if ( ( ++i ) < argC )
      {
        strcpy( fbname, args[i] );
      }
    }
    else if ( strcmp( args[i], "-j" ) == 0 )
    {
      if ( ( ++i ) < argC )
      {
        strcpy( jobfile, args[i] );
      }
    }
    else if ( strcmp( args[i], "--help" ) == 0 )
    {
      printf( "USAGE: %s %s\n", args[0], USAGE );
      return 0;
    }
  }

  if ( !( jobfile[0] ) || ( !( fbname[0] ) ) )
  {
    printf( "USAGE: %s %s\n", args[0], USAGE );
    return 0;
  }

  /**  */
  /* Initialize and get factor base. */
  /**  */
  initFB( & FB );
  if ( loadFB( fbname, & FB ) )
  {
    fprintf( stderr,
       "Error loading factor base from %s!\n", fbname );
    exit( -1 );
```

```
    }
    setLogs( & FB );


    /**  */
    /* Get parameters */
    /**  */
    if ( parseJobFile( & Job, jobfile ) )
    {
      printf( "Error parsing job file. Cannot continue.\n" );
      exit( -1 );
    }

    msgLog( GGNFS_LOG_NAME, "GGNFS-%s : MPI sieve", GGNFS_VERSION );

    startTime = sTime();

    // Do MPI classic sieve
    if ( Job.type == SIEVE_CLASSICAL )
      res = MPI_Classic_Sieve( & Job, & FB );
    // Do Lattice
    else if ( Job.type == SIEVE_LATTICE )
      printf( "ERROR: Lattice Sieve unavailable\n" );


    now = sTime();
    msgLog( GGNFS_LOG_NAME, "MPI sieve: SieveTime: %1.1lf",
       now - startTime );

    // MPI shutdown
    MPI_Finalize();
    return 0;
}
```

16.3.6 Avoiding Interleaved Messages

The use of `MPI_ANY_SOURCE` when you are receiving two messages with different buffer sizes from each process can cause major problems. MPI guarantees ordering of messages from the same process; however, it is possible that you will get interleaved messages from different hosts. For example, consider the code that sends and receives three messages of different types and sizes (Listing 16.3) [MPIStandard97]:

LISTING 16.3 Message Interleave Example

```
#define MASTER 0
...

int count = 0;

for (i = 0 ; i < BIG_BOUND ; b += numprocs)
{
  /* Do something */

  count++;

  if ( taskid != MASTER )
  {
    // Send an integer to the master
    MPI_Send(&my_int, 1, MPI_INT, MASTER, 0, MPI_COMM_WORLD);

    // Send an array of 100 integers to the master
    MPI_Send(&my_int_arry, 100, MPI_INT, MASTER, 0, MPI_COMM_WORLD);

    // Send a long to the master
    MPI_Send(&my_long, 1, MPI_LONG, MASTER, 0, MPI_COMM_WORLD);

    /* ... */
  }
}
/* end for */

/* Master receives from children */
if (taskid == MASTER )
{
  // How many msg should the Master receive?
  int numMsgs = BIG_BOUND - count;

  for (i = 0 ; i < numMsgs ; i++ )
  {

    // Receive an integer (FROM ANY SOURCE....BAD IDEA!)
    MPI_Recv (&my_int, 1, MPI_INT
              , MPI_ANY_SOURCE, 0, MPI_COMM_WORLD, &status);

    // Receive an array of 100 integers (FROM ANY SOURCE....BAD IDEA!)
    MPI_Recv (&my_int_arry, 100
```

```
                , MPI_INT, MPI_ANY_SOURCE , 0, MPI_COMM_WORLD, &status);

        // Receive a long (FROM ANY SOURCE....BAD IDEA!)
        MPI_Recv (&my_long, 1
                , MPI_LONG, MPI_ANY_SOURCE , 0, MPI_COMM_WORLD, &status);

        /* ... */

    }
}
```

Assuming that the code in Listing 16.3 is run by two processes, possible message arrivals are the following:

Host 1: Integer
Host 1: Array of 100 integers
Host 1: Long
Host 2: Integer
Host 2: Array of 100 integers
Host 2: Long

However, this is not always the case. Messages could arrive in the following sequence:

Host 1: Integer
Host 2: Integer
Host 1: Array of 100 integers
Host 1: Long
Host 2: Array of 100 integers
Host 2: Long

MPI does guarantee the ordering of messages within the same process. However, when dealing with many messages, arrivals could be *interleaved,* thus throwing the following *message truncation* error, which is very common among beginners on parallel programming:

```
Fatal error in MPI_Recv:
 Message truncated, error stack:
MPI_Recv(198):
MPI_Recv(buf=0xbffff018, count=1, MPI_LONG
```

```
 , src=-2, tag=0, MPI_COMM_WORLD, status=0xbffff020) failed
MPIDI_CH3U_Post_data_receive(1486):
 Message from rank 2 and tag 0 truncated;
 564 bytes received but buffer size is 4
rank 0 in job 1  vm-rhl8.ibm.com_32782
caused collective abort of all ranks
  exit status of rank 0: killed by signal 9
```

The previous listing can be fixed by specifying the child number in `MPI_Recv(…)`, thus the code in Listing 16.4 should fix the truncation errors seen earlier:

LISTING 16.4 Fixing Interleaved Messages in `MPI_Recv`

```
// Master receives from children
if (taskid == MASTER )
{
    // How many msg should the Master receive?
    int numMsgs = BIG_BOUND - count;

    // Child number
    int childNum = 1;

    for (i = 0 ; i < numMsgs ; i++ )
    {
        // Child number must not exceed the number of tasks
        if ( childNum > (numprocs -1) )
                childNum = 1;

        // Receive an integer
        MPI_Recv (&my_int, 1
                  , MPI_INT, childNum , 0, MPI_COMM_WORLD, &status);

        // Receive an array of 100 integers
        MPI_Recv (&my_int_arry, 100
                  , MPI_INT, childNum , 0, MPI_COMM_WORLD, &status);

        // Receive a long
        MPI_Recv (&my_long, 1
                  , MPI_LONG, childNum , 0, MPI_COMM_WORLD, &status);

        /* ... */

    }
}
```

16.3.7 Compilation and Runtime Data

The runtime data in Figure 16.3 shows an impressive performance gain even using a single machine ring—imagine the sieve running in a dozen servers simultaneously!

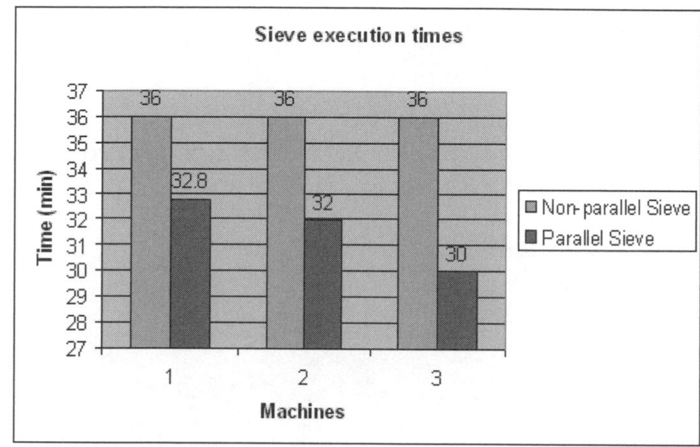

FIGURE 16.3 Sieve performance data.

The hardware used for this test consisted of an IBM ThinkPad T30 P4 i386, 40 GB HD, and 1.5 GB RAM. The software used was Red Hat Linux 8.x on VMware 4.5.

16.4 MPICH2–WS-GRAM INTEGRATION

WS-GRAM supports interfaces for adding support for new schedulers using scripts written in the PERL language. This section explores such interfaces targeted to the portable implementation of MPI dubbed MPICH2.

16.4.1 Scheduler Interface for MPICH2

The scheduler interface is implemented as a PERL module, which is a subclass of the `Globus::GRAM::JobManager`. Its name must match the scheduler type string used when the service is installed. For example, for MPICH2, the name is `mpich2`; thus, the module must be named `Globus::GRAM::JobManager:mpich2` and stored in a file named `mpich2.pm`. The following methods must be overloaded by this and all scheduler interfaces: `submit`, `poll`, and `cancel`.

The module starts by performing initialization operations as shown in Listing 16.5.

LISTING 16.5 `mpich2.pm` MPICH2 Scheduler Interface

```
use Globus::GRAM::Error;
use Globus::GRAM::JobState;
use Globus::GRAM::JobManager;
use Globus::Core::Paths;

use Config;

# NOTE: This package name must match the name of the .pm file!!
package Globus::GRAM::JobManager::mpich2;

@ISA = qw(Globus::GRAM::JobManager);

my ($mpiexec, $mpdlistjobs, $mpdkilljob);

BEGIN
{
    # Paths to mpich 2 executables
    $mpiexec     = '/opt/mpich2/bin/mpiexec';
    $mpdlistjobs = '/opt/mpich2/bin/mpdlistjobs';
    $mpdkilljob  = '/opt/mpich2/bin/mpdkilljob';
}

#**************************************************************************
# fork_and_exec_cmd: A sub to fork and execute a command string.
# The parent process will not wait for the child to complete
# Arguments: command string (example: fork_and_exec_cmd "/bin/date"
#**************************************************************************
sub fork_and_exec_cmd
{
    my $pid = fork();

    return undef unless defined $pid;
    if ( $pid == 0 )
    {
       # child
       $SIG{INT}  = 'IGNORE';
       $SIG{QUIT} = 'IGNORE';
       #open STDOUT, '>>/dev/null';
       #open STDERR, '>&STDOUT'; # dup2()
       #exec { $_[0] } @_;
         exec @_;
       exit 127;
```

```
        }

        # parent
        #waitpid($pid,0);
        $pid;
}
```

16.4.1.1 Submit

All scheduler modules must implement the `submit` method. This method is called when the job manager wants to submit the job to the scheduler. The information in the original job request RSL string is available to the scheduler interface through the `JobDescription` data variable. This is usually the hardest and longest method to implement (see Listing 16.6).

LISTING 16.6 `mpich2.pm` MPICH2 Scheduler Interface Submit Method

```
#*************************************************
# submit: Fires when a Job is submitted thru MMJFS
#*************************************************
sub submit
{
    my $self =   shift;
    my $description = $self->{JobDescription};

    # debug
    # $self->{JobDescription}->save( "/tmp/mpich2job_submit.$$" );

    $self->log("Entering pbs submit");

    if( $description->directory eq '')
    {
            return Globus::GRAM::Error::RSL_DIRECTORY();
    }

    chdir $description->directory() or
            return Globus::GRAM::Error::BAD_DIRECTORY();

    $self->nfssync( $description->executable() )
            unless $description->executable() eq '';
    $self->nfssync( $description->stdin() )
            unless $description->stdin() eq '';

    if( $description->executable eq '')
    {
```

```
                return Globus::GRAM::Error::RSL_EXECUTABLE();
        }
        elsif(! -f $description->executable())
        {
                return Globus::GRAM::Error::EXECUTABLE_NOT_FOUND();
        }
        elsif(! -x $description->executable())
        {
                return Globus::GRAM::Error::EXECUTABLE_PERMISSIONS();
        }
        elsif( $description->stdin() eq '')
        {
                return Globus::GRAM::Error::RSL_STDIN;
        }
        elsif(! -r $description->stdin())
        {
                return Globus::GRAM::Error::STDIN_NOT_FOUND();
        }

        # Submit
        my $job_stdout = $description->stdout(); #"/tmp/mpich2_job.out";
        my $job_stderr = $description->stderr(); #"/tmp/mpich2_job.err";

        my $cmd  = "$mpiexec -n " .  $description->count()
                   . " "
                   .  $description->executable() . " 1>$job_stdout"
                   . " 2>$job_stderr";

        #print "CMD=$cmd, PARENT PID=$$\n";
        # Fork process, do not wait for child
        my $pid = fork_and_exec_cmd $cmd;

        $self->log("job submission successful, setting state to PENDING");
        return {JOB_ID => $pid,
            JOB_STATE => Globus::GRAM::JobState::ACTIVE };
    }
```

16.4.1.2 Poll

The purpose of this method is to check for the status of a job. Poll works by querying the underlying OS for process information using the process ID returned by the `submit` method (see Listing 16.7).

LISTING 16.7 `mpich2.pm` MPICH2 Scheduler Interface Poll Method

```
#*****************************************************************
# Method overloaded by MMJFS to poll for the status of a Job
# By querying the OS for process information using the process ID
# returned by the submit method
#*****************************************************************
sub poll
{
    my $self = shift;
    my $description = $self->{JobDescription};
    my $state;

    my $jobid = $description->jobid();

    if(!defined $jobid)
    {
        $self->log("poll: job id defined!");
        return { JOB_STATE => Globus::GRAM::JobState::FAILED };
    }

    $self->log("polling job " . $jobid);

    $_ = kill(0, split(/,/, $jobid));

    if($_ > 0)
    {
        $state = Globus::GRAM::JobState::ACTIVE;
    }
    else
    {
        $state = Globus::GRAM::JobState::DONE;
    }
    if($self->{STDIO_MERGER})
    {
        $self->{STDIO_MERGER}->poll
            ($state == Globus::GRAM::JobState::DONE);
    }

    return { JOB_STATE => $state };

}
```

16.4.1.3 `Cancel`

`Cancel` must be overloaded by all schedulers. The purpose of this method is to cancel a running job. As with the poll method described earlier, this method will be given the job ID as part of the `JobDescription` object held by the manager.

LISTING 16.8 `mpich2.pm` **MPICH2 Scheduler Interface Cancel Method**

```
#*************************************************
# Cancel a job by killing the process id ($description->jobid()
#*************************************************
sub cancel
{
    my $self = shift;
    my $description = $self->{JobDescription};
    my $pgid;
    my $jobid = $description->jobid();

    if(!defined $jobid)
    {
        $self->log("cancel: no jobid defined!");
        return { JOB_STATE => Globus::GRAM::JobState::FAILED };
    }

    $self->log("cancel job " . $jobid);

    foreach (split(/,/,$jobid))
    {
        $pgid = getpgrp($_);

        $pgid == -1 ? kill($signo{TERM}, $_) :
            kill(-$signo{TERM}, $pgid);

        sleep(5);

        $pgid == -1 ? kill($signo{KILL}, $_) :
            kill(-$signo{KILL}, $pgid);
    }

    return { JOB_STATE => Globus::GRAM::JobState::FAILED };

}
```

16.4.2 MMJFS Service Configuration

The server configuration deployment descriptors `server-config.wsdd` and `local-server-config.wsdd` must be updated to include a new MMJFS service instance for the new scheduler by inserting the service XML shown in Listing 16.9.

LISTING 16.9 Server Deployment Descriptors Configuration

```
<!-- MPICH2 MMJFS-->
<service
  name="base/gram/MasterMPICH2ManagedJobFactoryService"
  provider="Handler"
  style="wrapped"
  use="literal">
  <parameter
    name="relabelOriginators"
    value="true" />
  <parameter
    name="installPath"
    value="/opt/gt32" />
  <parameter
    name="operationProviders"
    value="org.globus.ogsa.impl.ogsi.FactoryProvider
org.globus.ogsa.impl.security.authentication.SecureNotificationSource-
Provider" />
  <parameter
    name="persistent"
    value="true" />
  <parameter
    name="instance-schemaPath"
    value="schema/base/gram/managed_job_service.wsdl" />
  <parameter
    name="activateOnStartup"
    value="true" />
  <parameter
    name="schemaPath"
    value="schema/base/gram/mmjfs_service.wsdl" />
  <parameter
    name="sweeperFrequency"
    value="1000" />
  <parameter
    name="baseClassName"
value="org.globus.ogsa.impl.base.gram.mmjfs.MasterManagedJobFactorySer-
vice" />
```

```
  <parameter
    name="targetFactoryService"
    value="/ogsa/services/base/gram/MPICH2ManagedJobFactoryService" />
  <parameter
    name="handlerClass"
    value="org.globus.ogsa.router.RedirectProvider" />
  <parameter
    name="starterClass"
    value="org.globus.ogsa.impl.base.gram.mmjfs.proxyStarter.HostingEn-
vironmentStarter" />
  <parameter
    name="className"
    value="org.globus.ogsa.base.gram.mmjfs.MasterManagedJobFactorySer-
vice" />
  <parameter
    name="gridmap"
    value="/etc/grid-security/grid-mapfile" />
  <parameter
    name="allowedMethods"
    value="*" />
  <parameter
    name="factoryCallback"
    value="org.globus.ogsa.impl.base.gram.mmjfs.MasterManagedJobFac-
tory" />
</service>
<service
  name="base/gram/MPICH2ManagedJobFactoryService"
  provider="Handler"
  style="wrapped"
  use="literal">
  <parameter
    name="instance-schemaPath"
    value="schema/base/gram/managed_job_service.wsdl" />
  <parameter
    name="className"
    value="org.gridforum.ogsi.NotificationFactory" />
  <parameter
    name="operationProviders"
    value="org.globus.ogsa.impl.ogsi.FactoryProvider
org.globus.ogsa.impl.security.authentication.SecureNotificationSource-
Provider" />
  <parameter
    name="baseClassName"
    value="org.globus.ogsa.impl.ogsi.GridServiceImpl" />
```

```
  <parameter
    name="hostOsVersion"
    value="2.4.18-14" />
  <parameter
    name="hostCpuType"
    value="i686" />
  <parameter
    name="instance-baseClassName"
    value="org.globus.ogsa.impl.base.gram.jobmanager.ManagedJobImpl" />
  <parameter
    name="hostManufacturer"
    value="pc" />
  <parameter
    name="sweeperFrequency"
    value="120" />
  <parameter
    name="x509CertDir"
    value="/etc/grid-security/certificates" />
  <parameter
    name="allowedMethods"
    value="*" />
  <parameter
    name="instance-operationProviders"
    value="org.globus.ogsa.impl.security.authentication.Secure-
    NotificationSourceProvider" />
  <parameter
    name="instance-lifecycle"
    value="persistent" />
  <parameter
    name="globusLocation"
    value="/opt/gt32" />
  <parameter
    name="hostOsName"
    value="Linux" />
  <parameter
    name="schemaPath"
    value="schema/ogsi/ogsi_notification_factory_service.wsdl" />
  <parameter
    name="securityConfig"
    value="org/globus/ogsa/impl/base/gram/jobmanager/factory-security-
config.xml" />
  <parameter
    name="lifecycleMonitorClass"
    value="org.globus.ogsa.repository.DefaultServiceDeactivator" />
```

```
  <parameter
    name="instance-deactivation"
    value="120000" />
  <parameter
    name="instance-name"
    value="MPICH2 ManagedJob" />
  <parameter
    name="persistent"
    value="true" />
  <parameter
    name="instance-className"
    value="org.globus.ogsa.base.gram.ManagedJobPortType" />
  <parameter
    name="managerType"
    value="mpich2" />
  <parameter
    name="handlerClass"
    value="org.globus.ogsa.handlers.RPCURIProvider" />
  <parameter
    name="factoryCallback"
    value="org.globus.ogsa.impl.base.gram.jobmanager.ManagedJob-
    FactoryImpl" />
  <parameter
    name="jobMonitorType"
    value="scheduler" />
  <parameter
    name="instance-activateOnStartup"
    value="true" />
  <parameter
    name="instance-securityConfig"
    value="org/globus/ogsa/impl/base/gram/jobmanager/security-
config.xml" />
  <parameter
    name="name"
    value="MPICH2 ManagedJob Factory Service" />
</service>
```

16.4.3 Packaging Advice

Packaging of the scheduler interface must be done using the Grid Packaging Toolkit (GPT). This will make it easy for users to build and install. Even though this section has demonstrated a manual and quick integration way, you should package the interface files if you plan to distribute them. Such a task can be time consuming, see the developer's guide [WS-GRAMGuide03] for details on building a distributable package.

16.4.4 Testing and Troubleshooting

The following section describes testing and debugging tips for interfacing MpI with WS_GRAM.

16.4.4.1 Pre WS-GRAM (GRAM2): Registering a Gatekeeper Service

An entry in the Globus Gatekeeper's service directory must be created and the PERL module must be copied to the correct location. The program `globus-job-manager-service` performs both of these tasks. When run, it expects the scheduler PERL module to be located in the `$GLOBUS_LOCATION/setup/globus directory`.

```
$GLOBUS_LOCATION/libexec/globus-job-manager-service
-add -m mpich2 -s jobmanager-mpich2
```

Start a gatekeeper configured to run a job manager using the new scripts. Running this will output a contact string (referred to as `<contact-string>` in the following code), which can be used to connect to the new service.

```
% globus-personal-gatekeeper -start -jmtype mpich2

GRAM contact:
 vm-rhl8.ibm.com:32778:
 /O=Grid/OU=GlobusTest/OU=simpleCA-vm-rhl8.ibm.com
 /OU=ibm.com/CN=globus
```

A test job can be run by using the command: `globus-job-run <contact-string> <executable>`. For example, to run the `mpich2` default `cpi` program that computes the value of PI by numerical integration in three nodes, run the following:

```
% globus-job-run
vm-rhl8.ibm.com:32778:
/O=Grid/OU=GlobusTest
/OU=simpleCA-vm-rhl8.ibm.com/OU=ibm.com/CN=globus -np 3
/opt/mpich2/examples/cpi

Process 0 of 3 is on vm-rhl8.ibm.com
Process 1 of 3 is on vm-rhl8.ibm.com
Process 2 of 3 is on vm-rhl8.ibm.com
pi is approximately 3.1415926544231323
 , Error is 0.0000000008333392
wall clock time = 0.041725
```

16.4.4.2 WS-GRAM (GRAM3)

1. Start the OGSA container: Verify that the MPICH2 job factories are shown on standard output (see Figure 16.4)

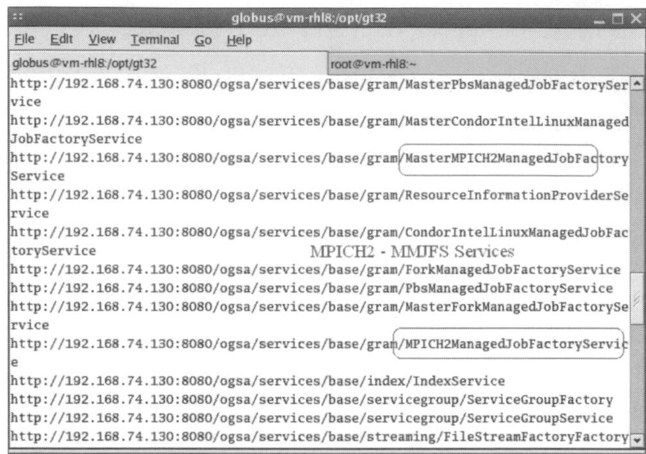

FIGURE 16.4 Standard job factories in GT3.

2. Create a Job Submission RSL file, as shown in Listing 16.10.

LISTING 16.10 MPICH2 WS-GRAM Job Submission RSL File

```
<?xml version="1.0" encoding="UTF-8"?>
<rsl:rsl xmlns:rsl="http://www.globus.org/namespaces/2004/02/rsl"
         xmlns:enum="http://www.globus.org/namespaces/2004/02/rsl/enum"
         xmlns:gram="http://www.globus.org/namespaces/2004/02/rsl/gram"
         xmlns:xsi="http://www.w3.org/2001/XMLSchema-instance"
         xsi:schemaLocation="
            http://www.globus.org/namespaces/2004/02/rsl
            ./schema/base/gram/rsl.xsd
            http://www.globus.org/namespaces/2004/02/rsl/gram
            ./schema/base/gram/gram_rsl.xsd">
    <gram:job>
        <gram:executable>
            <rsl:path>
                <rsl:stringElement value="/opt/mpich2/examples/cpi"/>
            </rsl:path>
        </gram:executable>
        <gram:directory>
            <rsl:path>
```

```
        <rsl:stringElement value="/home/globus"/>
    </rsl:path>
</gram:directory>

<gram:stdin>
    <rsl:path>
        <rsl:stringElement value="/dev/null"/>
    </rsl:path>
</gram:stdin>
<gram:stdout>
    <rsl:pathArray>
        <rsl:path>
            <rsl:stringElement value="./cpi.out"/>
        </rsl:path>
    </rsl:pathArray>
</gram:stdout>
<gram:stderr>
    <rsl:pathArray>
        <rsl:path>
            <rsl:stringElement value="./cpi.err"/>
        </rsl:path>
    </rsl:pathArray>
</gram:stderr>
<gram:count>
    <rsl:integer value="3"/>
</gram:count>
<gram:hostCount>
    <rsl:integer value="3"/>
</gram:hostCount>
<gram:jobType>
    <enum:enumeration>
        <enum:enumerationValue>
            <enum:mpi/>
        </enum:enumerationValue>
    </enum:enumeration>
</gram:jobType>
<gram:gramMyJobType>
    <enum:enumeration>
        <enum:enumerationValue>
            <enum:collective/>
        </enum:enumerationValue>
    </enum:enumeration>
</gram:gramMyJobType>
<gram:dryRun>
```

```
            <rsl:boolean value="false"/>
        </gram:dryRun>
    </gram:job>
</rsl:rsl>
```

3.Run the *managed-job-globusrun* script as shown here:

```
$ managed-job-globusrun
 -factory
http://192.168.74.130:8080
 /ogsa/services/base/gram
 /MasterMPICH2ManagedJobFactoryService
-file mpich2.xml –o

Process 0 of 3 is on vm-rhl8.ibm.com
Process 1 of 3 is on vm-rhl8.ibm.com
Process 2 of 3 is on vm-rhl8.ibm.com
pi is approximately 3.1415926544231323, Error is 0.0000000008333392
wall clock time = 0.041725
```

16.5 MPICH2–MDS3 INTEGRATION

MPICH2 jobs can be easily integrated with MDS by writing an information provider script in combination with the default Globus `ScriptExecution` provider. The following script demonstrates this technique. The script should be named `globus-gram-mpich-provider` and placed in your `$GLOBUS_LOCATION/etc` folder.

16.5.1 An Information Service Script for MPICH2

The following script uses the `mpich2` command `mpdlistjobs` to query for job information. It then parses the data and dumps XML compatible with GT3 index service. It can be run from the command line for testing purposes (see Listing 16.11).

LISTING 16.11 `globus-gram-mpich-provider`, an Information Service Script for MPICH2

```
#!/bin/sh

# MPD Job info command
mpdlistjobs=/opt/mpich2/bin/mpdlistjobs

#
# Emit MPD Job information in XML format
#
emit_JobXML()
```

```
{
    # XML namespace
    NS=
 "xmlns:rips=\"http://www.globus.org/namespaces/2003/04/rips\""

    # MPD job info cmd
    data=`$mpdlistjobs`

    if [ "$data" == "" ] ; then
            return -1
    fi

    # check if the MPD daemons are running
    echo $data | awk '/mpdlistjobs failed/ {exit -1};'
    if [ $? != 0 ] ; then
            return -1
    fi

    # MPD daemons are running
    # Query Job info
    echo "<rips:MPICH2_Jobs $NS>"
    $mpdlistjobs | awk '{

NS="xmlns:rips=\"http://www.globus.org/namespaces/2003/04/rips\""
          if ($1 != "") {
                  if ( $1 == "jobid")
                          print "\t<rips:Job rips:jobid=\""$3"\" "NS">"
                  else if ( $1 == "pgm") {
                          print "\t\t<rips:"$1">"$3"</rips:"$1">"
                          print "\t</rips:Job>"
                  }
                  else
                          print "\t\t<rips:"$1">"$3"</rips:"$1">"
          }
      }'
    echo "</rips:MPICH2_Jobs>"
}

#
# Main
#
emit_JobXML
```

16.5.2 Configuration and Testing

Figures 16.5 and 16.6 show the XML format created by the script in Listing 16.11, as well as the script execution with the Globus *service browser*.

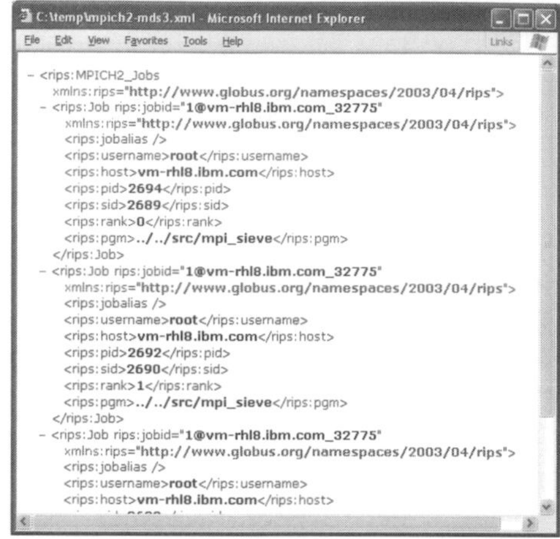

FIGURE 16.5 MPICH2 MDS information provider XML.

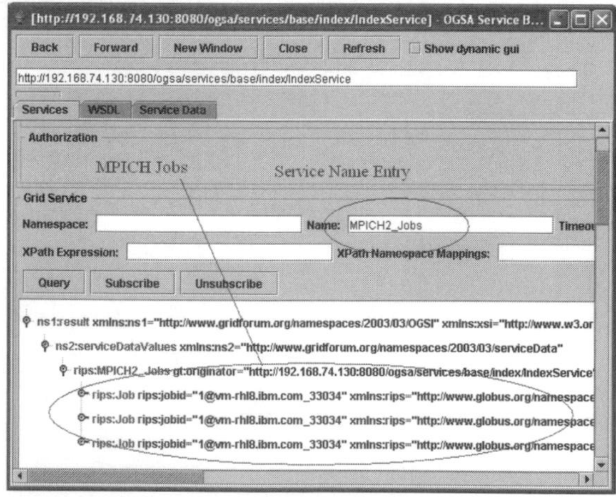

FIGURE 16.6 MPICH2 information provider service browser.

16.6 SUMMARY

MPICH2 is a free implementation of the MPI standard and runs on a wide variety of systems, including the following:

- Workstation networks, Beowulf clusters, individual Workstations, or SMP nodes running MPMD programs
- Grids through a globus2-enabled implementation of MPI
- Symmetric multiprocessors for shared-memory systems
- MPPs and others by means of their own MPI implementations

MPICH supports Fortran 77, Fortran 90, and C/C++ languages. It has been tested on every major OS platform, including many flavors of Unix, Linux, Windows, and others. This chapter has provided a practical overview of MPICH2 including installation, configuration, and testing scripts. Furthermore, practical examples and integration with the Globus Toolkit GRAM and MDS3 protocols are provided.

REFERENCES

[ANLMPI01] ANL Mathematics and Computer Science. The Message Passing Interface (MPI) standard. *http://www-unix.mcs.anl.gov/mpi/.*

[BriggsThesis98] Matthew E. Briggs. "An Introduction to the General Number Field Sieve." Thesis submitted to the Faculty of the Virginia Polytechnic Institute and State University, Blacksburg, Virginia, April 17, 1998.

[Cohen96] H. Cohen. "A Course in Computational Algebraic Number Theory." *GTM 138,* Springer, Berlin. Third corrected printing, 1996.

[Lenstra93] A. Lenstra and H. Lenstra, H. (Eds.), "The Development of the Number Field Sieve." *Lecture Notes in Mathematics 1554,* Springer-Verlag, Berlin, 1993.

[LenstraNFS] A. Lenstra, B. Manasse, and M. Pollard. "The Number Field Sieve." Tidmarsh Cottage, Manor Farm Lane, Tidmarsh, Reading, Berkshire, RG8 8EX, United Kingdom.

[MonicoGNFS] GGNFS. A public domain implementation of GNFS by Chris Monico. *http://www.math.ttu.edu/~cmonico/software/ggnfs/index.html.*

[Montgomery95] Montgomery, P., "A Block Lanczos Algorithm for Finding Dependencies Over GF(2)." *Advances in Cryptology—Eurocrypt '95, Lecture Notes in Computer Science 921,* 1995.

[MPICHAdminGuide96] Gropp, Lusk, Ashton, Buntinas, Butler, Chan, and Ross. *MPICH2 Installer's Guide Version 0.4.* Mathematics and Computer Science Division Argonne National Laboratory. *http://www-unix.mcs.anl.gov/mpi/mpich2/downloads/mpich2-doc-install.pdf.*

[MPICHUserGuide96] William D. Gropp and Ewing Lusk. "User's Guide for MPICH, a Portable Implementation of MPI," ANL-96/6, Mathematics and Computer Science Division, Argonne National Laboratory, 1996.

[MPIStandard97] The Message Passing Interface (MPI) standard. (c) 1995, 1996, 1997 University of Tennessee, Knoxville, Tennessee. Permission to copy without fee all or part of this material is granted provided the University of Tennessee copyright notice and the title of this document appears, and notice is given that copying is by permission of the University of Tennessee. *http://www.mpi-forum.org/docs/mpi-11-html/mpi-report.html.*

[WS-GRAMGuide03] WS GRAM: Developer's Guide. *http://www-unix.globus.org/toolkit/docs/3.2/gram/ws/developer/scheduler.html.*

Appendix

A Source Code

ON THE CD

The following programs are included in the companion CD-ROM in the following directory `Code/SupportSoftware/WebSphere/CH11_jCertServices`.

Program Name: SimpleCA.java

Requirements: Java CoG Kit 1.1

This program is an implementation of a simple Certificate Authority (CA) for the Java language. It has the following features:

- Certificate request generation in Privacy Enhanced Mail (PEM) format
- Certificate request signature
- Certificate information such as issuer, lifetime, strength, and so on

Creating a Certificate Request

To create a certificate request, the following command can be used:

```
Java org.globus.grid.ca.SimpleCA  req
–out /tmp/rq.pem
–keyput /tmp/key.pem –pwd "mypwd"
```

Optional arguments are as follows: `–dn "O=Grid, OU=Ogsa, OU=IT, CN=John Doe" –bits 1024` (*note:* `O`, `OU`, `CN` are case sensitive).

Signing a Certificate Request

To sign a certificate request, run the following command from your OS prompt (Windows/Linux):

```
Java org.globus.grid.ca.SimpleCA ca –rq /tmp/req.pem –out /tmp/cert.pem
```

For this command to work, a trusted (CA) certificate must be installed in the user's `$HOME/.globus/CA` directory, with the names `cacert.pem` and `cakey.pem` for the certificate and key, respectively.

Optional arguments are as follows: `-cacert` <path to CA cert> `-cakey` <path to the CA key> `-capwd` <CA pwd>

Getting Information on a X.509 Certificate

To get information about an X.509 certificate, use the following command (Windows/Linux):

```
jcs x509 -in /tmp/cert.pem -info

Subject: C=US, O=Grid, OU=simpleCA, CN=John Doe
Hash: 945769
```

ON THE CD

A sample output of this command is available on the companion CD-ROM.

Program Name: CertGenerator.java

Requirements: Java CoG Kit 1.1

CertGenerator.java is a program to generate X.509 Certificates and private keys using the RSA PKI APIs provided by the Java CoG kit. It is also capable of creating Globus credentials used by the Grid Security Infrastructure (GSI) for mutual authentication and authorization. The code for creating a certificate request and private key is available on the CD-ROM.

ON THE CD

Program Name: CertSigner.java

Requirements: Java CoG Kit 1.1

This is a program to sign X.509 Certificate requests and is used by the simple CA implementation mentioned earlier. It emulates functionality of software such as OpenSSL, and it can be easily modified to work with any type of J2EE application.

Program Name: CertManager.java

Requirements: Java CoG Kit 1.1

This is a program to load, save, and initialize user certificates and Globus proxies.

Program Name: Certrq.jsp

This, and the following programs, is a Web-enabled application that uses most of the subroutines implemented in previous sections within a Web environment. The purpose of these programs is to aid administrators in managing security on a grid within an organization by using simple Web-based tools for user and host certificate generation and signature.

Program Name: self-sign.jsp

This is a Web tool for self-signed certificate creation.

Program Name: userhost.jsp

This is a Web tool for user or host certificate creation.

Appendix

B About the CD-ROM

The following are included on the companion CD-ROM:

CH05_GridPortletsJetspeed: The portlet projects for Chapter 5 written for the Apache Jetspeed portal server including resource management (GRAM), remote data transfer (GridFTP), and Information Services

CH05_GridPortletsWPS: Grid portlet applications for IBM WebSphere portal server

CH08_OGSAFactorizationService: A large integer factorization service for GT 3.2 or later

CH10_jCertServices: Web tool for digital certificate creation and signature

CH10_ProxyCert: A Web application to demonstrate grid proxy creation, compatible with GT 2.x or later

CH11_GRAMClients: Miscellaneous Java clients for resource management under GT3

CH12_GridFTP: Remote data transfer programs

CH13_MDS2Client: Information Services client

CH13_MDS3RemoteSchedulerProvider: An MDS3-based remote cluster information provider; supports OpenPBS, Condor, and Sun Grid Engine

CH14_JavaCoG: Java CoG kit examples

CH15_WSRFFactorizationService: A large integer factorization service for GT 3.9 Alpha; precursor to GT4

CH17_MPIExamples: Miscellaneous MPI examples

CH18_MPIParallelSieve_ggnfs302: A parallel sieve implementation used by the Number Field Sieve for large integer factorization; written in C and based on the open source algorithm GGNFS

Index

H

I

J

N

O

P